Residential Treatment of Adolescents

Residential Treatment of Adolescents

Integrative Principles and Practices

Don Pazaratz, Ed.D.

 Routledge
Taylor & Francis Group
New York   London

Routledge
Taylor & Francis Group
270 Madison Avenue
New York, NY 10016

Routledge
Taylor & Francis Group
2 Park Square
Milton Park, Abingdon
Oxon OX14 4RN

© 2009 by Taylor & Francis Group, LLC
Routledge is an imprint of Taylor & Francis Group, an Informa business

Printed in the United States of America on acid-free paper
10 9 8 7 6 5 4 3 2 1

International Standard Book Number-13: 978-0-415-99708-9 (Hardcover)

Library of Congress Cataloging-in-Publication Data

Pazaratz, Don.
   Residential treatment of adolescents : integrative principles and practices / Don Pazaratz.
      p. ; cm.
   Includes bibliographical references and index.
   ISBN 978-0-415-99708-9 (hardback : alk. paper)
   1. Adolescent psychotherapy--Residential treatment. I. Title.
   [DNLM: 1. Adolescent. 2. Affective Symptoms--therapy. 3. Adolescent Behavior. 4. Behavior Therapy--methods. 5. Models, Psychological. 6. Residential Treatment--methods. WS 463 P348i 2008]

RJ503.P39 2008
616.89'140835--dc22   2008034592

Visit the Taylor & Francis Web site at
http://www.taylorandfrancis.com

and the Routledge Web site at
http://www.routledge.com

In loving memory of my parents

Contents

Preface   xiii

1   **Principles and Practices of Residential Treatment and of the Four Phase System**   1

The Hard-to-Service Adolescent   2
Theoretical Principles   4
Organizational Relationships   7
Treatment Phases   10
General Principles of Treatment   11
The Efficacy of the System   13
Summary   15
Integrative Treatment Principles and Practices   17
Conclusion   26

2   **Evaluation**   29

Referral Information   29
Psychological Assessments   30
The Psychosocial Assessment   31
Treatment Plan (Case Formulation)   32
Residential Placement   33
Group Home Layout   34
Group Home Interactions   35
An Integrative Approach to Reinforcements   38
Phases of Treatment   39
How Change Occurs   42
Treatment Motivation   43
The Difficult Youngster   45
Confrontation   46

The Impact of Treatment 48
Treatment Impasses 50
Dealing With Conflict Contextually 52
Anger Directed at Youth Workers 54
Affect and Its Expression 57

3 **Psychosocial Assessment by Child and Youth Care Workers** **61**

Childhood Development 62
Assessment Process in Residential Treatment 66
The Psychosocial Assessment 68
    Background of Youth (Social History) 69
    Social Functions 70
    Psychological Functioning 73
    Ego Functions 75
Personal Characteristics 79
    Habits 80
    Drug Therapy 82
    Interests and Hobbies 82
    School (Academic Functioning) 83
    Diagnostic Formulation 84
    Treatment Plan 85
Guide for Writing a Discharge Summary 86
Discussion 88
Summary 88
Conclusion 89

4 **Group Living** **91**

Contextual Goals of Treatment 91
The Socialization Process and Development of Values 92
Staff–Youth Relationship Building 94
The Element of Integrative Counseling 96
Power Struggles 97
Front-Line Interactions 98
Stabilizing Interactions 100
The Living and Learning Environment 101
Actions That Sustain the Group 102
Group Interactions 103
Staff Roles Contextually 106
Positive Peer Pressure 106
Subgroups 108
Summary of Group Dynamics 110

5   **Family Work in Residential Treatment**   **113**

Family Dynamics   115
Residential Placement   117
Treatment Issues   118
Placement Conditions   121
Family Assessment   123
Family Work   124
Treatment Emphasis   126
Family Treatment Plan   128
Family Counseling   130
Discharge From Treatment   131
Summary   132
Conclusion   133

6   **Modifying Behavior Through the Use of a Level/**
    Reinforcement System   **135**

Behavior Modification   136
Application of Reinforcements   138
Behavior Shaping   139
Benefits of Reinforcements   140
A Systems Approach   143
Rationale of Reinforcements   144
Critical Factors of Reinforcements   146
Limitations of Behavior Management   148
    Explanation of Levels   149
    Explanation of Credit and Point Scale   150
    Variable Factors   150
Discussion   152
Summary   153
Conclusion   154
Point Scale   160
Explanation of Reinforcement Categories   161

7   **The Role of Direct Care Staff in Residential Treatment**   **165**

Purpose of Policies and Procedures   165
Policy and Procedure Manual   166
Parenting Skills   168
Theory and Practice of Therapeutic Activities   172
Interviewing and Counseling Skills   173
Child Care Work Methodology   175
Family Work   177
Treatment Planning (Plan of Care)   179
Theory and Practice of Working With Groups   180

Community Resources   182
Ethics, Standards, Identity, and Responsibility   183
Communication Skills   184
Interpersonal Skills   185
Unit Functioning   185
Job Responsibilities   186
Teamwork   ·   186
Treatment Planning   187
Summary   188
        The Role of Youth Workers   188
        Group Home Management   188

8   Positive Discipline   191

Causes of Maladaptive Behavior   191
Confrontation Versus Control   193
Confrontation as an Encounter   194
Supportive Confrontation   196
Strategies for Emotional Interventions   198
Counseling Strategies (Psychotherapy)   199
The Group Home Environment   202
The Integrative Practitioner   203
Preventing Deterioration   205
The Nature of Conflicts   207
Counseling in the Here and Now (Contextually)   208
Summary   210

9   Therapeutic Programming   213

Treatment Components   213
Activities Program   213
Life Skills Program   214
Theory of Therapeutic Activities   215
Social Skills Development   216
Group Activities and Community Use   216
Structured Activities   218
Sustaining Interest   220
Games and Sport   221
Therapeutic Effects of Activities   221
Summary   222
Conclusion   225

10   The Role of Education in Residential Treatment   227

The Public System of Education   228
Educational Options   231

Behavior Control of Students 233
Parental Influence on Learning 235
The Need for Special Education 237
Treatment Classes 239
What Types of Youngsters Require a Treatment Class? 241
Curriculum Design of the Treatment Center Class 243
Academic Assessment 244
The Role of the Treatment Class Teacher 247
Discussion 249
Summary 251
Conclusion 252

11   Residential Treatment of a Disturbed Adolescent:
      A Case Study 257
Family Dynamics 258
Residential Treatment 260
Treatment Issues 260
Group Interactions 262
Case Study 263
Formulation 266
Discussion 267
Conclusion 268

12   Afterword 271
Introduction 271
The Four Phase System 272
Integrative Treatment 273
Psychosocial Assessment Overview 275
Reinforcements 276
How Evaluation Informs Behavior Management 278
Oppositionalism and Defiance 280
The Treatment Class 282
Activities 284
The Child and Youth Care Worker's Role 285
Family Counseling 288
Summary 289
Conclusion 291

References 293

Index 315

Preface

This book focuses on the core issues of the residential treatment of emotionally disturbed children and adolescents. It is based upon the principles and practices that were developed in working with "hard-to-serve" and "hard-to-place" adolescents, who were admitted into a continuum of treatment known as the Four Phase System of Metropolitan Toronto that operated from 1973 to 1990 (Pazaratz, Randall, Spekkens, Lazor, & Morton, 2000). The book describes the course of treatment, the way in which a milieu or residence should operate, and how its environment can be used therapeutically to shape and to influence a youth's emotional growth, intellectual development, and characterological potential.

This book details the theory, rationale, and practice of residential treatment, and reviews the problems faced by front-line staff in working with difficult youth individually and from a group care perspective. It is composed of 12 chapters that address the clinical advantages of integrative or multimodal treatment, and describe how it is enacted. This book can be used as a standard text for all front-line practitioners such as child and youth care workers, correctional workers, and special education teachers. It can also be a resource for those adjunct professionals, such as social workers, psychometricians, psychologists, and psychiatrists, who work less intensely with children or adolescents placed in group care facilities.

Emotional disturbance occurs in children and adolescents due to a complexity of biological or neurological factors and manifests itself in a broad range of interpersonal and behavioral problems. Other disorders may coexist that contribute to developmental problems and delays. There are various treatment rationales and intervention models that are efficacious when dealing with youngsters who need residential placement for treatment of their disorders. This book is a discussion of the essential integrative principles and practices that are fundamental to working with "hard-to-serve," at-risk young people. Central to residential treatment and care is the role of the child and youth care worker, which, briefly, is to help the youth move to a higher level of functioning. The clinical intervention strategies that are detailed in this book have been tested and proven facilitative and efficacious in a number of residential treatment and care facilities throughout Canada and the United States, with females and males, ages 10 to 19, displaying the full classification or spectrum of diagnostic disorders (Pazaratz, 1998a, 1999, 2005b).

This book will provide the practitioner with conceptual theories and practical tools for working with extremely demanding young people in various community and educational settings, such as residential treatment facilities, children's mental health centers, therapeutic group homes, psychiatric hospitals, detention centers, treatment classes, in the youngster's home, or from a storefront. The book offers the direct care worker and adjunct professionals (psychologists, psychiatrists, psychometricians, social workers, teachers, and so forth) an overview of the field of therapeutic youth work and the method of special education, and provides all practitioners with a broad and current understanding of the precise nature of the high-risk youngster. The book emphasizes how integrative counseling is practiced, its connection to residential treatment, and how direct care staff interface and coordinate their efforts with families, the educational system, and other professionals.

As a guide for those entering the field of residential treatment, it is hoped that the individual worker will become familiar with the organizational structure of residential programming, and the culture of youth work and its philosophical orientation. Developing a conceptual framework and technical skills and understanding youngsters in context are essential when providing treatment and care to youth who are disordered, disturbed, delinquent, mentally ill, or especially suffering comorbidity. For example, some youngsters upon placement feel more secure and, therefore, to avoid further emotional turbulence increase defensiveness. Others overrely upon staff members and therefore discount their strengths (Laursen, 2000). There are realistic intervention strategies and facilitating parameters when interacting with youth in care. These must be carefully articulated in enacting a reinforcing milieu, a holding environment, or a modifying ecology. There are also a number of practical approaches as well as clinical instruments that are fundamental to group work. However, developing staff–youth relationships is central to the role of front-line staff during their daily interactions, so that they can fulfill the developmental, emotional, social, and attachment needs of youngsters in treatment (Maier, 1987). Thus, the youngster's potential for growth and change is contingent upon staff members and the ever-evolving sociocultural milieu being made secure and meaningful, that is, the peer social system is supportive, and staff members are deeply understanding.

Residential treatment and care are founded on a discipline that is distinct in terms of the populations and problems they target and the modalities they utilize. Residential care as a philosophy is geared to resocialize youngsters through experience, to reeducate through relearning, and to redirect through counseling (Bettelheim, 1960). There are various practices, techniques, and guidelines for enacting interventions. The rationale for employing any particular engagement flows from the nature of the worker–youth relationship, and occurs in the context of the youth's pathology. This means that different behaviors necessitate different strategies (Garfat, 2003). But approaching youngsters with an inflexible treatment style can lead to power struggles and avoidance behaviors, and hinder the youth worker from anticipating and stopping maladaptive behavior patterns. Effective interventions are a function of knowledge, skill, caution, exploration, discovery, and working within existing forms and structure (Pazaratz, 2000b, 2000c, 2000d). The youth worker is influenced by a combination of the youth's maturity, emotional development, and thinking style; the nature of the referral problem(s); the youth worker's skill level; the culture of the group home; the youth's previous experiences with treatment (placement); and the context of the current situation, or how past problems impact the immediate moment.

Because an organizational structure is basic to residential treatment, the ideas presented here should help to clarify the way in which a residential program operates and how it fits into the community and uses the community and its resources. This book also aims to give the reader an appreciation of how theory and practice are integrated in the diagnosis and treatment of disturbed youth. There is recognition that not all divergent or conflictual family issues can be reconciled (such as parental attitude, availability, or cooperation); therefore, some unresolvable issues may have to coexist and be tolerated (Wachtel, 2004). Nevertheless, a range of techniques and theories will be reviewed. Some preferred practices or guidelines for dealing with aggressive, suicidal, and other extreme forms of acting out, regressed, or withdrawn behaviors will be discussed. The book also addresses themes in treatment and provides a view of adolescents in treatment: what they face, their access to opportunities, the nature of transition issues, the importance of family relations, and specific strategies that assist with community reintegration.

A fully detailed account of residential treatment is beyond the scope of this book. Nevertheless, the youth worker's job description, as defined in the context of the work environment, the utilization of resources, programming directions, ethical practices, and clinical skills, is a core theme. Briefly, direct care staff provide counseling and care to a wide variety of youngsters who have a complex range of needs, problems, strengths, and weaknesses, and who function at different developmental levels. Ultimately, youngsters in residential placement can be helped by humane, dignified, and competent staff members who interact as a team within clearly defined job descriptions (Pazaratz, 2000b, 2000c, 2000d). Critical to treatment planning and youth workers enacting their role is their ability to evaluate the youngster's and group's responses to expectations. Unless front-line staff members can get youth to adhere to their treatment goals and the rules of the program, the youngsters will feel unsafe, disconnected, and frustrated, and the social order will become chaotic (Polsky, 1962).

So what is the change process? How does it occur? How do front-line workers know when they are being effective? These are the most frequently asked questions in staff supervision (Pazaratz, 2005a). In short, the seasoned youth worker has come to understand that careless or nonspecific approaches to residential treatment and disturbed youngsters often engender unnecessary conflict between the youth and the worker. There are two approaches in dealing with disturbed youth: managing disruptive behaviors and understanding diagnosis or the reasons for the behavior (Whittaker, 1979). The former is based upon a particular approach such as learning theory and behavior modification, whereas the latter means that interventions will be formulated on the basis of change mechanisms that fit the case. Both approaches can be realized when residential treatment programs focus on developmental issues, utilize integrative treatment principles, incorporate elements of the milieu as reinforcements, and foster a positive peer culture (Vorath & Brendtro, 1985).

This book includes specific step-by-step procedures and behavioral approaches for both overt and withdrawn behaviors. It differentiates between interventions considered preferred, best, and mandated practices. It emphasizes the use of treatment principles that guide integrative practice. These principles organize the milieu or conceptualizations about the milieu, priority of programming, and types of interventions that are utilized. The book addresses the concepts of working with a group of youth, and the individual youth, in a structured or an unstructured context. There is an overview of staff roles and responsibilities, counseling rationale, bonding issues, methods to support extreme emotions or to lessen aggressive behaviors, the teaching of life skills, the effective use of language, and the reference group or norm to which children and adolescents in treatment are compared. There is an attempt to answer the question "What exactly takes place in residential treatment?"

This book provides the reader with a firm orientation of integrative child and youth care methodology and its practical advantages. Integrative therapy with youngsters relies heavily upon self-psychology and object relations (see Goldstein, 2002). In daily interactions, practitioners focus on stabilization, on distinguishing those factors that lead to onset versus those that maintain dysfunction, and on determining the fit between the youth's personal goals and available options. There is an emphasis on the youth achieving object constancy in relationships (Kohut, 1977). However, no treatment approach can provide all the answers for every youth. Therefore, this is the rationale for employing divergent theories and concepts that provide the youth worker with different views, practices, and knowledge, and a balanced approach to youth. Programming in integrative practice utilizes phenomenological methodologies in order to assist the child and youth worker to understand the treatment experience from the perspective of youngsters in care and the importance of family support (Pazaratz, 2005d). The discussion of treatment transactions makes the connection between staff training and staff evaluation, offers an understanding of assessment methods, and clarifies the application of theory. The book can also be used in supervision of youth workers to bridge the gap between abstract concepts and clinical practice, to help improve training, and as a direction for practice, for both the individual youth worker and a group of youth workers (Pazaratz, 2005a). The book is both accessible and relevant, emphasizing the practical over the technical, offering suggestions, and stressing "how to's."

Ultimately, the meaning and impact of any residential treatment program are revealed by looking at one essential variable, the nature of staff–youth relationships. In effect, the efficacy of residential treatment is the direct result of positive staff–youth connections (Fewster, 1990). This means that in order for staff members to develop healthy relationships, they must understand youngsters contextually, or how they are affected by developmental pressures, family issues, intrapsychic conflict, and peer relationships. The youth's social interactions inform the youth worker of who the youth is trying to be. The youngster's social skills, or lack thereof, help the youth worker to comprehend the nature of the youngster's cognitive, emotional, and verbal abilities. This information assists the youth worker to evaluate the degree to which the disturbed youngster is limited in his or her options.

Finally, this book provides an overview of the problems that need to be dealt with by the youth in order to complete treatment. For example, when addressing the reasons for placement, the youth worker will become aware of the youngster's conflicted background and problematic family relationships. The youth worker may even encounter or become the target of the parents' projection of their psychological difficulties or extreme behaviors. The parent–child conflict may also be viewed during their interactions, revealing the basis or function of the child or adolescent's main symptoms. But, ultimately, the focus of residential treatment and the youth worker's role is informed by the youngster's abnormal emotional development, the interactional pattern of the child–parent relationship that influenced the family's and their child's distress, the changes the youth must make in order to be discharged from treatment, and the way in which parents can be supported so that they are receptive to their child's return home (Ainsworth, 1997).

There are various clinical practices that help to stabilize the disturbed youth in residential group care, and these techniques are described and discussed. Of central importance in residential programming is the creation of structure and safety for the at-risk youth. Staff must be able to make relevant observations of youngsters' behaviors in the residence, at school, in the community, and during contacts with their family; kinesthetic abilities; awareness of self; and interpersonal skills. Therefore, there is an emphasis on the role of direct care staff and the way in which the worker monitors the youth's progress or lack thereof. Boundary issues are also an integral aspect of treatment and are fundamental to the care function of group work. This means that when a disparate population of disturbed children or adolescents who function at different developmental stages and levels is grouped together, there is a need for values clarification, awareness building, and skills acquisition. Children's rights cannot be overlooked in the treatment process, and therefore the worker's responsibilities are reviewed. Various theoretical approaches are utilized by staff members with different youngsters; however, it is the standardized approaches to treatment and programming that provide the consistency necessary to develop group harmony.

Residential treatment of severely disordered adolescents can be difficult and challenging because they ignore boundaries, violate social decorum and rules, and often overreact or withdraw excessively. For example, during social activities or community outings, even though a youngster has experienced a fun sense of adventure, playfulness, and warmth, nevertheless the youth can also rapidly digress into sullen moodiness, or extreme hostility, over a perceived slight or an inadvertent comment. Thus, the purpose of residential placement is to stabilize the disturbing aspects of youngsters, and to assist them to overcome hurt and pain that are manifest as alienation, social isolation, and often severe academic difficulties, if not failures (Waller, 1996). Therefore, a central aspect of residential treatment is to reinforce the young person's self-efficacy, personal control, and adaptive coping strategies. In this effort, the youth's attribution of cause and responsibility for difficulties and problems is assessed. The assessment process then becomes the basis for the treatment plan, which is implemented through contracting, targets the acquisition of skills, and embraces self-actualization. Change is thus experienced in behavioral terms, with the young person acquiring social competencies and improved cognitive abilities, organizing his or her emotions and life patterns, admitting to having problems, and experiencing trust, relevance, and commitment.

Prior to admission to treatment, most youngsters have been assessed. Generally, assessments identify a youth's problems and development relative to age-appropriate or normative functioning. Assessments also seek to provide information on the young person's strengths, needs, and goals, and the nature of family relationships. Nevertheless, existing psychological assessments may need to be updated. They may not provide current or sufficient information for treatment planning and intervention. Thus, during the course of treatment, additional information is often required. The Psychosocial Assessment that is discussed in Chapter 3 is a practical clinical instrument for evaluating and updating the youth's adjustment to placement. It is typically completed by child and youth care workers who seek to determine the way in which a resident views and interacts with the environment, the types of controls that are effective, the nature of the resident's defense system, the resident's stress tolerance, reality testing, the adequacy of the resident's psychological resources (resiliency), and the resident's self-concept. Addressing these issues enables staff members to set realistic treatment goals and to determine best practices. The Psychosocial Assessment also describes the least intrusive techniques to effect, monitor, and maintain change.

In summary, this book will show that current practices within residential treatment evolved from standards that were first articulated as principles of the Four Phase System that operated in Metropolitan Toronto. This book emphasizes that residential treatment, to be effective, occurs on many levels. As a process, it relies heavily on staff–youth interactions. It is enacted by youth workers employing clinical instruments such as assessments, rationale for treatment, treatment plans (or plan of care), contracts, and techniques for shaping behaviors (reinforcements). In essence, this book reviews and discusses the following information:

1. Philosophical principles and ethical practices concerning the purpose and context of residential treatment and care as developed by the Four Phase System.
2. Specific techniques and interventions that are employed to diagnose, understand, and treat adolescents and their families.
3. Criteria employed to evaluate and reinforce behaviors, and for identifying change.
4. The core elements of resocialization and developing group harmony.
5. The relationship of the family to the treatment program.
6. The nature and structure of a reinforcing milieu.
7. The theory and practice of child and youth care work.
8. Strategies for engaging youth in the change process and overcoming resistance and defiance.
9. The rationale and methods employed to establish and to enact therapeutic activities.
10. The nature and scope of the treatment class and its place within the overall educational system.
11. A case study that demonstrates the complexity of working with high-risk youth and the rationale for implementing an integrative treatment approach within a therapeutic milieu.
12. Epilogue: a summary of the practices utilized that form the core principles of the integrated treatment model.

CHAPTER 1

Principles and Practices of Residential Treatment and of the Four Phase System

Emotionally disturbed children and adolescents have a wide range of presenting problems and distinct mental health needs. There are a number of different treatment models, and various forms of community intervention. Some programs treat the whole family, whereas others focus primarily upon the youth-in-residence. Nevertheless, urban-based residential programs appear to have a number of common features, such as having an organized system of communication, employing direct care staff, providing feedback of information, using the community as a resource, utilizing therapeutic activities, teaching social and life skills, and emphasizing behavior control. This chapter discusses the theoretical structure, philosophy, principles, and practices that were utilized to create a comprehensive mental health service for the "untreatable adolescent" known as the Four Phase System of Metropolitan Toronto, which existed from 1973 to 1990.

The Four Phase System that functioned as a continuum of treatment and care for severely disturbed teenagers had and continues to have a tremendous impact and legacy today on residential treatment programs for children and adolescents. The Four Phase System was based on the concept that a coalition of independent service providers could be enlisted to act in concert to coordinate and to provide a variety of mental health services to teenagers and their families. As a network of agencies, the Four Phase System's goals were to stabilize the highly troubled adolescent, and to treat the youth by offering movement across various program categories and different degrees of service intensity, in accordance with the youth's changing treatment needs (Pazaratz, Randall, Spekkens, Lazor, & Morton, 2000). The strength of the system was its comprehensiveness and flexibility, whereby each treatment facility within the coalition specialized in one aspect of treatment in order to match the specific mental health needs of each adolescent.

As an alternative to institutionalization, the Four Phase System created a continuum of care that was youth centered, community based, and clinically eclectic. Continuum models are based on the theory that normal and abnormal personality exists on a continuum or gradient of pathology and that common features are identifiable, differentiated partly by their degree of intensity (Andrews, 1989). Placement decisions within the system were determined by the diagnostic and clinical needs of the youth and those of his or her family. In response to significant growth or regression, the youth could be moved within the system to a less or more structured program (Pazaratz et al., 2000). Ongoing feedback between agencies ensured relevance, organizational resilience, and treatment efficacy. Treatment parameters and objectives were based upon social learning, group theory, and behavior therapy. In short, the treatment process that was enacted was structured to be multimodal (that is, the interventions were educational, therapeutic, and socializing). But the quality of treatment and care for young persons referred to the system occurred due to the sensibility and skills of direct care staff translating treatment rationale or theory into practice (Pazaratz, 1998a).

In order for each treatment program to be clinically sound and efficacious, its organizational structure (administration) and the program operation (treatment) had to come together on both practical and theoretical levels (Pazaratz, 1999). This was the concept that was utilized in developing the Four Phase System. The system's contribution to the field of residential programming (to be discussed) included the knowledge gained from providing a comprehensive array of community-based treatment services. However, even though the system was established to treat the most disturbed adolescent, some youngsters placed in the system were considered to be "untreatable." Eventually, shifting political priorities and social pressures transformed the focus of the Four Phase System. This change in emphasis and funding resulted in the system's dissolution by 1990 (Pazaratz et al., 2000).

THE HARD-TO-SERVICE ADOLESCENT

A 1967 study of services for emotionally disturbed children and adolescents in Ontario, Canada, found that there was an unequal access to treatment and care for adolescents and a lack of general structure for future services development. At that time, children in Ontario with emotional problems were generally cared for by a patchwork of organizations, such as Children's Aid Societies, who placed children with behavior problems in foster homes, and a number of small institutions that had started out as orphanages. Some children were also being cared for and supervised by religious organizations such as Catholic Charities and the like. Prior to 1967, in Ontario, there were only two residential programs that accepted teenagers directly into treatment. All of the other residential programs that existed were established for children; and when a teenager was in care, that youth had been initially admitted as a child.

This 1967 study concluded that children's residential services were inadequate to meet the needs of troubled adolescents and their families because of limited resources, poor organization, lack of planning, and situations of inadequate coordination of existing services (Ontario Government, 1967). This meant that most adolescents did not receive any type or level of therapeutic intervention. As a result, overburdened families were stressed, and many youth, who then reacted to family conditions, were becoming offenders. Troubled teenagers were rarely considered for residential placement and were often discharged if they "acted out" in placement. Aggressive and psychotic adolescents who "acted out" their problems were frequently placed in a detention facility, a training school, or a psychiatric hospital. This meant that training schools often housed adolescents who were more disturbed than delinquent. There were also cases in which adolescents who wound up in a psychiatric setting remained institutionalized until adulthood. Therefore, it was concluded that many adolescents were not receiving the mental health care that they needed and, when placed, were often detained in environments that were in effect detrimental to their mental health.

It was also noted in the study that adolescents who displayed behavioral or emotional problems and came from an affluent background would be sent to private boarding schools by their families. In effect, a two-tier system for troubled youth was created. Therefore, in order to provide more appropriate, humane, and equal access to treatment for adolescents, the minister of health recommended the need to transfer and consolidate a variety of treatment programs to the Ministry of Health from the Ministry of Welfare (Ontario Government, 1967). By 1969, a new set of regulations were enacted that developed mechanisms for coordinating services for adolescents. Eight regions were established that would provide troubled teenagers with comprehensive health care from a mental health perspective and not from secure custody or hospitalization. This new approach emphasized cost-effective community-based alternatives to highly restrictive and expensive institutional long-term facilities.

The Province of Ontario as a whole was divided into eight geographical areas, each with a Regional Centre, designed to provide in-patient, out-patient, day care, and community consultation and education. Metropolitan Toronto was one of the eight geographical areas. It was also subdivided into four regions, and each region into four phases, but interconnected on the metropolitan level. Each phase was to establish a collaborative effort between existing programs (which were prepared to change their focus from children to teenagers) and to create new agencies that would be part of this continuum or system of treatment. Duplication of services was to be prevented by treatment programs having very specific parameters. To reduce length of stay in treatment, youngsters would be placed in a program (treatment phase) designed to deal with their specific needs or type and level of behavior problems. With four treatment phases, this flexibility meant that teenagers would no longer be sent to inappropriate placements or institutional settings, such as mental hospitals and training schools (Finlay & Randall, 1975), and become institutionalized or regressed.

Youngsters could be referred to the Four Phase System from any source such as a Children's Aid Society, a youth court, probation and aftercare, a detention facility, a training school, a psychiatric hospital, or a psychiatrist. Upon referral to the system, an intake worker was assigned from Phase One and became the case manager. An overriding clinical emphasis was to stabilize families with home care or "wrap-around" programming immediately. In this effort, direct care staff were placed in the family's home to make the home as therapeutic as residential placement and to offset the potential for youngsters being expelled from their home (Pazaratz et al., 2000). Thus, wherever possible the treatment objective of the Four Phase System was to maintain the family unit, and to unburden the family's mental health problems with clinical process and therapeutic strategies. This was especially important for adolescents considered at risk for developing more serious emotional disturbance (Pazaratz, 1998a). However, when home care was deemed insufficient or unworkable, and the youth had to be placed, each residential treatment facility within the Four Phase System was structured as a "holding environment" that could accommodate any adolescent with severe mental health problems. Hardy's (1991) observation that disturbed adolescents should be treated not only from a psychopathological perspective but also with understanding of the youth's potential for growing to self-awareness, self-direction, and autonomy was in practice the essential treatment principle of the system. This type of treatment philosophy, according to Winnicott (1965), is considered essential for those adolescents whose early environment had failed them.

THEORETICAL PRINCIPLES

At the time the Four Phase System was established, it was a new model or paradigm of practice and treatment. Yet today in North America, the clinical concepts and treatment rationale that were innovative and somewhat radical are considered commonplace and standard. The Four Phase System's clinical direction, treatment methodology, and design of the work environment were shaped through service agreements and refined through ongoing dialogue between agencies. The system's clinical intervention was adolescent focused. It ensured that if adolescents could not be stabilized in the home, then their placement needs would be met appropriately. The system was designed to obviate treatment stagnation or deterioration by offering a variety of treatment resources that allowed adolescents to mature, make progress, or even regress if necessary. As an adolescent stabilized and improved in placement or did not, the youth could be moved to an environment that reflected the youngster's current situation and ever-evolving treatment needs. Each treatment program was designed to have inclusive parameters, but to integrate and coordinate their efforts and methodology with those of other phases. Individual treatment plans were designed to be short or long term in scope. All treatment plans focused on the youth's safety, self-awareness, autonomy, developmental strengths and weaknesses, and family relations. The overarching emphasis on self-control and self-organization in treatment planning is described by Glasser (1965) as essential for working with adolescents.

According to recent research, establishing collaboration in a system of care is not easy to achieve, because building a system of care is both a process and a product (Hodges, Nesman, & Hermandez, 1999). Nevertheless, this was a fundamental task and operational principle of the Four Phase System. Each region of Metropolitan Toronto consisted of four phases. Each phase agreed to specific treatment parameters and practices and followed defined communication channels. In practice, each agency within the system agreed to the Four Phase's mission statement, core values, treatment practices, and philosophy. From its inception, member agencies were able to reach consensus about the system's operation because they were committed to a common theory of change and process.

Each of the phases had a definite structure and function. Phase One provided assessment and coordination of services, and articulated the system's philosophy to referral agencies. Phase Two consisted of two locked settings for crisis management. These hospital-based programs served all four regions of Toronto. Phase Three operated long-term residential treatment, in urban and rural settings, with some use of wilderness experiences. Phase Four provided short-term urban-based treatment, or reentry programs that emphasized life skills and teaching youngsters how to fit into the community and to use it as a resource. Additionally, all phases offered distinct treatment stages that combined aspects of psychological and social development. Each phase interconnected and coordinated its efforts with all those of the other phases, thus operating as a treatment team.

Kruger (1986) believed that teams create more effective programs and greater satisfaction for workers. This result was observed in the system. In fact, during interagency team meetings, the Four Phase agencies developed congruent definitions of clinical process, systemic objectives, and case management standards, and believed that a system of care led to better outcomes for youth and their families. During interagency team meetings, the clinical approach to adolescents and their families was the strengths-based model, and no treatment plan was implemented that did not attain consensus. This strategic planning improved system-wide coordination. Thus, as a mental health network, communication occurred on many levels, which improved treatment options and direction. All Four Phase agencies were enriched by membership in the system, because they were able to share costly resources that would not otherwise be available. In effect, by organizing a number of programs into a modern business corporation, the Four Phase System improved access, efficacy, aftercare, and savings. Consequently, more funds were subsequently available for direct contact with its client base.

In order to make the connection between theory and technique, or to implement interventions that would work, each individual phase or program had to develop a distinct approach and treatment methodology specific to its role, while maintaining treatment constancy and providing for casework continuity with the other agencies in the system. Because each treatment program approached youngsters from different or multiple perspectives, the overall system was integrative. This eclectic philosophy required that each program operate on two levels: the abstract, for higher functioning youth who could think about ideas and their actions, and behaviorally for those youngsters who could not reflect upon the self and were limited to concrete operations, due to developmental delays and dual diagnosis. Simply put, the aim of treatment was to gear each adolescent's awareness for change, accept the need for change at her or his level of comprehension, and get the youth to cooperate with the behavioral change process. This treatment philosophy for engaging adolescents at their cognitive-emotional level, according to Prochaska and Norcross (1994), provides for a youth's psychological adjustment, but also accommodates for a lack of adjustment. Thus, each phase's approach to treatment could be classified as multidimensional, or a "stage flexible intervention."

The clinical advantage of this mental health model is that adolescents moved across various program categories or levels of service intensity, depending upon their response or lack of response to treatment. Treatment phases were not a set of sequential steps that had to be taken serially, or progressively. Yet, treatment continuity was maintained by ensuring that the unique needs of the individual were paramount. As an adolescent moved from one phase to another, the essence of her or his treatment plan was maintained, but also carefully adapted or adjusted to the youngster's new needs and goals. This is consistent with Polsky's (1962) observation that treatment agencies have the task of creating an environment that not only responds to present behaviors but also offers an opportunity for future change. This philosophy was a central tenet of the system as it offered a continuum of services that were geared to future changes, including regression.

In summary, all programs within the Four Phase System focused on what Sherradan (1992) believed to be the essential features necessary in treatment programs, that is, the remediation of individual difficulties (relearning), emotional-cognitive development (insight), and resocialization (developing social skills). These clinical goals were pursued by seeking to stabilize a youngster's symptomology, teaching youth functional aspects of interaction, and inculcating the negotiation skills needed to participate cooperatively in groups (for example, the family, at school, and within the community). The intake process and regular case reviews identified the particular service that was most beneficial to the individual youngster. Direct care staff were positioned as the most critical clinical component in every phase. Youngsters were continually socialized into the attitudes, morals, and orientations of treatment staff, and to the norms of the community at large. Evaluating adolescent behaviors and understanding how they dealt with their environment, or reacted to it, were basic to treatment planning. The knowledge gained by clinical staff within the system, such as the efficacy of various treatment approaches, the best practice for each diagnosis, and the factors to be considered for successful community reentry, was distilled to referral agencies and private practitioners. This critical knowledge of how to plan for and intervene with high-risk adolescents, how to operate residential programs, and the skills to be developed during staff development and training was part of the legacy of the Four Phase System (Pazaratz et al., 2000).

ORGANIZATIONAL RELATIONSHIPS

The Four Phase System created the framework for the growth and development of mental health services to adolescents and their families by defining the role of community-based treatment programs in Metropolitan Toronto, and eventually the Province of Ontario. The system endeavored to treat all adolescents experiencing severe emotional or mental disorders, while ensuring the safety of the adolescent and the community, in the least restrictive environment consistent with effective treatment (Finlay & Randall, 1975). Treatment varied widely and included psychoanalysis, psychoeducational therapy, milieu therapy, transactional analysis, rational emotive therapy, behavior therapy, reality therapy, and peer culture models. Where more than one treatment approach is enacted in a clinical program, the treatment rationale is termed *integrative*. Because the different phases within each region employed different treatment techniques, the system in total is considered integrative. However, in their daily experiences youngsters learned about the self by youth workers focusing on youngsters being connected and emotionally stable, learning competencies (life skills), and pursuing developmental tasks (relevance), all of which were described as essential by Hooper, Murphy, Devaney, and Hultman (2000). To this end, youth workers incorporated techniques from a variety of models that maximized the potential for youth to become receptive to daily structure, a variety of programming and counseling.

Phase One's role included the intake responsibility for each regional system and provided access information to potential users. As the gatekeeper, Phase One dealt with the expectations for service, and coordinated the referral information. Upon receiving a referral to their region, Phase One performed the family assessment and developed an initial treatment plan. The intake procedure required Phase One to evaluate what the youth and his or her family needed in order to be stabilized. The youth's evaluation was based upon symptomology and developmental adjustment. The family's assessment focused on the family's strengths and resiliency and addressed their psychological needs. Detailing a family's resiliency is consistent with a strengths-based intervention model and is expanded upon by Rapp (1998). However, the family assessment also served to ensure that admission criteria were met. Upon a youth's acceptance to the system, Phase One immediately provided home care to maintain the adolescent and his or her family until the appropriate placement became available (Pazaratz et al., 2000). In consultation with other phases, a determination was made as to the phase and specific program within the region that was the most suitable placement. In analyzing effective placement decisions, Whittaker and Pfeiffer (1994) supported the idea that placement decisions should be based upon matching the program's characteristics with the youth's problems.

Phase One monitored all treatment plans, provided treatment consultation, became involved in discharge planning, and managed aftercare services. Phase One also provided home care, outreach, and day treatment programs for adolescents who were awaiting availability of a placement or who were unwilling to be admitted to any residential placement. On those occasions when a Four Phase agency was unable or was not prepared to admit a youth, then Phase One would program for that youth, in her or his home, until that placement or an alternate placement became available. There were circumstances when a youth could not be safely held in a program or was experiencing a crisis of decompensation; when this happened, Phase One provided support by adding staff to that program or by moving the youth to a more secure setting. Phase One also provided consultation, support, and education to community agencies outside the system, especially to those agencies that accepted the less severely disturbed adolescent deemed inappropriate for placement in the system.

There were two Phase Two programs that operated at preexisting or established facilities serving all regions of Metropolitan Toronto. Both functioned as secure, locked units (psychiatrically based). Adolescents considered self-injurious, suicidal, or dangerous to others, or experiencing mental health problems with symptomology of behaviors that required constant management, were referred to either hospital unit for stabilization (Pazaratz et al., 2000). Hospitalization provides a physically safe environment that protects youth from acting out suicidal impulses. It also allows time for a more thorough evaluation. Upon admission to Phase Two, youngsters were assessed for a 20-day period. This included observable data gathered from intensive individual and group therapy, and from the youngster's reaction to behavioral expectations and controls. Phase Two's 20-day treatment aimed to make the youth feel safe and to bring about a reduction in symptomology.

Within each of the Phase Twos, there were containment procedures and secure areas that provided additional controls, restrictions, or supports. Both hospital settings emphasized comprehensive structured activities, reality orientation, and social learning experiences. Youth were encouraged to express aggressive and hostile feelings appropriately and to modify troublesome behaviors. Most importantly, dangerous acting-out behaviors were controlled through firm and consistent interventions, as well as with psychotropic medication when this clinical intervention was determined therapeutic. Containment allowed adolescents to safely experience or discharge feelings that they were unable to verbalize. This type of crisis intervention was described by Masterson and Costello (1980) as being critical to the development of a therapeutic alliance, or a precondition for working through intense and debilitating feelings of shame, anxiety, anger, and depression.

Operating as a community-based program was the treatment rationale for most Phase Threes and Fours. However, some Phase Three programs were located in rural and wilderness environments far removed from Metropolitan Toronto. Phase Three provided long-term treatment for up to 2 years and sometimes longer, because some adolescents were too regressed and "stuck" in their pathology, whereas others needed to regress in therapy. Phase Three's role as a therapeutic "holding environment" offered and created structure to foster the release of painful affect caused by intrapsychic and interpersonal conflict. Trauma was dealt with psychodynamically. Teaching adolescents to learn about themselves, others, and the world at large was the primary treatment focus.

Phase Fours, as community-based reentry programs, were designed to be short-term and less intensive, employed fewer staff, and utilized interventions that focused on living in the here and now. Phase Fours emphasized learning from real-world experiences, developing personal responsibility, and accepting the community's legal standard of right and wrong. These ideas, which focused on self-agency and were originally developed by Glasser (1965), proved especially comprehensible to many adolescents, because they quickly understood the connection between making life choices and the results or consequences that followed. Winnicott (1965) found that a milieu can be more effective when staff members emphasize the development of greater self-acceptance and actualization instead of staff focusing on the youngster's personal pain. This was often the direction of treatment, especially for those youth who were emotionally strong enough or sufficiently integrated to benefit from this existential approach. All phases within the system offered treatment classes (see Chapter 10) or a school component, structured residential programming, group process, positive peer pressure, and family work. The decision for reintegration directly into the community from Phase Four was based upon multiple measures of adaptation and the availability of social supports (Pazaratz, 1998a).

TREATMENT PHASES

There are significant disadvantages when residential treatment programs operate as a single entity or in isolation. This includes having limited experience, knowledge, perspectives, management structure, clinical skills, program flexibility, staff growth, and emergency responses, and limitations in the development and implementation of program evaluation. As Curry (1991) pointed out, with limited resources, a residential program can be ineffectual and even become demoralized in attempting to fulfill the overwhelming expectations of the community, especially when dealing with "hard-to-serve" clients. Menzies (1979) added that when human service organizations address complex and difficult problems with inadequate resources, they can too easily develop dysfunctional cultures such as low staff morale, cynical ethical attitudes by staff, and ineffective employee performance. By contrast, Anderson (2000) has found that in communities where systems of care have been implemented, these represent a fundamentally different way of delivering mental health services, so that systems of care sustain interagency collaboration or the potential to be more comprehensive as a service provider.

Treatment collaboration was experienced as a real advantage for those agencies belonging to the Four Phase System. The Four Phase System was good at getting complete information about a youth's history and character and the nature of family relationships. The system utilized multidisciplinary clinicians most efficiently because their roles and process were defined. The agencies of the system were proficient at stabilizing, counseling, reeducating, and reintegrating high-risk adolescents. This occurred because each youngster's treatment status and progress were constantly evaluated. Treatment outcomes were generalized to a sample of adolescents receiving residential treatment for the same problems, and thereby interventions and the use of resources were maximized. Importantly, costs were contained because services were provided in the community and duplication of services was kept to a minimum in the system (Pazaratz et al., 2000).

Other strengths of the Four Phase System were its abilities to define service accessibility and stick with it, and to be immediately responsive to families in crisis. Placement decisions were based on a match between the program's characteristics and an adolescent's reasons for referral, and not upon the availability of a bed. Linking of a youth's pathology to treatment resources was supported by Whittaker and Pfeiffer (1994). Additionally, it has been shown by Well (1991) that treatment programs achieve "goodness-of-fit" by defining the types of problems that they are effective with and why. Goodness of fit occurred in the system, because each regional treatment team met regularly to discuss treatment plans, programming issues, interagency communication, and issues that flowed from clinical practice. Aftercare programs critical to a youngster's successful community reintegration were integral to treatment planning. Treatment outcome was measured in terms of psychosocial adjustment, or absence of symptomology, as well as functional aspects of behavioral change in family, school, community, and so on (Pazaratz et al., 2000).

GENERAL PRINCIPLES OF TREATMENT

All treatment programs under the Four Phase System were classified as *children's mental health centres* (known as *residential treatment facilities* in the United States), and they were funded at that level. A residential treatment facility has been defined by Tuma (1989) as a 24-hour facility, not licensed as a hospital, which provides mental health treatment programs for mentally disordered children. This definition as coined by Tuma is similar to the mandate of the Four Phase agencies that were required to be exceptionally strongly resourced programs. The programs were designed for the hard-to-serve adolescent, who typically came from a highly dysfunctional family. The family was frequently very rejecting or was unable to involve itself in the therapeutic process. However, there was no requirement that parents participate in the adolescent's treatment. There was a focus on the adolescent as an individual. Yet, throughout the placement period, there was an active outreach to parents encouraging them to connect positively with their child, through visiting and by providing updated information on the youngster's progress. Whenever there was a potential to facilitate the adolescent's return to the family unit, this was the major focus of treatment and the discharge goal. But, when an adolescent was not able to return to his or her family upon discharge, the goal was to support any kind of family connection that was advantageous for the youth (Pazaratz et al., 2000).

The typical profile of an adolescent admitted to the Four Phase System included inadequate coping mechanisms and poor resiliency skills, so that the youth was unable to function adequately within his or her family, the community at large, and the local public school district. Upon admission to the system, rarely did any adolescent demonstrate a commitment to any part of the treatment process. Therefore, in order to stabilize youngsters, external controls were placed on them at the least intrusive level, or sufficient for safety until they were able to develop internal controls. Ultimately, success of placement was based on the program's (staff's) ability to provide residents with experiences, which strengthened their self-image and locus of control. This competency-based approach was enacted through structured achievement experiences that were developed for youth, which helped youngsters to measure their progress against themselves, other youth, and the world in general. According to Prochaska and Norcross (1994), helping youngsters to increase knowledge about problems through interactions with others and by helping them to develop observation and interpretation skills is essential. For those youngsters who would never return to their family, but would move to independence, life skills training was deemed critical to reinforce the capacity for self-care (Pazaratz et al., 2000).

Case histories of youngsters placed in the system revealed background conditions in their families, with peers, and at school that had served to isolate and alienate the youth from other people. Additionally, most youth had never experienced their parents or family as a supportive constellation, nor had they ever learned to rely on others in a trusting way (Finlay & Randall, 1975). Thus, another benefit for youngsters placed in the system was an environmental change that helped to lessen the influence of subcultural attachments that Prochaska and Norcross (1994) believed reinforce negative behaviors. There was also a strong effort on the part of each individual treatment program to provide experiences where youth could develop a sense of cooperative dependence within group interactions. Residents were taught cause and effect, or to understand the impact that their negative behaviors had on the environment, including significant others.

According to Serin and Brown (1996), a major treatment objective involves increasing a youth's motivation for treatment, and this was always a focus of casework and the contracting process. Experiences with contractual processes underlined the concepts of trust and commitment. This distinction is viewed as critical and elevates treatment above containment (Pazaratz, 1999) even though residential treatment is based upon safety derived in containment. However, due to the severe nature of their pathology, the process of change for many youth was often slow and incremental. Resistance to treatment was often encountered. Resistance is perceived to occur because the individual is less motivated and, therefore, makes fewer behavioral changes (Preston & Murphy, 1997). In addition, resistance to treatment was understood conceptually as the youth's need to defy and challenge external controls, the youngster's inability to trust authority figures, and the fact that most youth did not have a supportive family or hope for the future (Pazaratz et al., 2000).

All Four Phase programs created therapeutic social milieus through group work. They also made provisions for academic remediation and nonacademic skills development. The general treatment approach enacted by direct care staff was psychodynamic, or the interpretation of communication and interactions. This approach emphasizes discussions so that youngsters could learn from their peers and by reflecting upon experiences (Bandura, 1977). Individual treatment plans were developed for each youth, and the youngster participated in the contractual process. Unless residents define their problems from their perspective, articulate their life goals, and commit to a method and a time frame for changing, then the treatment process and the youth's progress will be impeded. Contracting as a clinical tool was fundamental to bringing about behavioral change (Pazaratz, 1998a). Treatment completion was based upon multiple measures of adaptation and the youth's ability to reflect upon his or her progress, and to identify new needs. The average length of stay in the residential portion of the system was 18 months followed by support from aftercare and community care programs enacted by Phase One. Some adolescents needed supportive services into their adulthood.

THE EFFICACY OF THE SYSTEM

The Four Phase System never had a written mission statement or definition, but rather service agreements developed between agencies that defined the process. Even though there was a concept of how the system would operate and evolve, member agencies cooperated because there was both an "idea of purpose" and no divergence on how they defined emotional and behavioral disorders and the criteria for change. Ultimately, the member agencies were effective at articulating the system's mandate, and this enabled referring agencies and workers within the system to believe that the system would be efficacious. Tichy and Ulrich (1984) argued that energizing staff or getting them to subscribe to a common goal requires this sort of transformational leadership. Clearly, participation in the development of an innovative treatment system for the high-risk adolescent motivated staff members.

Over time, specific decision-making procedures were developed that strengthened the system (i.e., each agency's functioning and interagency cooperation). However, there were no policies for dealing with disputes between member agencies, or for minimizing interagency disagreements that occurred in part because all agencies retained their independence and an autonomous board of directors. Yet, despite some discord, there was an atmosphere where everyone felt free to contribute, and to a large measure did so (Pazaratz et al., 2000). Moss (1974) discussed how cooperative team functioning is related to positive clinical outcome, and this was experienced within the system.

The Four Phase System has been regarded as efficacious by Pazaratz et al. (2000) because it did not deviate from its clinical focus of defining service accessibility and "tracking" of adolescents. Case management and systems theory were incorporated as clinical practices. The team concept added to treatment integrity as it forced agencies to be open in their treatment approach, to collaborate around each case, and to follow established case management standards or principles (Pazaratz et al.). Dumphrey (1978) was correct in his findings that organizational metaphors and myths serve as a unifying theme. The workers within the system developed a feeling of the specialness of their efforts. An open discussion of their clinical approaches allowed other agencies to evaluate treatment efforts, and to provide input or criticism. Ultimately, the adolescent benefited because it was not taken for granted that all decisions were right. No case was discharged until the youth's treatment needs were resolved (Pazaratz et al.).

Although not all clinical interventions with every youngster were successful, the system developed critical knowledge and practical recommendations on how to establish, organize, and provide direct care to families and to operate residential programs that are relevant for today. There was ongoing sharing of critical knowledge among and between agencies in an effort to minimize interagency struggles, to recognize the equal status of agencies, and to establish an atmosphere to which everyone felt encouraged to contribute. Each agency's service plan relative to its mission statement and goals was communicated to agencies within and outside the system. As agencies evolved or refined their clinical process, these new procedures were shared with other member agencies in order to maintain the balance between the system's security function and its treatment and care protocols.

The fragmentations that occur when agencies perform the dual function of treatment and control, as described by Finch and Hewling (1978), never became a system problem because the Four Phase System operated contextually, continually adjusting its services to the changing needs of adolescents. The system responded to societal trends and family problems, and recognized how changes in family lifestyles and society led to increased problems for some youth. The system had an effective consultative function with other community agencies such as Children's Aid Societies, family courts, school boards, detention facilities, probation officers, government policy makers, and the like (Pazaratz et al., 2000). Importantly, The Four Phase System was a precursor to the Child and Adolescent Services System Program (CASSP) enacted by the U.S. government in 1984 (as described by Stroul & Friedman, 1986), whose mandate is to provide support for communities to develop mechanisms for coordinating services among agencies that serve children and their families with multisystem needs.

Though there were many successes, major problems remained unsolved. First, it proved unworkable to have only severely disturbed youth in any one program. For many staff, it was unrewarding to work with youth who made little change over a long time frame. The theory that all clients would be treated effectively, if centrally accessed and monitored, proved unrealistic, because the system could not accommodate the sheer number of adolescents needing services. As a result, there were some youth who were rejected as being too difficult, even though the Four Phase System was developed and sold to funding authorities as meeting the need for hard-to-serve, high-risk adolescents. With a limited number of beds, it was not possible to treat all referrals. The design was too idealistic, as well as insufficient! As a result, "treatment beds" had to be purchased outside of the system.

The unloading of difficult clients is not an uncommon problem in the mental health sector. This situation was encountered by the Four Phase System, whereby some referring agencies would label an adolescent as "crazy" or would manipulate the youth's presenting diagnosis to fit admission criteria. Thus, in order to have access to the system, some agencies were not totally candid with their referral information, purposefully leaving out the adolescent's strengths (Pazaratz et al., 2000). Stoner (1985) decried clinical exaggeration, or downplaying positive aspects of an individual's personality, as intellectual and clinical dishonesty that is prejudicial and detrimental to a patient. This was encountered as a problem for the system, because symptomology was often described to fit admission parameters.

The most problematic aspect to the smooth operation of the Four Phase System proved to be that none of the programs funded in the system were compelled to cooperate with other Four Phase agencies or to even accept youth from any other Four Phase agency. The board of directors of each individual Four Phase agency held the position that they were autonomous and that their responsibility was primarily to their immediate community and secondarily to the system. Eventually, the cooperation and coalition building among the agencies and between the four regions of the Four Phase System waned, especially when some boards of directors were fearful of losing their autonomy and decision-making capabilities to the system. Disagreement also evolved between those clinicians who believed in advocacy and those who championed case management (Pazaratz et al., 2000). Bardach (1977) discussed this type of service dilemma as arising when conflicting expectations of stakeholders and the pressures from constantly shifting social and political agendas undermine a program's specific goals and become an obstacle to success. Hargrove (1975) noted that the reality of the political process is that groups vie for control, or defend programs from any criticism, and this precipitates the redefinition and delivery of mental health services. Not only did this occur, but also the Four Phase System finally was doomed when the Ontario government changed its priorities and reallocated funding from this project to support social services, outpatient health care, housing, education, and the like. Chandler (1991) stated that when policy makers and planners come to view mental illness and its manifestations more as a reflection of social disability, there is a resounding shift in priorities.

SUMMARY

The Four Phase System was set up by the Ontario government to find a more compassionate and effective way to treat hard-to-serve, disturbed adolescents. The system was created when a need was identified from a thorough evaluation of the clinical, educational, and social problems of the high-risk adolescent (Finlay & Randall, 1975). The system was composed of agencies that linked specialized individual treatment programs in a unified whole. Unfortunately, funding for the Four Phase System excluded an evaluation component. This inability to statistically validate its efficacy effectively undermined the system, because its impact and relevance were never measured quantitatively. According to Dryden (1996), to bridge the gap between research and theory, treatment evaluation is necessary so that the immediate relevance becomes reflected in the methods utilized. Shapiro, Freiberg, and Bandstein (2006) added that adopting evidence-based practice provides a balanced coverage of child therapy, theory, research, and practice.

On the federation level, the Four Phase System provided an idea of purpose to which individual agencies and their workers felt connected. The system was clear at defining its services and method for accomplishing its goals with adolescents and their families. The system created opportunities for families to access specialized services according to their needs. This was important for the ever-changing and evolving nature of families. The Four Phase System was at the vanguard of reflecting policies, behaviors, and attitudes that were cross-culturally focused by offering culturally congruent services, which Benjamin and Isaacs-Shockley (1996) stated are critical for publicly funded organizations to have credibility.

In attempting to meet too many and diverse service needs for an ever-expanding spectrum of difficult youth, crucial problems arose, such as high staff turnovers, some adolescents being too regressed for the system, and others tying up beds because of the severe nature of their pathology. Naïvely, the system tried to treat all hard-to-serve youth. Extremely difficult adolescents would block the system for a year or so. By design, it was not possible to put up a "no vacancy" sign. As a result of not being able to fulfill the demand for treatment beds, service providers had to develop a system outside the system. Additional treatment agencies were recruited to handle some excess cases (Pazaratz et al., 2000). Out of necessity, intervention strategies had to be shifted from treatment to prevention, and this proactive process is described more fully by Rappaport (1981). Without a funding increase, this shift in priorities depleted limited resources for residential treatment.

Clearly, some adolescents referred to the system were better served in other settings. This was realized with the development of treatment alternatives. To their credit, the service providers within the system were abreast of the interaction between changes in the system and how this affected treatment response. Cohen and Cohen (2000) stressed the importance of this particular flexibility, wherein social service organizations develop realistic goals and priorities, but are also able to redefine organizational structure, thereby repositioning an agency through successful coalition building and reorienting staff to cope with change.

The Four Phase System as a coalition of service providers was largely successful at adapting to evolving priorities. In this regard, staff education was actively promoted as critical to the provision of quality services to youngsters and for improving treatment outcome. Additionally, organizational metaphors and myths were utilized by the system to bolster staff morale and served as a unifying theme. Dumphrey (1978) has shown that people who respond to a "unifying theme" internalize pictures of the workplace, and this confers meaning on its various members. Many direct care staff who worked in the Four Phase System came to believe that they were the elite in their field, because they worked with the most difficult youth.

The Four Phase System was effective with most adolescents placed in treatment. However, increased pressure developed to redeploy limited resources to nonclinical community-based programs and service models. Scull (1993) pointed out that when mental health is linked to social process or is seen as replacing the function of the family, it is then reformed or restructured by policies that pursue more sociocultural development. Over the life of the Four Phase System (1973–1990), government policy makers increasingly sought to help disturbed adolescents by changing environmental factors and by modifying the delivery of social support.

Eventually, the Four Phase System became unsustainable when a difference of opinion arose between policy makers and clinicians over the cost-effectiveness of the system. Thus, some of the clinical parameters of the system were reduced and replaced with social assistance programs. Nevertheless, the demise of the system is an example of how social policy decisions should be made on the basis of data gained from practice, research and outcome studies, or the blending of political action with scholarly and clinical experience, and not on the basis of political pressure from lobby groups. With the demise of the system, individual community-based treatment facilities in Ontario no longer offer a richness and diversity of therapeutic resources.

Although the Four Phase System had no formal measure of treatment outcome, it was observed by senior clinicians that youth with greater ability for developing interpersonal relationships, intellectual capacity for language and problem solving, absence of concretistic disordered thinking laden with primitive ideation, and acute as opposed to chronic onset of problems progressed more favorably (Pazaratz et al., 2000). These conclusions, as noted over a 17-year period concerning treatment prognosis and progress, have been corroborated in the literature, especially by Erker, Searight, Amanat, and White (1993). In addition, Anderson, Kooreman, Mohr, Wright, and Russel (2002) have found in their research that systems of care produce successful outcomes in their involvement with families while containing costs of care.

INTEGRATIVE TREATMENT PRINCIPLES AND PRACTICES

The Four Phase System established some essential treatment guidelines that are now standard treatment principles and child care practices. The central tenets concerning residential treatment are that it is an integral part of caring, it should focus on improving an adolescent's or a child's capacities to deal effectively with both feelings and behavior, it should aim to modify that which is dysfunctional, and, ultimately, this fundamental change assists in the process of socialization. For many youngsters, receiving immediate therapeutic intervention is required to ensure their safety, which is often predicated on the control and modification of destructive behaviors. Therefore, there must be effective treatment strategies that can be quickly brought into play as a planned response for difficulties being experienced by youth. The Four Phase System's guidelines for enacting an integrative treatment methodology include the following:

A. PRINCIPLE: refers to the philosophical and ethical stance concerning the purpose and context of treatment and care. Basic principles are fundamental to the structure and operation of a therapeutic milieu and should pervade any interaction with all children, adolescents, and families of theirs that receive treatment.

1. *Normalization*: As defined in the context of residential treatment, this ensures that the individual's needs are met. In order for this to occur, the patterns and conditions of everyday residential life are as close as possible to those that are the normal patterns of the mainstream of society (Wolfensberger, 1971) and are to be promoted by direct care staff. Therefore, the living conditions are typical, and at least as good as those of the ordinary youngster not in treatment. The purpose of these conditions is to foster the development of the youth's full potential. Application of the normalization principle has social implications that are used to shape the treatment milieu, such as the layout of bedrooms, personal space, and the like.

2. *Individualization*: The services offered in a treatment program should meet the individualized needs of residents. Treatment programming takes into account the normal as well as the special physical, psychological, developmental, and environmental tasks of each young person and his or her family. The treatment agency provides for the necessary physical and human resources to implement its service response at the levels of a specific population and the individual case.

3. *Acceptance*: This principle implies the creation of a treatment environment whereby the child or adolescent and his or her family are accepted as they are, in their totality, including strengths, weaknesses, and the full range of their feelings—anger, sadness, love, etc.—thereby always maintaining a sense of the person's innate dignity and personal worth. Acceptance does not mean approval or tolerance of a behavior that is destructive to the self or others. It does mean that a problematic behavior is dealt with in a way that maintains an atmosphere of acceptance of the person as a whole.

4. *Purposeful expression of feelings*: This principle also implies an atmosphere that permits the recognition of the total range of a child's, adolescent's, or parent's feelings—and provides realistic opportunities for the safe expression of those feelings, again in ways that are not destructive to the self or others, and as part of the therapeutic process.

5. *Self-determination*: This principle emphasizes the active participation of the youth and his or her parents in the delineation and carrying out of the treatment plan, including the right to make

choices and decisions. It is understood, however, that the resident's right to self-determination is limited by his or her capacity for positive and constructive decision making and by the framework of civil and moral law.

B. TREATMENT PLANNING PROCEDURES: *Procedures* refer to the means of establishing accountability and responsibility within the agency, and ensure that principles and practices remain well integrated. In residential treatment, the treatment plan or a plan of care is essential to casework. A written treatment plan for each youth and his or her family should be available and known to all staff (also see Chapter 5).

1. The treatment plan should include:
    a. formulation of the problem,
    b. a treatment approach of choice,
    c. a school or work plan,
    d. treatment goals,
    e. treatment strategies to be employed,
    f. specific monitoring procedures and timelines, and
    g. a discharge plan.

2. The treatment plan is based upon and affects the following:
    a. All behavioral events that elucidate the youth's problems or bear directly on the established treatment goals. This means that daily events are recorded on the day when such events occur. Review of these notes (recordings) occurs during staff changeover as well as during supervision.
    b. Progress notes such as month-end reports in relation to defined goals are recorded by appropriate staff at intervals determined at initial goal setting.
    c. Regularly scheduled team meetings to review individual treatment plans and progress take place at suitable intervals. This allows for specific techniques to be monitored and evaluated regularly to assess their effectiveness in relation to achieving treatment goals. Any treatment approach should be stopped if it is not producing beneficial results.
    d. Changes in treatment plans and the setting of new goals (including the possibility of discharge) are based on thoughtful decisions to which all relevant staff, the youth, and the family contribute. Included in this process are those professionals from the community who are currently or likely to be involved with the youth and his or her family.
    e. To make treatment more relevant to the lives of youngsters, and to establish connections between personal and societal opportunities, all youngsters and their parents should know (in a general way and in advance) the types of treatment

interventions that may be used, and the purposes thereof. Informed consent forms should be developed by individual agencies that reflect their philosophy and their treatment rationales.

C. TREATMENT PRACTICES: *Practices* refer to specific techniques and interventions that are used to treat youth and their family.

1. Although the youngster is understood in the context of her or his family, the youth is often, out of necessity, the primary focus of intervention. The young person's treatment plan should be based on the youth's vision. The plan and its method of implementation should assist the youngster to want to change and grow, and to learn from experience. However, in the process of change, some techniques are more effective at different treatment stages. There should be a process whereby the youth is encouraged to interact and to connect with her or his family, staff, peers, and the community.

    In those circumstances where the youth's family is rejecting, or is unable to be involved in a therapeutic process, it would be unrealistic to require the family to be involved. However, there should be a continuous outreach to the family in an effort to engage them to connect positively. A major focus of treatment and a goal with respect to discharge planning is the potential for facilitating the family's reconnection with their child. The criteria for an effective intervention program include identifying the strengths and resources of the family, engaging them in the treatment process, and using contracting or a short-term treatment model (Berry, 1997). Where youngsters cannot live with their family following discharge, the treatment goal is to support whatever level of improvement that is possible in the youth–family relationship.

2. Youngsters who are referred to residential treatment typically lack impulse or behavioral controls. This means they display poor reality testing and problem-solving strategies necessary for satisfying social, emotional, or behavioral interactions. External controls are placed on youngsters until they are able to develop frustration tolerance and effective internal controls. Where a youngster's ability does not exist, staff should not expect a commitment to the treatment process, and front-line staff should also understand that there often will be a lack of motivation and a good deal of resistance (Pazaratz, 1998a).

3. Success and achievement experiences are essential for a youngster's development of a positive self-concept. The effectiveness of any treatment plan is largely based on its ability to provide the resident with experiences that strengthen the youngster's

self-image. Residential treatment offers opportunities for social and negotiation skills development. Learning from peer–adult interactions, the social environment, and community experiences provides the context by which young persons discover themselves and measure their progress against themselves, each other, and the world in general.

4. *Accepting reality*: Inappropriate behavioral responses are frequently an attempt by youth to gain control over their environment or relationships. Life skills training reinforces the capacity for gaining self-control and for self-esteem development. Unfortunately, some residents can never return to their family, but move directly to independence. They need practical information in order to live and function autonomously and in the real world.

5. *Responsibility for behaviors*: Contractual processes emphasize the concepts of personal accountability, trust, commitment, and developing realistic goals. Youngsters need help in setting practical, obtainable goals, and encouragement to follow through on their goals and to pursue prosocial and proself behaviors. Residential placement should provide experiences that help residents to develop a sense of cooperative dependence with peers and staff. This occurs through learning improved communication and interactional techniques.

6. *Treatment progress*: Adolescents do not make rapid changes when problems are severe. Due to the intensity and duration of their problems, the process of change is slow and incremental. Counseling aims to bring about change in the youth's personality and a reduction in symptoms. However, treatment resistance by youth occurs on many levels and includes testing or rejecting external controls, lack of trust in authority figures, and lack of supportive family connection. The treatment period for any youth may be short term (under 6 months) or from 1 to 2 years. However, change is more likely to occur when youth realize that the benefits of changing are greater than the cost of maintaining unhealthy behaviors. Upon discharge, there may be a need for a supportive but less treatment-oriented experience.

7. *Treatment program components*: The treatment program should offer a range of specific activities and experiences for the individual as an individual and as part of the group. Individual treatment plans are developed for each adolescent and focus on individual needs (see Chapter 2). An individual's treatment plan includes behaviors targeted for change and skills to be learned. Contracting as a clinical tool is fundamental to treatment plans. Individual counseling occurs in the context of the situation or

the environment (life space), and when it is deemed appropriate. Discharge planning is a part of each case review throughout placement, and the referral agency is kept appraised and involved in this process.

8. The general treatment program should include the following:

   a. *Activities component*: Specific therapeutic activities should occur in the group home and the surrounding community. Activities emphasize cooperative group interaction, help the participants to gain enjoyment, and provide individual interest development (see Chapter 9). Child care workers are directly involved in designing and giving leadership to individual and group recreational activities, including activities programming on weekends.

   b. *Life skills component*: This component teaches youngsters how to live in the real world, to look after themselves, and to utilize their inner resources in relation to their daily needs. The intent of life skills is to show youth where to put their vitality and creativity, and how to understand and to cope with problematic situations. Life skills can be essential in encouraging treatment participation and for shaping behavior. As a learning opportunity, life skills inform adolescents of successful ways of handling the demands of the world while relying on their own talents and knowledge. Life skills training involves practical information in basic aspects of independence and daily functioning such as shopping, cooking, locating a place to live, finding and keeping a job, using the transit system, budgeting, constructively using leisure time, engaging in personal health care, developing friendships, and resisting negative influences.

   c. *Group interactions*: The ability to communicate within a group and to learn from others is the primary purpose of the group treatment component. Utilizing the group format requires staff to coordinate the activities and participation of a disparate group of youngsters, and mobilize them to act in concert (positive peer pressure) and cooperate with the program's goals. During formal groups and unstructured groups, the importance of peer interactions cannot be overemphasized. It is through the group process that youth increase their knowledge about their problems. This occurs with staff support that includes staff labeling, explaining, or distilling complex interlocking problems and conflictual situations so that youngsters can make sense of these transactions.

   The group format and staff interpretation provide a vehicle for communication, feedback, and understanding of different points of view. Groups provide opportunities for residents to come together or coalesce around common themes and values. Groups stimulate a youth's ability to observe the self, to know the self, and to understand which internal values and beliefs need to be changed or adjusted. Groups offer youngsters practical situations where they can learn to deal with negative emotions that are related to unhealthy behaviors. Participation in support groups has been found to be beneficial to individual residents (Pazaratz, 1998a).

d. *Individual counseling component*: Competency in counseling requires that staff utilize communication and interactional skills on a level the youngster can understand. Staff need to know what kinds of information should be sought from youngsters, how it can be obtained, and how it should be utilized. Staff counseling skills include dealing with disruptive behaviors or externalized problems. This means that staff must be able to recognize and respond to emotional symptoms or internalized problems, have knowledge of substance-related problems, and be able to support a youth both in the residence and in the community.

e. *School component*: Various programs within the Four Phase System, such as the Oshawa/Whitby Crisis Intervention Centre (a reentry, Phase Four treatment program), developed highly structured day treatment programs. Day treatment included a school component, and it was considered essential for youngsters who could not attend any community school. Day treatment programs as a distinct resource had as their focus practical skills development, learning of life skills, and engaging in work preparation training (Pazaratz, 1998c). Basic to the academic portion of day treatment were remediation and support for the emotional-behavioral adjustment of students (Pazaratz, 2001). The academic assessment was considered an important function of the local board of education's support services that ensured an appropriate educational curriculum specific to each individual's learning style. Upon a youth becoming behaviorally and emotionally stabilized, reintegration into the regular school system could be enacted on a gradual or part-time basis. The day treatment model is now known as a treatment class, and it is described in Chapter 10.

f. *Staff training*: Focuses upon clarifying the staff member's thinking about the relationship between treatment goals and the strategies used to reach those goals. Staff training encourages those who work with children and adolescents in residential treatment to be as clear as possible about their "theory of change," i.e., to ensure that staff think about the therapeutic choices and decisions they make. This approach provides a fresh perspective and generates new strategies for change. It is particularly important to keep "long-term" residential treatment as short as possible and not to institutionalize youngsters during their placement (Pazaratz, 2000a).

g. *Psychosocial Assessments*: It is assumed that most, if not all, youngsters are usually assessed by a psychologist or psychiatrist prior to admission to residential treatment. However, some psychological assessments do not always provide a sufficient basis for proper treatment planning. During the course of treatment, additional information is often required that helps with the youngster's adjustment to placement and documents this process. This critical information can be elicited in a highly structured format known as a Psychosocial Assessment (see Chapter 3), which is recorded by a child and youth worker and builds upon a psychological and/or psychiatric assessment. Such issues as the resident's way of viewing the world, effective behavioral controls, stress tolerance, reality testing, adequacy of psychological resources, relationship with family, and self-concept are important to the identification of realistic treatment goals and suitable strategies for reaching those.

h. *Milieu treatment*: A *milieu*, in the broad sense of the term, means "a school for living" and is the context whereby residents learn from their experiences and interactions with others during group discussions, activities, and their environment. Milieu treatment includes life space counseling, which occurs when indicated or, as needed, in the moment and in the situation. Some youth need additional therapy for problems that are beyond the education and training of child and youth care workers. These clinical sessions can be conducted more formally in individual or group therapy by a social worker, by a psychologist, or by contracting with community resources.

i. *Staff development*: Direct care staff must be able to deliver a host of services to youngsters with multiple problems and needs. Staff development includes acquiring knowledge of and the building of skills across a wide range of relevant topics such as symptom patterns, clinical codes and categories, ethical and professional responsibilities, documentation (case notes), treatment modalities, behavioral patterns of the youth population in treatment and their deviation from the norm, and the impact of learning problems or disabilities. Front-line staff must also understand group dynamics, understand how to help youth to achieve program and contract goals, help youngsters to develop a vision of themselves, promote their independence, and teach life skills and job readiness (Pazaratz, 2003b). These staff skills are realized through effective communication, cooperation, and coordination with team members, supervisors, and clinical consultants (see Chapter 7).

j. *Staff support*: Even when staff are well qualified through education and work history, a strong background does not prevent workers from experiencing intense job-related stressors, feeling emotionally drained, and becoming negative, inflexible, or withdrawn from residents (Kreisher, 2002). According to Robbins (1992), symptoms of burnout can be revealed in recurrent bouts of tension, anxiety, irritability, headaches, insomnia, substance abuse, and the like. When treatment staff feel overwhelmed emotionally, there can be inattention to the residents' needs, rigid adherence to rules, inability to concentrate, and even abusive behaviors or blaming youth for their own problems (Arches, 1991). It is the multiple roles and tasks that front-line workers must handle in a rapidly evolving environment that are challenging for staff members and the treatment team. Continuous staff training and development assist staff to cope with and understand their emotional reactions and job-related stressors. Although individual counseling of staff is neither intended nor appropriate, nevertheless on occasion personal issues do surface in supervision (Pazaratz, 2005a). For example, some direct care staff will blame their supervisor or the agency when they are confused or make mistakes (Pazaratz & Morton, 2002). At times, individual support and assistance from a consultant such as a psychologist, a psychiatrist, or other resource personnel can help to promote staff effectiveness, tenure, and stability within the program (Pazaratz, 2003b).

k. *Program evaluation*: Ultimately, the effectiveness of any mental health or social service organization has to be evaluated in terms of the efficaciousness of outcome measures. Although a control group is basic for a scientific measurement of effectiveness, a control group is especially hard to set up in examining any applied group or residential setting (Helgerson, Martinovich, Durkin, & Lyons, 2005). Nevertheless, Davidson-Methot (2004) made the case for the utility of qualitative methods in improving our understanding of the reasons for the success or failure of mental health services. Davidson-Methot believed the question of program effectiveness can indeed be addressed through both formal and informal means. Evaluative measures should include feedback from residents, their families, and other stakeholders such as referring agencies and collateral service providers (within the community). But in examining how children and adolescents adapt to treatment, self-reported developmental and social attainments are often more revealing of adjustment than are changes in symptomatic behaviors (Pazaratz, 1999).

CONCLUSION

The Four Phase System was established as an adolescent-centered service for the extremely disturbed youth. Wherever possible, it attempted to repair family relationships. It consisted of community-based treatment programs that provided a continuum of care in an effort to coordinate and develop mental health services for adolescents. It was a totally new way of service delivery for North America in 1973. Its treatment rationale and approach have today become the standard for defining mental health services not only to adolescents but also to children and their families. Its innovative use of day treatment for learning disabled and behaviorally disordered youth has changed the way in which school districts understand the unique learning and developmental needs of this special population of at-risk youngsters.

The Four Phase System relied upon a multiagency service plan where youth could move across various program categories or levels of service intensity. Each treatment program within each phase of every region specialized in one aspect of the adolescent's treatment such as assessment and placement, crisis management and stabilization, long-term treatment, and reentry or discharge. Ultimately, the most profound legacy of the Four Phase System was its contribution to the knowledge base of working with extremely disturbed adolescents in the community, in their homes, and within the school system. It downsized the need for acute in-patient adolescent psychiatric hospital beds with the placement of seriously disturbed teenagers in community residential care. The Four Phase System also demonstrated that many of these same youngsters, who were initially placed in Children's Mental Health Centres, could be serviced in less costly therapeutic group homes and that the length of placement could be reduced. It underscored the fact that adolescents who came into contact with the justice system also had emotional problems and needed treatment as well as or instead of detention.

The Four Phase System established the advantage and effectiveness of an integrative therapeutic rationale as the basis for operating individual programs and systems of care. Unfortunately, the Four Phase System also attempted to deal with all social and family breakdown from a clinical perspective. This led to an increasing number of referrals, which overwhelmed the system (Pazaratz et al., 2000). However, England and Cole (1992) have substantiated what was demonstrated by the system: that the provision of a comprehensive and coordinated mental health system of care to youngsters with severe emotional disturbance is both feasible and more effective than depending on a single system of care. Clearly, the existence of the Four Phase System for 17 years is a testament to its effectiveness.

CHAPTER 2

Evaluation

REFERRAL INFORMATION

When youngsters are referred to residential treatment, the following background information is needed: age, reasons for referral, treatment history, and the youth's legal status (for example, ward of a children's aid society or county social service agency, young offender, persons in need of supervision, and so forth). Included in the referral package should be a social history, psychological assessment, medical report, mental status examination (for psychotic youngsters), case history, and academic evaluation or school records. This information details the youngster's psychological functioning (incompleteness), cognitive abilities or limitations, quality of relationships, type of self-indulgence, nature of impulsivity, strivings for recognition, protective barriers, and emotional weaknesses. The youngster's capacity for change and reintegration, the youngster's objects of identification, and the nature of conscious and unconscious conflicts need to be addressed (Aldridge & Wood, 1998). A comprehensive psychosocial profile helps the treatment team to understand the source of behavioral problems and social conflicts experienced in the youth's family, and the factors that led to the youth's apprehension, detention, placement, and the like. Of importance is what has been tried with the youth and his or her family, the nature of progress, and the probable reason for any failures, such as their socioeconomic situation, relationship problems, community conflicts, and school adjustment difficulties (Kamphaus & Campbell, 2006).

It is important for the treatment team to have an accurate picture of the youth's background experiences. These should include a description of behaviors: whether the youth is aggressive and violent, sets fire, commits theft, is a victim of physical and/or sexual abuse, or is physically (sexually) abusive of family members or others in the community. Youngsters can present with a range of problems such as being sexual perpetrators, runners, and addicts; and having experienced family suicide, a family member being jailed, or a family member being hospitalized (as mentally ill). The youngster may be hyperactive, be learning disabled, have suicidal tendencies, or engage in self-mutilation (Bertolino & Thompson, 1999). Frequently, youngsters referred to treatment have experimented with substance use or abuse (Pazaratz, 2005c). But, generally, a youth's antisocial behaviors have resulted in, or were caused by, family breakdown or the youth gravitating toward a countercultural lifestyle. These issues must be identified and detailed (Tremblay, Hartup, & Archer, 2005). A preplacement interview and/or a preplacement stay of a week in duration (when possible) can be beneficial. This helps the treatment team to develop an impression of the youth, to formulate the treatment approach, and to define intervention strategies. Preplacement visits also allow youth to prepare for leaving home or their previous placement and transition to residential admission. A preplacement interview conducted prior to a youth entering the program allows the youth an opportunity to negotiate a contract for placement and to establish discharge criteria (Taylor & Alpert, 1973).

PSYCHOLOGICAL ASSESSMENTS

The purpose of a diagnostic or psychological assessment, as part of the referral package, is to provide the treatment program with an overview of the youth's level of functioning and maturation. It also describes the youngster's relationship to and position within his or her family (Kandel, 2005). The assessment attempts to identify the nature of the family's pathology, such as the degree to which the youth and/or the family are stuck in their behaviors, and what the treatment goals are. A balanced assessment addresses developmental areas, the youth's strengths (Laursen, 2000) and weaknesses relative to age- and phase-normative behaviors, and the adjusted functioning of a similarly aged youth. The assessment focuses on the youngster's needs. It details those supports that must be built into a treatment plan in order to stabilize the youth to get him or her to be responsive, to assume self-control, and to interact prosocially (Kamphaus & Campbell, 2006).

The Psychological Assessment provides treatment staff with the methods and rationale to assist youth to develop self-understanding, the skills necessary to resolve conflicts, and the procedures for attaining goals. Relevance is ensured by identifying a youth's unique needs and goals and by noting which changes in the youngster's past (whether positive or negative) have affected the youth. The assessment is the basis for the treatment plan as it seeks to determine the factors that led to the onset of maladaptive paths versus those that led to the maintenance of psychopathology (Pazaratz & Morton, 2003). This means that problematic behaviors are understood in terms of age of onset, antecedents, and long-term consequences. In order to resolve conflictual behaviors, the assessment especially focuses on solutions or opportunities (goals) to improve the youth's condition (Sattler, 1988).

Some factors and conditions may have changed between the youth's referral and admission. Thus, additional information is often required in order to make the treatment plan relevant (Dyer, 2006). Of major interest is the resident's object relations and the defense mechanisms that are employed. Additionally, the psychological assessment should inform the placement agency of the techniques prescribed to stabilize the youth, the ability to understand cause and effect, and the nature of self-concept. Addressing these issues helps in setting realistic treatment goals and suitable strategies for reaching them.

Upon placement, the youth's treatment plan flows from the psychological assessment, is devised in discussions with team members, and includes identifying specific types of interventions that will stimulate growth. This process challenges youth at a realistic level so that they do not become overwhelmed, too dependent on staff members, or institutionalized (Pazaratz, 2000a). Staff members' assistance is essential in order to help youth to understand the social system, interactional patterns, and program expectations and to modify goals as needed. Staff members will need to be available to evaluate each youth's mood and emotional potential. This knowledge helps staff members to define and implement limits and structure, and the direction in which the youngster should be socialized.

THE PSYCHOSOCIAL ASSESSMENT

The Psychosocial Assessment (as detailed in Chapter 3) is written by direct care staff. It is the basis for understanding each youth and his or her behaviors in context, such as social needs, behavioral patterns, and adjustment in his or her environment and among the people within it. This psychosocial assessment follows the themes developed in the Psychological Assessment that is prepared by a registered psychologist, who provides a clinical diagnosis. The Psychosocial Assessment focuses on whether there is treatment progress or lack thereof. The Psychosocial Assessment addresses specific questions:

1. What are the reinforcements to the youth's current level of functioning?
2. How great a stake does the youth have in his or her behaviors?
3. What are the possibilities that the community can react in new and more adaptive ways to the youth (and the converse of this question)? In other words, can the youth deal with his or her problems in a less structured setting?

The Psychosocial Assessment as a document will inform staff members of the following information for each youth:

1. Range of programming requirements such as activities, responsibilities, choices, etc., and whether the youngster's abilities are consistent with the demands of those circumstances and opportunities..
2. Types of support, encouragement, and rewards that the youth will respond to, and those consequences that will or will not work with a particular youth.
3. Those opportunities for developing new skills that should be explored.
4. Those adult and peer role models, in the program and in the community, that should be made available.
5. Those opportunities for problem solving and decision making that are likely to induce further growth experiences.
6. Those work, volunteer, or communal opportunities that will help to develop social interaction, purpose, and goals, and those experiences that will provide a degree of normalcy and will help the youngster to connect with reality, or the real world.

In sum, the Psychosocial Assessment brings together all relevant background information from previous Psychological Assessments; medical investigations; the youngster's academic profile; contacts with social services, courts, and the like; and any subsequent clinical investigations. It is used as the basis or template for the treatment plan. The emphasis is on formulating those new communication and interactional skills that youth must learn and that should be practiced. Unless youth engage in a treatment contract and define the nature of their problems, there is not treatment, only containment (Pazaratz, 2000a). Youth are assisted by staff members to articulate their problems in relation to self, family, peers, social and life skills, school, and discharge and transition issues. Understanding the resident's inner experiences of treatment, or what is most important and helpful, can improve communication and enhance connection (Crenshaw & Hardy, 2005).

TREATMENT PLAN (CASE FORMULATION)

Establishing a treatment plan at admission is fundamental to proper case management and an important guide for residents. The treatment plan is essentially a hypothesis about the causes, precipitants, and ongoing dynamics that influence a youth's psychological, interpersonal, and characterological development. Treatment plans include descriptive information that supports or justifies the hypothesis. Treatment recommendations flow from the hypothesis. The plan helps to organize complex and contradicting information about a resident. It serves as the basis for normalizing the treatment and care experience. A treatment plan (case planning) offers a real-life picture that helps all staff to understand each youth. It assists workers to be aware of and to predict problems that will interfere with treatment. The descriptive component lays out the central facts of the youth's life and current conditions (Pazaratz, 2000a).

Adhering to treatment plans is essential in order for staff members to function as a team. The treatment plan identifies those issues that have caused and are perpetuating a youngster's interpersonal, intrapsychic, or behavioral problems. It tells youth workers what residents need to do in order to feel better about themselves. The treatment plan identities long- and short-term goals. Youngsters benefit when a treatment plan is adhered to. This does not mean that youth workers should become so invested in a formulation (the nature of the problem) that they are unable to listen to (or hear) a youth, or accept behaviors that do not fit the diagnosis. The treatment plan should assist youth workers to understand even those behaviors that do not fit the formulation. It should allow youth workers to think about the resident in new but systematic ways. Finally, treatment plans give residents a voice in terms of the care that they want to receive and to help them experience success (Pazaratz, 1998a).

Adherence to treatment plans is monitored by staff and reflected in daily log notes. Additionally, log notes document behaviors, and this protocol is a licensing requirement, linked to program accountability, accreditation, and case planning. Documentation is based upon objectives and clearly defined goals that are specific rather than vague. This means that the nature of interventions is understood precisely and fits the current needs of the individual, rather than blending all residents together into the needs of the treatment program. Documentation (note writing) of each youngster's behaviors is a daily requirement that assists youth workers to focus on the treatment needs of individuals and those of the group. It becomes the basis for reports and assessments; keeps residents, their families, and referral agencies abreast of progress, indicating where change has occurred; and identifies those areas for potential growth. Documentation sums up why treatment has or has not been completed successfully.

RESIDENTIAL PLACEMENT

Many youngsters entering residential treatment display uncertainty, trepidation, and even fear. They do not know what to expect. They are unsure of their ability to cope and to deal with the profound changes to their lives and the challenges of treatment (Kagan, 1996). How do youth workers help youngsters to settle in, accept placement, or deal with their sense of dislocation and a mix of intense emotions? Youth workers make residential treatment a reliable and safe environment by conveying genuine interest in youth. Without staff members demonstrating understanding and providing reassurance, the youth's emotions will escalate to unbearable levels. Residents are made to feel safe when they gain information that helps them to comprehend placement and to understand the process that they can experience (Maier, 1987). In this effort, they can be reassured that placement does not make them permanently separate from their families, even though they may feel abandoned. This means that although a youngster's family lives in a different location, nevertheless ongoing contact and interactions can be maintained on a regular basis.

Although meaningful staff–youth connection and collaboration take time to develop, staff members can build toward trust by emphasizing the importance of human interactions and meaning in relationships (Noshpitz, 1993). Youth workers can point out the opportunities that are available to youngsters in placement, things of interest, and the fun youngsters can have with staff. Ultimately, the principle of normalcy, or offering the same living conditions that would be found in a regular family, provides stabilization. If youngsters cannot relate to staff members and the milieu (which is considered the therapeutic cornerstone), or if staff members fail to ensure safety, then it is predicted that all other therapies will fail (Polsky, 1962). Therefore, in order to reduce the likelihood of such a catastrophe, the central aim for youth workers is to encourage and support each resident, so that residents do not feel alienated, overwhelmed, and totally alone in their new environment.

The nature of the facility's or group home's culture and social system is revealed in the context of staff–youth and peer-to-peer interactions. Residents are integrated into the social organization through the use of language, ideas, common tasks, or sets of goals, and in shared group dilemmas and psychological processes (Crenshaw & Mordock, 2005a). A systems view of group interactions requires youth workers to use a collective approach, to enact the group home's purpose, to function smoothly, to maintain rules and programs, to provide for individual needs, and to develop group cohesion. Youth workers should be cognizant that all youngsters are different developmentally, have an outer originality (uniqueness), and possess their own understanding and knowledge base. Staff members should be mindful that unresolved conflicts lead to heightened differences, affect the treatment environment, and impede the smooth functioning of the social system (Pazaratz, 1998a). Staff members provide counseling to resolve differences and to improve understanding and connection. Problem resolution helps to maintain harmony in the social system.

GROUP HOME LAYOUT

Group homes in urban communities are typically located in single-family dwellings in residential neighborhoods, but duplexes work well too. A group home floor plan is designed to facilitate a natural flow and interaction of youngsters and staff (Pazaratz, 2005b). A ranch-style (single-story) dwelling is the preferred type of building, offering the most flexible layout for conversion and for supervision of youth. The facility as a home should be sufficient in size to provide for common purpose areas that include dining, relaxing, and recreation. There should be areas where youth can separate from each other according to their interests. Rooms used as "living" spaces should allow for television viewing, listening to music, reading, and interacting. There should also be areas that can be solitary spaces for residents to relax, and separate areas for staff members to work in (Bettelheim, 1960). Youth workers require an office where they can counsel, write reports, keep a first aid kit, ensure that records and any medications are secure, and store various supplies. Residents often share a room with at least one other youth, and sometimes two. Personal possessions are always a problem in group living arrangements. Youth are entitled to the safeguarding of their possessions, even though they should be discouraged from bringing valuable items into the group home.

Residents are provided closet space and a chest of drawers in which to keep their clothes and personal belongings. Youngster's bedrooms are personalized as they would be in their own homes. Bedrooms are arranged to accommodate each resident by creating an environment of permanence and belonging. Bedrooms should symbolize for youngsters that they have a secure and safe place within the group. The bedroom provides a personal environment and a place where the youngster has an opportunity to do homework, leisure activities, and hobbies. Ensuring a private space for each individual offers a balance where youth can enjoy solitude or be with others. It is hoped residents will become more of a participant and connected socially if they do not feel that they have to hide within the group, or away from others, but can find and be involved in those activities that are satisfying and enriching for them, at their pace (Bettelheim, 1974).

The group home culture usually allows that any public or common space can become an exclusive-use area when these spaces are occupied by individuals for that purpose. Residents are encouraged to feel at home and to behave as they would in their own homes. Common living areas are standard communal spaces that encourage youngsters to interact with each other directly, or indirectly, and to include their community friends, without interfering with other residents' private spaces. Common spaces can be areas for planned or casual gatherings. These allow for all residents and staff to come together. Sometimes, the living room or dining area is used for visitors and families to associate, and those residents not directly involved are asked to use some other space (Bettelheim, 1960).

GROUP HOME INTERACTIONS

Direct care staff should have working knowledge of the developmental characteristics of emotionally healthy and well-adjusted youth. Higher-functioning youth are considered a reference group. They provide an opportunity for comparison, a view to the change process, and by contrast an understanding of pathology. Direct comparison of youngsters to similarly aged peers not in treatment provides youth workers with a method to understand disordered behaviors, or the degree to which aberrant acts are problematic and the degree to which they are a deviation from the norm (Ariel, 1997). This may mean that some behaviors are merely negative attention seeking or normal manifestations of childhood silliness, or are adolescent exploration, discovery, and expression. For example, attention-seeking behaviors can be a compensation for low self-esteem, or exhibited as an act of affirmation (actualization). Disturbed behaviors are understood in context (i.e., as being self-defeating, self-harming, antisocial, and not goal enhancing; Ellis, 1994). Conversely, the well-adjusted youth not in any form of care displays the capacity to tolerate psychic tension during self-observation and self-reflection, and, therefore, does not engage in destructive acts to deal with anxiety and stress.

The group home's social system offers youth workers the opportunity to view and to evaluate a youngster's interactional style during routines such as meals, doing chores, use of leisure equipment, and peer interactions over time and space. Of interest to staff members is the way in which youth give into or withstand negative peer pressures. In other words, the question that is asked is whether the youth can find his or her own identity in term of choices, interests, activities, and style of interaction. Additionally, youth workers want to determine how residents deal with peer differences or conflicts. Do they turn to staff members for assistance, or keep staff at a distance? What type of intervention do youngsters find supportive (e.g., interpretation of conflicts, affirmative measures, probing for details, and/or reflective listening)? Ultimately, staff members want residents to understand that resolving interpersonal issues and conflicts builds trust and connection, and provides an opportunity for youngsters to contemplate roles and responsibilities, and be future oriented (Fewster & Garfat, 2001).

The social dynamics that occur in group interactions are similar to those in a family constellation where siblings share one or two adults. They will display similar feelings of rivalry, the fear of loss of favoritism or specialness, and the fear of rejection and corresponding feelings of shame. Group meetings help youth to realize that their peers also experience the same types of feelings or similar types of problems. Groups create the opportunity to assist someone else with similar problems. Residents also derive knowledge and skills by watching staff members help peers to deal with their problems. They learn how to cooperate and to await their turn. Each group member can discuss personal and family problems in the group format, or privately with one staff member (Yalom, 1983). All residents are encouraged to develop their own solutions. Yet, some will have limited ability to be open about their feelings; to share objects of attachment, possessions, and resources; and to cooperate with others in a time–space continuum.

Groups offer family-like interactions that teach youth how to regulate distance and closeness appropriately, understand boundaries, identify and solve problems, share responsibilities, develop interpersonal awareness and skills, share resources and turn taking, deal with issues of dependence, develop independence, and improve reality testing and frustration tolerance (Corder, 1994). But relationships within small groups are not necessarily easier to establish and maintain, because with fewer persons present, the dynamics and interactions can become much more intense and appear more intrusive. This means youth workers should be concerned that youth do not overpower or are not overpowered by peers, that rivalries do not develop, not to show a preference for one youth over another, and to ensure that each individual's rights to privacy are respected.

When encountering and confronting negative behaviors, youth workers at first want to determine whether the youngster understands and accepts what is being said about the problem. The youth worker then makes the youth aware of the natural or logical consequences that can directly result from a behavior. The youth worker should suggest alternative behaviors and offer choices that are goal oriented and self-enhancing. The youth worker restates what is logical in the context of the situation (i.e., positive behaviors draw people together and are inclusive, whereas negative acts have the opposite effect and drive people away). Staff members are cautioned not to apply rules or hold expectations mechanically or rigidly, ignoring the youth's individual needs. Youngsters cannot be motivated by threats, and must not be frustrated in their growth (impeded in the maturational process) or pushed beyond their abilities so that they experience repeated frustrations and failure (Kiraly, 2003). Nevertheless, goals are typically attained gradually. Progress or a lack of progress toward a goal is revealed through indicators. When goals are set, a timeline is utilized, as are staff supports, or controls as needed. Controls are utilized when youngsters are not able to undertake responsibilities safely. They should be designed to be both facilitative and supportive (Pazaratz, 1996b).

It is important for youth workers to realize that disturbed youngsters will misbehave, act out, and be oppositional or defiant, because that is what disturbed youngsters do. This does not mean that youth workers should accept these behaviors. However, for youth workers to become upset or angry, or to moralize about a situation with youth for doing what they were referred to treatment for, is illogical and destructive. Disturbed behaviors should not prevent youth workers from accepting a resident, or from realizing that the youth is human and therefore fallible. It is the behavior and not the youth that is inappropriate and self-defeating (Ellis, 1994). Youth workers cannot allow conflicts to disrupt the worker–youth connection, or permit the resident to engage in self-downing. Staff members want to develop mutual regulation, and cooperation with residents, around issues of behavior control, expectations, and consequences. Mutual regulation ultimately means that staff members and youth can both come to expect that the other will be reliable, constant, and mutually fulfilling (Pazaratz, 2000b, 2000c, 2000d).

AN INTEGRATIVE APPROACH TO REINFORCEMENTS

Most youth in residential placement are not always cognitively capable of abstracting, or thinking about their problems. They have difficulty understanding themselves through introspection. Therefore, structured counseling sessions that include goals and procedures that help organize their thinking strategies, choices, and self-care are paramount. Individual counseling sessions should be followed up on by all youth workers operating as a team. Most treatment programs that focus on behaviors emphasize the importance of social interaction in order for residents to feel safe and connected, learn from experience, and develop protective factors. Maintenance behaviors by treatment staff stabilize youngsters and are supportive, educational, and (where necessary) pharmacological in nature. Most importantly, residents are taught to contemplate and to understand themselves and others systematically, intellectually, and developmentally.

How is a therapeutic environment created that offers consistency, is not intrusive, and can teach the youth to think of the future? The emphasis of integrative practice is to make the unique treatment goals of the individual fit within the structure of the program. In effect, this requires that the youth's goals are practical, solvable, and achievable in the real world. To incorporate goals within a treatment plan, data are collected on observable problematic behaviors, and how and when these behaviors occur. Then these behaviors are described specifically in order to be graphed and reinforced for adaptive and positive changes (Pazaratz, 2000a, 2003c).

A weekly behavior management checklist or chart is a useful clinical instrument because it can reflect progress and identify ongoing problematic areas. A comprehensive reinforcement system supports and discerns (through contracting) the needs of each individual youth, in spite of the youth's particular intellectual ability or skill level. A reinforcement system that includes a behavior checklist helps youth to understand those expectations that apply to them, so that they can be maintained safely by programming (even before the youth comprehends or even agrees to a treatment plan). The checklist also helps youth to understand his or her emotions in the context of social interactions, to identify emotional triggers, and to locate where and when stressors occur. A reinforcement system utilizing a checklist graphed on a spreadsheet aims to teach youth self-evaluation and self-monitoring skills that help them to track how they deal with expectations or any given conflictual situation. It aims to get youth to identify the triggers or onset of their feelings during interactions, and to stay in control. A reinforcement system promotes the idea that youth should seek help from staff members and peers, that they need to cooperate when staff members offer help, and that they can benefit from following instructions (Pazaratz, 2003c).

There are, however, criticisms and some practical disadvantages of all reinforcement systems. The main problem with any reinforcement system, or the application of contingency management and a token economy, is that they are artificial even though they are created to provide necessary structure and feedback of behaviors. It has been argued that a reinforcement system or token economy, if not applied judiciously, is a contamination of the care aspects of treatment, because it can be intrusive, nonobjective, and controlling. In other words, over time there can be a deleterious, almost punitive effect, especially if there is not an emphasis on generalizing from the immediate moment to the future. Another criticism is that a behavioral reinforcement system where a checklist is employed can cause some staff members to ignore the importance of developing relationships with residents. There will also be youth who misunderstand the intent of reinforcements and get upset, believing that they are being penalized for displaying their mistakes, ignorance, poor performance, and bad choices (Pazaratz, 1999).

Even though residents largely benefit from a reinforcement system that focuses on competency and skill development, nevertheless all programs ultimately rely upon the treatment skills of direct care staff and their subjective ability to understand youth. However, youngsters need more than contingency management (Pazaratz, 2003b). Prosocial and self-enhancing behaviors need to be taught, because these comprise the central focus of the youth's treatment plan. Counseling needs to take place that allows youngsters to feel that they can be open about their inner difficulties and lack of knowledge. It is difficult for youngsters to learn self-control, especially if their environment and people within it are unpredictable, critical, and emotionally distant, or if a behavior management system appears punitive and arbitrary (Crenshaw & Mordock, 2005a). In integrative practice, youth are encouraged to take emotional risks and to not fear that they will be punished for being wrong, not knowing, making mistakes, or being different.

PHASES OF TREATMENT

Based upon Margaret Mahler's (1979) stages of separation individuation, it is argued that there are three distinct phases that youngsters experience in residential treatment. Although these phases are broader than those defined in integrative practice, nevertheless these consist of dependency, interdependence, and separation. The first phase is one of profound adjustment for some youngsters, especially for those who feel disillusionment toward adults and the world, and conclude that neither are reliable or provide safety. This belief arises from abandonment and/or abuse that has led to feelings of depression and rage (Pazaratz, 2003a). Prior to residential placement, all youngsters have tried to deal with their problems in some fashion (Kagan, 2004). But, upon admission, some youth conclude that they have failed again. They now believe that they have been rejected, are defective, or are the cause of all the family's problems. These types of thoughts lead to more anger and resentment. Additional acting out may occur because they surmise that they have nothing more to lose. Magical thinking may also arise whereby they think that their rage will cause parents or adults to give into their wishes and take them home. Yet, for many youngsters, residential placement offers relief, safety, and hope for the future. It provides an opportunity for a new beginning (Dror, 2002).

Upon placement, youth workers enact a number of strategies that provide emotional support, structure, and limits. As part of the treatment team, they understand that the nature of the worker–youth relationship sets the tone for the treatment process. In this regard, youth workers encourage youngsters to discuss their feelings about placement. Some youngsters deny that any of their behaviors led to placement. They blame others for being taken from their homes, such as a social worker, probation officer, judge, even parents, and the like (France, 1993). This defensiveness means that they will often avoid discussing personal information, being truthful, and providing relevant facts. There are also youngsters who are unresponsive, uncooperative, and misleading. Some use denial due to unresolved anger over placement. Their anger may escalate into negative behaviors. But the labeling and interpretation of emotions and communications by youth workers help to unravel complex issues and to stabilize the disturbing aspects of youngsters. For example, asking youngsters such questions as "Why are you angry?" "Why are you swearing?" or "Do you know you are yelling?" can help youth to recognize emotions and behaviors that they take for granted or use as a weapon. Provoking attitudes can be dealt with by getting youth to look at the situation more realistically (i.e., they were sent into treatment to deal with their intense emotions, and placement provides their parents with time to deal with their emotions and those issues that affect the youth; Aldridge & Wood, 1998).

Oppositional attitudes, acting-out behaviors, and "smoke screening" make connecting with some youngsters difficult (Ariel, 1997). But, youth should not be allowed to opt out of any aspect of the program. Allowing residents to dictate, or to pick and choose, when and under which circumstances they will participate, or cooperate, only gives youth a greater sense of power. Getting residents to discuss the successful, enjoyable, and positive experiences that they have had provides them with a reassurance that staff members do not judge them. Often, youngsters do not realize that they do more things right than wrong. Yet, they tend to focus on what has gone wrong, accept blame for situations that they were not responsible for, and overlook their positive efforts and strengths (Aldridge & Wood, 1998). They may not realize that even though people in general do the right things in life, sometimes they do not get what they want or the right results. But, although people feel frustrated with unfortunate results, not everyone gives up or reacts negatively. Ultimately, residents are taught to tolerate the reality of being in treatment and to accept controls. Until this occurs, resistant behaviors will emerge as a reaction to experiencing disconnection, feeling hurt, and being emotionally overwhelmed and out of control.

As youngsters move into the second phase, or interdependence, they face the challenge of developing self-control, dealing with their low frustration tolerance (discomfort anxiety) and their tendency to self-denigrate. The young person's internal conflict generally arises from simultaneous attempts at self-preservation and self-transformation. Self-critical beliefs, or self-downing, can cause negativity toward others and become lifelong rage (Kagan, 2004). Because some youngsters believe they cannot control events, they try to manipulate or overpower others to get what they want. This especially occurs when residents encounter differences of opinion with other youth and staff, which adds to their sense of not being able to do things right. Their frustration with others (and self) may lead to additional acting out. Counseling under these circumstances focuses on a persuasive exercise to motivate youth to adhere to their contract, to develop improved self-knowledge, to talk about feelings, and to settle into the give and take of relationships (Brendtro & Shahbazian, 2004). Ultimately, a youngster's internal and external conflict is reduced when he or she develops acceptance and tolerance, learns from experiences, has an improved awareness of social interactions, and enjoys relationships for what they are (Ellis, 1994).

In every phase of residential treatment, developing and maintaining a positive staff–resident connection with some youth will be difficult. This means that some youth will regress emotionally when they cannot adjust to the next developmental phase. With others, transition from one phase to the next will happen with less angst. Improved cooperation occurs when youth workers communicate on the youth's level of comprehension, or ability to incorporate information. A positive empathic attitude by youth workers is essential in order to convince youth that meaningful relationships are supportive but based upon both parties giving (Fewster, 1990). Development of a therapeutic alliance is often slow, sometimes gradual, and certainly ongoing, and it demands staff patience. Staff members may become extremely frustrated with some youth because their defensive or avoidance behaviors make it impossible to connect and establish a relationship with them. In fact, some youth enjoy frustrating staff or having staff give into them on any level, so that the youth wins or causes staff members to chase after him or her (Redl & Wineman, 1957a). These youth have difficulty bonding. They can be quite hostile, bitter, sarcastic, uncooperative, self-harming, and even dangerous. They have a profound anger toward most adults and resent any kind of adult authority. Nevertheless, for these youngsters to successfully navigate the second phase requires them to accept the reality of having been admitted into care. How they respond to ongoing expectations will affect the course of their placement.

The success of residential treatment relies upon the completion of the third and final phase, known as *individuation/separation*. This occurs when residents acquire a locus of control, and become self-directed and self-sustaining. In other words, the referred or identified problems are considered manageable by the youth, who has internalized the requisite skills to tolerate those problems. The youngster has also adapted to the reality of adult expectations, interacts positively in the outside community, and uses the community's resources to advance his or her independence. Successful discharge can be described in terms of absence of readmission or recidivism. But, for many severely damaged youth, they will be in need of a system of support for most of their adolescent years and into their early adulthood. It takes consistent effort to overcome a history of neglect and abuse. Setbacks are not unusual!

A planned discharge from residential placement is usually enacted when the youngster has internalized pro-self and pro-social behaviors. This means the youngster displays a profound developmental change (self-awareness) and emotional growth (self-control). In practice, the youth has learned to become better organized, less chaotic, and more focused (Brodie, 2007). With changes to self-image and identity, the development of self-acceptance and tolerance for others has also evolved. The youth displays greater objectivity and improved social-emotional adjustment, is more flexible, and is less critical and demanding of others (Beaumeister & Leary, 1995). In sum, treatment has to do with teaching youth how to adapt to their environment, to live with themselves, and to connect with others. Ultimately, treatment outcome and successful community transition (reintegration) are directly affected by the degree and nature of the youth's psychopathology, intelligence, and motivation, and the ability and keenness of staff (Pazaratz, Randall, Spekkens, Lazor, & Morton, 2000).

HOW CHANGE OCCURS

What are the central characteristics of disturbed behaviors that need to be changed? Youngsters who are disturbed have a deficit in the self and are unable to accurately identify or think about their behaviors, and to tolerate how other people react to them (Kernberg, 1984). Their emotional interactions and behavioral responses are either excessively controlled or minimally controlled. Their emotional tone can be volatile, phoney, excitable, rigid, shrill, or flat. They have difficulty sustaining their emotions within the normal or acceptable range of affect. Some youth are almost always out of control (such as hyperactive), and in need of controls, as they have problems with attention, agitation, or anger management. Some have severe mood swings, erupting into anger and hostility, then fleeing or receding into withdrawal, sullenness, depression, and self-harming acts. They act out compulsively (drug use, inhalants, promiscuity, violence, self-harming, etc.) and do not realize that their behavioral responses are based on feelings of shame. They are unable to decipher the source of their emotions. They act out to discharge intense pain. But they do not learn from experience (Brodie, 2007).

Emotionally disturbed youth have developmental delays so that they have not differentiated themselves as autonomous individuals. To maintain psychic equilibrium and emotional balance, they often become dependent upon others. Uncertain of their own emotional survival, they are overly concerned with the possibility of psychic harm or injury, real or imagined. They develop a fake self with which to deal with others and world conditions, and to defend against their fears of anxiety or of having no sense of self (Kohut, 1977). They create a false self to deal with the pressures in life, shaped by the demands of others, rather than derived internally. They have difficulty thinking their thoughts, feeling their feelings, and thinking about their feelings calmly. Self-observation and self-reflection or thinking through are higher-order developmental attainments that the disturbed youth cannot even contemplate. Developmental deficits mean that the sense of self is quite precarious, and therefore, the youth is more concerned with the immediate moment (survival of emotions) than with fulfillment (goals) (Freeman & Reinecke, 2007).

Emotionally disturbed youngsters are often confused or even overwhelmed by their emotions, and misperceive how other people feel. They have difficulty comprehending that they affect others and are unable to perceive how other people see them. They do not realize that their self-harming or destructive behaviors are signs of an emotional imbalance. When told that they need help, they are offended (Brodie, 2007). They deny and bury feelings. Their disorders entail a deficit in their ability to recognize the cause of their emotions. They believe that they are justified when they are angry and defiant. They cannot see that their angry outbursts or sullen withdrawal is problematic. Their intense emotions are a defense against experiencing more guilt, shame, and self-downing. When they have physically acted out, they are afraid or unable to examine and understand the real reason and meaning for their behaviors. They do not understand how their problems interrelate with those of their families, which compounds their present placement predicament. Instead, they believe that if they were only allowed to move back home, everything would be better.

Ultimately, change in disturbed or regressed youth occurs when an internally derived sense of self is fostered and developed (Bleiberg, 2001). This occurs when youth workers encourage the emergence of the youth's sense of self. However, the desire to change the self and to attain genuine interpersonal progress must be the resident's; otherwise, the youth's attempt to fit in with the expectations of others will perpetuate his or her predicament. Only when the capacity for self-observation and self-reflection has emerged will the youth develop a genuine sense of self (Kohut, 1977). Ultimately, the youngster will have learned to appreciate the opportunities for new interpersonal experiences. The youngster has learned to reconcile the need for interpersonal relatedness with the reality of his or her separateness.

TREATMENT MOTIVATION

Many youngsters placed in residential treatment are resistant, viewing it as merely doing or serving time. This defensiveness occurs when placement is conveyed as a fixed term, or misunderstood because the specific problems the youth and his or her parents need to work on have not been identified accurately or accepted. Resistance also arises when youth do not want to be in treatment or are not motivated to look at issues. They have little interest in complying with and following their treatment plan. Some youngsters resent being in any form of placement and would prefer to find their own way on the streets. Others merely lack abstract reasoning skills. They have difficulty separating the self from their behaviors. They are unable to be calm and in control of their thinking (reflective), and to examine how they construct or misconstrue meaning and reality (Cotton, 1993). But not all extreme expressions of affect are signs of treatment resistance. Some resistive behaviors result from deficiencies in comprehending, for example, social interactions, other people's intentions, one's own affect, and how to deal with or resolve two different points of view, that of someone else's with that of oneself. Many youngsters in placement display low frustration tolerance, which can be viewed as resistance.

Oftentimes, those behaviors that are viewed as resistant may not actually be treatment resistance, but occur because the youth is stuck in his or her pathology (i.e., a comorbidity of disturbances that are overwhelming, such as a mix of psychological and social deficits). This means that when youth underreact (freeze), or overreact, in stress-provoking situations, they have not developed appropriate modulation of emotions, self-control, or problem-solving responses. They are not able to identify and to express their intense feelings calmly (Stein, 1995). They do not know how to seek support in dealing with overwhelming emotions. Treatment compliance also takes longer for youth who have a co-occurrence of disorders because these need to be dealt with separately. For example, regressed and undersocialized youngsters have limited and imprecise language skills that make it difficult for staff members to evaluate the relationship between the youngster's narrative expression of ideas and an accurate understanding of experiences (Sattler, 1988). But, nevertheless, improving communication skills assists youth to comprehend and convey ideas more cogently, to interact with greater understanding, and to act more calmly.

Treatment resistance includes noncompliance, or oppositionalism and defiance. Nevertheless, all youth need to feel accepted, to feel safe, and to have a sense of personal worth, meaning, and purpose in life. These fundamental existential needs can be met within the context of staff support. Nonconditional acceptance of youngsters by staff members facilitates healing through meaning and enhances the youth's sense of validation (Maier, 1987). Youth especially cooperate with and relate to staff who are capable of interpreting value-laden issues and who can deal calmly with emotionally complex issues. When youth are connected to staff members, they feel interpersonal value. As they become more self-accepting, they are less likely to need others for validation and to be dependent on someone else for love and approval.

They are self-sustaining and more capable of handling rejection, neglect, or the disapproval of others (Kronenberger & Meyer, 2001).

All youth in placement have experienced failures and frustrations in many areas of their lives, such as educational, interpersonal, physical, and recreational. The self-loathing and tensions that resulted from these disappointments compound the negative view of self, which interferes with developing learning strategies and better problem-solving skills. These skills deficits impede further change, growth, and social connection. In fact, higher-functioning peers often treat them as losers, dumb, crazy, or nonentities. Peer criticism, bullying, and distancing result in pain, greater self-doubt, and increased emotional turmoil. A vicious circle evolves whereby the youth feels even more rejection and shame, which causes the youngster to fall further behind academically and socially relative to his or her peers. In fact, these youth are less likely to risk undertaking new activities or social relationships.

THE DIFFICULT YOUNGSTER

Extremely difficult-to-handle youngsters typically have had multiple placements, are often older, and have fewer family connections and supports. They usually display an excess of aggression, paucity of good feelings for others, and undue reliance on the external environment for self-esteem regulation. They suffer emotionally because they do not have significant others who remain constant in their lives. They are viewed as incorrigible, untreatable, and likely to become offenders (Tremblay et al., 2005). Some are psychotic, whereas others have limited intelligence or display severe learning impairment. The regressed or undersocialized youth can be a physical and an emotional drain on staff. Psychotic youngsters are even more difficult to stabilize. They are often maintained safely in detention facilities, psychiatric wards, or secure treatment until they can be supported in an open setting.

Youngsters who do not respond to treatment typically are not genuine in their social interactions, and do not talk about their feelings or are insincere. They lack motivation, anxiety, distress, and the desire to change. They do not find uncertainty intolerable. They do not feel that their emotional conditions and problems are unbearable, are solvable, or need to be solved. They are not necessarily concerned with their future. They do not feel the need for assistance, or know how to relate to someone who is supportive and to accept support, empathy, or connection (Brodie, 2007). Some who resist treatment may be afraid that accepting treatment means that they are ill or defective, or that they will be forced to give up on themselves and their beliefs, family, and friends. Some do not want to reveal personal information because they believe to do so would make them vulnerable or appear weak. Thus, they conclude that the costs of cooperating with staff outweigh the benefits. Some feel ashamed; others, vulnerable and unable to trust. Still others believe that by talking and opening up to staff, they would betray their parents or some family secret (Pazaratz, 1996b).

In order to help all youngsters, front-line workers must do more than to share in the youngster's daily experiences. Youth workers are required to go beyond mere interpretation of disturbed behaviors, insight, catharsis, or a description of communication patterns. They need to awaken residents from their self-defeating attitudes and from dwelling obsessively on negative feelings. This is accomplished by inculcating the acceptance of things as they are, however bad reality may be. It means showing youth how to live in the here and now, yet plan for the future. It is when youngsters stop dwelling on their emptiness and anger, become conscious of obtainable opportunities in the real world, and see themselves as capable of functioning in it and deriving pleasure from it that change can occur (Krugen, 2004). But, there are also the highly motivated youth who will work hard at changing, persevere in difficult situations, and realize that they will benefit from placement. These youth can be an especially positive influence with peers and uplifting for staff (Brendtro & Shahbazian, 2004). Accordingly, youngsters are responsive to treatment when the following occur:

1. They accept the reality of their placement and can be persuaded to make the best of it rather than to merely serve time. They also realize that it is self-defeating to hang onto behaviors, addictions, compulsions, and so forth (Ellis, 1985).
2. They have learned to deal with issues from the past. Their anger toward parents is tempered by realizing adult limitations. They recognize that they and their parents need support and help in dealing with family problems (Ainsworth, 1997).
3. They have developed an understanding that their problems are repetitive patterns of misbehavior or avoidance, which can be characterized by an internal struggle between opposing desires and moral dictates (Ellis, 1994).
4. They hold a belief and trust that the program and staff members can help them get better. They are able to see that others have already benefited from the program. They recognize the advantage of risk taking, being open, and seeking staff support (Pazaratz, 1999).
5. Their personal disappointments with life, others, and the self do not prevent them from pursuing self-acceptance and tolerance for others (Ellis, 1994).

CONFRONTATION

Negative peer interactions can produce, or be the result of, rivalry, disagreements, hassles, and conflicts. Yet, not all conflicts between peers escalate to the point of requiring staff intervention. However, staff confrontation may be required to interrupt, block, or redirect some behaviors that are contentious, negative, problematic, dangerous, or interfering. Confrontation can be directed at an individual, or the group (Yalom, 1985). As an intervention technique, confrontation can be quite uncomfortable for many adolescents and even staff members. In addition, there are many youth who need reminders of limits and boundaries, or who need to be assisted to deescalate; thus, confrontation can be beneficial. Confrontation does not include aggression or discipline. It challenges the youth's specific avoidances. Confrontation, like clarification, directs the youth's awareness toward usually obscure themes. If confrontations are not handled skillfully (genuinely), then both staff and youth may overlook the fundamental requirement of dealing openly and honestly with each other. They may forget that all behaviors in a social system affect the system and its members. Therefore, it is vital that residents realize that confrontation is part of the treatment process and is not an attack, but the means whereby balance, cooperation, and harmony are reestablished. Without proper confrontation, none of the residents can begin to change or to understand how they affect others. They may even deny that they have any significant problems. They will either tolerate or ignore inappropriate behaviors by their peers, or they will fight each other to get their own way (Ghurman & Sarles, 2004).

Confrontation can be effective when it is reality based and used to penetrate such defenses as denial, repression, projection, and intellectualization. By modifying a youngster's defenses, staff can help the youth develop new cognitive and emotional skills. Confrontation stirs up passions because it is anxiety provoking and forces self-examination, probing the youth's level of honesty and openness (Lilberman, Yalom, & Miles, 1973). Some adolescents become upset when confronted because they believe that they are being devalued. Others have a sense of grandiosity and believe that they are entitled to have their own way, or that staff members should not interfere in their affairs. Some residents cannot reveal who they are due to shame, or an uncertainty as to who they are (Kohut, 1977). Interpretation is used to show how these themes underscore related issues, why they recur, and how certain topics that were avoided can be contemplated. Confrontation is an active and focused intervention intent on improving communication, getting past resistance, and creating conditions for change. Confrontation requires staff members to clarify the essential problems within behaviors (that is, what happened, as in a sequence of cause and effect). Confrontation is a reminder of limits, accountability, boundaries, and the rights of others. It is inclusive because it emphasizes responsibilities, the rights of peers, and the significance of group membership and participation (Lilberman et al., 1973). It is vital during acting out because it reminds youth of appropriate behaviors and expectations, and the goals of their treatment plan.

Confrontation that emphasizes the teaching of new facts and procedures is a highly useful intervention technique with aggressive or withdrawn youngsters, who are often fearful, or unsure of group participation and membership. Improved understanding during confrontation occurs when youth use reflectiveness and a conscious effort to make better choices. Confrontation as a process is positive as it encourages youth to deal with social values of empathy, integrity, fairness, cooperation, respect, motivation, and the like. It cuts through antisocial attitudes, such as misleading, lying, oppositionalism, avoidance, magical thinking, bullying sexism, racism, and the like, all of which are employed to manipulate or hurt others (Lilberman et al., 1973). When residents take confrontation personally, they are to be informed that it is their behaviors or attitudes that are being questioned, or that their behaviors are unacceptable and disruptive. Confrontation of conduct-disordered youngsters by peers can be problematic because they often attack each other or view that they are being attacked (Shulman, 1957). However, their personal value is not being rated. For those youngsters who are identified as bullies and predators (they like to believe that their behaviors are "cool," and they get "turned on" by having power over others), confrontation can expose their grandiosity, warped sense of superiority, and status seeking. For some residents, confrontation reveals their isolation based upon a fear of involvement and participation. They relate better to objects, or animals, than other humans. When confrontation is used in conjunction with support and caring, then staff members are modeling the parental role and employing empathic attunement.

THE IMPACT OF TREATMENT

How does the youth worker understand the impact of the treatment process contextually? Treatment can have both a settling and unsettling effect. Residents can feel trapped or stuck. They can have a fear of being harmed emotionally or physically by peers. They speak of feeling insignificant, disconnected, out-of-control, crazy, and always watched. However, the positive effects of treatment occur when residents trust youth workers and allow them to get close. When residents believe that staff members will not be harsh, critical, negative, retaliatory, or disapproving of the resident's behaviors, then they feel connected. They will also come to believe that staff members will mediate their issues fairly. In effect, the youth worker has been permitted to enter into the youth's world and to discuss meaning from transactions (Polsky & Berger, 2003). The youth is now responsive to the worker's requests, accepts limits and redirection, seeks proximity to the worker, and openly shares issues (fears and hopes). Staff members no longer have to use confrontation, but can make subjective interpretations. The worker is allowed to reflect upon the youth's behaviors without the youth reacting.

When a resident attempts to manipulate a youth worker, this is a test or challenge of the youth worker's resourcefulness, knowledge, and skill. Nevertheless, staff members need to remain focused and in control emotionally. They should not overreact or avoid dealing with the youth. It is how the youth worker deals with testing, attention seeking, acting out, or manipulation, and how he or she resolves these potentially conflictual behaviors, that determine the kind of worker–youth relationship that will develop. Some residents are skilled at questioning the fairness or sincerity of youth workers. Others will question the youth worker's ability to care or to be ethical. There are residents who will try to continually provoke, or are constantly demanding, negative, and needy. There are youth workers who react with frustration, and anger. Others are immobilized and uncertain of how to respond to the intensity of accusations and issues raised by youth. Some staff members may feel helpless and inadequate and experience a sense of despair, especially when overwhelmed by a youth's emotional volatility. There will be youth workers who feel disillusioned because they cannot get a resident or the group to calm down and cooperate. But youth workers are cautioned that residents can and do experience a full range of emotions, as do staff. Interactions become more complex when both youth and staff members are emotional (Pazaratz, 2000b, 2000c, 2000d).

How can youth workers deal with oppositional, defiant, or even non-caring youth without becoming incensed and punitive? Youngsters vocalize intense emotions, or negative attitudes, because they have not developed the ability to be reflective, self-modulating, resilient, and positive. Some youth workers cause residents to escalate beyond being verbally abusive to becoming physically out of control. This can occur when youth workers are too cautious, or give the residents too much power and control over which rules they will follow. There are also workers who see residents' acting out as a challenge, and therefore something to be provoked. Daring youth to be defiant will lead to additional problems that take away from the focus of working on goals. Provoking residents will also make them apprehensive or cynical toward staff. Aggressive confrontation will remind some residents of their parents' irrational actions. They will conclude that the worker does not truly care about them or their needs (Pazaratz, 2003b).

Youth workers can avoid power struggles when they do not convey that they must win, or that they are always right and the resident is wrong. There are times when it is more expedient for the worker to allow youth to have their say, or to accept that youth cannot relate to the worker's ideas. The youth worker does not need to overpower residents intellectually to gain cooperation. It is also important for staff members to acknowledge when they have made mistakes, and when their approach was incorrect. Truthfulness and candor by staff members help youth to realize that the worker is also human and vulnerable. In this way, youth workers convey that a respectful relationship is more important for them than to win every dispute or to be infallible. Staff members must not act or pretend that they know everything based upon their position or due to a power differential. Instead, more can be gained in the worker–resident relationship when staff members are to be perceived as genuine and professional (Pazaratz, 1996b).

Youth workers will experience mixed emotions triggered by the pressures of residential treatment. Powerful reactions toward a youth or a group of youth can interfere with the treatment process and the goal of relationship building. However, the emotions that are evoked can be a useful source of information, even though the worker is not always conscious of the meaning or the nature of these emotions (Pazaratz, 2005c). Staff's negative feelings toward youth can be subtle but powerful. These emotions can come out indirectly, be masked, or be disguised in actions toward youth. Youth workers should be aware of or cautious not to develop intense negative emotions (countertransference) toward any youth. Some youth workers justify treating youth with the same angry emotions that youth direct at them in order to mirror to the youth the youngster's negative behaviors. Openly venting negative feelings toward residents by staff for any reason, even to help youth better understand their negative attitudes, is termed counterresistance and is destructive. In fact, for youth workers to use the term *mirroring* to justify this type of behavior is incorrect, because mirroring as a theoretical concept coined in Bowlby's attachment theory (1969) means to reflect positivity and acceptance.

Youth workers may not always be aware of the negative feelings that are invoked in them during their interactions with residents. But when workers become aware of their negative attitudes toward residents, this comprehension should be used to discover the reasons behind their intense feelings. Although these feelings can be reflective of communicational impasses or ongoing oppositionalism, they are considered vital sources of information. Other less destructive negative feelings, such as frustration, concern, suspicion, annoyance, and irritability, can also arise during interactions. These less intense negative feelings are by no means terrible or horrible, nor is the worker a reprobate for having these emotions. However, all intense emotions, though not considered functional, are quite human (Ellis, 1985).

TREATMENT IMPASSES

The youth worker has to determine how accurate residents are being when they reveal personal information. For example, when youth are being confronted on behaviors, staff members need to determine whether the explanation or response they receive is sincere and factual. This question includes whether youth have the capacity and willingness to observe and describe themselves (their situation and background) openly and honestly. To gauge a resident's sincerity, the youth worker must be aware of how the youth views adult or staff relationships. Residents have a variety of attitudes toward youth workers. Some youth see staff as helpful, whereas others feel staff obstruct them. Youth can also force youth workers to take control. This occurs when youth set up power struggles, chaotic interactions, or "chase me" games, or are aggressive toward others. At times, residents will try to outsmart youth workers by maneuvering them into being all knowing and controlling. They may also seek condemnation or punishment by threatening to or actually engaging in emotionally manipulative behavior. Some youth test or challenge staff. Others become competitive with youth workers. They question or dispute workers' knowledge, or maneuver them into dilemmas (similar to the relationship they experienced with their parents; Pazaratz, 2003a).

Youth realize that manipulation is a challenge to workers. When residents manipulate, there is enormous pressure on workers to respond. But how do youth workers understand what is going on so they can stabilize the situation rather than be caught up in games and escalating power struggles that often lead into issues of control? Some staff feel pressure to do something about defiant, challenging, or vulgar language and manipulative attitudes. Some staff members react to a lack of respect. Others feel overwhelmed by situations they have not anticipated or do not understand. They become anxious and fearful (Pazaratz, 2003b). All reactive staff behaviors can prevent the worker from approaching the youth and the youth's behaviors calmly, systematically, and logically. When a youth worker's uncertainties, fears, and doubts are telegraphed or identified, then the youth either is frightened or feels satisfaction. Staying calm and remaining intellectually in the moment, even when the youth worker feels unsure or confused, help the youth worker to focus and to be solutions oriented. When staff members maintain self-control, they can engage the youngster in problem-solving techniques.

In daily interactions, some ordinary situations can escalate if staff are too quick to believe that the youth's attitude is a challenge to the worker's ego or authority. Even though youth workers enact structure and limits, and regulate the flow or movement of residents within program boundaries, these fundamental youth care practices, although seemingly routine and innocuous, can cause some youth to react. Reminding residents of their treatment plan also places the youth and their behaviors in perspective, or reminds the youth of the issues that led to placement (Pazaratz, 2000a). When youth workers offer youngsters choices, or ask questions, these techniques can help to decipher chaos in communication and deescalate behaviors. The youth worker can also stabilize potentially volatile situations or change the sequence of events by asking such questions as the following: What part did you play in the problem? Why must you keep old disturbances alive? Why must you upset yourself? What can you do to make yourself feel in control of your emotions? Where are you going with this? In what way does your behavior make you feel better? Did anything really, really bad happen to you? What are your long-term goals? Where do you go from here (if you decide to give up)? How do we fix things today?

The way in which workers comprehend communication patterns, the purpose of interventions, and the nature of their duties will influence how workers talk and interact with youth (Pazaratz, 1993). However, understanding theory does not always mean that the youth worker has good interactive or engagement techniques. There will always be direct care staff who have different philosophies and styles, even though they work in the same setting, and this may make some workers feel out of sync with their colleagues. Staying connected with youth when they are out of control, focusing on issues, and not being duped or misled become hard for staff if they doubt themselves. But having an approach, a rhythm (style), and an intervention strategy helps workers with difficult engagements. It allows workers to feel that they are able to deal with uncertainty, self-doubts, and continuously changing demands, and to make youth feel secure, even though the youth workers do not understand everything that is happening (Pazaratz, 1999).

In emotionally charged encounters, to understand the negative emotions and defense mechanisms, staff enter the internal experience of youth and hear their trouble. However, in spite of staff's best efforts at deescalation, some situations will escalate from strong resistance to power struggles (Pazaratz, 2000b, 2000c, 2000d). Staff may unwittingly create more oppositionalism by being too stern or forceful or too quick with consequences, or foolishly give consequences as punishment or out of anger, thereby further provoking the youth. Staff members can learn to deescalate emotionally charged situations through eye contact, by reducing physical presence or closeness, by voice tone, by being reflective, or by not needing to prove that they are all knowing and powerful. When youth are listened to and workers remain in control of themselves, youth have an opportunity to feel understood and to calm down. Once youth are calm and prepared to talk or listen, then staff can verbalize or label the essence of the problem and its solution. Youth may agree or admit that they had been attention seeking, disturbing or controlling of others, acting out negative emotions (fears, anxiety, and anger), being defensive, projecting their feelings onto others, and so on. But they may also remain in denial. Impasses may lead to more acting out, especially if staff members are overly determined to establish control as opposed to seeking stabilization (Pazaratz, 2003c).

DEALING WITH CONFLICT CONTEXTUALLY

Within the milieu, interpersonal conflict results from rivalries, competition, grudges, and overreactive youth. Limited successes with problem solving and poor social skills lead to escalating interactions. Conflict can also arise because some youth are so angry with their life, with others, or with their conditions that they just want to bully or hurt someone else (Crenshaw & Mordock, 2005a). Nevertheless, youth workers are required to keep all youngsters safe and defuse conflicts. The youth worker makes residents aware of what they are unaware of, or dimly aware of. The worker identifies the conflict that creates anxiety or anger, and the issues that need to be addressed and resolved, or accepted as unchangeable. During conflict resolution, some youth will react by feeling anxious or misunderstood, or believe erroneously that the worker is against them or strongly dislikes them. Nevertheless, the worker aims to have youth give up extreme emotions, to live with an unpleasant outcome, and to accept being controlled and directed by staff. When youth relinquish the power struggle, they are in effect giving up on their anger and defiance and accepting staff's point of view or conditions as they are (Pazaratz, 1996a, 1996b).

Ultimately, youth create their own anxiety. They must learn to cope with their dread. They need to recognize that cooperating with staff and obeying rules are not as bad as they make them out to be. An attitude adjustment is a challenge to the youth's characteristic ways of relating and experiencing parents, adults, or staff. This may not occur until the youth actually acknowledges certain painful realities, or experiences the intensity of empty feelings of shame, guilt, abandonment, hurt, and alienation. In effect, youngsters must relinquish the belief that they could get better without facing these painful emotions. This may mean that the youngster will have to trust staff and let them get close. Learning to trust adults and to open up is the essence of residential treatment (Pazaratz, 1999).

All youngsters possess a healthy cooperative side and a negative resistive side. Youngsters in treatment experience dilemmas such as being defiant versus cooperative, and wanting connection versus being left alone. Youngsters can feel emotionally overwhelmed when they are unable to make a decision and stick with it. It is when youth recognize both sides of their position, and can calmly talk about their fears of being wrong or making matters worse, that their feelings are understood. Some youngsters need assistance to comprehend both sides of an issue and the implication of their choices before they can relate to the youth worker's point of view (Glasser, 2000b). As comprehension improves, a balance develops and a clear path evolves. Negative attitudes diminish. Gradually, the youth begins to understand how his or her emotions are a function of his or her fear of relinquishing oppositionalism or accepting help. By degree, the youth's behaviors shift toward stability and away from anxiety and defiance. The youth's actions are based on self-enhancing decisions. With improved self-understanding, there is a reduction in control issues.

At times, youth workers are exposed to tremendous pressures to understand what is going on with an individual or dyad, or between group members. To help youth generate the longest-lasting and most profound change possible, the youth worker needs to gather information systematically, not jump to conclusions, and possess the ability to interpret dynamics or transactions. The youth worker's approach to collecting and sorting through complex problems requires the use of psychological, cognitive, behavioral, interactional, and commonsense techniques. The youth's history, previous assessments, and treatment goals help the worker to understand the youngster contextually. Some events from the resident's past created some of the problems, whereas other problems are a result of how the youth learned to deal with problems. The worker must also be aware of how the events of the present affect the individual and how the individual affects others (Cotton, 1993). The following points illustrate the issues of resistance contextually:

1. Resistance is considered an interactive behavior that does not have one underlying cause. It is the result of the mutual influence of a number of interrelated factors or conflicts with others and can be considered a coping mechanism or, conversely, a means of sabotaging treatment adherence (Ellis, 1985). Resistance includes such behaviors as defiance, oppositionalism, stubbornness, and rationalization.

2. Behaviors of noncompliance, uncooperativeness, and hyperactivity are also considered resistance. However, when these behaviors occur, staff can entice the resident to cooperate with parts of his or her treatment plan and the therapeutic program (Pazaratz, 1993, 1996a).

3. Defiance, resistance, or a lack of treatment adherence can occur in any form of placement, including foster care, because placement away from family and friends is seen by many youth as coercive and aversive. These reactive beliefs can be diminished when youth workers listen to residents so that they have a voice and are encouraged and supported to utilize it (Pazaratz, 2003c).

4. Acting out of emotions is the way in which some youngsters deal with the extreme interpersonal or intrapsychic conflicts that they do not fully comprehend. When youth learn to focus on their thoughts, instead of their feelings, they reduce the overpowering intensity of their emotions and can begin to express their ideas calmly (Durrant, 1993).

5. Acting out is employed by youth for dealing with their or other people's anger and anxiety. Acting out of intense emotions is a learned or acquired behavior pattern that continues in placement when adults prevent youngsters from having their own way (Pazaratz, 1996a).

6. Many youth are classified as high risk or "untreatable" because of their extremely disruptive behaviors in previous placements. Their difficulties are severe and originate in the borderline area, or as a personality disorder that is manifest as poor reality testing and poor impulse control. Therefore, change comes about slowly. The main treatment effort is to focus on stabilization (Pazaratz et al., 2000).

ANGER DIRECTED AT YOUTH WORKERS

Many youngsters admitted to any form of placement have difficulty controlling their anger. What techniques can youth workers employ to help residents understand and express their feelings of anger appropriately? The youth worker must first understand the nature or purpose of the resident's anger (Maier, 1979). Some anger arises in the course of the events that occur in the environment (Noshpitz, 1993). Many youngsters are predisposed to vocalize their anger. For example, the way parents behave when they are angry, especially toward family members, conveys a strong message to their children of how to deal with anger, such as for venting or to punish others (Crenshaw & Mordock, 2005a). The youth worker needs to determine whether the resident's anger is merely venting or whether it will escalate to the level that the youth is out of control. Notwithstanding the role the youth worker may have played in causing the youth's anger, it is more likely that aggressive youngsters with a history of being physical will become assaultive. The youth worker also needs to anticipate that the resident's anger might lead to physically acting out, directed at peers, destruction of property, or self-harm. By keeping calm and knowing the source of the resident's anger, the youth worker is better positioned to defuse, deescalate, and channel the youth's thinking and problem solving (Kingery, McCoy-Simandle, & Clayton, 1997).

How does a youth worker remain objective and personally detached when a resident is verbally explosive and reacting with criticism, rage, profanities, insults, and the like? The worker needs to remember that angry outbursts are due to low frustration tolerance, discomfort anxiety, and poor impulse control (Ellis, 1977). Also, the youngster is behaving in characteristic ways that are the reasons for the youth's placement (Perls, 1969a, 1969b). It may be impossible for the worker to know whether she or he did or said something or overlooked some issue that was upsetting. Therefore, unless the underlying issues are identified by the youth, these cannot be fixed. Some youth are habitually angry with others (for example, with adults, women, minorities, or peers) but also project anger onto authority figures (Crenshaw & Mordock, 2005b). They seek to confirm or to justify being angry (i.e., they were treated unfairly or without respect). Still others will test workers to see if they can control workers through their anger as they do their peers or parents. Youth workers should not take insults and profanity personally. Even though staff members believe they have a connection or bond with the youngster, they should not be surprised to learn youth can at times be intentionally provoking (Pike, Millspauch, & DeSalvator, 2005).

Some workers believe that they should always be in control and may feel ashamed that a youth's angry outbursts or threats have angered or upset them. Others may not be able to deal calmly with their strong emotional reaction (counterresistance). These staff members may want to retaliate when they are sworn at, degraded, or insulted. But the desire to retaliate is counterresistance and impedes therapy. Belittling, negative, or retaliatory comments that may be disguised as psychological insights or interpretations are inappropriate and will only cause the situation to worsen. Workers making statements that humiliate or intimidate will inflict damage to the worker–youth relationship and prolong the power struggle (Pazaratz, 2000b, 2000c, 2000d). Any ill-conceived comments by staff members could escalate an already volatile situation and lead to serious legal consequences. Unfortunately, there are workers who believe that they have failed in their youth care role when they encounter a youth's angry outbursts, verbal harangue, or physical assault. Some youth workers even believe the youth's anger is justified.

Anger includes resentment, showing spite or vindictiveness, deliberately annoying other people, blaming others for one's mistakes, and being touchy or easily annoyed by others (Ellis, 1977). Sometimes anger can be triggered inadvertently because someone (a peer or staff member) said something that came out the wrong way. There is the possibility something was misunderstood by the youngster, such as in a flight of ideas. The youth's anger could have been activated by touching on topics replete with shame, rage, or fear. The youth may be experiencing confusion or anxiety, or feeling ashamed of not being able to deal with expectations, competition, feelings, issues, or questions; consequently, the youth's anger is defensive (Farrington, 2004). The resident may anticipate confrontation, loss of privileges, or consequences (discipline), and becomes anxious and angry. The worker also needs to know whether the youth is angry only about the issues that occur in the moment, or whether there are underlying issues. The youth may be obsessed with events outside the home concerning family, friends, and so on (LaPointe & Legault, 2004).

There are numerous reasons for a youngster's anger and a variety of factors that reinforce it. For example, anger can be a means of creating more distance between the youth and worker, or employed to bring the worker closer. Some youth have difficulty in dealing with boundaries and knowing optimal or appropriate distance in relationships; thus, they become upset when they cannot attain what they want in a relationship (Pazaratz, 1993). In some families, anger is the major or only means by which people achieve any kind of intimacy (Ge, Conger, Loreng, Shanahan, & Elder, 1995). Anger can be a defense against feelings of sadness, powerlessness, shame, jealousy, or other emotions (Ellis, 1977). Anger can be a form of manipulation, whereby the youth enjoys power struggles. Many individuals are addicted to anger. Anger can be the way by which youth deal with a buildup of anxiety. Some youth have never learned techniques for being assertive (Grych & Fincham, 1990). Anger can occur because the youth is not noticing, learning from, and putting together connections (social cues and adopting appropriate social responses).

It is important for youth workers to process and resolve any negative reactions the youth has toward the worker. The youth worker needs to determine whether the resident's anger is personal, or symbolically directed at the youth worker as an authority or parental figure. In other words, the youth worker wants to determine whether the youth has unresolved feelings from the past toward a parent, authority figure, or the like. When this occurs, frontline staff become in the minds of youth that hated object (that is, parents or other persons of great emotional significance). Thus, some youngsters who get into interpersonal conflicts are able to justify and explain any behavior. In so doing, they are more clever than they are genuine (Tremblay et al., 2005). This means that when they are held accountable, they focus on any perceived unfairness or adversity to explain why they acted the way they did. Looking for patterns in the youth's behaviors often confirms the referral problem, such as reactive attachment disorder, infantile rage, conduct disorder, or oppositional defiance (Hardy & Laszloffy, 2005). Behavior patterns also indicate the direction for intervention and ongoing issues that need to be dealt with.

Youth workers who overreact to a youth's behaviors are often personally frustrated by their lives and ambitions. Some are consumed by ideas absorbed from family and society, and the values of success and failure. It would be better for them to give up on their own idea of how things should be, not only in their lives but also in the group home. This means that they need to be committed to their professional responsibilities, yet relaxed and unattached to outcomes (Kagan, 2004). Personal needs can get in the way of what the worker desires to happen at all levels of life. The worker can allow him- or herself to be in the present and to explore the unfolding of the moment. In terms of a youth's anger, the worker needs to be mindful and in the present, and not to overreact. When the youth is vocal or aggressive, the worker embraces the youth's energy (but not the youth's intent) and redirects it. The worker speaks calmly and reminds the youth that there are no failures unless the youth has rigidly set goals based upon a belief of winning, losing, being approved of, or being rejected (Pazaratz 1993, 1996a, 1996b). The worker and youth can both realize that life is not a controlled environment, but is filled with surprises (as is the group home) that require a fluid approach to living if the youth as an individual is to meet all its challenges. Life is about adaptability and learning how to flow, no matter what the circumstances. Ultimately, life can be fulfilling when individuals do not stop learning and experiencing.

AFFECT AND ITS EXPRESSION

It is important for youth workers not to minimize, deny, or denigrate a youth's feelings. Sometimes, feelings of infatuation toward a staff member become the problem and interfere with the therapeutic process. Even though a youth's feelings can be stressful, workers need to grasp the inner meaning in terms of the youth's self-object functions and then to supply what is missing (Williams & Thurow, 2005). However, there are youngsters who have a vivid fantasy life and make-believe that they have a special relationship with a worker or workers. They hold onto their beliefs and behaviors in order to hang onto relationships. This type of identification and attachment can become problematic (Bleiberg, 2001). These intense feelings can make some youth workers uncomfortable and uncertain of how to interact with the youth. Nevertheless, to get the relationship in balance, youth workers emphasize the nature of boundaries and clarify the role of staff members (Pazaratz, 2003c).

It can be difficult for youth workers to sort out emotions when youngsters talk incessantly. When youth ruminate and/or whine about a problem, or conditions, these types of complaints can be tedious as the youth worker tries to help the youth settle down. Some youth get frustrated when the worker does not fix the problem, and they can become reactive or resentful toward the worker. This may make the worker perplexed and angry because the youth will not listen and is being difficult (Aldridge & Wood, 1998). Some workers will want to distance youth who are emotionally needy, clinging, and immature. Some worker–youth conflicts occur when youth constantly place demands and pressure on staff for attention or for special treatment and are resentful when they do not receive it.

Emotional manipulation of staff by youngsters interferes with the course of treatment. These behaviors must be managed carefully so that staff–youth relations do not degenerate into a battle of wills. Manipulation is a compulsive pattern which consists of a goal conflict whereby youth act deceptively and disguise the deceitfulness of their activities, but feel contemptuous delight, especially when they are able to con staff and/or other youth (Redl & Wineman, 1957a). Any form of manipulation, oppositionalism, or "chase me" games is sustained by a secondary gain that is highly rewarding and reinforces the youth's sense of grandiosity and ability to frustrate staff. This behavior is also motivated by envy and resentment. The youth has a need to win and therefore to retaliate and to "outmaneuver" staff. The power struggle can begin by the youth asking for a privilege that is beyond what would normally be allowed or that the youth is not entitled to; when the privilege is denied, that is used as an excuse to be angry. Manipulation is a battle for control and ultimately aimed at undermining staff's ability to maintain control and order. Setting up staff in order to resist them allows residents to have a sense of outrage and to justify breaking rules (Axline, 1998).

The manipulative behaviors that youth engage in with staff should also be addressed in their treatment plan. Manipulation is often part of the youth's defense system. It can be triggered by the staff's attitude toward the youth (which may cause the youth to be deceptive in order to gain control or to refuse to be controlled). Examples of manipulative (defensive) behaviors are denial, projection, and intellectualization. These are revealed in words and acts. The purposes of manipulation include getting away with not following daily programming and getting staff members to overreact to the youth's laziness (as did parents). Manipulative behaviors are designed to block change, hide the truth (openness), and mislead the worker or peers. Manipulation protects the youth from the fear of staff (or others) getting too close, or to bolster a weak, damaged ego (poor sense of self). Manipulative behaviors are also a sign of poor reality testing and derail the course of treatment. When youth workers confront deception, lying, or conning, this may result in the youth becoming more openly angry. Staff monitoring and confrontation can be utilized to counter manipulation, but may also lead to a more intense power struggle. The preferred technique for dealing with manipulation is to channel oppositional behaviors into positive efforts (Pazaratz, 2000b, 2000c, 2000d).

Deception by youth can also include phony affect, or transparent behaviors, such as pretending, imitating, or simulating appropriate language and affect, but actually being insincere. Insincerity is designed to gain control over others and interactions. It should be recognized as oppositionalism (Ellis, 1985). The youngster has not internalized the systems of values and meaning that are central to treatment. Some youth will say anything in order to be liked and approved of, to look competent and knowledgeable, or to appear cooperative. But a phoney attitude, when confronted, will invariably be seen to be superficial and short-lived. This pretense of cooperation is self-enhancing and geared to break rules or to violate other people's rights (Ross, 1996). Some youth resort to these behaviors in order to exploit, hurt, or control the worker. This urge to hurt others can be replaced with empathy when self-criticism becomes less irrationally harsh and with the development of values. This occurs as the youngster attains a more coherent sense of identity, knowledge, and personal power, which flows from experiencing benign relationships based upon affective commitment, friendship, and positive feedback (Rogers, 1951).

CHAPTER 3

Psychosocial Assessment by Child and Youth Care Workers

The Psychosocial Assessment was developed to provide treatment staff with a comprehensive profile of adolescents placed at the Oshawa/Whitby Crisis Intervention Centre, a reentry program of the Four Phase System (Pazaratz, 1998a). This assessment model is typically performed by direct care staff in order to augment the psychological or psychiatric assessment that is typically included in the referral package. It specifies a youngster's developmental attainment relative to established age-expected norms, or the behaviors of similarly aged peers. Even though most youth placed in residential treatment have been classified based on the *Diagnostic and Statistical Manual of Mental Disorders* (*DSM-IV-TM*; American Psychiatric Association, 2000), subsequently the Psychosocial Assessment provides a structured format for the collection of additional data. It identifies the young person's difficulties, and establishes a direction for treatment. It assists the treatment team to develop multiple perspectives of a youngster, in relation to social skills, self-regulating behaviors, and peer and adult relations. It also describes ego functioning, cognitive and communicative abilities, group home adjustment, interaction with family, and the range of behaviors at school and in the community. Because this assessment is concerned with all aspects of a youngster's life—past, present, and future—and circular causality, it addresses the resident's pathology, or deviation from the norm, and identifies any blocks in the change process.

CHILDHOOD DEVELOPMENT

The influence of Freud's theory of the psychosexual development of children revolutionized the field of child psychology as he identified the roots of adult behavior in childhood. He believed that all living organisms have the purpose of self-preservation and preservation of the species. He believed that babies, like all humans, act in ways that reduce stress, which forces the child into relationships with others. The infant has biological needs, and in an attempt to meet those needs the baby's personality is developed. Thus, Freud felt the determining factor in human life can be found in the interaction between inherited dispositions and accidental experiences. Freud established his theory of child development based upon case studies (Freud, 1975). He also believed that attachment of the infant to the mother is formed as a result of the consistency and predictability of the parent in meeting the child's biological needs.

Behaviorists attempt to be more scientific than psychoanalysts. They believe the weakness of the case study method employed by Freud is that it generalizes from a small sample and cannot compete with rigorously controlled experiments and meticulously controlled surveys. In their method, behaviorists correlate how preceding events or stimuli will influence behaviors (Watson, 1919). In discussing childhood development, behaviorists dispensed with the theory of intangible mental states (psychoanalysis) and confined their observations and clinical interventions to overt or measurable behavior.

Skinner (1938) recognized that children enter the world with a genetic endowment; nevertheless, he was primarily concerned with how environments shape behavior. Skinner's position on childhood development has been to demonstrate through experiments that the child's behaviors can be controlled by the application or withdrawal of reinforcements. Unlike Watson, Skinner's model of conditioning was not Pavlovian (i.e., concerned with response behavior that was a result of a stimulus). He believed that operant behavior played a greater role in human life than did respondent behavior (reflex response). Operant conditioning involves learning of voluntary responses and weakening or strengthening of responses by the use of reinforcers or consequences. This means that negative behaviors in children, such as attention seeking, can be extinguished by the adult withdrawing attention when the child seeks it inappropriately.

Events that are experienced internally, such as thoughts, feelings and drives, are recognized by behaviorists, but only as a weaker or covert form of behavior. However, due to unmet needs, children may experience images of reality, or pain, but these are not distinguishable unless they are expressed in behaviors that are measurable. Behaviorists do not believe that thoughts or emotions can cause behavior; rather thoughts and feelings, are the results of prior reinforcements. For Skinner (1938), the explanation of drives (cause of a behavior) is not the fulfillment of an inner need, but rather a behavior that has a high probability of occurring that serves as a reinforcer for other behaviors. Crain (1993) elaborated upon this view, stating that drives such as eating and drinking have no special utility as reinforcers, but the behavior of an infant who eats well should be reinforced—not that an inner need is met.

Erikson (1963) advanced psychoanalytic theory by focusing on child development as a psychosocial experience. He viewed the child as a social being who incorporates experiences through the five senses in order to form the beginnings of ego functions (thinking and reasoning) and, thereby, gains impressions of the world outside the self. Central to Erikson's psychoanalytic theory is the concept that a child resolves a particular crisis before moving on to the next stage, such as in the conflict or tension that arises from the absolutes of trust and mistrust. Because parents are unable to sufficiently meet all of a child's needs, that is, to help the child to avoid painful experiences, the child learns to trust with a measure of discernment (Erikson, 1963). However, to create conditions for trust, parents need to convey a profound sense of dependability, and that there is meaning to what they are doing together.

The contribution of Piaget's (1974) work on child development theory has been a comprehensive understanding of the intellectual development of children. For Piaget, age is not an important consideration because he recognized that children pass through stages at different rates. Nevertheless, the developmental process means that children move through stages in the same order. Stages are viewed as incremental ways of thinking, and are not genetically determined because children are naturally inquisitive and constantly trying to make sense of their environment. Natural curiosity, according to Piaget (1974), is intrinsically motivated, and cognitive development is a spontaneous process. Children develop cognitive structure on their own without direct teaching from adults. Spontaneous learning means that the child makes intellectual progress merely by exercising his or her innate curiosity to explore his or her environment. New experiences are assimilated and accommodated through adaptation. This means the learning of new experiences is integrated into existing thoughts or behavior (adaptation), or where thoughts or behaviors are altered to accommodate a new experience.

Kohlberg (1969) expanded upon Piaget. He believed that the development of mature thought in individuals is the result of experimental problem-solving situations, or an active change that arises in thinking patterns between the organism and the environment. Accordingly, individuals progress from one stage to another when they interact with persons at a higher stage of moral development. This view discards the dichotomy between environmental and maturational types of learning. Thorton (1995), in establishing children's capacity to solve problems, also disagreed with age-dependent developmental theory. Problem-solving competency for Thorton is dependent on the child's ability to process language, and children are born with the requisite equipment to interpret and to draw influences from the stimuli in their physical and social environment.

Maslow (1968) disagreed with behavioral approaches, and he argued that children's feelings are essential to learning and that many social factors influence an individual's development. Therefore, in as much as healthy children seek fulfilling experiences, they should be allowed to control their own behaviors and to make choices. Bandura (1977), a social learning theorist, argued that children learn through observation in social situations, that is, by vicarious conditioning and learning from models. In other words, children learn by their attention to the model; they imitate or reproduce behaviors of the model. By watching others, the child learns how behaviors are increased or decreased in relation to the rewards or punishment that the other person received for a behavior. For example, children's use of language, social behaviors, and attitudes is facilitated through imitated behaviors. For learning theorists, unlike psychoanalytic and cognitive theorists, children's development has nothing to do with internal events or developmental stages, but rather occurs due to the reinforcement and shaping of behaviors. Bandura (1986) explained childhood development in terms of learning as a function of environmental factors, whereas maturation is a more organistic result, or a qualitative property of the organism itself.

Bowlby (1969) believed the tendency for individuals to seek proximity to members of the same species is biologically driven so that the adult complements the infant's attachment. Bowlby's views on childhood development arose from his observations of child–mother interactions, which led to his conclusion that there are three types of childhood attachment: secure, anxious avoidant, and anxious resistant. The attachment style either assisted normative development or impeded it. Thus, children shape their own experiences so that development is a combination of internal and external factors. Ainsworth, Blehar, Waters, and Wall (1978) added that children form secure attachments when mothers soothe their child's cries, hold them close, and are attentive to their feeding needs.

Kohut (1977) saw the child's development as dependent on appropriate responses from the parents (specialness, idealizing, empathy, and mirroring), or because the child derives pleasure from the parent–child relationship and not solely from the satisfaction of physical needs that the caregiver could provide. In order for the child to manipulate the environment, a mental representation of the self, others, and the environment is established. Klein (1957) emphasized the importance of the mother for bonding and attachment experiences that must be established in order for the infant to feel secure enough to explore the environment. Honig (1985) supported the importance of the parent–child relationship, having found that children's responses to parental requests for compliance or limits were positively associated with parents demonstrating sensitivity, acceptance, and understanding in their interactions with their child. This means that a child is more likely to thrive and form attachments if he or she has a positive affectionate relationship with a parental figure. Therefore, according to the object relations school, children can be understood developmentally as they outgrow phases, and they encounter experiences throughout life that stimulate a dialectical interplay in the mind (Ogden, 1986).

Empathy has been identified as a significant childhood attribute that arises from child–parent interactions. Kegan (1982) stated that the ability to identify feelings of others is the first sign of morality. Prior to 2 years of age, children have an appreciation of right versus wrong, that is, a moral emotion such as fear, shame, or guilt. These emotions are experienced when a child thinks that he or she has actually violated a moral standard (Kohlberg, 1981). Therefore, when a child experiences violence or aggression as a parental response to his or her behaviors, the moral emotion will be eradicated. With an increase in punishment, it becomes easier for the child to transgress, even though the child continues to know when he or she has violated a moral standard, because the emotions that have kept behaviors governed and controlled are no longer active (Pazaratz & Morton, 2000). According to Pazaratz (1996a, 1996b), this is central to understanding personality deficits observable in conduct-disordered children and adolescents, who lack conscience formation.

Bronfenbrenner (1986) believed the nature–nurture controversy is out of date. He stated that childhood maturation is the result of the interactions between the developing organism and its total environment. He saw human development as an ongoing process influenced by environmental factors, including fetal exposure to toxins, the infant's biological endowment, and how the infant takes in her or his environment. This in effect means that when the infant's surroundings are in sync with her or him, such as parents who are caring and supportive, then the baby can grow emotionally and develop an interest in the world. Bronfenbrenner's childhood developmental theory blends the impact of geneticists with that of environmental influences. Thus, at any point in space and time, it is either the internal features or external factors of the organism, or a combination of both, that may interfere with maturation of a particular function. According to Thatcher (1994), there appears to be an increased agreement that heredity and environment interact in childhood development.

In conclusion, these different theories as to the impact of external factors not only can be understood as an indication of various approaches and interpretations of research, but also underscore that there is still incomplete knowledge of the effects of genetic inheritance, neonate conditions, parenting styles, the child's environment (culture), and economic-social conditions. Additionally, although heredity and environment interact to shape personality, individuals not only respond to stimulation but also seek out the stimulation that they respond to (Ferguson, 1968). This means that the questions still unresolved are how much heredity (or to what degree the environment) influences development, when each factor has its specific impact on childhood growth, as well as why the child selects the stimuli that he or she will or will not respond to. These questions are central to conceptualizing childhood problems that bring children into therapy, some to foster home placement, and others into residential treatment. However, once a youth is placed in residential treatment, these issues need to be addressed in order to understand the child developmentally.

ASSESSMENT PROCESS IN RESIDENTIAL TREATMENT

Children and adolescents can be viewed as growing toward autonomy, from short-term interests to long-term goals, and toward increasing self-direction and self-awareness (Hardy, 1991). Children and adolescents pass through developmental stages where cognition, physical growth, and coordination more closely affect intellectual functioning than in adults (Winnicott, 1965). Children and adolescent's mode of thinking, or of solving the same problem at different stages, represents the capacity to make sense of a greater variety of experiences and is indicative of the youngster's development. Movement from one stage to a later stage occurs because the youth is more adaptive and the next stage is more fulfilling (Kohlberg, 1969). For the adolescent, this means that his or her quest for individuation or to advance through developmental stages occurs by making those aspects of the self, which are enmeshed with parents, autonomous (Silverberg & Gondoli, 1996).

Notwithstanding the apparent instability of a young person's personality and intractable behavior patterns, most clinicians are aware that developmental change is predictable in childhood and adolescence (Kagan & Klein, 1973). When there is a lack of normative development or where normal development has stopped and has been replaced by pathology, children and adolescents are placed in residential treatment. Integral to the Psychosocial Assessment is understanding which factors have prevented normal development, or phase-appropriate functioning (Shervin & Shectman, 1973). The Psychosocial Assessment requires collecting and collating factual data regarding the youngster's experiences in a number of areas, in order to determine where the child's or adolescent's rate of development is accelerated, arrested, delayed, regressed, or uneven. Its purpose is to identify the supports that need to be built in and how to get the youth to understand cause and effect, or the impact of choices. All assessments, such as this psychosocial model, aim to be persuasive in terms of prioritizing intervention techniques that may be more efficacious (Reiser, 1988) and considering which controls should be lessened.

The Psychosocial Assessment also helps front-line staff to assist the youngster's adjustment to the group home environment and provides the direction for treatment. Therefore, it must be remembered by staff members performing assessments that any difference between the conclusions of an assessment and the direction of treatment would be problematic (MacKinnon & Michaels, 1971). This is supported by Perls (1969a, 1969b, 1969c), who believed that the aim of counseling is to help the fragmented individual to become whole, fully alive, and capable of experiencing positive emotions.

Pazaratz and Morton (2003) added that if a child's problems are not dealt with at the time that his or her symptoms are identified, then the findings and recommendations of the Psychosocial Assessment would be meaningless.

The Psychosocial Assessment process requires that both positive and negative behavior patterns are identified. It considers the nature and degree of the youngster's feelings and moods, and the quality and intensity of the youth's social interactions; and it describes the stressors and supports in the youth's life. The assessment evaluates the development and structure of the youth's personality, the strength of the youth's ego, and the capacity or range of the youngster's stimulus barrier. To be valid, a Psychosocial Assessment requires close observation of the youngster's physical appearance, motility, coordination, cognitive abilities, perceptual functions, emotional reactions, as well as fantasies and dreams. Children and adolescents are understood in the context of their family background and its history. For example, rituals bond families together, help children and teenagers to succeed at school, assist youngsters to engage in prosocial activities, and enable them to experience lower levels of anxiety than those children in unstructured or chaotic families. Disintegration of rituals is often the first sign that a family is falling apart (Pazaratz & Morton, 2003). Therefore, when a child's or teenager's development is arrested or delayed, the contributing factors can be identified.

Social interactions are central to the way in which youth express the self. A youth's development is critically linked to his or her age, and to whether the youth functions at his or her age relative to youngsters of the same age. For example, while a youngster is in placement, those activities, interests, and hobbies that are engaged in as well as those that are not pursued reveal his or her level of emotional adjustment and cognitive growth. This means that the character of activities and a youth's general behavior in an activity can be more significant for the treatment team because the youth's social experiences provide additional information beyond verbalization (Pazaratz, 1997). Once a diagnostic formulation is established, then the treatment plan considers the presence of complicating intrapsychic issues such as the young person's capacity for attention, frustration tolerance, impulse control, and self-concept, as well as the youngster's age and gender needs.

Ultimately, a youngster's treatment plan, or plan of care, is based upon the identification and formulation of the youth's problem. A treatment plan's effectiveness relies upon conceptualization of the problem by the child or adolescent, the choice of issues identified for change by the youth and/or parents, the context or environmental conditions that affect the youth, the receptiveness and motivation of the youth to treatment, and the fit of the youngster and his or her family with the therapist (Rogers, 1951) or treatment program. In the treatment plan, a range of intervention techniques are hypothesized that may provide beneficial results in the change process. Accurate and comprehensive information that is detailed in the treatment plan contributes to better management of organizational resources (Hoge, 1999).

THE PSYCHOSOCIAL ASSESSMENT

The intake process has shown that children and adolescents with mental health disorders are not a homogeneous group (i.e., their families, their situational factors, and the youngsters themselves are in fact quite dissimilar from each other; Skinner & Blaskfield, 1983). The Psychosocial Assessment provides an orderly means for the collection of data. Much of childhood development can be understood as the child's ability to integrate disparate aspects of experience into ever wider wholes (Piaget, 1975). The Psychosocial Assessment provides an analysis of the various factors that affect a youth's ability to be able to comprehend information and to utilize it. It also identifies the youth's strengths, weaknesses, adjustment level, style of functioning, and social skills, and the quality and nature of the youth's interactions. The Psychosocial Assessment as an instrument seeks to understand and to describe youngsters in the context of their environment and the nature of their significant relationships. It therefore requires a degree of information on the youngster's family and its history.

The Psychosocial Assessment identifies how the youth and his or her family have dealt with major developmental milestones and any family crises. It is used as a reference point to identify delays and/or growth in specific areas, to predict future patterns, and to communicate about the youth (Sparrow, Fletcher, & Cicchetti, 1985). It is greatly affected by the direct care worker's ability to draw upon direct observation, be reflective, be aware of information and interpretation variance, and identify gaps in information and fill in those gaps (Fuller & Hill, 1985). In spite of the assessment's utility to help treatment staff to organize and prioritize the youth's problems, youngsters are not always able to see that they have problems or to agree about their problems. Nevertheless, residential treatment cannot proceed until the youngster develops some awareness of his or her behaviors and their impact upon others, and learns to assert some self-control (Pazaratz, 1996a, 1996b).

In daily interactions, the direct care worker is constantly faced with behaviors that are problematic or can become problematic and knowing when and how to intervene. Diagnosis is one way in which mental health disorders are classified so that workers can respond uniformly but also respond to individual situations and unique needs (Skinner & Blaskfield, 1983). The assessment, therefore, becomes the basis of the youth's treatment plan and for the types of interventions that are efficacious. It informs staff of which supports will likely be effective and which supports and controls need to be changed. But during the assessment process, staff should proceed cautiously so that information is not collected selectively, even though it may confirm initial diagnostic impressions. The assessment can also be distorted when exclusionary information is ignored by the observer, creating a correlation where none exists (Silver, 1984). Ultimately, the assessment is informed by the youth's narrative and requires the youth worker to think about the nature of the youth's reality, the concept of age-appropriate development, the relationship between the young person and front-line staff, and the knowledge base of psychology (McLeod, 1998) and residential treatment.

The Psychosocial Assessment builds upon the referral package that includes a psychological or psychiatric assessment that typically recommends the appropriate method of treatment. The following format, as a descriptive instrument, is designed to evaluate children and adolescents during their residential placement, for writing of reports, and, according to Jordan and Franklin (1995), for ensuring that there is the linkage of assessment to clinical decision making. It is based upon qualitative methods that include ethnographic interviewing, process recording, graphic methods, and participant observations. It evolves from routine youth work with children and adolescents. When writing the Psychosocial Assessment, the worker should neither introduce nor imply judgments about the youngster. Diagnostic terms and definitions can only be used by youth workers when citing or referencing a psychological or psychiatric report already in the youth's referral package.

Background of Youth (Social History)

1. An opening statement is needed to describe the youth's background, and the events or issues that led to the youth's placement. The social history includes living arrangements, involvement in social agencies, criminal proceedings, cultural and religious influences, and past history of treatment and the effects of treatment. This information provides an initial impression and a hypothesis about the youth that are compared to the final diagnostic conclusion as well as to subsequent assessments. Included in the opening is whether the youngster entered treatment willingly, and what was said to the youth about placement.

2. Briefly describe the youth's age, the youth's physical appearance, the socioeconomic life of the parents, and the relationships between the youth and his or her parents, the youth and his or her siblings, and the youth and his or her social group. Are there cultural, ethnic, or religious issues that the youth grapples with? Do these affect the choices available to the youth, and if so, in what way?

3. Parental attitudes and communication patterns clarify how family dynamics affect the youth. For example, dysfunctional families are often a closed system in which the youngster has few, if any, outside resources for correcting distorted perceptions of the self and for dealing with confusing or hurtful experiences that may occur (Minuchin, 1974). List all family members present (and absent) at intake, and describe family dynamics: chaotic, anxious, rejecting, broken down, codependent, disengaged, rigid, diffuse, enmeshed, or supportive. Who is the youth closest to, and who gives him or her the most problems? What are the family's stressors and strengths? How

has the youth adjusted to others in his or her home, at school, and in the community?

4. Have the youth and family experienced other forms of counseling, and were there any treatment impasses? Has any family member been hospitalized, incarcerated, or placed on probation? Has the youth experienced any prolonged periods of separation from his or her primary caregivers, and for what reasons?

5. What are the youth's problem areas identified in the referral: delinquent (antisocial), suicidal, withdrawn, unmanageable, undersocialized, aggressive, substance abuser, sexual perpetrator or victim, destructive to property, or the identified patient (scapegoat)?

6. The process of adolescent individuation includes deidealizing parents, being less dependent on parents or less angry, and seeing parents as people with strengths and weaknesses (Steinberg & Silverberg, 1986). How realistic is the youth's view of his or her parents? Is the youth aware of his or her feelings (behaviors) toward others and the impact these have? Does the youth deny, project, or displace blame? Can the youth separate personal problems from those of family members such as parents, siblings, etc.? Does the youth appear inhibited, lack spontaneity, or behave compulsively? Is the youth allowed to make choices and decisions, or is she or he always told what to do?

7. Medical history: Discuss the nature, duration, and impact of illnesses on the youth's life, activities, and relationships. What medication is the youth on? Does any other family member have any major illness? Does the youth suffer from headaches and stomachaches? How frequent are these, and when do they occur?

Social Functions

Child and adolescent maturation occurs in a social context. The developmental task for the youth is to master the facts of his or her existence and to be able to coordinate his or her efforts for meaning and happiness within the context of family and community. As individuals, youngsters actively construct reality from their social world. The young person's relationship to his or her social environment and those individuals within it is cognitive, or a dialogue between the youth's construction of reality and the structure of the environment. The youth's awareness of how to deal with others derives from thought and symbolic interaction (Kohlberg & Meyer, 1972). Of interest to the assessment process is a description of the youth's motives (i.e., what were the reasons for his or her behaviors that led to placement, and what should or could he or she have done instead?). These questions are intended to get youth to reexamine their judgment in relation to others, opportunities, and life issues. Of importance is whether the youth has learned from his or her experiences, and whether he or she repeats these problematic behaviors in similar circumstances. Making proself and prosocial decisions is a sign of emotional stability, maturity, and critical-thinking skills (Glasser, 2000a).

Both children and teenagers who have developed normally are drawn to their peers, deriving pleasure from social interactions. Those youngsters who generally feel secure in peer relationships have already discovered who they are within their family. However, the youth with severe family problems, or who experiences a dysfunctional parent–child connection, has not (Elkind, 2007a). Children and adolescents with difficulties in social functioning have underdeveloped reflective capacity, or an inability to attribute mental states to others. This includes a limited awareness of other people's desires, beliefs, and boundaries. Without these insights, the youngster is unable to feel empathy (Gottman, Gonso, & Rasmussen, 1975; see also Fonagy & Target, 1997). Critical to understanding youngsters is discovering whether they have the capacity to feel for others, and under what circumstances, or if the youth is overly involved with him or herself. The youth worker also wants to examine what the youngster says about his or her personal and family life, or how the youth makes meaning of experiences from his or her existence (Kegan, 1982).

Peer–Sibling Relationships   According to Sullivan (1953), latency-age and adolescent friendships immunize youth against severe psychological illness because they are of such paramount importance. In groups whose structure is sound and whose tasks are clearly defined, disturbed youth may in fact behave well, whereas in subcultures or antisocial groupings, the well-adjusted youth may succumb to negative peer influences and regress rapidly into aberrant behaviors (Pazaratz & Morton, 2000). This category looks at the quality of the youth's relationships, how the youth is affected by peers, and the impact the youth has on others.

1. How does the youth interact with peers in the group home? With peers in the neighborhood, and at school? Does the youth have the ability to form adequate relationships appropriate to his or her developmental level? What is the quality of his or her relationship with peers (e.g., timorous, boisterous, grandiose, bully, exploitive, victim, assertive, insecure, follower, or leader)? To what degree is the youth affected by negative or countercultural elements? Can the youth resist or cope with negative peer pressure; or does the youth have a delinquent ego, as described by Redl and Wineman (1957b), and align him or herself with other youth in order to justify behaviors or to defy and frustrate staff and to violate rules? When the youth feels overwhelmed, is there social isolation, a vulnerability to irrational thoughts, loss of motivation, or an inadequate sense of self? Can the youth separate him or herself from personal problems experienced by peers?

2. Does the youth mix primarily with the same sex (i.e., males or females)? With one peer? Does the youth date? Is the relationship

serious, platonic, casual, sexual? Are the youth's friends older, younger, or the same age? Is there an inability to feel intimacy and closeness, so that relationships with peers are impoverished? What activities or issues does the youngster engage in with peers? Is there a lack of recreational interests and activities?

3. Cohen and Cohen (1996) believed that deviant values in adolescents are indicative of a conduct personality disorder. What values does the youngster subscribe to in terms of personal integrity? Are the youth's values indicative of psychopathology, or are they merely different? Is the youth a loner, excessively cautious, reckless, easily distracted, or obsessive? Does the youth have good or poor social skills? Is the youth insightful into other people? Can he or she learn about him or herself from these relationships? To what degree do peers influence the youth's ideas, beliefs, concepts, attitudes, behaviors, lifestyle choices, knowledge, and goals? What does the youngster admire in peers? Are the youth's friends and their value system in direct conflict with those of the youth's family?

Adult Relationships   The key to working with adolescents, according to Hanna, Hanna, and Keys (1999), is to develop a therapeutic relationship based upon respect. Nevertheless, adolescents often view therapeutic techniques suspiciously, such as by perceiving them as adult manipulation or a threat to the youth's quest for freedom (fun) or independence (Van Wagner, Gelso, Huges, & Diemer, 1991). Therefore, adolescents in treatment do not often view their behaviors as dysfunctional, but instead see adults as controlling.

1. What kind of interactions or relatedness does the resident have with staff? With teachers? With other adults? Are there issues of trust or mistrust, wanting adults to remain the same or to change, getting too close or too far away, coercing or being coerced, or autonomy or dependence? Is the youth rebellious, submissive, ingratiating (manipulative), passive-aggressive, adultlike (parentified child), enmeshed, dependent, disrespectful, belligerent, aloof, detached, affectionate, engaging, pleasant, helpful, courteous, passive avoidant, seeking codependency, passive resistive, oppositional defiant, seductive, or physically threatening?

2. Are the resident's interactions primarily with female or male staff? Does the youth feel comfortable and confident with both sexes? Is the youth sexually suggestive, or does he or she misperceive interactions as sexual?

3. What role are staff allowed to play? Does the youth see a staff member as a confidant, a friend, a disciplinarian, authoritarian, a referee, aloof, enmeshed, a rescuer, a teacher, or an equal? Are staff permitted to share insight and understanding? Does the youth respect adult

boundaries and allow adults to use consequences, give directives, or have control?

4. Some youngsters communicate by being provocative, and this may cause staff or teachers to be frustrated, weary, and distant. What feelings does the youth evoke in adults (anger, frustration, caring, protectiveness, fear, suspiciousness, etc.)? When staff intervene in the youth's main conflict areas, does this involvement create enough tension so that the youth's predominant defenses and structural organization emerge? What are these?

5. Has there been a failure to differentiate from parents? Are the youth's conflicts, fears, and anxieties a result of his or her uncertainty of parental love and approval? Are trauma and violence a part of the youngster's lifestyle, or is he or she able to see that not all adolescents, as proposed by Flaherty and Horowitz (1997), have to give into the idea that violence is integral to the adolescent population? Risk taking can also be part of the adolescent's behavior pattern. It can be viewed as an angry power struggle with parents, i.e., part of the challenge or means for youth to find out who they are and to determine who they will become (Pazaratz & Morton, 2000). Does the youth engage in risk taking, and what are these risks? What are the reasons for risk taking? Consequently, has the youth suffered any serious injuries due to risk taking?

Psychological Functioning

Youngsters aged 6 to 12 are considered well-adjusted when they display secure and comfortable feelings and confidence about their ideas and about themselves as persons. Peers and teachers are an important part of their lives. They display curiosity about learning and are interested in trying different activities, trying new skills, and seeking challenging social situations. They have a sense of industry. However, when some children fail, they become discouraged from trying. They conclude that they do not measure up. They feel inferior, or have a negative self-image (Erikson, 1963). When youngsters are labeled slow, or defective, they tend to match their behaviors to expectations (Hebb, 1980). In the 13 to 18 age range, the major developmental crisis for adolescents is role confusion, or problems of sexual identity and career choices. When adolescents have an integrated sense of self, identity develops. They adjust to new and demanding experiences (Erikson, 1963). This section examines the way in which self-concept or belief about the self is influenced and shaped.

Self-Image   Erikson (1968) believed identity is shaped by understanding oneself and others. Failure to fulfill this task leads to either distress or protracted indecision and personal fragmentation. For Kohut (1977), the development of the self occurs by the child's subjective experiences with others. When there are interpersonal problems, disorders of the self emerge. These are manifest in emptiness and anxiety about fragmentation. Attempts to avoid these existential anxieties can lead to self-indulgent and self-destructive behaviors.

1. General impression: How does the youth describe him or herself? Does he or she act immature, needy, with learned helplessness, delinquent, deviant, handicapped, as a nonperson, grandiose, or self-assured? According to Clausen (1975), teenagers view their physical maturation relative to that of their peers (i.e., beginning early, on time, or late). Is this an issue for the youth? For others? Is the youth overweight, obese, underweight, or anorexic? Is the youngster too short (small, or underdeveloped) or too tall (or well developed) in consideration of age? Are physical development and appearance issues? Are there physical defects such as scars, burns, or acne? Are there tattoos, body piercing, etc.? What are the reasons for these markings: self-image, status, identity, body enhancement, cover-up of (self)-mutilations, as a statement about the self, to indicate gang affiliation, or for what others should think about the youth?

2. What is the youngster's general attitude toward life: gloomy, bitter, pessimistic, sad, negative, defensive, angry, accepting, or hopeful? Is the youth agreeable and emotionally stable? Does the youngster have a good grasp of reality, such as an understanding of cause and effect, or how his or her behaviors contribute to or exacerbate problems? Does he or she learn and habituate quickly from experience? Are natural and logical consequences effective forms of discipline, or does the youth defy any types of rules, boundaries, limits, and controls?

3. The youth's neatness in clothing or lack of it reflects self-care. Is he or she careless in personal organization such as grooming, attire, belongings, and personal space? Are clothes and dressing style used to convey a message such as being tough, cool, athletic, etc.? Is the youth conscientious and respectful of other people's rights, living space, and belongings? Does the youth take other people's belongings, or steal, misuse, or deliberately damage other people's possessions?

4. Youth who have a history of physical abuse, have been victims of neglect, commit property crimes, and have poor relationships with staff or experience difficulties with attachment and separation are more likely to be runners. This means that youngsters run away when they feel threatened by thoughts they have tried to repress or when situations get to be too intense. Some youth externalize their inner conflict and use the environment as a release (Kashubeck, Pottenbaun, & Read, 1994). Does the resident have a history of running away or being AWOL? Does he or she violate group home rules,

societal rules, or other people's rights, or intrude in other people's affairs? Does the youngster demonstrate an understanding and appreciate the moral difference between right and wrong? Does the youth accept accountability for his or her acts, or does the resident always have an excuse, justify his or her behaviors, and never admit to being wrong? Does the youth try to create crises, confusion, chaos, negativity, or passive resistance in the group home? Does the youth try to take advantage of other people's misfortunes?

Ego Functions

The ego is regarded as having the task of balancing the demands of the real world. This occurs with the emergence of defense mechanisms of isolation, affect, and rationalization that help to separate personal issues from those of other people. The ego has to control any unacceptable thoughts, emotions, or instinctual drives in such a way that the youngster suffers the least discomfort and yet is able to continue to function (Goldstein, 1995). The most important ego functions include reality testing, impulse control, thought processes, judgment, synthetic-integrative functioning, mastery–competency, and primary and secondary autonomy (Bellak, Hurvich, & Gediman, 1973). The following categories help the front-line worker to understand where the youth is having specific difficulties.

1. *Intelligence*: Is the youth below average, average, or above average in intelligence? Is the youth progressing to greater adaptation, differentiation, and integration in his or her means of thinking? What are the youngster's intellectual strengths and weaknesses? This includes the ability to organize, abstract, analyze, and synthesize ideas. How are these manifest in behaviors?

2. *Cognition*: Self-reflection increases during adolescence. The cognitive functions that emerge are the serializing and separating of objects into various groups. This means that the abilities to plan, to understand another's viewpoint, to recognize the validity of another's argument that differs from one's own, and to reflect on thinking emerge as youth age (Nurmi, 1991). Cognitive skills include sensory perceptions, integration, memory (sequential information storage), and the ability to reason, including output (retrieval of information) or access for comprehension and memory. Does the youth have problems in any of these areas? Does he or she use compensatory devices? The capacity to understand and conceptualize also indicates the youth's cognitive level. Are there any deficits or difficulties with comprehension, nonverbal and verbal working memory, planning, verbal fluency, response preservation, motor sequencing, or sense of time? Does the youth understand complex ideas? Can she or he use

symbols as the means and method to reduce the world or culture around her or him? Is there a history of brain injuries or seizure disorders?

3. *Speech*: This includes the use of language, ideas, and information processing. In evaluating the youth's verbal fluency, speech reflects cognitive level. The use of words facilitates a more precise communication with others, reflects more adequate reality testing, and underscores better impulse control. What is the youth's first language, the language background of his or her parents, and the communication patterns in the family household? Is the use of words, grammar, and syntax appropriate? Are there oral inaccuracies or disfluency in speech? Can information be elicited from the youth? Is there excessive talking, limited verbal ability, difficulty conveying information, neologisms, echolalia speech (expressive language disturbance), overuse of profanity, hip language, rapid talking that is difficult to interpret, stuttering, slurring, or a lisp? Is there language delay or lack of spoken language, inability to initiate or sustain a communication, or stereotyped and repetitive use of language? Is the quality of speech whining, monotonous, or too soft or loud? How is the youth's style of speech affected by his or her moods? Does the youth's expressive language difficulties interfere with academic or occupational achievement or social communication? Does the youth respond to questions in an irrelevant or oblique manner? Is the speech delayed in conveying ideas because of too many tenuously related ideas? Disorders in thought and misuse of language indicate there may be genetic causes of the youth's problem or a communication disorder. Thus, it is important to distinguish between language comprehension and language production difficulties (Andreasen, 1979).

4. *Motor skills*: Considering both fine and gross motor skills (e.g., handwriting and riding a bike), are they below what is expected given the youth's developmental age and intelligence, such as dropping things, clumsiness, or being uncoordinated, hyperactive, or left- or right-handed? Does the youth have difficulty in any activity or sport, or only in certain areas? Are there physical limitations or handicaps? Is there a developmental coordination disorder? In what areas does the youth excel?

5. *Social interest*: According to Adler (1938), social interest is the basis of normality and mental health. When individuals belong as equals, they are secure within themselves, and they maximize their potential. Is the youngster socially aware? Is he or she awkward? Is the youth's level of social interests broad, or is the range limited and underdeveloped? Does the youth try too hard to fit in with peers, is the youth too needy for peer approval and validation, or is he or she a loner? Do the youth's belief system and values come from within or

from someone else? Internally driven individuals reflect ego autonomy (Goldstein, 1995).

6. *Capacity to relate*: Does the youth relate or attach to people? Is the youth able to take another person's point of view? Does the youth prefer to interact or to be with animals rather than people? Does the youth relate mainly to objects (i.e., computer games) instead of people? What is the quality of relationships with people: insincere, distant, separate, superficial, warm, involved, friendly, open, or meaningful? Does the youth withdraw or become inordinately mistrustful with peers or adults? Some youth who want to disown or rationalize their own hostility perceive others as hostile. Does the youth justify his or her negative behaviors toward others, or is the youth able to reframe the context of the issues with others, or reinterpret the emotional content of a stimulus? In other words, can the youth establish or reestablish rapport after a conflict? Is the youth responsive to reassurance, and can he or she deescalate? Does the youth become excessively compliant and/or exceptionally depressed after a conflict with others? Does the youth associate intimacy with aggression? Seductiveness? Approval? Is the youth shunned by peers? Why?

7. *Affective life*: Emotions are conveyed through language and nonverbally. Is the youngster capable of a wide range of affect, or is the affect flat, stunted, or constricted? Is there poor eye contact and/or lack of vocal inflection? Is there a difficulty in expressing rather than feeling emotions? Is the youth's affect superficial in order to appear appropriate, sincere, interested, connected, and the like? Can the youth describe his or her feelings or inner life? What can be said about the youth's ability to trust, to feel guilt and shame, or to be anxious? Can the resident modulate his or her anxiety, or is the youth paralyzed by it? Is the young person withdrawn or disinterested in others and their emotional life? Are the resident's emotions easily aroused? Do the youth's emotions get out of control? Does he or she need constant pressure to settle down? Are there separation reactions? How does the resident deal with compliments or praise?

8. *Impulse control*: Dreikurs, Grunwald, and Pepper (1982) stated that children and adolescent behaviors are purposive, or goal directed, and their actions are intended to gain attention, achieve power, seek revenge, or display inadequacy. According to Wexler (1991), most behaviors represent a youth's attempt to cope with anxiety and to maintain a cohesive sense of self. Even bizarre or self-destructive behaviors reflect an attempt to rebalance or to protect the fragile self. Self-control is revealed in attention span, resistance to environmental distractions and disruption, the ability to return to a task following disruption, and the ability to appropriately match behavioral

states to social context (Putman, 1991). Adolescents with attention deficit hyperactive disorder (ADHD) are restless, talk excessively, act impulsively, interrupt others, and value immediate rewards over future ones (Barkley, Fischer, Edelbrock, & Smallish, 1990). Youngsters with organic deficits of the central nervous system are more vulnerable to anxiety; they overreact to stimulus and have difficulty controlling impulses. They are easily hurt and may react with aggression or withdrawal (Silver, 1984).

The question to be answered is to what degree can the youth self-manage and self-soothe? What is the quality of this control? Can he or she delay and postpone gratification? When the youth is frustrated, what form does anger take: destructiveness to property, people, or self; verbal assaults; temper tantrums; withdrawal; passive-aggressiveness; passive resistance; avoidance; running away; or escape in the use of illegal or mind-altering substances? Is anger rigidly controlled to the extent that there is no manifestation of the same? Is the youth frightened by his or her anger or impulsivity? Does the youth become grandiose when under stress? What kind of controls does the resident respond to: verbal (logic and reason), sanctions, consequences, or bribes? Does the youth become out of control to the point of needing crisis intervention or restraint? How does the youth express his or her aggression, e.g., toward adults, peers, animals, or property? For youth at risk for violent behaviors, it is essential to describe the connections of their conduct problems to the behavioral disorder (Borum & Verhaagen, 2006). What are these? According to Fitzgerald (2005), there are high rates of family violence and animal abuse in the background of violent youth. Is there any information on this issue?

9. *Defense system*: Defense mechanisms in a healthy youngster are integrated into the personality, function smoothly, and do not stand out (Shafir & Shafir, 1992). For the well-adjusted youth, the main defense is repression, which aids in keeping anxiety about new situations or conflicts under control. Some use of repression is reassuring whenever anxiety is too great. Repression assists in pressing down unwanted thoughts, feelings, or awareness. It is used to forget painful issues, but these can emerge as symptoms. When repression fails, other defense mechanisms such as displacement and projection come into action to deal with painful ideas.

Many children and teenagers without a background of abuse can overuse defenses in an effort to cope with overwhelming stressors, expectations, losses, or fears in their lives (Donovan & McIntyre, 1991). There is a natural tendency for youth to react in progressively more primitive ways when encountering potentially dangerous and inescapable threats, so that they resort to behaviors appropriate to earlier developmental stages (Ludburg, 1972). For the emotionally troubled youth, one or more defenses are notable, and the defenses stand out. The youth worker's task is to help youth to become aware of the overuse or rigid employment of particular defense mechanisms. When the youth feels stress, what ego functions does he or she use to cope? What defenses does he or she use? Against what (blame, shame, etc.)? Is there splitting of or difficulty accepting good and bad aspects of the self? Of others? To what degree does the defense system operate: overly strong superego, no spontaneity, diffuse anxiety, excessive intellectualization, or rationalization? What kinds of defenses need to be built in? What defenses need to be loosened? What are the defenses against? What types are predominant?

10. *Reality testing*: Overt behaviors reveal what is intact or defective in reality testing. In order for youth to change, they have to want to change, realize what their problems are and how they contribute to them, and, most importantly, take ownership of their treatment plans and their lives (Bromfield, 2005). Youth with poor reality testing hold illusions about their specialness or entitlement. Their capacity for anticipating the consequences of their behavior is limited. Some youth distort reality through their use of primitive defense mechanisms. How important is the youth's past or the triangulation of emotions? In other words, does the youth have the urge to express who he or she is? Is there a willingness to discuss and to understand how the past affects him or her in the present? Can the youth learn from experience? Can the youth set and pursue realistic short- and long-term goals? If not, what are the impediments to these actions? Does the youth lack a sense of reality, sense of time, or sense of place? Are there excessive fantasies? Are there episodes of delusions? Hallucinations? Derealization? Depersonalization?

PERSONAL CHARACTERISTICS

Thinking, according to Riegel (1975), can be explained from the point of view of the social task of the moment. The social task to be enacted dictates the level of thought required. Thus, most workers are capable of assessing a youngster's problem-solving abilities and social skills compared to those of other children or adolescents. These ordinary, everyday behaviors reflect the youth's personality and maturation level and ability to make use of the environment. The youth worker is required to identify specific habits, peculiar to the individual youth and to his or her natural abilities, that elucidate and expand understanding of the youth's psychological and social functioning. This section deals with the resident's sense of meaning, at-risk issues, and resiliency behaviors.

Habits

1. *Eating habits*: Are these messy or controlled? Does the youth eat well, is he or she fussy or suspicious, or does he or she refuse food, overeat, binge, or hide food in his or her bedroom? What foods does the youth snack on? Does the youth convey a lack of control over eating, or a feeling that she or he cannot stop eating, i.e., control what or how much she or he is eating? Is self-evaluation unduly influenced by body shape and weight? Does the youth engage in self-induced vomiting, or the misuse of laxatives, diuretics, or enemas? Does the youth chew and spit out large amounts of food? In the youth's background, has food been deprived, used as a reinforcement, or withdrawn as a punishment?

2. *Sleeping habits*: Does the resident have trouble getting to sleep or staying asleep, or experience nonrestorative sleep or difficulty waking up? Is he or she restless? Does he or she experience nightmares? Snoring? Bedwetting? Sleepwalking?

3. *Sexual development*: An attempt should be made to distinguish between normal and pathological behaviors, such as a natural interest in reproduction versus sexually reactive behaviors or extensive (obsessive) sexual behaviors. Has the youth been a victim of a sexual or a physical assault? Does the youth talk about his or her masturbation, or engage in it openly? Does the youth masturbate with others, or engage in other types of sex acts with peers? Is the youth curious about sex, disgusted by it, or disinterested? Is the youth interested in pornography? Does the youth expose him or herself or attempt to watch others in the process of dressing or undressing? Does the youth touch him or herself, or other people, inappropriately, seeking such contact through hugging or bumping into others? Does the youth stand too close to others? Is the youth a sexual predator; is the youth coercive, forcing or manipulating another into sex; or does the youth exchange sex for money, favors, or prohibited substances? Does the youth collect pictures of younger children? Does the youth have a sense of sexual identity, maleness, femaleness, or undifferentiated?

4. *Nervous habits*: Does the youth have difficulty sitting still? Is the youth constantly on the go? Are there unusual patterns of motor activity such as nail biting, scratching, thumb sucking, nose picking, rubbing of genitals, pulling out hair, or experiencing facial or other tics? Does the youth engage in repetitive acts such as rocking, seemingly driven and nonfunctional behavior, hand shaking or waving, foot tapping, head banging, mouthing objects, self-biting, picking at skin or bodily orifices, or hitting one's body? Is there soiling and/or enuresis? Is there an inability to have normal bowel movements? Does the youth display daily rituals, such as an order of events for

getting ready for school, bedtime, etc., which when interrupted for any reason create a reaction? Does the youth's need for structure and control interfere with spontaneity of thought, feeling, and action?

5. *Drug use*: Dreikurs (1972) identified three main problems behind the increasing use of drugs that begins in childhood and peaks during adolescence: (a) overconcern with excitement, so that overcoming boredom justifies violent and hazardous acts; (b) defiance: defiant youth choose behaviors for so-called identity; and (c) escape from reality and responsibilities. Is there use of restricted or illegal substances such drugs, alcohol, or tobacco? If so, what? What are the amount, frequency, methods, and consequences of use? How are these substances obtained? Is there glue or gasoline sniffing, or the use of any other life-endangering inhalants or compounds?

6. *Behaviors*: How does the youth create distance when she or he feels emotionally vulnerable, threatened, insecure, etc.? Have there been any self-harming behaviors, or behaviors that reflect extreme risks? Are there examples of unpredictable, impulsive, poor-judgment, or inappropriate actions? Is there self-piercing or body tattooing? Are there any self-mutilating behaviors or suicide gestures? Are these for attention, to avoid punishment, to control anxiety, as a result of guilt, for power, or for secondary gain? Has the youth engaged in any assaultive or intimidating acts? Does the youth enjoy fighting; hurting others; being physically hurt; tormenting, torturing, or killing animals; or fire setting? Does the youth experience more injuries of various sorts than other youth? Does he or she operate equipment or utensils, or play in activities, unsafely? Learning disabilities and ADHD increase the probability of chronic behavior problems (Bromfield, 2005) and delinquency, such as aggressive assaults, vandalism, stealing, lying, truancy, running away, fire setting, robbery, cruelty to animals, sexual coercion, abuse toward others, and weapons use. Has the youth been charged with any of these offenses, and if so, what is the current disposition of the matter? What does he or she say about these issues?

7. *Fears*: Siegler (2000) believed five basic fears are formed in childhood: fear of the unknown, fear of being alone, fears about the body, fears of the voice of conscience, and fears about the self. These fears are transformed during adolescence. What fears does the youth have? Has the youth experienced any frightening (traumatic) or violent situations? Denial and repression are ways of separating unpleasant thoughts, feelings, or experiences from conscious awareness (Goldstein, 1995). Denial is a normal defense when undergoing physical or emotional shock. Prolonged denial to block awareness or put off taking responsibility for certain feelings or actions can become problematic. Make believe is another coping mechanism used to redefine the youngster's experiences, identity, and power (Putman, 1991). Some indulgence

in fantasy and role playing is, however, developmentally appropriate. Cantwell and Baker (1985) believed that resiliency behaviors can be activated to deal with stress or crisis. Does the youth employ resiliency behaviors to deal with crisis?

8. *Illnesses*: During the youngster's stay in residence, describe the nature and course of physical illnesses. Does the youth seek comfort from staff during illness or turn away into solitude? What medication has the youth been on? Are there factors that led to changes in the symptoms or illness? Any evidence of psychosomatic disorders? Is the youth able to distinguish physical sensations from emotional feelings? Hypochondriacal behavior may reflect the youth's experience of being badly mothered, or inadequately cared for or mothered. Does the youth have any dental problems, or impairment of hearing or vision?

Drug Therapy

In residential treatment for some childhood disorders, a trial of medication is often considered when potential benefits are considered to significantly outweigh risks. Nevertheless, there are many parents and professionals who oppose pharmacological intervention because they understand that there are psychological explanations for a mental disorder or for significant contributions to it. Yet, the etiology of all psychiatric disorders is multiply determined. To assess the potential benefits versus risks of a specific medication, each case must be evaluated on an individual basis.

Medication is considered where the maturation and development of a youngster are being disrupted or delayed by a mental illness (Green, 1991). There are also times where medication will augment other treatment modalities. The determining factor is whether a drug will significantly increase the response to other treatments or prevent (stabilize) deterioration.

Therapeutic drug use requires that goals of treatment and time frames to reach them are established. Drugs must be used in effective dosages for sufficient time periods as determined by a medical doctor from an evaluation, and require continuous clinical observation. It is the role of staff members to ensure that treatment response and the emergence of adverse effects are monitored closely. The drug dosage should be adjusted accordingly, and appropriate treatment for emergent adverse effects must be instituted as quickly as possible by the attending physician.

Interests and Hobbies

Youth who participate in sports exhibit fewer behavioral problems, earn better grades, interact better in the classroom, have fewer behavioral problems outside the classroom, drop out less frequently, and attend school more regularly (Jeziorski, 1994). This means that it is the pleasure derived from the activity that is symbolically significant. Additionally, physical activities are shown to have a positive influence on self-esteem in youth, with the greatest beneficial effect for youth with disabilities (Gruber, 1986). However, talents are the result of the acquisition of a sequence of skills. The acquisition of these skills is facilitated by opportunities in the individual's environment. For example, children and adolescents cannot become good at a sport unless the opportunity to participate is made available, which includes proper equipment, good facilities, and coaching. Therefore, development of talents is examined and understood in relation to support, constraints, and changing tasks (Van Lieshout & Heymans, 2000).

1. What interests and hobbies does the youth have? Are these challenging, stimulating, pleasurable, or too easy? What are the emerging social interactional patterns with peers and adults? Does the youth seek out younger peers and/or activities appropriate for a younger child? Is the youth open to new ideas and curious; does he or she demonstrate diverse interests and imagination? What sports and games does the youth pursue? What is the youth's skill level in activities relative to those of same-aged peers? In her or his self-expression, is there a sense of playfulness, whim, and spontaneity, or is the youth unable to let go?

2. During activities, is the youth enthusiastic, creative, perseverant, compulsive, disinterested, or scattered? Is the youth repetitive or restricted, and therefore engages in stereotyped patterns of behavior in interests and activities, or lacks a varied approach? When frustrated, does the youth persist with difficult tasks or withdraw? Is there a difference in the youth's attitude toward, or is there a preference for, individual or group activities? How does the youth deal with conflicts in sports? Does he or she comply with rules? What are his or her attitudes toward competition, winning, and losing?

School (Academic Functioning)

1. What grade is the youth in? Is the youth at grade level in his or her curriculum? Has the youth been held back or skipped grades? Are there academic achievement tests in reading, arithmetic, spelling, and written language, or specialized skill areas? Are there difficulties with performance, such as being underproductive, uncooperative, demanding of assistance, or unable to work independently? Does the youth express extreme effort to attain educational goals? Is there a short-term memory problem? Is there a diagnosis of a learning disability or an inborn information-processing problem? Does the youth prefer vocational over academic pursuits? Is the youth enrolled in treatment, special education, or regular (vocational) class?

2. The way in which the youth makes meaning of his or her world depends on the way in which the youth understands and describes

his or her perception of the world (Ysseldyke & Christenson, 1987). What is the youth's attitude toward school? Does the youth see school as an opportunity for social connection, sublimation, and object finding? Is the youth overly serious and perfectionist? Are there solid, realistic thinking strategies? What educational difficulties does the youth have? How does the youth make sense of his or her difficulties, and what options are available to him or her? Is there attention to school work, homework, and projects? Is the youth easily distracted, forgetful, disinterested, or overly worried, and does he or she lose homework? Does the youth complete all the work expected of him or her? What changes need to take place in order for learning to occur? What are the supports and constraints the resident needs? What are the youth's problems in the context of academics and interactions in the school? In what way will the youth's problems be solved?

3. What would the youth like to do when he or she leaves school? Has the youth ever had a job? Is working important for the youngster? How does the youth spend his or her money? Is there careful management of funds?

Diagnostic Formulation

The establishment of a diagnosis integrates the diverse findings into a comprehensive view of the youth, assisting in treatment and the type of therapy and intervention to be attempted. Consideration should be given to the possible causal relationship between observed and self-reported client behaviors, as well as inferred client characteristics and the impact of environmental factors (Hayden, 1987). In terms of the youngster's referral information, the following questions should be asked:

1. What diagnosis (in gross terms)—neurotic, psychotic, deprived, oppositional, conduct disorder, reactive attachment disorder, etc.— has been applied to the youth by a psychiatrist or psychologist?

2. What is the rationale given for the diagnosis (by a psychiatrist or psychologist) in behavioral terms such as the youth's unconscious conflicts that may be contributing to his or her difficulties? Does the youth feel persecuted by peers, staff, teachers, or parents? Are there delusional or hallucinating experiences? Or perceptual distortions? Are there grandiose fantasies?

   A. Evaluating defense mechanisms is essential to understanding youngsters in treatment, as are managing oppositionalism or withdrawal, clarifying conflicted behaviors, and engendering more adaptive functioning. Usually, two or more defenses are at work at the same time (Clark, 1998). Are there a description and discussion in background and clinical reports of defenses used (e.g., repression, projection, obsessive-compulsive, reaction–formation, displacement, etc.)?

B. Defenses help to manage infantile rage, dependence, psychosis, low self-esteem, and abandonment. Narcissistic defenses may develop in order to cope with fears of abandonment and loss of approval. How do the youth's defense mechanisms improve or hinder her or his acceptance of reality and the understanding of cause and effect?

C. What is the youth's coping style? Does the youth have the ego capacity expected of his or her age? Does the youth suffer from feelings of injury, shame, and humiliation with accompanying feelings of powerlessness, helplessness, and rage? Does the youth have reflectivity, the capacity to see or understand things in their larger sense?

D. Are there any problems that were previously considered less serious or more serious, or that went unrecognized, in other placements?

3. Differential diagnosis: This is appropriate where there are two or more significant difficulties or possible explanations for behavior, e.g., mental retardation and emotional disturbances, or psychotic functioning and extreme anxiety. According to Offerd, Boyle, and Racine (1991), social skills deficits are an indication of a learning disability. There is also an overlap or comorbidity of conduct disorder, ADHD, and learning disability. In this respect, have other disorders (e.g., retardation or physical handicaps) been identified by a psychiatrist or psychologist, and does this question indicate, substantiate, or complement the intrapsychic difficulty? If indicative of other disorders, to what extent are they felt to be primary or secondary? Disorders that are commonly complicated by comorbidity are anxiety and mood episodes, psychosis, and substance abuse (Wetzer & Sanderson, 1997). Are these currently a factor? Were these discussed in the referral information?

4. Strengths-based interventions for youth who experience behavioral and psychological challenges are more efficacious than pathology-based approaches (Laursen, 2000). What are the perceived areas of ego strength or deviations from the norm such as talents, interests, capacity to abstract, or use of language?

Treatment Plan

Treatment planning is a process that moves from the assessment of the problem, to the formulation of the problem, and then to the implementation of treatment. Treatment is expedited when changing behavioral patterns are identified and understood. This section deals with the formulation of the treatment plan or the enactment of the Psychosocial Assessment.

1. What are the conclusions of the data and how best to match the youth's needs with the appropriate program intensity, which is especially important for high-risk youngsters or youth who have been abused, are suicidal, or are a delinquency risk (Skinner & Blaskfield, 1983). In order to accomplish this, identify the nature of problems, and the goals that have been established. Detail the indicators and the review dates.
2. Where does the youth now stand in terms of normal functioning in consideration of age? What needs to happen in order for the youth to feel happy, secure, or well-adjusted?
3. What factors have caused the youth to resist change? What mechanisms and devices does the resident use to defend against treatment adherence and therapeutic progress? Describe techniques to be used to change maladaptive functioning. Several studies support the view that adolescents can improve on multiple variables, regardless of whether these problems were specifically targeted by treatment (Powell & Oei, 1991). This means that adolescents especially need to feel heard and understood. When they are heard, cooperation hinges on adult validation, reinforcements, and the building of positive relationships. Does the adolescent need more empathy, or should he or she be pushed to change? What skills does the youth need to learn, such as assertiveness, relaxation, or management of emotions that target anger and anxiety? Does the youth lack reasoning or abstract thinking skills? Can pleasurable activities and generating alternatives reduce stress?

GUIDE FOR WRITING A DISCHARGE SUMMARY

The Discharge Summary is considered to be part of the assessment process and should be written up after the resident has been discharged from the treatment program.

A. Referral
   1. Identification of the youth, including age and brief description
   2. Referral route
      a. Who referred the youth?
      b. For what reasons?
      c. What was the precipitating event, i.e., why was the youth being referred at that point in time?
B. Background information
   1. What was the presenting problem(s)?

    2. What was the duration of problem(s)?

    3. Describe the coping mechanisms in the family with relation to presenting problem(s).

    4. Brief description of the family, significant members, and patterns of operating, e.g., symbiotic tie between mother and youth.

    5. Summary of previous investigations.

C. Diagnostic description

    1. Identify the major maladaptive behavior patterns and whether or not there has been evidence of change.

    2. Describe self-image and ego functions.

    3. What is the major conflict at this time?

    4. What progress occurred in terms of eating, sleeping, sex, nervous, drug, or alcohol habits?

D. Special investigations

    1. What investigations were carried out?

    2. Did these investigations indicate other difficulties (e.g., retardation or physical handicaps), or do they substantiate and complement the intrapsychic difficulty?

    3. If indicative of other difficulties, to what extent are they felt to be primary or secondary?

E. Diagnostic formulation

    1. Diagnosis (in gross terms): neurotic, psychotic, deprived, etc.

    2. Diagnosis in behavioral terms with rationale

      a. Defenses used, e.g., projection, obsessive-compulsive, reaction–formation, denial, or repression. An excellent resource that explains defenses is Goldstein (1995).

      b. Defenses against what? E.g., infantile rage, dependence, or psychosis.

    3. Differential diagnosis: This is appropriate where there are two or more significant difficulties or possible explanations for a behavior, e.g., mental retardation and emotional disturbances.

F. Recommendations

    1. Treatment plan: was it considered a success or a failure, and why?

    2. Techniques used to change maladaptive functioning (description of).

    3. Where does the youth stand now in terms of normal functioning in consideration of age?

    4. Specific recommendations.

    5. What follow-up has been planned?

DISCUSSION

The Psychosocial Assessment is a vital factor in the delivery of residential treatment. It identifies the adjustment level of the young person and describes problem areas, which help to inform treatment and to make it relevant. This assessment model can also help to provide an understanding of the youth: what the youth looks like and why, what his or her needs are, what factors have affected or shaped the youth, how change has occurred in the youth, and a baseline to measure treatment progress (Scherer, 1985). Therefore, the written assessment should also contain the language and ideas of the youth, as well as quotes, in order to inform the treatment team and referring agencies of how to enter the youngster's world and what the youth is trying to accomplish (Horner, Sugai, Todd, & Lewis-Palmer, 2000).

According to Achenbach (1980), the lack of positive or adaptive behaviors and the failure to progress on developmental tasks are extremely indicative in the recognition and diagnosis of pathology. Thus, the Psychosocial Assessment requires that goals are specific, objectives are clear, and interventions are tailored to develop the youth's uniqueness. This means that the criteria for the youth's discharge are program completion. Nevertheless, it is important that the practitioner and treatment team not only look for psychopathology or emphasize deviance and neglect, but also detail the youth's strengths, adaptive behaviors, and assets (Barton, 2006).

SUMMARY

When children or adolescents present with comorbid disorders, they are the most difficult to treat. This requires the treatment staff to be cognizant of the co-occurrence of disorders, to determine the most pressing or interfering problem, and to treat these first and then, when these identified features are under control, deal with the others. This means that attention needs to be given to the developmental issues that have contributed to, or are currently contributing to, the present problem (Shirk & Phillips, 1991). This includes modifying undesirable social behaviors and developing new behaviors in the group home, at school, on home visits, and in the community. It is not enough to break negative behaviors or to focus on what the youth does wrong, but new adaptive behaviors must be established and positive behaviors are to be strengthened. This includes a plan to develop the young person's creative potential and to help the youth to increase his or her confidence by reviewing how the youth has coped successfully with other problems. When the youth believes that he or she has completed treatment, the criterion employed to evaluate this assertion is whether the youth can demonstrate greater flexibility, cooperation, self-control, and personal responsibility.

CONCLUSION

The Psychosocial Assessment examines the youth's transactions in his or her current placement, whether in residential treatment, a foster home, or a treatment class. It addresses the interrelated effects of biological, psychological, and social factors on the evolving youth. It examines situational influences on the youngster within the context of her or his family, at school, with peers, and in relation to social class, ethnicity, culture, religion, and sexual maturation. It examines in detail and in depth the influences of the family and its impact that led to internalized and externalized problems. It is an evaluation of how a youth deals with the expectations placed on him or her.

The objective of the Psychosocial Assessment is not only to evaluate the young person's developmental attainment but also to understand how the youth has dealt with his or her emotional experiences and connection with other people. It is a process that is structured to help the individual staff member to discern what the youth's responses are to the normalization process of residential treatment, or any placement, and it uses social indicators to measure or describe the youth's adjustment. It assists teamwork and underscores the treatment staff's link to the youngster. It is a dynamic document that is updated during the youth's stay in placement. It reflects any major changes in problems, definition, goals, objectives, interventions, or maturation. It is defined by content and by description.

In a well-crafted and thoughtful assessment, a comprehensive picture of how the youth as an individual emerges, and the way in which the youngster deals with life, issues, and other people. It addresses stabilizing factors for future mental health; high tolerance for frustration, good sublimation potential, effective ways for dealing with anxiety, and a strong urge toward completion of development (or for growing up and becoming independent and self-reliant). Because not all children or adolescents placed in residential treatment manifest the same extreme emotions and behaviors, not all areas of each category of the assessment will be observed or relevant for every resident. The Psychosocial Assessment has four distinguishing characteristics:

1. It details the connection between the young person's current problems and his or her past.
2. It describes the resident's emotional-behavioral problems in relation to his or her immediate social environment and experiences.
3. It identifies the resident's needs; thus, treatment can be specific and time limited, and its effectiveness is based on the youth's unique characteristics.
4. It determines whether treatment had any impact, and if the reevaluation of behavioral changes, the nature of problems, or the attainment of goals is deemed unremarkable or regressive, then treatment can be restructured.

CHAPTER 4

Group Living

CONTEXTUAL GOALS OF TREATMENT

Children are mainly shaped and socialized by their parents. Children's values and attitudes are a direct result of the quality of parent–child interactions. Effective socialization occurs in families when the child is made to feel safe and secure, and strongly experiences love, approval, validation, and closeness (Elkind, 2007a). The parameters of firm and consistent expectations, with clearly defined limits and structure, inculcate youngsters with the parent's value system and connection to family. But, when parents discourage or punish closeness and intimacy, and discipline is inconsistent, random, or excessive, then the child's sense of self and maturation are disrupted and delayed. Eventually, the confused and/or embittered youngster may gravitate toward subcultural ideals or seek approval on the streets. This likelihood is diminished when parents are nonconditional in their acceptance of their children and subscribe to society's core norms and values (Wachtel, 2004).

Most adolescents in residential facilities display an overlay of psychiatric, emotional, or antisocial symptoms. Many of these youngsters, classified as at risk by social service organizations, have been involved in illegal acts. Of those youngsters detained or incarcerated in juvenile facilities and/or facing the justice system, many have serious mental health issues (Pazaratz, Randall, Spekkens, Lazor, & Morton, 2000). Generally, when youngsters commit antisocial or delinquent acts, they are adjudicated to the youth justice system (Canada) or to the juvenile justice system (United States). But, when children and adolescents act out their emotional problems within their families, they are regarded as being more disturbed than delinquent, and viewed to be at risk or in need of protection. Consequently, they may be apprehended by Child Protective Services or Children's Aid Societies, or referred to social services and placed in the mental health system. However, disturbed adolescents can also wind up as youthful offenders or in the juvenile justice system, according to their misdeeds. Depending on the way in which youth are identified, as needing or responding to controls, they are either placed in treatment or adjudicated to detention.

Upon admission to a residential facility, most youth have similar reactions. At first, they comply with the rules and ingratiate themselves to staff members. But, as they interact more with their peers, and try to fit in and to hide their fears, they often display grandiosity and bravado. Youngsters who align themselves with the power of the peer subculture, or even display outright defiance toward staff, typically justify their oppositionalism by stating that they are only reacting to staff because their behaviors are always being monitored and their choices controlled. These reactive attitudes that are manifested as defiance, oppositionalism, or defensiveness are termed *resistance* and impede treatment. The youth worker's task is to overcome resistance, and to motivate the resident to cooperate, to open up, to have hope, to learn, and to change.

Guiding youth in the contracting process is a crucial step in gaining treatment adherence. Contracts provide youth with an opportunity to identify their problems, work on goals, elicit help, and prepare for discharge. Treatment contracts employ timelines, become tangible reminders of goals, and require the development of new skills and improved attitudes. Contracts help youngsters to experience placement as purposeful, concrete, specific, and goal directed. Contracts address issues of loss and connection, and provide a format to share feelings, fears, hopes, confusion, and uncertainty. Contracts review the youth's accomplishments, reinforce adaptive responses, and instill a sense of pride (Pazaratz, 2000c).

THE SOCIALIZATION PROCESS AND DEVELOPMENT OF VALUES

Upon admission to residential treatment, the youth typically undergoes complete psychological testing, which includes intelligence and projective testing. Psychological testing identifies the type of pathology the youth is experiencing and the intervention techniques to be employed. Medical problems are not overlooked as either the cause or the result of emotional problems. Upon identification of the youngster's problems, a treatment plan is formulated that includes the goals as established by the referring agency. The youngster's treatment plan includes family issues and an academic plan, and identifies criteria in the change process, contextual factors, and co-occurrence of problems.

In spite of careful testing and long-term planning, one of the difficulties in working with youngsters admitted to treatment is that they lack motivation. In fact, they lack many self-sustaining values and often have alternative values.

They gravitate to passive hostility and dependency. They typically exhibit identity confusion, lack of motivation, and defiance. Oppositional behaviors may include passiveness, denial, constant complaining, hyperactivity, destructiveness, boisterousness, or refusal to cooperate and an inability to deal with the give-and-take demands of relationships. Defensiveness makes it especially difficult to engage youth in meaningful treatment strategies. For some youngsters, the pervasive nature of their negative reactions interferes with their ability to cooperate with staff or peers. Many youth have difficulty making progress because they are easily misled or manipulated by their peers. There are others who are habitually misleading, deceitful, or outright pathological. Sometimes, a severe learning deficit or extreme moods contribute to them being stuck in their behaviors.

How, then, does the youth worker engage youngsters and build a cooperative relationship? The youth's use of language conveys a message and negotiates the type of relationship that he or she wishes to have (Tannen, Kendall, & Gordon, 2007). Additionally, how the youth talks informs the worker of the defenses that need to be lessened, or built in to stabilize the youth and to teach adaptive control over impulse discharge. Of interest to the youth worker is to understand how the youth deals with sexual and aggressive drives and narcissistic needs. This knowledge will assist the staff member to determine the developmental forces that have influenced identification, affect regulation, and frustration tolerance. Additionally, it is vital to know the way in which parents shaped the youth's ability to form secure attachments, close or meaningful relationships, and gender specificity and its organizational power. This background information clarifies how the youth has dealt with or can deal with trauma or psychic danger. There may be unconscious or unspoken fantasies to repeat a trauma or strong unfulfilled wishes (Constantino, Dana, & Malgady, 2007). It is especially important that the youth worker realizes how the youth is influenced by the worker's personality and whether this leads to acting out. Surviving a youth's acting out or challenges, and learning the meaning of these behaviors and how they are connected to the youth's past experiences, is crucial (Kagan, 2004).

Many youth in residential placement have given up on themselves. They have been subjected to adult rejection, peer humiliation, and societal labels. These debilitating experiences have made some of them feel like "failures" or "crazy." Some youngsters fear that staff may hold or develop similar negative views once they get to know them. Some youth overreact to expectations and limits, believing that these controls are belittling. Others will react to controls and expectations because they have never encountered any, or any on a consistent basis. Still others may interpret staff members as being bossy. They may also misperceive or fear expectations. There are youngsters who view youth workers as unfair, stupid, or intrusive, or find them threatening. There are youth who will feel that rules are too difficult and believe that they will fail at following them and be punished. They may initially internalize or somatize their feelings; yet eventually they may even act out physically to release their anxiety.

To prevent negative attitudes toward rules, youth workers encourage youngsters to voice their concerns in all aspects of programming, and to discuss problems, goal setting, choice of activities, and the like. Because many youngsters tend to blame their environment and the people in it for their troubles, youth workers can deal with this negativity by using milieu interactions to transmit a sense of inclusiveness. Supportive confrontations, feedback, and verbal reinforcement (acknowledgment or praise) by youth workers (and peers) will quickly and explicitly lead to improvements in a resident's self-understanding, communication skills, and choice of interactions. Standard situations involving conflict with parents and other adults in authority can be discussed. Instruction can then be given for dealing with problematic situations. Rehearsals in conflict avoidance or resolution are helpful problem-solving strategies (Pazaratz 2000b, 2000c, 2000d).

STAFF–YOUTH RELATIONSHIP BUILDING

Most youth in residential placement have not developed sufficient social awareness, insight, or reflectiveness (understanding of their own or others' mental processes). They are unable to comprehend, relate to, or process others' feelings, or respect the boundaries of others. This impediment is based on a lack of interdependency, inclusiveness, and trust. Nevertheless, most youngsters can be resocialized and taught to overcome interactional and interpersonal deficits. They can learn to open up, share, understand affect, accept limits, follow directives, and even abide by the difficult and complex reality of living in a social group. This contextual approach is realized when youth workers share insight into youth developmentally, or the association between a resident's cognitive and emotional functioning and what the youth does, imagines, and says (Williams & Thurow, 2005). But this requires that discipline and consequences are used judiciously by youth workers in order to build rather than to weaken the bonds of attachment. Staff members also need to convey caring by recognizing the uniqueness of the individual; demonstrate that they will persevere with the relationship, especially when the youth is not making progress or is being defiant; and not be judgmental or reject the youth.

Abused youth see themselves as victims of external circumstances, powerless in the hands of forces they cannot control. Nevertheless, they can be taught to shift their thinking so that they can experience control at least over their emotions. They can also embrace the idea of self-acceptance, give up self-rating, and reject self-denigration (Ellis, 1994). Youngsters do not have to be ever growing, or to become competent at anything, in order to accept themselves and to be happy. They undoubtedly have made mistakes that are part of being human. Yet, they continue to act out their feelings of shame, because they believe they are defective, unlovable, and useless. They under-standably react to the criticisms they have received. Many have been treated as if they were worthless. Some have been physically traumatized. Many are emotionally oversensitized! Too often, they look for any unfairness to confirm their view of their own worthlessness. When they are confronted or admonished, a distortion sets in. They believe that they are being devalued (France, 1993). As a result, some childhood and adolescent disorders clearly develop because irrational thinking styles make them prone to illogical reasoning. Nevertheless, these reasoning errors can be corrected. Youngsters can be taught to stop thinking like a victim and not to equate their value with some-one else's rating of them. They can learn that not every disagreement is an attack. Learning to recognize inferences and their leap in logic or to dispute negative beliefs can assist youngsters to correct and to control their thinking process. They can teach themselves to calm down and to control the urge to act out or retaliate (Ellis, 1994).

To develop positive relationships, front-line workers need to convey non-conditional acceptance. Whatever traits, characteristics, and values the youth has are to be respected and regarded as valuable. Intellectual limitations, personality quirks, unique interests and hobbies, and even negative attitudes and avoidant behaviors should be utilized to stimulate change and growth. Negative or reactive behaviors can be redirected to become strengths. Many imperfections can be reconstructed so that they are utilized in productive ways. Indeed, there may be unique behaviors in every youth that have not been recognized. There are behaviors or traits that can be deemphasized. When youth discover meaning or value in what they are interested in and what they can do, this adds to their awareness and purpose. Ultimately, a youth must acknowledge mistakes (deal with denial) and redress those behaviors in which he or she has invested, however unwisely. If positive and adaptive experiences or behaviors are not noticed, but ignored, then residents will dis-count themselves, and falsely conclude that their interests are not worthwhile (Durrant, 1993; Johnson, Rasbury, & Siegel, 1997).

All people are more than the sum of their parts. Teaching youth to develop a positive view and to be flexible is called a *second-order personality trait*. These features are essential characteristics of a resilient individual. It is when youngsters recognize and take advantage of opportunities that come their way that they will benefit from discovery and learning, and move beyond being to becoming (Ghurman & Sarles, 2004). Teaching youngsters how to incorporate this information into their construction of reality will increase reflectiveness or self-awareness. Self-awareness is essential when appraising the significance and meanings of a variety of emotional states (Ellis, 1994). This discovery into the self indicates the development of a higher level of inte-grative capacity. This process includes accessing affective memories, or reflec-tive awareness that permits multiple perspectives on the self, on others, and about the meaning of life. Developing insight is a prerequisite for achieving emotional maturation and behavioral potential.

THE ELEMENT OF INTEGRATIVE COUNSELING

Does integrative counseling have a concept of what it is for youngsters in placement to be "adjusted" or "adaptive"? And if it does, how do youth workers help youth to experience or attain such a self-concept? Integrative practice is based on the premise that a youth's age appropriateness or level of emotional and cognitive development reflects the youth's adjustment. Thus, staff members aim to understand youth contextually, in relation to the demands of their environment and their behaviors relative to behaviors of similarly aged youth not in treatment. The youth's psychosocial functioning in placement is affected by the fit between the youth's developmental needs and the environmental context. Youth workers redirect pathological misbehaviors and help youth to enhance their strengths while minimizing weaknesses. Staff perform this function by emphasizing fairness and respect in transactions, modeling genuine behavior, and providing information dispassionately, so that youth become receptive to correcting distorted thinking and modifying maladaptive behaviors.

As treatment progresses, the focus of integrative counseling is on the identification and understanding of affects that are not fully recognized (by youth) interactively or internally. Residents often have a host of painful feelings about themselves, believing that they are defective, inferior, and unchangeable. These debilitating beliefs can permeate all aspects of subjective experiences. Holding on to self-loathing has a profound impact on a youngster's outlook and interactions (Ellis, 1977). In some circumstances, feelings of total worthlessness so dominate a youth's self-view that no other focus of treatment can be initiated until this all-consuming shame has been eased. Youth worker interventions are directed toward the elimination of self-downing and self-pitying emotions, which are typically expressed as anger, anxiety, depression, substance abuse, sexual acting out, and the like. Daily staff–youth interactions aim to modify the cognitive belief system so that youngsters are less self-destructive and more aware of their potential (Rose, 1998).

Many explosive (conduct-disordered), learning impaired, and/or sexually aggressive (predacious) youth suffer from the effects of stress and anxiety. The ability to express oneself in words during states of intense emotions is an important achievement in self-regulation (Pazaratz, 2003a). Youth can learn to reduce the effects of their symptoms and to be in control of their behaviors. Improved cognitive reflexivity occurs when youth restructure attitudes and beliefs, and change destructive self-talk or inner dialogue, that lead to outbursts. Developing assertiveness also helps to counter interpersonal fears and fosters confidence in one's ability to control stressful emotions. As youth deal less emotionally with problems and relinquish physical acting out for stress reduction, this approach will lead to mutual and reciprocal empathic bonds with youth workers. With the mastery of affective states and improved interpersonal relations, the youth's self-concept is enhanced (Pazaratz, 1996a, 1996b).

POWER STRUGGLES

Most youngsters in treatment are fearful, suspicious, and wary of revealing their weaknesses. Many of them cannot bear to be judged or to be an object of criticism, rejection, control, and discipline. Some youngsters even regard supportive confrontation as an attack on them personally. Some react to staff merely because they are always being watched. As a result, staff will find that there are residents who are difficult to comprehend or to interact with, as they avoid staff, violate rules, and fail to listen. Yet, they boast and exaggerate about themselves, do not feel that they are listened to (understood and respected), and often want to do all the talking. When these youngsters realize that they cannot continue to manipulate, con, or get staff to give into their demands, they often become hostile, oppositional, and defiant. Some youngsters become more defensive when their selfish attitudes are confronted, controlled, or interrupted. There are also youth who escalate in their defiance, and purposefully break rules, run away, withdraw, lie, manipulate, retaliate, and the like. They do not want to change! Anything that prevents the youth from doing or feeling the right thing, or making the healthy choice, is treatment resistance, which is the basis of the power struggle.

When residents engage in provocative, defiant, and aggressive behaviors, these function to control others, distract the group, or manipulate the group's emotional tone. Some negative behaviors are calculated to gain status within the group. Overreaction by staff members can quickly lead to more verbal hostility, power struggles, withdrawal, and the like. Therefore, youth workers should be cautious when they respond. Conflict resolution and affect regulation are ongoing themes in youth work (Fewster & Garfat, 2001). Defiance can be based on anxiety, shame, and anger, or due to a disorder (conduct, reactive attachment, oppositional/defiant, and so forth). Defiance and oppositionalism are best handled when youth workers are aware of how their interventions are being experienced (such as a fear, humiliation, or challenge). This helps workers to understand why a youth resists or escalates interactions into a power struggle. Distancing of staff, shunning or avoidance, and the defensive organization (negative reactions) of emotions, cognition, and behaviors show a lack of staff–youth alliance, bonding, or attachment. But when youth feel connected to staff and the program, this sense of security and trust allows for the expression of individual differences and provides a sense of shared meaning.

Power struggles are minimized when youth workers emphasize understanding and listening, rather than attempting to convince residents that they are not seeing things correctly. When youth workers try to prove that they are right (and youth are wrong), or that they (staff members) are only being helpful, intelligent, and so forth, this superior attitude can antagonize youth. But there are also youngsters who are not easy to reason with. How, then, does a youth worker deal with the intensity of a youngster's emotions? Youth work is an intersubjective experience. Acting-out behaviors or passive defiance affects some youth workers' sense of authority, ability to be in control, and capacity to be reflective and thoughtful. Youth workers' reactions flow from their negative subjective feelings toward a particular youth, or a group of youth, into feelings of dislike, disgust, or even anger. When faced with rapidly escalating behaviors, some youth workers do not remain in control (calm), are not objective, or do not maintain their ability to focus, be rational, or be reasonable. By remaining emotionally available (not angry or distant) and by being reassuring (as opposed to being punitive, holding a grudge, or being offended), staff can teach youth to be in control of their feelings and responsible for their behaviors (Fewster & Garfat, 1998).

Objectively pointing out misbehaviors with a view to problem solving helps to redirect and to limit the negative impact on a youngster's vulnerable sense of self. When youth are confronted or redirected, they can be taught to understand that their experience of shame arises from their misattributions, and that they are not in fact being evaluated or criticized by staff. However, encounters between residents and youth workers can become emotionally charged when language is loud, aggressive, and escalating so that each person affects the other. The youth worker must be cognizant of the resident's moods, rules, boundaries, stress tolerance, fantasies, desires, values, and goals, or lack thereof. Staff should avoid using misbehaviors, mistaken beliefs, misuse of language, and distasteful ideas or values against the resident. Some ideas, issues, or behaviors may be disturbing for staff. But youth workers can nevertheless remain objective and accepting of youth, while disapproving of misbehaviors or wrongheadedness. Staff availability and reasonableness help youth to change attitudes. This is unlikely to occur if staff condemn or react toward youth (Pazaratz, 2000b, 2000c, 2000d, 2003b).

FRONT-LINE INTERACTIONS

A youth worker's authority and power are to be used judiciously (fairly), and never for revenge or self-gratification. Youth workers need to know how to calm residents when they are angry and to teach them (how) to delay their impulsive desire to "blow up," act out, or retaliate. Stabilizing residents occurs when youth workers show them how to recognize cues to impulsivity, deescalate emotionally, and curtail the urge to "get even." Self-control is based on the ability to tolerate uncomfortable situations, to deal with the pain of emotional turmoil, and to stay focused in the moment. This ability to deal with discomfort anxiety arises when the youth learns to change self-talk, stays with volatile issues (fears) that trigger emotional turmoil, and talks calmly to others about issues (Ellis, 1994). Once these competencies are internalized, youth will experience the positive effects of clear, nonemotional, problem-solving communication.

What can youth workers do when they realize that some youth are not interested in cooperating or compromising? What can youth workers do when some youth mock, scorn, or argue with everything they say or do? What can youth workers do when some youth attempt to manipulate them? Ultimately, youth workers want youngsters to feel connected, to experience trust, and to discuss the reasons for their oppositionalism. Yet, staff members are better prepared for disappointments and power struggles when they realize that residents can be skilled manipulators and good at avoidance. Youngsters in placement can be quick to make up excuses, deny responsibility, blame others, or apologize without sincerity. Some youngsters never acknowledge any of their misdeeds. They have rigid defenses! They rationalize or justify all irresponsible behaviors. There will be times when neither insight, nor talk about feelings, nor reconstruction of cognitions will help in the change process. But acting-out and negative behaviors do not just occur because of impulsiveness, compulsion, or passion. These defiant, defensive acts can be purposeful and deliberate, whereby the youth is seeking power, revenge, control, or attention.

Can youth workers expect to form relationships that are mutually trusting yet therapeutic? Yes! This is achievable, especially when staff members emphasize the principles of fairness and respect in social interactions. Youth will react negatively, especially if their behaviors are judged harshly, consequenced punitively, or used to manipulate them. Inducing youth to feel shame about their behaviors, ideas, or values will contribute to their anxiety, sense of insecurity, and feelings of unworthiness. Youth will not see the worker as someone they can trust and rely upon for support if the youth worker is perceived to inflict pain or be caustic or degrading. When youngsters feel that they are valued and their wishes and needs (conscious and unconscious) are understood, they trust workers and learn to see them as genuine, caring, and reasonable. An empathic approach will assist staff to uncover the root of problems. When staff deal with the cause behind symptoms, this intervention will break down the youth's defenses, build understanding, improve connection, and reduce the likelihood of future power struggles.

There are times when a youngster's volatile behaviors and interpersonal attitudes are similar to the youth worker's own experiences. The worker may not be aware of these coincidences. Sometimes, these are buried issues in the youth worker's life, or past, that are touched upon or aroused by concerns and difficulties raised by youth. Frustration or even anger toward residents may be an attempt by the worker to cover up his or her own inferiority and shortcomings, or to push away personal issues. Any intense emotional response toward youth by staff is called *countertransference* and interferes with being objective. This can be problematic if the worker acts upon countertransference, because to do so can lead to a battle of wills or counterresistance. However, when staff have an awareness of the cause of their reactive feelings, this can help them to curtail inappropriate feelings. By staff understanding the source of their feelings and the nature of the youngster's, they can overcome these, which puts them in a better position to connect with residents (Pazaratz, 2000b, 2000c, 2000d).

STABILIZING INTERACTIONS

When direct care staff draw upon aspects of various therapies, this combination of techniques provides greater flexibility. Certain modalities such as behaviorism, positive peer pressure, and the like are typically employed to create structure that assists with the goals of reeducation, resocialization, treatment, and care. When staff combine different theories of behavior change (integrative), these new perspectives can add to the discussion of daily issues (Pazaratz, 1999). This means that staff should have good verbal skills, be able to use language effectively, and have the social and linguistic framework for understanding and expressing feelings. Feelings are comprehended by deciphering emotional content embedded in social and cultural discourse (Pazaratz, 2005b). Understanding the real meaning, or metamessage, during communications is fundamental to problem solving. Staff should be able to combine the theoretical aspects of problem solving with practical methods or real-life examples. This approach can help expand a youth's understanding of communication and relationships.

Many youth workers believe that insight-oriented discussions should be the principle treatment technique and that a worker's competence is based upon the ability to get youth to talk. When staff employ or rely upon only one approach, they reduce the possibility of being effective, such as misunderstanding the youth or not developing strategies that meet the unique needs of the individual. Integrative theory emphasizes that individuals are understood contextually and that more than one intervention strategy, or intervention technique, can be efficacious. For example, teaching the use of reflection and observation can prompt residents to question themselves (i.e., attitudes and behaviors) and ask themselves whether they are contributing to the problem. Emphasizing the use of neutral language and being solutions focused help youth to deescalate tense and conflictual situations. To create group cooperation and treatment adherence, staff members utilize a balanced and controlled emotional tone. These integrative techniques are more likely to be successful than when staff are rigid, inflexible, and authoritarian.

All youngsters will pass through various treatment phases. Not all youth will encounter these sequentially. However, encountering or experiencing a phase means that youth pass through stages of awareness and reflectivity. They will also engage in behaviors that reflect the phase they are in. In integrative practice, the treatment phases consist of being obsequious (honeymoon), seeking validation (closed or superficial), acting out (reaction to treatment), building a therapeutic relationship or trust (bonding), processing the past or dealing with abandonment (abuse, neglect, etc.), living and being in the present (acceptance), setting and pursuing goals (future oriented), and, finally, negotiating and implementing discharge–community reentry plans (transition, individuation, and separation).

THE LIVING AND LEARNING ENVIRONMENT

Integrative practice is based upon a philosophy and a set of principles that promote self-sustaining and socially appropriate behaviors and goals. In enacting an educative and socializing environment, integrative practice emphasizes improved reality testing and the importance of good social skills, such as problem solving or how to function and to interact with others. Daily social interactions inform and provide each resident with opportunities to understand the self, others, life, and the world. Effective social skills can be acquired as a competency and underscore the importance of the self (i.e., to learn to function as an autonomous individual, and to employ problem-solving and critical-thinking strategies; Brodie, 2007). Youth workers' effectiveness at instilling self-caring values and teaching communication skills hinges on their ability to motivate youth and to convey the enormous benefits of changing.

Creating a homelike environment for children and adolescents in residential placement and providing for their daily emotional and developmental needs are the care functions of youth work. The treatment aspect of placement is enacted when youth workers employ stimulating programming and a supportive structure, and by keeping youth involved and connected to critical areas of their lives such as family, school, and community. Both the care and treatment aspects of residential placement require minimizing abrupt and drastic life and relationship changes. By enacting a balanced approach to care and treatment, residents are encouraged to let down their defenses and to reveal how they deal with, and have dealt with, the important areas and relationships in their lives (Schoenberg, 1994). Once direct care staff experience the real youth (i.e., what the youth feels and does, what the youth defends against feeling and doing, and what the youth understands or does not comprehend), staff members can teach youth how to deal more effectively with social interactions and the feelings that arise during emotionally charged situations.

In spite of staff members' best efforts at problem solving, some youngsters make their problems worse by being stubborn or hypercritical. They do not know how or refuse to deal equitably with others, even though they demand to be treated with fairness and respect. Their defeats, disappointments, and failures are used to justify a negative view of the self, others, and conditions. Their self-defeating and self-denigrating attitudes need to be replaced with opportunities to experience success in relationships and in activities. They need to learn not to self-rate, and to demand love, approval and validation, or fair treatment. They need to comprehend the difference between desiring and demanding recognition or respect. They need to learn how to tolerate their disappointments. These philosophical shifts provide youth with an opportunity to accept the self, others, and conditions no matter how unfair or difficult they appear (Ellis, 1994).

ACTIONS THAT SUSTAIN THE GROUP

The residential environment and the living group symbolically become the new home and family for all youngsters. Youth workers provide residents with the protection, gratification, and emotional-intellectual stimulation found in a family. Youth workers promote psychological growth by encouraging residents to reexperience the issues of (emotional) trust and connection. To this end, youth workers should be warm and seek involvement in the resident's daily activities. This approach is the basis for connection and becomes the fundamental fabric of the social system. This means that youth workers are careful not to replicate the negativity and rejection that these youngsters have experienced with other adults in their lives (Kettler, 2001).

During daily interactions, there will be a larger ratio of youth-to-youth interchanges than youth-to-staff ones. More frequent contacts with peers predict the development of greater peer influence than that of staff. This means that youth workers cannot have the same degree of social impact on youngsters or offset the need for peer approval. Staff are also frequently viewed negatively and with suspicion. But staff can maximize their influence with residents through friendship, modeling, and supportive interactions. However, if youth workers are insincere or have unclear, underdeveloped, or antisocial (subcultural) values, then residents will have values confusion and continue to function in antisocial ways, or become entangled in dysfunctional behaviors.

It is improbable that the two primary groups (staff and youth) can always complement each other. Often, they will be at odds! Peer approval is attractive, and peer group interactions are complex, composed of a competing subsystem. Thus, many youth will become overwhelmed and confounded by conflicting ideas and values of staff and various subgroups vying for their allegiance. Divergent viewpoints can create confusion and add to some youngsters' inner turmoil. Some youth also buy into a negative view of adults and their rules (Redl & Wineman, 1957b). They impulsively engage in a conflict with staff over the use of language and ideas, and subscribe to the myths within pop culture that tend to reinforce (glamorize) antisocial attitudes expressed as defiance or some sort of rebellion.

Many youth in placement can be described as having limited verbal skill and as displaying lower than normal intellectual functioning (below potential), minimal previous successful experience at most activities, and a history of acting out (or extreme withdrawal). Quite often, youth enjoy the power derived from acting out. Youngsters can also be very impulsive, attention seeking, and easily influenced. To make the peer group work, and to eliminate antisocial attitudes in the individual, the youth worker employs a task-oriented focus (Pazaratz, 2000a). Youth workers also influence and shape the social dynamics or the way an individual and the group reach out for one another. This means that the youth worker actively intervenes to diminish negativity, the use of foul language, the glorification of violence and drugs, coercive interactions, and bullying. The youth worker wants to establish interactions that are based on positivity. Once youngsters realize that staff are committed to being supportive and nonpunitive, meaningful exchanges and cooperation can occur. It is when youth understand that staff are genuine that they will begin to value staff and staff members' ideals more than those of their peers.

GROUP INTERACTIONS

As part of the overall program, group counseling has many similarities to the group living process. Group interactions are a powerful medium that creates tension and regulates it. The group process is the training ground where youth practice communication skills, learn to identify and talk about feelings, and develop problem-solving strategies. The group format is the main social testing ground for youngsters to understand themselves and their relations with others (Rose, 1998). The group experience also provides an opportunity to learn through imitation and modeling and a forum for practicing new roles and attitudes (toward substance use, sexuality, etc.) (Daley & Thase, 2000). Group discussions deal with relationship dynamics, communication, meaning making, and boundaries. Articulation of group norms informs residents of the importance of self-care, making friends, the expression of affect, developing competency skills, the learning of new interests, and the advantages of proself and prosocial behaviors (Lee & Gaucher, 2000).

The use of the group format is an integral part of integrative practice. The group format is an intervention method directed at individual change and group harmony. The group is used as a means as well as a context for the achievement of goals (Yalom, 1985). When front-line staff lead groups, they underscore program expectations. This means that they are required to demonstrate thoughtfulness in planning groups, provide good introductions for new members, and integrate new members into the group culture. To promote belonging and competence, youth workers emphasize modeling between and among peers. To enhance problem solving, youth workers use verbal activity and nonverbal cues. Group rules and norms are employed to reinforce the principles of normalization. The group format is employed to enact connection and relevance (Yalom, 1983). To ensure that youngsters do not leave treatment with ill feelings or a sense of abandonment, the group enacts a meaningful separation ritual, which is devised so that the youngster's progress is emphasized (Page, Campbell, & Wilder, 1994). In the group format, the leader puts the group and its members to work for each other by being:

1. the central person and the object of identification;
2. a symbol and spokesperson of desired norms and values;
3. a motivator, stimulator, and definer of individual goals and tasks;
4. a reinforcer of roles;
5. a stimulator of activities; and
6. a catalyst for change.

Goals are achieved and maintained in the social environment and daily living experience when the group leader focuses on the following:

1. Commonality of purpose; this principle binds individuals to the group, and is essential in a therapeutic community. Commonality emphasizes that whatever one individual does affects others (Newman & Newman, 2001).
2. Teaching group members to be clear, direct, and unemotional in communication.
3. Teaching social skills and responsibilities that are used in everyday life within the program or community, i.e., during peer interaction, with staff, and in family life.
4. Motivating youth toward self-caring, self-assertion, and maturity.
5. Teaching residents to understand themselves and to develop a new sense of self.
6. Empowering residents to feel good about themselves and others by being genuine when sharing thoughts and feelings and interacting with peers.
7. Formal groups that look at the following:
   A. Authority (external controls) versus self-responsibility (self-control)
   B. Individual versus group rights
   C. Individual and group rights versus staff duties and institutional accountability
   D. Tolerance and acceptance of individual differences in ideas and preferences. This means that during the group process, value-laden issues such as violence, sexuality, isolation, scapegoating, substance use and abuse, and cultural, religious, and gender diversity are not avoided but are dealt with factually (Urberg, 1992).
   E. Group members share in decisions, participate in counseling of peers, involve themselves in the planning of activities, and allocate household responsibilities. Emphasizing the commonality of all residents helps youth to identify with the agency and its social norms to a greater degree.
   F. Group focus is on resocialization, not institutionalization. Topics include background experiences, family problems, issues of

    transition and discharge, staying in control, managing emotions, and learning to identify the need for help, to ask for help, and to be receptive to help.

8. Youth often misunderstand and mislabel their emotions and those of others, which also adds to their inability to problem solve. Some youth have anxiety (fears) and/or an excess of defenses. Group treatment includes disputing irrational beliefs and correcting misinformation and prejudices (Rose, 1998).

Groups have cycles of equilibrium and disequilibrium (Yalom, 1983). Within the group experience, there are moments of conflict, playfulness, humor, arguing, tedium, confusion, calmness, and productivity. Youngsters talk about parents, staff, the program, and all kinds of unfairness. Some ask questions, others jump to conclusions, and still others talk indirectly. Sometimes, the group process leads to in-depth discussion and exploration of certain topics. Peer support and discussion with others, who have similar experiences or problems, comprise the essence of group interactions (Yalom, 1985). Sometimes, peers are sympathetic to another's concerns; at other times, they are disinterested or come down on each other. Some point out that each individual is responsible for his or her problems and therefore should not blame others. Some understand the importance of limits and that these are tied to the principles of contingency management. The youth worker refocuses the discussion when derailment or personal attacks take place. The worker explains why these problematic behaviors occur and helps participants to deal with the emotional part of conflicted topics. When participants watch others and are reflective, or show others how to approach their difficulties, insight is gained.

Participants learn from peers, who struggle with the same issues, and relate in similar ways with ideas of reference. Participants learn to think about intentions (i.e., their own and those of others; Yalom & Rand, 1966). Some youth are adept at picking up on other's feelings and linking them to self-esteem issues. Some are capable of examining problems and being solutions focused. There are youth who can confront others calmly, whereas some criticize staff, and others talk of feeling defective because of a lack of relationship with parents. Some youth feel responsible for others and their progress, and offer advice on too many issues. Some confrontations are harsh and unfocused, and do not deal with real problems. But other confrontations are too critical and inflexible of others' misdeeds. Group members are more likely to acknowledge their behaviors when they witness similar behavior occurring in others, or someone with whom they identify (Yalom & Rand, 1966). As group members speak of their personal problems, peers are encouraged to offer suggestions and support. A recurring theme in group work is that life within relationships consists of competing and cooperative motives. This helps group members to overcome feeling different, labeled, categorized, or diagnosed. It is through a creative mix of discussion and activity that doing, thinking, and feeling combine to renew the quality of life, personal development, and relationship fulfillment. Ultimately, the group process is effective when youngsters understand the interaction and balance between passions and values, and freedoms and constraints (Corder, 1994).

STAFF ROLES CONTEXTUALLY

The socializing agents of the family (for example, parents and siblings) are replaced, replicated, or enacted in residential placement by youth workers and other youth. Residents are guided into acceptable behaviors by staff members conveying the idea that all youngsters can benefit from the social system and the norms of the milieu. Youth workers also explore and discuss with residents what they understand of social interactions and how they experience themselves and the environment. Youth workers intervene when residents employ primitive and destructive behaviors, or merely seek assistance.

During conflicts between residents, the youth worker deals with each youth separately. This gives each youth space and time to think about his or her respective experience without having to defend his or her actions in the presence of an equally upset peer. The youth worker models the capacity for observation and reflection, so that each youth can understand a different perspective and learn a negotiated approach to conflict resolution. However, residents ultimately need to learn to rely upon their own judgment and internal resources. Some youth are afraid to trust their own ideas and are reluctant to confront peers even with staff support.

During counseling, staff translate, or interpret, for youth the psychological, interpersonal, or intrapersonal reasons for the youth's behavior into plain language. Staff describe for each youth the effect that others are having upon the youth. Youngsters are shown how their beliefs are affected by their environment, or socially mediated communication. In effect, their emotional reactions are a response to environmental and social pressures (Freeman & Reinecke, 2007). Ultimately, the youth worker needs to differentiate learned behavioral responses, such as when the resident merely copies other youth who have equally poor problem-solving skills, from those behaviors that occur due to an innate emotional problem or a mental disorder. Thus, for the youth worker, pathology is understood in terms of how much behaviors are learned (for example, as a result of imitating dysfunctional [deviant] models within a youth's environment) or whether the behaviors are due to intrapsychic conflicts.

POSITIVE PEER PRESSURE

In any treatment environment, group interactions can be positive and socializing, or negative and/or chaotic, creating unhealthy group dynamics. When the peer group is comprehended as a social system, the interactions of its members can be shaped or directed toward working and learning together (Vorath & Brendtro, 1985). Positive peer pressure can be cultivated as an environmental force and method that is enacted by youth workers utilizing a nonauthoritarian, persuasive approach. In developing positive peer pressure, youth workers foster leadership, teach assertiveness skills, and promote group harmony (Brendtro & Shahbazian, 2004). Supportive dynamics evolve when youth workers provide youth with knowledge of how to engage others in a negotiated relationship based upon reflectivity, understanding, sincerity, and clarity of language. Peers offer the potential for mutual support, that is, residents assisting each other with the development of skills, strategies, and ways of thinking things through to modify habitual avoidances and distortions (Moody & Lupton-Smith, 2002).

If youth interact primarily with staff, if staff dominate group interactions (ideas), and/or if group members are mainly passive (watching and listening), positive peer pressure will not develop. In other words, too much staff control of discussions will impede residents from acquiring or demonstrating their abilities and strengths (Lee, 1996). However, when staff members stimulate discussion between group members and encourage an exchange of ideas, positive peer pressure can be elicited and shaped. Ideas and discussions flow freely when group members believe that they are being treated equally, or when they receive praise and their ideas and feelings are respected in the decision-making process (Davis, Hoffman, & Quigley, 1988). Positive peer pressure does not mean that staff members do not have a significant voice and cannot be involved. In fact, youth workers are required to monitor the intensity and direction of group interactions, discussions, and ideas, and to mediate discussions that may escalate out of control.

There are various treatment protocols and safety or care constraints that shape the content and the ultimate nature of the group process. Youth workers may have to remind group members that certain behaviors that are problematic in the group home (but are endured) may have more severe consequences if displayed or acted upon in the community. Positive peer pressure does not mean an absence of disagreements, or that residents will always support each other and interact reasonably, or eliminate outward expressions of hostility. Peer bonding and the relationship-building process may first require some negative dynamics to be worked through (Tannehill, 1987). To bring forth the potential for positive dynamics, youth workers may have to intervene and redirect some interactions. For example, youngsters are often overly focused on their own needs, and, therefore, they do not always respect the rights of others. They can be overly intrusive. When group members do not resolve differences, establish consensus, or have a direction, this means the group process involves too much discussion or bickering, or is unfocussed. To help implement decisions, youth workers redirect transactions or suggest choices to help with consensus or resolution (Rose, 1998).

In order for positive peer pressure to be effective, there are times when the youth worker needs to assume the leadership role, or to be the main force within the group. Leadership becomes especially important when there are group members who do not participate or when members are upset and quarrelling. Positive peer pressure arises from learning how to convey prosocial attitudes, developing knowledge of empathic interactions, and enacting appropriate confrontation (Stein, 1995). Youth workers might find it frustrating when not all group members participate or cooperate. Youth workers may in fact be unsure of how they might get every youth involved in programming. This can occur when they explain the purpose of positive peer pressure and encourage each youth to take part in decision making. Positive peer pressure helps all youth to develop communication skills, to learn about themselves by risk taking, to learn to respect differences, and to benefit from group dynamics. Positive peer pressure encourages each individual to take responsibility for the social system and the home operating harmoniously (e.g., rules being followed and cooperation around chores).

A residential setting must not be regimented to the degree that its warmth is replaced by a sterile environment. To develop a congenial atmosphere, staff members emphasize the benefits of positive relationships. Staff members also encourage personal dreams and use every opportunity to identify each individual's potential for self-development. Supportive statements, gestures, and specific comments should include all youth. Staff members also encourage active participation (Fewster & Garfat, 1998, 2001). This means that all youth have an equal opportunity in discussions and are protected from ridicule. Staff members help youth to become positive and adhere to the program by modeling commitment, assigning importance to routines, monitoring daily interactions, and placing emphasis on the cleanliness of the living unit. Fostering inclusiveness helps each resident to see him or herself as part of a "family" and prevents the emergence of subgroups, negative attitudes, or one youth dominating the others for selfish motives. Inclusiveness helps all youngsters to feel invested in what happens in and to the group, and to the individual. When youth feel connected and believe they are valued, the residence functions more smoothly (Springer, 2006).

SUBGROUPS

Subgroups do form within residential treatment programs. They can occur naturally in any group process. Some subgroupings can be fully compatible with the overall objectives of the larger group. Subgroups can also be destructive, especially when they are formed for, or due to, manipulation, secret bargains, and powerful alliances. When subgroups are formed for the wrong reasons (i.e., an individual or a number of residents have given up something, or violate some rule, for a more comfortable emotional position with peers), this is known as a conspiracy or a negative alliance.

Youth in placement are often guarded and do not necessarily talk about their real feelings. Their emotional burden is buried or projected. In this respect, peer alliances provide safety or rescue from others and can protect youth from feeling isolated and alone. Feeling connected to peers even on a superficial level can help to defend against feelings and thoughts that are too painful to deal with. Alliances are a means of gaining power over, control of, or protection from fears, insecurities, and emptiness. But, alliances can also lead youth into behaviors that perpetuate problems of scapegoating, bullying, and antisocial acts, or may lead to getting caught up or entangled in petty bickering and distractions. Sometimes, conflicts with others provide youth with excuses not to change, a means of having fun or power by deliberately creating chaos (Rose, Beardon, & Teel, 1992).

In integrative practice, when dealing with issues or conflict, the youth worker should not overly focus on bringing out insight, meaning, and perfect understanding. Instead, the youth worker can encourage residents to look at and to live their reality in more flexible and open ways. When youth workers encourage residents to see more possibilities in group interactions and hope in their situation, they are performing their leadership role. Some key aspects of group dynamics that youth workers should focus on include the following:

- Youth and workers create rules, expectations, boundaries, and a social system.
- Rules are utilized to overcome resistance and to develop peer cooperation.
- Groups allow residents to experience emotional material that is otherwise difficult to access (Yalom, 1983).
- Youth can feel trapped in coalitions (as in their own families; Minuchin, 1995).
- Peers can assist those youth who have been victims to develop positive roles.
- Peers can help those youth who perceive themselves as helpless to achieve a sense of empowerment, connection, and control in their lives.
- Positive peer pressure helps to develop motivation and structure.
- Peers can help those youth who misunderstand their responsibilities and the tasks required of them to learn to deal with developmental issues, such as identity, and to understand complex relationships (i.e., to deal with the group's needs and emotional climate).
- Commonly encountered problems of groups are subgrouping, negative alliances, power struggles, anti-adult attitudes, and resistance. However, not all subgroups are negative, destructive, or countercultural.
- Staff define group protocols, structure the group process, build cohesion, manage conflict, regulate interactions and transactions, sustain progress by defining issues and goals, and implement transition.

SUMMARY OF GROUP DYNAMICS

Every youngster within a residential treatment facility interacts with a host of peers. Sometimes, peers are supportive and helpful. There are times, however, when peers deliberately hinder each other. Nevertheless, at various levels the group process of interactions stimulates knowledge, perception, memory, feelings, and thoughts. Consequently, each youth has feelings for every person within the program. Sometimes, these can be quite intense. Some youth are closed and will not reveal themselves. Others talk of previous experiences, the present, and the (unknown) future. There are those who express concerns over a range of issues and are ever changing. There are youth who have memories and unresolved feelings about relationships from the past and ideas and beliefs that they try to make sense of. In placement, they encounter a range of new experiences that are not always easy to process. Some experiences may be amusing, uplifting, and intriguing; others are exhausting, boring, and conflictual. Sometimes, youth share their dreams, hopes, fears, moods, preoccupations, and deliberations. Some youngsters have difficulty discussing their complaints about peers, staff, or family members. Sometimes, these conflicts define the tension within the group. At times, the issues may be beneath the surface and carefully disguised, but ever emerging. Some staff members are good at eliciting those thoughts that help youth to develop a better understanding of their feelings. Some youth can build upon old ideas, sometimes transforming them. Ultimately, staff members want youth to be open and genuine, to learn for themselves, and to live in the here and now.

Group interactions can be lively and fun, or complex, chaotic, and stressful, but an ever-changing reality. Most youngsters in placement will attempt to find something to identify with while they seek recognition and define their place and role within the group and the group home. Some talk of feeling picked on and rejected, which are often recurring themes in their lives. Staff members attempt to get all youngsters to experience acceptance, to feel connected to the group, to join in, and to interact as they would with family and friends. Staff members want youth to relate to each other in positive ways; to identify with peers and staff, and to see that they also have hopes, fears, and frustrations; and to experience the joy of relationships and the pleasure of knowing others (Kettler, 2001). Residents often relate to and know their peers superficially. But, they can come together on many issues. Eventually, youth may be genuine in their talk of themselves and their family background.

During group home interactions, many youth will talk about their daily experiences at school and in the community; their contact with friends, family, and social workers; and so on. Some of the discussions are interesting, some are task and issues oriented, and others are meaningless, repetitious, or unfocused. There will be youth who are constantly attention seeking or prone to prolonged venting. Some residents are skilled at connecting with their peers and staff members, and they interact quite well and openly; others are indifferent or purposely distant, closed, defensive, and hostile. Some talk of their dreams or fantasies, the music they listen to, the sports they like, and what they have seen on TV, at a show, or the like. They are excited about life and their ideas as well as those of others. Some residents may challenge a staff member's competence or authority, or make fun of the staff member's car, clothes, sexuality, ideas, and so on. They may also enjoy creating chaos, undermining the efforts of their peers to succeed, scapegoating a weaker peer, contaminating the interactional process with negatives, or taking pleasure in setting up power struggles with staff and peers. Some residents will remain silent, impassive, indifferent, or detached (Kettler, 2001).

When youth do not interact or do not talk with each other, it is difficult for staff members to develop a social system based upon understanding, compromise, and cooperation. The distancing or shunning of others affects the well-being of all group members. Under these circumstances, the system of interactions becomes stagnant, and sometimes negative and even destructive. There may be one or more youth who deliberately undermine the social process or make it conflictual. There are youngsters who enjoy and thrive on sabotage and will continually create conflict by misleading peers and staff through lies, backbiting, arguing over phoney issues, or having selfish demands. There are youth who play a role, such as being tough, being insincere (fronting), falsifying information, interfering with understanding, or enjoying manipulating others (Hardy & Laszloffy, 2005). But there will also be staff members and residents who see the manipulation for what it is and resist or counter it, and remain largely disappointed but not seriously affected.

Many manipulative behaviors by youth are based on the need to survive and to be in control. Manipulation can be a reflection of what youngsters have experienced within families, or based on their parents' behaviors toward social services, police, courts, and so on (Garbarino, 1999). There will be youngsters who understand what went wrong, or why interactions with others do not work. Sometimes, when youth reveal the depth of their troubles and conflicts, the nature of their problems and despair can overwhelm other residents and some staff members, neither of whom will know how to respond. Yet, some youngsters will feel relief when the group interacts harmoniously and the group home operates smoothly. These residents demonstrate positivity, change, and a reasonable degree of success. Their resiliency in the face of stress and adversity helps youth workers and other youngsters to realize that the treatment process does in fact have meaning and offers hope, repair, and renewal (Kagan, 2004).

CHAPTER 5

Family Work in
Residential Treatment

In residential treatment programs for emotionally disturbed children or adolescents, family work is often enacted by a social worker, a senior clinician, or sometimes even a child and youth care supervisor. There are any number of intervention strategies used with families whose problems are long-standing and embedded in structural patterns of communication and maladaptive relational skills. Generally, the family worker attempts to strengthen the parent–child attachment, to change dynamics that inhibit growth, and to improve relationships to promote positivity and meaning. This occurs by assisting parents to develop reasonable limits, teaching them to recognize their child's emotional needs, and emphasizing positive communication. When family members have a new point of view and act in ways that offer unique experiences of themselves, this reframing can bring about balance, harmony, and a direction for change. This chapter discusses the role and skills enacted by family workers in the Four Phase System that helped connect parents to the treatment process and their child.

Children and adolescents are admitted into residential treatment because of the severity of their emotional-behavioral problems and the inability of their parents to deal with them. As a result of ongoing parent–child conflict, marriages can become strained and siblings stressed. Residential treatment of emotionally disturbed children and adolescents begins where the family breaks down. It focuses on interpersonal transactions, intrapsychic conflict, the impact of the treatment process on the youngster, and the youth's conformance to staff expectations. Staff interventions include clarification of process, confrontation, control, redirection, support, reinforcements, and interpretation. At the same time, staff attempt to make the treatment process more responsive to the long-term goals of the individual youngster (Pazaratz, 1998a). Critical to this process is the "goodness-of-fit" between the resident and direct care staff. This connection is essential to the youth's well-being and adjustment (Germain, 1991). This means that the quality of care must meet the needs of the youth. A youth's concurrence with the treatment process develops when the young person interacts cooperatively with others and recognizes the advantages of maintaining positive relations with peers and staff (Pazaratz, 2000a). Concurrence also occurs because staff members do not exert pressures on youth where the youngster's abilities do not exist.

Structure and programming are essential in a residential environment to overcome negative attitudes and to assist residents to meet the expectations placed on them. As described in Chapter 3, treatment flows from the accurate and ongoing assessment of such issues as defense mechanisms, coping strategies, traumatic experiences, family relations and communication patterns, and the youngster's adjustment, or lack thereof, to the milieu, at school, or in the community. Direct care staff assist residents toward growth and adaptation in social functioning by making the milieu responsive to the youth's social needs, by using the environment to help change behaviors, and by stimulating developmental capacities. Staff focus on the youngster's strengths, interests, dreams, fears, insecurities, and difficulties or pathology, and bring about change by enacting a supportive relationship, setting achievable goals, and establishing a process that enables youngsters to focus on self and social interactions (Pazaratz, 1999).

Although there are multiple intervention strategies that are effective with different youngsters, the treatment of parents and resolving the issues of attachment are considered essential if youngsters are to return home (Whittaker & Pfeiffer, 1994). Attachment is the deep and enduring connection established between a child and his or her caregiver in the first few years of life (Bowlby, 1969). It profoundly influences every component of the human condition: mind, body, emotions, relationships, and values (Levy & Orlans, 1998). In treatment, this means that the parent–child conflict (reactive attachment) must be resolved before most youngsters will give up their maladaptive behaviors (Hughes, 2007). The preferred practice for resolving ongoing family distress is family counseling (Reiss, 1991). Family engagement differs depending on the agency and/or clinical skills of the family worker. Family counseling can include family therapy, family conferences, parent effectiveness education, and the like (Taibbi, 2007). The skills and knowledge required of the family worker vary according to the particulars of the family situation, as does the sequence of interventions (Ainsworth, Maluccio, & Small, 1996). The question that must be asked in conducting family sessions is "Which approach will have positive results for the child or adolescent and his or her family?"

FAMILY DYNAMICS

The parental role is to provide for those critical functions that are necessary for growth and the fulfillment of developmental needs that the child cannot perform for him or herself (Kohut, 1977). The parent's task includes to socialize, to teach, and to inculcate good judgment. The success at transmitting proself and prosocial values derives from the quality of parent–child interactions, such as the varying degree of parental warmth, acceptance, support, and mirroring. These caregiver behaviors are the basis for making children receptive to their parents and provide children with a sense of meaning, humanness, and partnership with others (Kohut, 1977; see also Elson, 1986). Sometimes, the parenting style can directly impede the child's ego development (i.e., a good self-image, or worthy self-concept; Laing & Esterson, 1970; Robin & Foster, 1989). Chronic empathic failure by the parenting figures will undermine a child's sense of self-cohesion and may lead to fragile self-esteem or disorders of the self (Kohut, 1984).

When parents are unavailable for their children, this emotional distance contributes to the formation of a weak ego, insecure identity, and the youngster's inability to master the requisite psychosocial tasks of various developmental stages (Erikson, 1959). As a result of disengaged family experiences, some youth develop emotional problems, poor reality testing, and/or adjustment difficulties (Minuchin, 1974). In a circular fashion, emotional disorders can be compounded when children have irrational demands of their parents (Ellis, 1994). For example, youngsters who do not receive unconditional parental love and approval may conclude that their parents view them negatively (such as being defective and unlovable). The resulting self-esteem problems can lead to insecure attachment and irrational feelings of separation or loss that are ongoing issues in the youngster's life (Mann, 1991).

Perhaps the most critical parental function that is directly related to a broad range of both positive and negative behaviors in children and adolescents is parental monitoring. Parental monitoring consists of close supervision of the youth's interests and activities. Various studies have concluded that when there is good monitoring, academic achievement is positively correlated (Kurdek, Fine, & Sinclair, 1995). Other studies have determined that poor parental monitoring is related to higher levels of externalized behaviors, such as delinquency, aggression, antisocial behavior, and violence (Patterson & Stouthamer-Loeber, 1984). Additionally, low parental monitoring is correlated to earlier initiation of substance use (Steinberg, Fletcher, & Darling, 1994). Nevertheless, few parents have any real knowledge about parenting, the broad range of challenges facing them and their children, or the risk factors that affect children, including family disorganization, disruptions of lifestyles (e.g., due to moving or illnesses), and the impact of economic difficulties (Patterson & Welfel, 1994). Likewise, parents are often unsure of what constitute reasonable levels of direct supervision, especially as youngsters mature, seek autonomy, and become more influenced by their peers and attuned to pop culture (Pazaratz & Morton, 2000). Many of these same parents are unable to cope with problems faced by their children as they evolve biologically into teenagers (Vernon, 1996).

Family and social conflicts become especially difficult for those youngsters who are vulnerable to criticism and loss, and, therefore, cannot formulate or implement realistic life or problem-solving plans (Boyd-Webb, 2003). Unfortunately, many children and adolescents who become entangled in their family's conflicts (or problems) do so because they are overly sensitive, yet are often seen by their family as the problem, or the cause of the family's difficulties. In response to the child's perceived misbehaviors, the parents displace or project intense emotions onto their child, or scapegoat their child because they believe the child is responsible for the parents' and family's misery (Stierlin, 1977). Children are also drawn into parental conflicts, inducing anxieties in them (Laing, 1965). The child's reactions to parental fighting may also include divided loyalties, extreme conflictual emotions, periods of depression, intense anxiety, and especially anger-related problems, which when overtly displayed confirm some parents' beliefs that their child has created all the family's problems. Lacking an integrated and cohesive sense of self makes adjustment to life stressors or family pressures difficult for the fragile or at-risk youngster (Kohut & Wolf, 1978). As a consequence, one in four teenagers are deemed to be extremely susceptible to high-risk behaviors and school failure, and another 1 million display moderate risk (Husain & Cantwell, 1992).

In some families, where parents are constantly in conflict with each other or have different agendas, there are children who perform the role of "rescuer," and others who want to remain uninvolved but accept being the family scapegoat, or the cause of the family's distress. When the child becomes the scapegoat for the family, family conflicts and frustrations become secondary, or are temporarily alleviated. Nevertheless, the child's emotional difficulties in reality are a response to parental distress, or adult conflict expressed or deflected by the child (Minuchin, 1974). This type of communication pattern and relationship dynamic leads to repeated family crises as the child feels pressured and then acts out, or is induced to take the blame for family problems. In a circular fashion, the child's reactive behaviors only increase tensions in the family by redirecting attention and responsibility for family problems away from the parents and onto the child. It is, therefore, important for the family worker to ascertain how a child's temperament and anxieties affect or are created by parental conflict or contribute to family dysfunction, and the converse of this question (McDermott & Char, 1974). When adolescents engage in at-risk behaviors such as alcohol and drug use, gang membership, sexual activity, and the like, it is necessary to determine whether it is due to cultural conditions or erosion of the family unit (Wicka-Nelson & Israel, 1991).

Not all family conflicts or marital problems create disturbed children. For example, individual factors exhibited early in childhood such as a difficult temperament or some antisocial behaviors have been found to predispose youngsters to difficulties later in life (Klein, 1995). In other words, all children have their own lives and changing characteristics, perceptions, needs, distortions, and capacities. There are also youngsters who have never been in a close or sustaining relationship with their parents. They are disengaged, and lack intimate feelings or loyalty, and their attitude can be characterized by a high degree of independence. Ultimately, the child does not relate positively or connect with his or her parents, family, and family goals, or the child believes that his or her family is dysfunctional (Hughes, 2007). Therefore, in spite of having loving and high-monitoring parents, some children will become disturbed or oppositional on their own. There are also children who feel distant, but paradoxically become entangled in family conflicts. Nevertheless, when a child or an adolescent becomes emotionally at risk due to a lack of family cohesion, attachment, or emotional bonding, and the parents become openly rejecting of the youngster, or when the child rejects the parents or is at risk of harm, a total intervention is needed to support the youth's deteriorating sense of self. As a form of intervention, residential treatment helps to provide relief from the unbearable tensions of repeated crises that can overwhelm both children and their families (Pazaratz, Randall, Spekkens, Lazor, & Morton, 2000).

RESIDENTIAL PLACEMENT

Youngsters who require residential treatment programs often present as having profound isolation and disconnection in their immediate social relationships with family members, authority figures, and peers (Pazaratz, 1996b). Nevertheless, Laing (1965) believed that some parents contribute to their children's difficulties by covertly molding and manipulating their children and undermining their attempts to be autonomous and self-regulating. There are also youngsters who experience interpersonal problems because they are confused by parental double-bind messages, or have difficulty accepting parental values (Satir, 1964). But there are also some youngsters who pursue different values and purposes that are directly counter to those expressed by their parents. These youth gravitate to subcultures, and become alienated by their family. According to Barkley (1997), adjustment issues arise because the child has experienced reciprocal and circular interactions that lead to conflict between the youth's inner desires and his or her outer life with parents, or parental expectations, and societal norms. In essence, the youth is faced with a dilemma as to who comes first, the parents or the self. Learning to balance two divergent viewpoints can be too complex or abstract for some youth to solve. Minuchin (1974) concluded that these kinds of dynamics that are embedded in family rules, values, structure, and boundaries are not easily resolved, especially for the at-risk youth, even though they are revealed in family transactions.

In order to survive in some families, a youngster's defense mechanisms, substance abuse, or physical acting out can become an escape and a protection from recurring bouts of insecurity, pain, or suffering (Haley, 1979). Additionally, some at-risk or acting-out behaviors by youngsters, although inappropriate, can be viewed as a coping strategy, or a means for developing independence and an identity (Pazaratz & Morton, 2000). Deficits in the caretaking environment that cause the youngster to feel deprived of the essentials of life can also comprise a factor that contributes to a youngster's negative attitude or hostility toward his or her family and others. This unresolved anger can be expressed as oppositionalism and defiance, or even as countercultural attitudes, none of which are easily modified as they exert a strong hold on the child's personality and interactions (Winnicott, 1965).

Optimal childhood socialization and emotional adjustment occur in families that do not follow a policy of conflict avoidance, that see other family members as resources rather than obstacles, that have not settled into a pattern that inhibits growth and differentiation, and in which relationships outside the family are not considered more fulfilling. The families also have clear generational boundaries and emphasize distinct separation between the status, power, and roles enacted by parents and children. However, maladjustment results in children because they come from families that have undifferentiated boundaries, overinvolved or uninvolved parents, unresolved marital discord, and hierarchical misalignments between parents and children (Minuchin, 1974). In addition, severe emotional and mental health problems can occur in youngsters when parents are too harsh, too punitive, sexually exploitive, or unforgiving of misdeeds. Thus, when parents are rejecting of their child or rigid toward the child, this usually indicates that the parents have severe problems themselves. Consequently, many youngsters who require residential placement are raised in a highly dysfunctional family where roles and expectations are not clearly defined, and/or parenting practices can be extreme and inflexible (Pazaratz et al., 2000). For many other youth, there is ineffective monitoring of their moods and interactions. This parenting style includes indifference and neglect of the basic needs of their children. Disturbed parenting can also arise due to unresolved anger or guilt, denial of problems, parenting skills deficits, and relationship issues (Pazaratz, 1999).

TREATMENT ISSUES

There are children and adolescents placed in residential treatment whose parents have considerable difficulty involving themselves in the therapeutic process or any aspect of the program (Pazaratz, 1999). These parents doubt that there are any real benefits to treatment. There are also parents who accept their child's placement, believing that residential treatment is what the youth needs, even though they doubt that progress will occur. Other parents see placement as providing a measure of perceived safety for their child and believe that the family benefits as it is protected from social stigma (Dunst, Trivette, & Deol, 1988). This acceptance may be a form of denial that their child was removed from the family home for child protection or endangerment issues. Some families acquiesce to residential placement because it alleviates the emotional-behavioral turmoil, interrupts the parent–child power struggle, and stabilizes their child. Notwithstanding these different attitudes toward placement, of critical importance is the question of whether parental involvement should be a precondition for residential treatment. A corollary to this question is whether any benefits are realized by forcing a family to participate in treatment. Under circumstances of child abuse, child abandonment, parental imprisonment, or mental illness, it is an absolute necessity that the youth be the focus of treatment. When children are at risk of additional abuse, parental counseling should be a precondition before there is any type or level of parent–child contact. This means that there should be a willingness on the part of the treatment program to treat the youth in the absence of family involvement or where involvement would be detrimental (Pazaratz et al., 2000).

It is important that residential placement not be conveyed to parents as the solution to their failures because this type of message is negative, is possibly accusatory, and most likely will cause the parents to feel hurt and resentful. Social workers and front-line staff need to realize that there is a power differential between themselves and parents. Clinical intervention in a family, no matter how helpful, can create what Bernheim (1982) called a burden on the family. The relationship with the family is the means by which the family worker and front-line staff provide help. Therefore, no worker can realistically proceed to help a family without first developing a positive relationship with that family. Establishing a therapeutic relationship with parents is essential for instilling hope and motivation (Perlman, 1979). This means that family members need to view treatment as a supportive resource for the family system. In this respect, family workers present themselves as having parenting expertise to help the family, but involve the family at their level of ability, in order to enact change and for joint problem solving. This approach is a positive model offered to the family and also reflects the nature and focus of residential treatment. The family worker, in effect, emphasizes that the youth's placement can assist both the youth and the family because the youngster is now away from any destructive elements that may exist within his or her community (McDermott & Char, 1974).

The separation caused by residential placement may be emotionally traumatic for some youth. This psychological crisis may intensify over the course of residential placement. The youth can deteriorate or experience separation anxiety if the break with the family is too long, or if the program assumes too much responsibility for the youth or not enough shared responsibility with the parents (Pazaratz, 1999). For example, if the youngster "acts out" in the residential program, and neither the youth nor the parents have to deal with each other, this may cause some youngsters to feel disconnected or experience a false sense of reality (i.e., they do not feel accountable to their parents or may even believe that their parents do not care; Pazaratz, 1996a, 1996b). This also reinforces the feeling of impotency that the family experienced when the youth was referred to the residential facility. Therefore, it is important for parents to be kept abreast of their child's progress and any difficulties the youth has encountered and how these were resolved.

Many parents are unsure of the role they should play, or are even distrustful that they should enact any role, especially if they have relinquished custodial rights (even though temporarily). Therefore, it is important for treatment staff to use the separation and the accompanying anxiety created by a young person's admission to residential placement as an opportunity to help the youth and his or her family to stay connected, and to work through or resolve conflicts (Pazaratz et al., 2000). By participating in their treatment plan, parents feel they are being listened to, and they begin to value the family worker and the program. They are then more likely to remain involved with the youth's progress and changing needs, and realize that giving up custodial rights does not mean that they have relinquished parental rights, or abandoned their emotional life with their child. With the family worker's help, the family can explore any intense separation feelings, so that all family members may be more aware of how to adjust to ever-changing family dynamics.

The immediate purpose of residential placement is to unburden the family's cyclical and engulfing conflicts, to stabilize the youngster and his or her family, to heal internal pain, and to help family members to think differently about themselves. The youngster's family is viewed from the perspective of the youngster's current and potential ability to deal with them. The importance of the youth's family connection and parent–child relations is not lessened with an emphasis on the youngster and on his or her problems. Throughout the youth's residential placement, there is an ongoing and active outreach to the family in order for them to participate in the youngster's treatment plan (Pazaratz, 1999). Facilitating the youth's return to his or her home will not occur unless parents are involved or abreast of their child's changes. Discharge goals are more likely to be realized if these are supported by parents. The youth's successful transition from residential treatment to his or her home or to independence is made easier if the parents remain involved and support whatever resources or services are available to assist the youngster. The family worker needs to convey respect to family members for their efforts and the difficulty and enormity of moving beyond their problems (Ainsworth et al., 1996).

PLACEMENT CONDITIONS

Residential treatment is an unfamiliar and unknown process for most parents. Therefore, in order for them to be involved and to feel comfortable with treatment, they need information. When parents learn about the intent of treatment, its methodology, or the process, and they and other family members feel understood and accepted, they will believe that they have a role. Parental cooperation increases when staff members offer open and shared communication, especially in those situations where staff members seek out and listen to family input (Pazaratz, 1999). Ensuring that parents participate and remain in contact with their child can help diminish excessive detachment or separation anxiety. Separation anxiety or feelings of alienation can also be alleviated by having ongoing purposeful contact with families, such as keeping them abreast of special activities and events; providing progress information, no matter how routine or minimal; having family members visit the facility; and ensuring that any of their fears and concerns are dealt with at the time these occur. However, unless family members are invited to participate, it is unlikely that a therapeutic alliance will develop. Ultimately, the treatment team and the youth directly benefit from the nature of the parent–worker alliance.

According to Bell (1963), most families are trapped between the need for change and the need to protect their current patterns, roles, and organization. In chaotic families, loyalty to the family and maintaining the family's precarious balance are more important than personal development or the well-being of individuals (Boszormenyi-Nagy & Spark, 1984). To secure the parents' interest in the treatment program and their child's treatment plan, the family worker must overcome what Hoffman (1981) believed blocks cooperation: the idea that all therapies can be perceived as adversarial. Many parents have had stressful experiences with social service agencies. Some parents have developed trust issues or are fearful of revealing their vulnerabilities and being judged. To avoid misperceptions and to alleviate doubts, the family worker should not be seen as attempting to "outwait" or "outmanoeuvre" the family (Wachtel, 1992). Rather, the family worker must convey genuineness and empathy for the family. A positive attitude directed at the family assists the family worker in treatment planning. Even though some families may accept the treatment staff's definition of the treatment plan, the family must not see therapy as something being done to them or their child, but rather believe that treatment is participatory (deShazer, 1985). By experiencing the therapeutic alliance in the form of a treatment contract, each party is assured that there is collaboration and a commitment to the objectives of the interactional process. Although there are families that resist contracting, or any level of overtures by treatment staff, some do in fact see treatment as providing a relief from distress. There are also parents who become cooperative simply when workers reach out to them (Anderson & Stewart, 1983).

After the diagnostic phase, or when the family assessment has been completed, family work is initiated. Family counseling is usually ongoing throughout the youngster's stay in treatment. Family counseling begins with the building of a communicative relationship with the parents. This means that the family worker negotiates a direction, a course of action, and the purpose (goals) of treatment (Epstein, 1992). When the family worker enlists the parents in defining the problem, and then identifies the tasks to be performed, this helps the parents to understand the steps necessary to solutioning (Webb, 1999). Importantly, the contracting process also aims to reduce any power differential, social distance, and treatment impasse between the family worker and the parents, and to promote parental competence (Bowen, 1978). The ultimate goal of family counseling, as expressed though contracting, is for the parents to accept treatment rather than to have the treatment process create a division between them and their child (Feldman, 1992). By the parents agreeing to the nature of short- and long-term goals, the child's connections to the family are maintained and the family's role in their child's change–growth process is accentuated (Germain, 1991).

As a result of a youngster being placed in treatment, feelings of distress, resentment, and resistance can emerge within a family. The parents' defense mechanisms may become destabilized as their grief evolves and their guilt expands, especially if their child is not making progress, or if treatment personnel do not meet their child's needs. A prolonged lack of change will undermine some parents' trust in staff. Because family workers and front-line staff are in a power position relative to parents, this differential can also heighten suspicion and resentment (Laborde & Seligman, 1983). However, in some families, unusual emotions of relief, joy, satisfaction, and freedom may also surface upon a child's placement. These feelings need to be explored and discussed! Nevertheless, families will typically come to believe in the benefits of placement upon encountering warmth, acceptance, and understanding from staff members. When parents are encouraged to become an integral part of the treatment process, they feel less threatened that their emotional life and connection with their child will be disrupted during the youth's placement. Family connection improves when staff members exhibit positivity and professionalism, and utilize negotiated techniques to share information. This concerned outreach by staff members is the basis for facilitating family cooperation and change (Luborsky, 1984).

In spite of the positive efforts by staff members to engage families, invariably the means by which youngsters are admitted to a residential program will affect the course, length, and ultimate success of treatment. If youth enter a residential program ungrudgingly, without feelings of parental abandonment or fear of punishment, but with the active support of their parents, then youngsters are more likely to enjoy a fulfilling experience and a greater degree of success. However, if youth are forced into treatment and do not want to be there, or feel displaced and disconnected, it is unlikely they will become cooperative, and the length of their treatment will be extended (Ainsworth et al., 1996). When treatment resistance is encountered, such as little or poor parental cooperation, no interest on the youngster's part in his or her problems or solving them, or no ability on the part of the youngster and/or the parents to engage in therapy, then the youth may view residential placement as coercive, or merely serving time (Anderson & Stewart, 1983). A negative attitude toward placement by a youth may then create the conditions for additional acting-out and hostile behaviors.

FAMILY ASSESSMENT

The family assessment is an evaluation of the family unit and a description of its interactions. The family assessment explains the family's particular living style and philosophy for dealing with life and the rearing of children (Boyd-Webb, 2003). The assessment does not pathologize; instead, it emphasizes and draws attention to the family's resources, abilities, and challenges. This means that the family assessment provides a description of the family's pattern of relating, or how its social system is organized. A description of the family system includes identifying and detailing the family's cultural background, its degree of acculturation, the role of extended family members, the family's developmental patterns, its style of communication, and its relationship to others and the community (Pennell & Anderson, 2006). Understanding the family's environmental conditions, resources, life events or stressors, strengths, and problem-solving capacities helps the family worker to locate the nature and source of emotional issues (Woods & Robinson, 1996). Describing how family members communicate, how affect is expressed, which problems are identified (and by whom), and whether or not these issues are resolved will indicate the "family type" (Minuchin, 1974).

In the assessment process, understanding the family type refers to the way in which family members interact with each other; their level of adaptability, cohesiveness, and style of communication; and how the family attitudes are a function of their (experiences) history (Olson, Russell, & Sprenkle, 1979). The family evaluation also attempts to explain the forces that have contributed to the family's healthy development or dysfunction, and the youth's pathology (Goldstein, 1995). Of importance for the family worker is to determine how the family's resources and strengths can be utilized in treatment (Rippel, 1964). Another critical question to ascertain is how the family responds to internal and external pressures for change. This information describes exactly who plays what roles, such as leader, rescuer, victim, or dependent (Minuchin & Fishman, 1981).

It is unlikely that the family will begin to change during the assessment process, or before the family has begun to trust (Minuchin & Fishman, 1981). Following the assessment process, the family worker engages the family in the counseling process. Family counseling can include teaching family members to identify problems, to listen to each other, to be empathic with other members, and to develop procedures for resolving problems. The family worker also focuses on the family's unique way of organizing itself in order to function in its environment and to deal with its daily needs. The family worker strives to determine what prevents change and whether it is a function of the counseling technique, the purpose of defense mechanisms, the nature of coping strategies, how decisions are made, and what is left unresolved and why (Stierlin, 1977). The family worker wants to ascertain the family's adaptability; its ability to change its power structure, roles, and relationships; and whether these occur as an adjustment to various situational stressors. The family worker seeks to understand the way in which past and present experiences give rise to the family dysfunction (Seruya, 1997). By being sensitive to a family's sense of identity, the family worker establishes rapport with the family, and this helps to create a facilitating relationship that assists with family counseling (Bowen, 1978). The worker's positivity allows for interpretations and confrontations as these are necessary. These techniques are used judiciously and should be congruous, rather than at odds, with the treatment objectives.

FAMILY WORK

Family work in residential treatment can be conducted by a family counselor or social worker. Not only does the family worker focus on improving communication but he or she also teaches parents how to establish a benign leadership over their children. Families become dysfunctional in a number of ways, for example when one or both parents redirect marital strife onto a child, by parents competing with each other for their children's loyalty, by one or both parents blaming one child for all the family's problems, or by a parent forming a coalition with one child against the other parent (Minuchin, 1974). There are also some extreme situations where the family is out of balance because children run the family, or one youth may be out of control and the parents are afraid of that child. There are also family units in which children are totally neglected, or they are unresponsive and uninvolved with other family members (Satir, 1964).

Ultimately, family work aims to rebuild order and harmony within the family system. The family worker's purpose is to strengthen the parents' relationship, to teach parents to cooperate, and to reinforce hierarchical boundaries or the executive subsystem (Minuchin & Fishman, 1981). This function includes guiding family interactions so that parents change what they do with their child and employ more realistic controls based upon clear communication and age-appropriate expectations. Sometimes, the family consists of only one parent or a parent and stepparent. Nevertheless, the family worker's focus and approach remain the same. Family structure is not and cannot be fixed, static, or permanent, but as a system it should be healthy and vibrant (i.e., fluid and evolving; Feldman, 1992). This practical definition of the functional family has realistic implications for how parents talk, interact, and keep their child safe, such as by demonstrating more involvement, patience, listening, monitoring, and flexibility (Pennell & Anderson, 2006).

In the course of therapy, the family worker will come to understand the family's communication patterns, characteristic ways of functioning, and methods for dealing with stress and conflict, and the rules and boundaries that tie the family together (Boyd-Webb, 2003). Their behavior in sessions is a crucial source of data. Families will also reveal how members attempt to clarify interactions. The family worker can use a structural intervention to strengthen the family system by reinforcing parental significance and leadership (Minuchin, 1974). The family worker engages the parents in a problem-solving approach. The family worker does not present him or herself as being superior to the parents. The family worker does not deal with them as if they are to be blamed and condemned, or as if they are incompetent. The family worker conducts him or herself as knowledgeable of children in general, and relates to the parents as knowing their own child(ren).

To understand the parental position, the family worker asks the parents to describe the nature of the dynamics that created the impasse between the parents and/or between parents and their child (Hoffman, 1981). The family worker seeks the parents' help by asking them to describe their feelings about their child, the nature of their relationship with that child, how the parent–child problem arose, and what maintains it (Madanes, 1984). The family worker will also ask the child(ren) to explain how relationships and family interactions have developed into their present shape. An open discussion helps family members to understand their role in the family, and the feelings and reactions of others. This technique also provides each individual in the family with a perspective on how he or she is perceived by other family members (Penn, 1982) and what roles they are allowed or expected to perform.

When the family worker interacts nonjudgmentally toward the parents, this approach increases the likelihood of the parents participating in their child's treatment plan (Minuchin & Fishman, 1981). The family worker will present strategies and relevant information that are helpful to parents (Wachtel, 1992). The family worker offers the parents suggestions and feedback regarding misunderstandings, conflicts, and impasses. For example, some parents may need to be taught to see their child as an individual, not to project their distorted views (of their child) onto the child. Parents should be able to deal with misbehaviors without condemning their child and to separate their views of the child from the child's behaviors (Wachtel, 1992). The family worker may have to point out to the parents how the child's behavior is shaped by the parents or is a reflection of the parents' behaviors. When some parents understand how they have influenced their child's attitudes, they are often able to achieve dramatic results in their child by making changes in themselves (Severe, 2000). Nevertheless, parents need to learn to deal with their child's current placement and behaviors, and resist bringing up issues from the past in a negative tone or for condemnation. The family worker counsels parents to be open to the positive qualities of their child and to use a different way of thinking and interacting. This requires the parents to employ the same child management techniques that the treatment staff utilize. The family worker also emphasizes and highlights each parent's strengths, draws attention to their knowledge of what has worked, and steers the family toward potential solutions (Woods & Robinson, 1996).

The family worker wants all family members to discuss the implications and consequences of their problems, or behaviors, in terms of the impact on the family unit (Hollis & Woods, 1981). This means that family intervention elicits themes of competence and connection. Family intervention includes modification of basic behavior patterns that encourages change in the nature of relationships (Malan, 1976). Ultimately, the family worker seeks to have the family move away from correcting old problems, and asks family members to envision desired futures and to develop new lives (Madsen, 1999). The family worker asks family members to specify what needs to be done, a question intended to improve the present style of family communication and cooperation. When family members change their perspective of each other and problems, they are better able to listen and to see the positive intentions of other members. As family members interact with each other in ways that create cooperative dynamics, this form of discourse provides an awareness of how their seemingly fixed entanglements were a function of ignorance, estrangement, or anger. Ultimately, family members are encouraged to be more flexible in their interactions, to seek out different ways of behaving, and to anticipate the creation of a more workable family structure. The family can begin to experience relationship arrangements that are consistent with who they wish to be. This means that they are empowered to change the family structure and negotiate new life experiences as family members grow and evolve (Wachtel, 2004).

TREATMENT EMPHASIS

Parents have different reactions to their child being placed in residential treatment. Some parents will become overly concerned, and almost intrusive, in their dealings with program staff, whereas others will resist being engaged. Just as staff members often feel they are being judged, there are parents who fear they will be judged by staff. Therefore, some parents are guarded about revealing any kind of information that might be too personal, or even incriminating. Some families will resist all overtures by treatment staff, whereas some others will regard staff members as providing a relief from distress (Anderson & Stewart, 1983). There are parents who will attempt to dictate or control the treatment process; they will not be willing to provide information, or respond to requests for cooperation (Laing, 1965). In fact, no amount of persuasiveness will convince some parents that their child is not the cause of all the family's problems.

There are parents whose disturbances include using their child as an extension of themselves. This attitude often reflects a scapegoating process, and it fails to acknowledge how other members contribute to or are affected by the problem (Madanes, 1984). Defensiveness by parents will prevent them from recognizing or accepting that they have unrealistic or rigid demands of their child. There are parents who are very angry with the social service system and will compete with and challenge the therapist. There are others who are quite open in their hostility to any form of counseling (Pazaratz et al., 2000). For those parents who need to control treatment, it can be a defense against their own fears, inadequacies, and vulnerabilities. Not cooperating with treatment staff can also be a way of parents punishing their child by undermining his or her hopes of returning home (Haley, 1979). Nevertheless, when parents do not take personal responsibility and will not modify their attitude toward their child, confrontation can be utilized to improve family functioning (Madanes, Kein, & Smelser, 1995).

It may be impossible to develop a working alliance with some parents who are reluctant to interact and to be involved with treatment. They often justify their extreme hostility to their child and will not give up destructive patterns (Tomm, 1988). There are also parents who expect the treatment program to assume total responsibility for their child. They do not want to be involved, or to participate at any level. They may minimize family difficulties or insist that their child needs to be "fixed" (Madsen, 1999). Some parents may see requests to participate in family counseling as an intrusion interfering with their new-found tranquility, daily activities, interests, values, and priorities (Pazaratz, 1999). Although many parents display weaknesses, fears, and problems, they also have life circumstances, strengths, and a unique history.

Some parents report that they have felt overwhelmed and left exhausted by the challenges of life, so much so that they agree to the proposition that their child's needs were neglected, or that they have blamed their own frustrations on their child. Clearly, these parents need help with their child, or even a time-out (Condrell, 2006). But, for whatever reason (trust, fear, etc.), some parents are unable to benefit from counseling (Patterson & Welfel, 1994). Nevertheless, there are in fact parents who are committed to their children, and are very eager for counseling in order to become more effective parents. Some parents will even accept that their child has been taking responsibility for the family's problem (Hoffman, 1981). This realization may occur when the parents' well-being improves, or their socioeconomic conditions are less stressful, and they develop an awareness and sensitivity to what has happened to their child (Kelly, 1999).

If treatment staff have a difficult relationship with parents, this impasse can be problematic for the youngster's treatment experience. Therefore, it is important for staff members to recognize this possibility and to get the parents to feel connected in some manner. There are parents who do become attuned to and supportive of treatment upon realizing their child's distress. There will be parents who become cooperative because they have a genuine need to help their child and not to repeat what happened to them as children. Some parents appreciate that their parental limitations and insecurities are the result of their own childhood experience and have nothing to do with their child's nature. Therefore, they do not want their child to endure similar pain, and they feel relieved to have the support of treatment staff. There are parents who will respond to counseling when the focus shifts away from child–parent issues to deal with the problems in the parents' lives. Other parents respond when counseling takes apart old stories that have organized family life and helps the parents to build alternative narratives that open up new possibilities for growth and change (Madsen, 1999). Ultimately, children prosper when they are loved and accepted, and where there are clear expectations for responsible behaviors (Smith, 1991). There will be parents who are receptive to this information and understand that parenting includes understanding and forgiveness.

In order for treatment staff to recognize how a youngster's home life can affect the youth's treatment experience, treatment staff need to be aware of the interactional similarities between the parents' relationship with their child and the staff–resident dynamics (Nichols & Shwartz, 1991). However, because not all family problems lead to disturbed children, some of the youth's behaviors need to be addressed from an individual perspective rather than a family view. In other words, the youth can be difficult even though he or she has loving and supportive parents. Yet, it is necessary to understand how the youngster's behaviors, anxieties, and temperament have contributed, and continue to contribute, to the family's problems (McDermott & Char, 1974). This may mean that there is a circular causality, beyond the youngster's biosocial difficulties, whereby the youth and parents affect each other. Nevertheless, the parents' reactions to their child can be lessened when parents and treatment staff cooperate in the youth's treatment plan. The youngster's attitude often improves when he or she no longer views the parents as uninvolved, disinterested, or punitive.

FAMILY TREATMENT PLAN

When a family agrees to participate in the child's treatment, a plan should be developed whereby the focus of family issues changes from the youth being the problem to the family having the problem. In other words, the parents will have agreed that their style of interacting may be the cause of the youth's emotional-behavioral difficulties (Minuchin, 1974). In effect, the parents become accountable for their behaviors and openly discuss methods to attend to the developmental needs of their child(ren). This type of intervention forces all family members to reevaluate their pattern of interactions. It also causes parents to change their conception of their roles and helps them to realize that some of their child's behaviors are a reaction to, or occur in spite of, the parents. This understanding strengthens the family hierarchy. This approach is consistent with child protection work where the youngster has been apprehended for "safety," yet the focus of the intervention is to build upon family resiliency, to stabilize it, and to strengthen the child and family's situation (Turnell & Edwards, 1999). This model recognizes how certain events, role transitions, and life issues affect a family's sense of well-being and functioning. As a clinical construct, it also takes into consideration that children from single-parent and reconstituted (blended) families may be more susceptible to problems than are children from intact, or traditional, families (Thomas, Farrell, & Barnes, 1994; and see Gagnon & Coleman, 2004).

The family treatment contract is similar in scope to the youth's plan of care or task-centered contract (Reid, 1996; see also Pazaratz, 2000a). The treatment plan or contract is the basis for working toward the youngster's discharge home by teaching family members to identify problems and goals, to develop new problem-solving skills, and to incorporate realistic methods for supporting each other. The family treatment plan is based upon the four tasks that the normative family performs. These objectives include creating an identity or the method for maintaining the family, establishing boundaries (rules), providing for physical needs (organizing roles), and regulating the family's emotional climate. The implications in this approach are not only that children's problems flow from the child's nature but also that the child's behavior is a result of ongoing dysfunctional interactions. Thus, the basis of the treatment plan and clinical direction for the family worker is to teach the family how the family's style of functioning has created, and/or continues to maintain, the problems the child is experiencing (Pinsof, 1981). The family worker constantly appraises how successful the family is and can become at changing destructive dynamics and building harmony. Additionally, the parents and their child are asked to monitor progress, as well as to reassess communication and interactional patterns. Changing family homeostasis (a given configurational relationship) requires members to be able to change the rules that maintain conditions within which behaviors can vary (Minuchin, 1974).

During ongoing family sessions, the youth and his or her parents are continually encouraged to review the nature of the family's problems, and the methods that are being used to solve interpersonal difficulties. The parents and their child are asked to discuss relational problems in a nonemotional and nonblaming manner. They are reminded to cooperate and yet resolve issues from their own perspective and not necessarily from the family worker's value system. However, critical to resolving different points of view in families is understanding the goals of other family members, and being able to identify what role each person plays in finding a solution. Once this process has been enacted, these dynamics are used to precipitate or direct the change process, and these are incorporated into the way in which the family usually deals with issues (deShazer, 1985).

FAMILY COUNSELING

Sources of family stress can occur because of specific events, or because of the changing needs a youth experiences during his or her maturation. The family worker's ultimate effort in family counseling is to reestablish the parents as benign leaders who are in control of their home, while encouraging the youth's cooperation. This approach provides the structure needed in order for the youngster to pursue his or her goals and yet abide by limits without disrupting family harmony. New life circumstances require new coping patterns, and parents may need help with understanding these ideas and in making personal and relational transitions (Vetere, 1993). This may mean that parents teach their children how to become more self-reliant and interconnected individuals, rather than dependent on or at odds with the family unit.

Many parents have not learned to listen to their children and to validate their children's concerns and needs (Dinkmeyer & McKay, 1989). Family harmony is a two-way process, and it hinges on good communication between parents and their children. Direct care workers as well as the family worker ensure that the parents' approach to child rearing and behavior management includes the same types of limits, expectations, controls, and positive reinforcements as are used in the group home. This means that instead of parents overly focusing on what their child has done wrong, positive behaviors are emphasized and rewarded. Growth-enhancing attitudes by parents are based upon acknowledging their child's uniqueness and encouraging the child's interests. Additionally, when parents are attuned to their children, they provide consistency and do not give into misbehavior. They convey that they like their children and do not find them to be a burden. They avoid criticizing their child, are patient with children who operate on a different schedule, create reasonable rules and clear expectations, make time for their children, and resolve negative behaviors through the use of positive discipline.

In order for some parents to change from being too rigid, enmeshed, chaotic, or disengaged, they may need a period of therapy. For example, where life stressors overpower one parent's or both parents' emotional balance, individual or couples counseling may be prescribed to lessen personal problems and marital issues. Parents may also feel overwhelmed by daily responsibilities and have trouble providing for the family's physical necessities. In addition, some parents may experience stressors that make it hard for them to create an emotionally stable and supportive environment (Dunst et al., 1988). Consequently, when parents feel displaced (not listened to) or blamed for their child's problems, they can become uncooperative in treatment. Resolving these adult problems may be necessary before child management can succeed. Additionally, the family worker should be careful not to display an overidentification with the child, and a sense of disappointment and irritation with parents and their style of parenting. To avoid the development of a rivalry or of bitterness toward treatment, family workers need to convey acceptance of parents, even though the worker will vocalize disapproval of destructive or abusive behaviors (Levy & Orlans, 1998). When parents define the role they wish to play in their child's treatment, family counseling can be more successful.

DISCHARGE FROM TREATMENT

When a youth is placed in residential treatment, there is both a physical and a psychological separation from the family. This separation will often cause the youth to experience shame and rejection. During family sessions and home visits, some youngsters do experience a form of reunion and even a more mature relationship with their parents. Before a youngster is discharged home, an evaluation should be undertaken that examines such issues as the parents' child management skills, the potential for the youth's maltreatment, anger management issues, the involvement of parents with substances such as alcohol and drugs (and their abuse), the nature of communication difficulties or social isolation, and the relational problems that must be resolved before the youth moves home (Hodges, 1994). This analysis also looks at the availability of extended family and community support, the perspectives of treatment staff, as well as the perspectives of the parents regarding the family's readiness for their child's return (Turnell & Edwards, 1999). The youth's discharge home will integrate the youngster's autonomy and attachment needs, as well as the good and bad aspects of self and family. Thus, the support and therapy given to youth and their families after discharge are as important as the care and treatment given during placement (Pazaratz, 1999).

Notwithstanding the way in which a youngster is discharged from treatment, whether preplanned or due to unforeseen circumstances, subsequent home and community adjustment relies heavily on the quality of support available to the youngster (Pecora, Whittaker, & Maluccio, 1992). To get one's needs met within families, there are times when it is easier for the youth to return to previous ways of interacting (Pearce & Pezzot-Pearce, 1997). Most parents will benefit from ongoing support upon the youth's reentering the family. When the family worker maintains a partnership with the parents, this relationship and ongoing worker–parent contact (although diminished in frequency) may prevent abuse, arrest reactivation of destructive problem solving, obviate the youngster's oppositionalism and defiance, and avert the dissolution of the family. Even though youngsters and their parents are made aware of predictable crises and are taught to anticipate conflicts, the family worker emphasizes that he or she will not take over the job of parenting.

A youngster's completion of treatment and discharge from residential placement are not a guarantee of successful reintegration of the youth into his or her family, the community at large, and the real world. Upon a youth's discharge to his or her family, family members will be forced to deal with various situational stressors, such as changes in power, structure, roles, and relationships (Olson, Portner, & Lavee, 1985). Nevertheless, the family can learn to deal with these transitions and the ever-changing developmental needs of the youth by being aware of these concerns and by preparing for them in a planned fashion. This means that the independent-oriented living skills that are taught to the youth can also be emphasized upon a youngster's return home. Parents can also be reassured that many children upon discharge from treatment do prosper because of improved relationships with peers and authority figures, at school, or in the community. In fact, it is the social bonds developed in the family and at school that tend to inhibit delinquency in childhood and adolescence in the first place (Sampson & Laub, 1993).

Upon a youth's discharge home, there is often a cumulative nature to the stress experienced by the parents and their child, and a profound uncertainty as to the likelihood of successful reconnection. However, community organizations can provide the youngster with an outlet and the belief that the youth can fit into their programs, enjoy participation, and become successful. Strong social bonds that are developed in community programs have been found to inhibit regression into delinquency in both children and adolescents (Sampson & Laub, 1993). Community-based resources help youngsters to feel connected, and therefore the youth is more likely to maintain treatment gains (Pecora et al., 1992). Support following discharge by community-based counseling services may include helping the family navigate the overlapping demands of multiple agencies and institutions, assisting the youth to deal with the pressures of the real world, and helping to prevent such diverse problems as substance abuse, school dropout, gang membership, sexual promiscuity, and pregnancy (Boyd-Franklin & Bry, 2000). Without community-based outlets for both the youth and family, their stress may lead to conflict and destructive parent–child relations.

SUMMARY

To understand a youth's adjustment or reaction to residential placement, treatment staff should be aware of the youth's background. There are a variety of family types and interactional patterns that may create difficulties for children, adolescents, and their families. For example, some families are characterized by authoritarian leadership, infrequent role modification, strict negotiation, and a lack of change. There are also families that manifest an uncertain leadership, dramatic role shifts, erratic negotiations, and excessive change (Olson et al., 1985). Some parents discount their child's ability to succeed or to change, and therefore they do not put much effort into the relationship. In effect, the message is that the child or teenager will never receive parental love, approval, or recognition no matter what the youth does. Because the youngster is not accepted, the youth is never really forgiven for anything, and maybe the metamessage is that the child or teen does not deserve forgiveness. Some parents never validate their child's or teenager's efforts because to do so would excuse the youth's irresponsible behaviors (deShazer, 1985) and shift some of the family's problems onto the parents, and in turn the parents would have to deal with their own harsh, rigid, or inflexible behaviors toward their child.

The aim of family counseling is to break the negative cycle of parent–child interactions and to teach parents alternatives to harsh punishment, overinvolvement, or no involvement. Family treatment emphasizes the positive aspects and resources of the family system as well as specific skills that are essential for nurturing children and adolescents. This includes teaching family members to be adaptive, to develop shared strategies for augmenting other family members' strengths, to develop interests, to overcome weaknesses, and to resolve problems so that disagreements over issues do not become destructive. Ultimately, healthy interactions must be substituted for negative or pathological behaviors that family members engage in. When family members learn to value each other and to give unconditional acceptance, this emphasis on meaning and meaning potential increases family cohesiveness, attachment, and emotional bonding. The family worker looks for indicators of these important attitudinal changes such as through the enactment of new communication patterns, family members volunteering information or self-reporting, and the parents being able to discuss how their behaviors or reactions have stimulated the youth's symptoms.

CONCLUSION

The nature of a family's problems are typically hidden by defense mechanisms, or are revealed in the aberration that prevents the child's or teenager's normal development, or where one member controls other members by emotional manipulation and coercion. The family therapy process is like the milieu itself, wherein the family worker both creates and conveys an atmosphere of cooperation and hope. This positivity can be enacted by helping family members to understand that no one has to be blamed for family problems. Also, when family members are not mindful, the solution can become the problem, and yet everyone can be part of the solution (Satir, 1964; Wachtel, 2004). Thus, during a counseling session, if any interactional pattern becomes destructive, the family worker points out the negative aspects of communication and the effect that these overpowering messages have on children (Gottman, Fainsibler, & Hoover, 1997) and all family members.

In family sessions, to facilitate a change in the family system, the family worker provides mediated learning experiences that enable youngsters and parents to develop the ability to interpret family life, and to understand how they have experienced it (Feuerstein, Rand, & Rynders, 1988). The family worker offers a variety of ways of sorting out negative dynamics for bringing about family harmony and the methods to change the family's homeostasis (Fausel, 1998). A strong indicator of family progress is a corresponding reduction in the youth's symptoms following home visits and an increase in a pleasurable home life. In summary, a family worker attempts to do the following:

1. Assist the family to form an alliance with treatment staff and the agency.
2. Emphasize and develop the family's strengths.
3. Enable the family to grow stronger by building upon its different and unique background and culture.
4. Help the family to benefit from the full scope of resources available to them in their neighborhood and community, and to use these resources upon the youth's discharge.
5. Provide the family with postdischarge support at the level of their needs.

CHAPTER 6

Modifying Behavior Through the Use of a Level/ Reinforcement System

When adolescents were referred to the Four Phase System, the treatment focus was to stabilize the youth and his or her family, to bring about a reduction in disruptive behaviors, and to teach youngsters to understand life's themes and conflicts. Thus, the treatment emphasis was on developing a locus of control that, according to Lefcourt (1982), is an essential treatment focus emphasizing social learning, positive attitudes, and ego strength. In their efforts, treatment staff relied upon the systematic application of intervention techniques that were based on learning theory, the psychodynamic understanding of emotional problems, and behavior therapy. Because all behaviors are observable and, therefore, measurable and changeable, behavioral change can be stimulated by altering contingencies and reinforcements and by the prescribed management of milieu interactions. Thus, a youngster's problematic behaviors can be modified over time by treatment staff controlling and directing environmental events and by applying or removing reinforcements as required. This chapter describes the theory and application of a modifying economy based on the principles of behavior therapy and positive discipline, which was developed at the Oshawa/Whitby Crisis Intervention Centre, a reentry program of the Four Phase System.

BEHAVIOR MODIFICATION

Most parents provide their children with comforts unconditionally. They typically emphasize adaptive behaviors that are appropriate and effective for optimum maturation and development (Pazaratz & Morton, 2000). They address their children's individual needs with strategies that incorporate behavioral principles that target common problems such as bedtime procrastination, sleep disturbances, getting along with siblings or friends, getting ready for school and other events on time, doing chores, and completing homework without fuss (Shiller, 2003). These parents recognize that behavior problems can become sources of frustration for them and their child, and are attentive to their children's developmental needs. Yet, some youngsters require a structured life apart from their families to increase their ability to overcome family conflicts, and mental or emotional impairment (Wozner, 1991). Youngsters admitted to residential treatment manifest behaviors that are unsafe and unhealthy, occur too frequently, are excessive and extreme, or are severely overcontrolled.

Residential treatment and care of children and adolescents are intense experiences that emphasize learning responsibility, handling choices, experiencing growth through emotional enactment, developing reflectiveness, and acquiring negotiation and problem-solving skills. However, bringing about change during residential placement is a highly complex interactive process. Treatment occurs on several levels at once. The change process is based upon staff–youth interactions that stabilize youth, make them feel safe, and resocialize them. The relearning of skills and the development of competencies are also critical. Variously, the youth's self-defeating behaviors are blocked, redirected, or confronted by staff members, whereas resiliency behaviors are stressed. Over time, the intrapsychic conflict that underlines the youth's symptoms will emerge in such a way that the systemic issues of the youngster's past and family dynamics can be explored and dealt with psychodynamically.

Not all problems that youngsters experience that lead to placement are the result of the same conditions, nor will all youth be helped by the same approach. Nevertheless, front-line staff will enact a balanced approach with youth that consists of person-centered counseling, behavioral management, and cognitive restructuring. Intervention techniques vary for each youth and for each situation. Thus, the approach is integrative. Yet there is an emphasis on residents learning to identify and to understand their problems, to develop strategies for change, and to pursue goals by entering into a task-centered contract or treatment plan. Contracting places problems in a broader context, articulates conditions that elicit the problems, and identifies the thoughts, feelings, and actions that reinforce the problem (Epstein, 1992). Contracting assists youth to realize that the problems are theirs, and that conflicts arise due to the way they perceive and react to others (or conditions), and are not always the result of being mistreated. Contracting provides residents with a direction for change, to feel in control yet connected to relevance (Pazaratz,

2000a). By adhering to the contract, residents learn to organize themselves, to develop life goals, and to share their thoughts and feelings. Self-caring skills are thus brought about by the therapeutic management and modification of the youngster's attitude and deportment.

Front-line staff are cautioned that they may become frustrated if they look to behavior modification as a means of controlling residents and their behaviors. Ultimately, behavior modification is meant to teach cooperation and self-management skills. Staff members are encouraged not only to rely on contingency management but also to think about youth from various perspectives and to utilize multimodal or integrative strategies. This means that staff members should aim to develop a relationship with youth in order to be able to engage residents in discussions of personal issues, problems, and daily experiences. Interaction and feedback between residents and youth workers create the context for the youngster to develop self-understanding, enhanced social skills, empathy toward others, and empowerment. Improving interpersonal relationships and becoming goal oriented provide residents with a meaningful direction, a purpose, and hope in treatment (Monk, Winslade, Crocket, & Epston, 1997). The development of positive peer relationships and supportive staff interactions informs the social process and the treatment context, to which residents are more likely to commit. In other words, through peer pressure and discussions with adults, a youth's self-development is influenced (Forehand & Wierson, 1993). Thus, the young person's emotional difficulties and needs are treated psychosocially, or in the reality of group living. The issues that are dealt with in these interactions are as meaningful as the discussions of abstract and hypothetical situations, or those involving distant reflections on past interpersonal events (Pazaratz, 1998a).

Behavior modification ultimately attempts to stimulate enhanced cognitive operations within youth by reinforcing them for trying new problem-solving techniques and/or seeking alternate solutions. In turn, as youngsters develop new skills and competencies, they improve their self-acceptance, self-caring, and tolerance for others (Fewster & Garfat, 1998). This occurs when an individual reassimilates or reowns what she or he has given up, or disowned, such as a sense of self, family, friends, and so on. The more a client (the youth) has disowned, the more impoverished, angry, or depressed she or he becomes (Perls, 1969b). Thus, residential placement provides residents with an opportunity to reclaim their lives through social connection (Pazaratz, 2000b). This healing of residents occurs by striking a balance between the aims of the program and the youngster's personal aspirations, or social development. This means that the hopes and dreams of each resident are not sacrificed to meet program design, or for the purpose of institutional expediency (Pazaratz, 2000c). In fact, residents are encouraged to develop and to be committed to a life plan (or goals), to pursue social relationships, to engage in creative or fun interests (sublimation), to confront their fears, and to strive for long-term pleasure. Chesterton (in Manguel, 2000) supported the thesis that happiness is a learned trait. In everything worth having, even in every pleasure, there is a point of tedium, or a pain that must be survived. Everything, in fact, has another side, and the individual must go beyond the obvious and seek out its meaning. These ideas of the richness and hopefulness of life are incorporated in each youngster's plan of care and treatment contract (Pazaratz, 2000a).

APPLICATION OF REINFORCEMENTS

All behavior patterns, including maladaptive ones, are learned. Therefore, undesirable behaviors can be described specifically and modified by detailing desired performance behaviorally (Bandura, 1977). Events following behaviors are called *contingencies of reinforcement* and are seen as controlling, or maintaining, conditions of the behaviors (Bandura, 1986). In a passive environment, a youngster's development can be accelerated or retarded with proactive intervention. New behavior patterns can be realized through naturalistic contingencies or self-observed reinforcers such as pride, sense of accomplishment, or self-scheduling pleasures or recreational activities. This in effect means that with appropriate stimulation, any youngster's development can be significantly influenced (Allyon & Azrin, 1968). Yet limitations in the change process should also be expected (Kazdin, 1984).

How, then, do staff implement behavior management, which includes the traditional goals of social learning and the relearning of social skills, and coordinate these dynamics with contingency management or apply the principles of cause and effect? All parties involved in the youth's treatment plan identify those behaviors that are inappropriate (and why) and those that are desirable. This is based on a systematic assessment to establish frequency, duration, and conditions under which problematic behaviors occur. After behaviors are observed and documented, they can be altered through the agreed upon or contracted use of valued reinforcers (Allyon & Azrin, 1968). Each resident is prescribed what he or she should or should not do. As a structured approach, behavior therapy allows interventions to be standardized. It is valuable for treating a variety of behavior problems, because reinforcements can be applied to strengthen and to increase the frequency of appropriate behaviors, and to shape or to mold new behaviors. Reinforcements can also be removed to weaken or eliminate inappropriate or unacceptable responses. Problematic behaviors can be extinguished when contingencies of reinforcement (antecedents or consequences) are changed. It is by modifying the nature of the stimulus and/or reinforcements that behaviors can be conditioned to occur as a substitute or replacement for undesirable actions (Freidman, Goorich, & Fullerton, 1986).

By providing youngsters with specific information on the nature or quality of interactions, and by teaching them to become reflective, this type of engagement is designed to enhance developmental maturation and to provide youth with essential information so that they can manage their present needs and fulfill future hopes and dreams (Beker & Feuerstein, 1991). In addition, cognitive change occurs as a youth understands the connection between the reinforcement and his or her behaviors, learns problem solving strategies, and understands how to make better decisions or choices (Glasser, 1998). This means residents will begin to comprehend that cooperation results in rewards, an increase in privileges, and greater freedom and independence (consistent with the adolescent's abilities). However, when the youth is not behaving responsibly and makes poor choices, these acts will result in an increase of controls and the loss of privileges.

Behavior therapy requires an agreed upon contract that is time limited and reviewed by staff and each resident. The conditions for identifying a baseline are established when target behaviors are agreed upon. The contract identifies those behaviors that should increase in frequency and distinguishes them from those that should be extinguished and/or those that should be replaced by other behaviors. This information assists in measuring progress or lack thereof and in identifying the types of reinforcements to be employed. Positive consequences of a behavior occur when a target behavior is followed by a positive reinforcement. This means that there will be an increase in the frequency of that behavior because the youth values the reinforcement and will continue to work to attain more reinforcements (Watson & Tharp, 1972). New behaviors can also be developed through procedures such as modeling, demonstration, and prompting, and by cueing and shaping (i.e., rewarding small steps that approximate desired behaviors; Bandura, 1986).

BEHAVIOR SHAPING

Observation of youth and their behaviors provides staff with information concerning general behavior patterns of high frequency. By the charting of a youngster's behaviors, staff can identify those contingencies or reinforcements that precede or follow target behaviors. This helps youth workers to understand where most of a youngster's problems occur: at which time of day, under which situations, and with what conditions. Charting also reveals behavioral patterns that will help staff to anticipate problem areas. To eliminate self-defeating behaviors, an alterative behavior is provided. Negative behaviors are discussed with youth and then rephrased into more positive, less punitive appearing, but more objective contingency management language. Contingency management is especially effective at stabilizing the high-risk youth's residential placement and, with improved adjustment, at increasing every youngster's personal and social behaviors (Pazaratz, 2003c).

Behaviors that are identified on contracts deal with argumentativeness, breaking rules, fighting, lying, self-injury, self-care, and responsibilities for the upkeep of one's living space. Behaviors that can be shaped by the application of reinforcements include all of the above as well as defiance, passive avoidance, dependability, asking staff members for help, and cooperation with authority figures and peers (Morris, 1985; Pazaratz, 1999). Behavior therapy has also been successful at changing conduct disorders (Christopherson & Finney, 1993), or modifying behaviors that are regarded as antisocial or an infringement of other people's rights. Thus, behavior modification can be therapeutic for adolescents who present impulse control problems and experience low frustration tolerance, self-esteem issues, learned helplessness, and difficulty with reality testing. And, according to Barkley (1997), there is some proven efficacy for assisting teenagers with attention deficit hyperactivity disorder (ADHD). In sum, utilizing reinforcements can modify social behaviors, the learning of new behaviors, and the development of self-control, and can inculcate accountability (Pazaratz, 1999).

By charting or monitoring the impact of intervention strategies, the treatment team also gains information on the effectiveness of different interventions, the abilities of different staff, and the types of reinforcements and consequences that can be employed successfully (Walsh, 1984). Staff cohesiveness results from approaching each youth in the same manner, and from the consistent implementation of basic intervention strategies (Pazaratz, 2000d). Conversely, when any staff is repeatedly having similar problems with a variety of youth, then team members can assist that particular staff to deal with the youth and those repeated problem areas differently and more effectively (Pazaratz, 2000b). Charting of observable behaviors as an indicator of habitative progress informs the treatment team of the specific types of intervention that are not effective with individual residents, assists in formulating and monitoring individual treatment plans, is a useful criterion in constructing program evaluation (Reid, Parsons, Green, & Schepis, 1991), and can provide an analysis of therapeutic programming (Pazaratz, 1999). By utilizing a standardized approach, such as a behavior chart, child and youth care workers ensure that problematic behaviors will be monitored, the treatment focus will be specific, and all staff members will be provided with a picture of the effectiveness of different aspects of the program (Freidman et al., 1986; Pazaratz, 2000d).

BENEFITS OF REINFORCEMENTS

For youngsters to be stabilized and integrated into a residential treatment program, the environment needs to provide a secure structure that is developed by staff members being consistent and constant in their interactions. Close monitoring of behaviors and limited freedoms are imposed upon youngsters until they demonstrate impulse control, frustration tolerance, and cooperative interactions with peers and staff. However, as the resident complies with staff expectations and develops positive peer interactions, there are fewer controls and a reduction in staff directives. Controls, but not monitoring, of behaviors will diminish consistent with the individual's adaptation or the development of self-control. The youngster's treatment plan can be continually adjusted to allow the resident to make choices where he or she can safely and responsibly manage these. Earning the privilege to make choices will serve to diminish oppositionalism, power struggles, passive-aggressive retaliation, and verbal bickering or fighting with staff (Pazaratz, 1999). Ultimately, staff want residents to increase their problem-solving strategies and to realize that their freedom to choose is directly connected to their ability to be responsible. More independence or autonomy is made available when a resident demonstrates prosocial behaviors and improved reality testing. For Perls (1969a), good habits are life supportive. They are part of the growth process, or the actualization of a potential skill.

Kazdin (1990) has determined that behavior therapy can be used in conjunction with other therapies. Thus, a modifying economy based upon principles of behavior therapy can be applied to all residents in any treatment program regardless of the youngster's maturity, learning impairment, or degree of manifestation of emotional problems (Pazaratz, 1999). This in effect means that most problematic behaviors can be continuously improved upon when youngsters are exposed to systematically rewarding reinforcements. Within clearly negotiated and defined boundaries, residents work toward their goals (as stated in their contract or treatment plan). As they learn and practice new ways of interacting, youngsters in effect experience growth and change (Kitchener, 1991). Staff–youth discussions clarify for residents the criteria used for earning reinforcements, the nature of problematic behaviors, or the behaviors that need to be changed and the reasons for change. During the discussion of interpersonal problems, staff feedback clarifies for residents the fundamental disagreement as to what or who is the cause of the problem, and who is reacting (Pazaratz, 1996a). Reinforcements offer residents external guidance and motivation, and are instrumental in stimulating a fundamental change to the way in which residents think about self-care, cooperation, and opportunities (London, 1977; Pazaratz, 2000a). The enhancement of reasoning skills enables youth to experience improved social, academic, interpersonal, and vocational adjustment. For Perls (1969a), the learning of skills is the discovery that something is possible.

A modifying environment (contingency management) is basic to the organization of a milieu or a group living unit, and it assists with the implementation of program policy. It deals with behaviors and events in the immediate context or moment. A behavior modification system can utilize any type of reinforcement such as money, tokens, and/or the earning of privileges (Allyon & Azrin, 1968). Residents are taught to value the system, the unit of exchange, and the concept of cooperation. Desired and selected behaviors are identified as being within the eventual competence of the youth. Reinforcements are rewards for adaptation, cooperation, and the acquisition of new skills and competencies. In practice, reinforcements can be based on earned checkmarks, or credits that can be exchanged for cash and/or movement on a level system. When a level system is integral to behavioral management, it exposes youngsters to greater challenges and opportunities for growth. Movement on levels also acts as a reinforcement. Each level has different expectations for behaviors of self-care and cooperation, and correspondingly there are greater rewards and challenges as the youth progresses through the levels. When a resident examines for him or herself the issues of self-control, and learns to monitor his or her progress within program parameters, competencies are developed and characterological growth is realized (Freidman et al., 1986). Ultimately, youth experience emotional healing and self-fulfilment as they make progress toward their goals (Pazaratz, 1998b).

In the implementation of a contingency management system, residents can be taught not to be distracted by staff evaluating and rating their behaviors. It is the youngster's acts or competencies, and not their worth, that are being assessed. Self-esteem difficulties will occur if residents equate their worth with either their positive or negative behaviors (Ellis, 1994), and with attaining or not attaining valued reinforcements. This systematic approach to behavioral intervention upholds the advantage of behavior therapy. It has little impact on the youth's sense of self because the youth's value as a person is never equated to, derived from, or known based upon his or her behaviors. In essence, each young person can create his or her own meaning by learning self-acceptance as espoused by Ellis (1994). Therefore, residents are counseled not to link their self, or self-worth, with their actions and achievements. Thus, an enhanced perception of their accomplishments and competencies can emerge with the acquisition of new behaviors (Forehand & Wierson, 1993). This means that disruptive behaviors can be defined as competency deficits. Nevertheless, the frequency, intensity, and duration of these behaviors can be reduced, and even extinguished, by the withdrawal of reinforcements, time-out from reinforcements, or the application of reinforcements for adaptive or alternative behaviors.

Charting of behaviors on a graph provides a comprehensive daily overview of each resident's functioning within the program. The chart informs staff of the resident's problem areas, and whether or not the youth is working on his or her contract. Intervention strategies can be immediate and communication more specific because even though different staff deal with each resident, all staff have a common focus of problematic behaviors. When extreme emotions and behaviors are identified and worked on, case management and staff coordination are improved (Pazaratz, 2000a). Nevertheless, staff must be aware of a less obvious problem, superficial cooperation. This includes such attitudes of inertia, apathy, and passive avoidance, which are unrewarding in life. These inclinations or choices can be overcome by encouraging risk taking and assertiveness, so that youngsters deal with procrastination tendencies and poor motivation (Beker & Feuerstein, 1991). The reinforcement system also ensures that the young person's "rights" and "obligations," which exist outside the group home, are maintained in the treatment facility (Erwin,

1978), because a behavior management system should uphold community standards of normative behaviors and, where necessary, consequences.

Instead of youngsters being self-absorbed, or focused on their self-worth, staff members aim to make residents aware of problematic behaviors and their ability to control and to change these. Staff aim to teach residents how many of their problems flow from choices that occur in the context of their interactions with others (Pazaratz, 1996b). A level system also emphasizes this perspective because staff teach residents management of emotions, development of social skills, and an awareness of how positive interactions can lead to progress through the levels. Staff–youth discussions have the purpose of clarifying misunderstandings, providing knowledge of the mechanics of the level/reinforcement system, helping with the development of attachment, and enhancing staff–youth cooperation. With an increase in staff–resident positivity, this improved dynamic can stimulate the youngster's participation in the treatment–change process while reducing behavior control questions (Pazaratz, 2000b). Additionally, when specific criteria are employed to monitor and reinforce behaviors, then negative reactions that arise from too much confrontation, or perceived criticism, have been seen to diminish (Pazaratz, 2000d).

A SYSTEMS APPROACH

A youth's behaviors are understood as they occur in their environment. Behaviors can be shaped by applying reinforcements, utilizing counseling, and emphasizing resocialization (Reid et al., 1991). A treatment facility becomes a modifying environment, because it has an organizational structure that consists of expectations and communication channels, all of which create conditions to support youngsters (Pazaratz, 2001). The modifying economy complements other strategies that are employed in the treatment of youngsters, who function at different developmental levels and stages of treatment. There are a variety of events, hobbies, sports, and recreational endeavors that are geared to promote skills development, pleasure, a sense of purpose, and feelings of connection, and to overcome negative attitudes (Pazaratz, 1998a). These activities are considered therapeutic because they enable youth to learn about themselves and life, and the way in which knowledge can be transferable to other situations. These experiences assist youngsters to observe their own emotions, to regulate these, to practice new behaviors, and to reconsider their own priorities. They are also taught to moderate and to control behaviors that arise out of conflicts, disputes, or competition. Teaching of skills for dealing with stimuli or emotional arousal is as important as the process by which behaviors are modified within a reinforcement system.

The modifying principles of a treatment program also offer treatment alternatives and create circumstances under which change can occur. In some situations, "time-out" from reinforcements as a behavior reduction technique, or removal of all positive events for a specified period of time, can be extremely effective (Kazdin, 1980). This is based upon the theory that if something negative reinforces a behavior (as in a power struggle), then either remove the reinforcer from the individual or remove the person from the reinforcer (Algozzine, 1985). Learning to interact cooperatively will provide youth with insights that help to improve attitudes and problem-solving strategies (Rose, 1998). Youngsters can also be taught to be reflective and focused, rather than to apply themselves randomly to situations or be scattered in their behavior (Kendall, Reber, McLeer, Epps, & Ronan, 1990). Residents are taught to think about their thinking, to self-regulate, to correct their errors, and to try new behaviors. The resident is continually asked to become conscious of him or herself and of others. Hopefully, the resident has also understood the idea of fragmentation. Perls (1969b) believed that an individual will feel disjointed or fragmented when his or her parts (self) are distributed in various places, such as relationships, past, and future.

Another important aspect of residential treatment is for the resident to develop a cohesive sense of self and organizational skills. This information can be acquired through direct teaching, with relationship-based counseling, and with the crucial use of staff modeling. Residents receive instruction on behavioral expectations. Behavioral expectations fall into two categories classified as instrumental and affective. Instrumental behaviors consist of any physical tasks such as chores, routines, and the like, whereas affective categories deal with a youth's emotional responses. Staff members explain the behavior that is expected in each instrumental and affective category, the degree of competency or level of performance required for minimal reinforcements to be obtained, and how the youngster can achieve greater amounts of reinforcements. The resident restates the actions that need to be taken and how these are to be performed. When a youth's behaviors are deemed ineffective or insufficient, the staff member looks for skills that need to be employed by the youth in order to deal with impasses or difficulties. This may mean that new strategies will be developed, that the resident may need to put in more effort, or that errors and mistakes are a result of a learning-based problem. Residents are asked to seek help and feedback from staff when they experience difficulty with processing information and during the enactment of a task. Even though a problem's attributes will require different problem-solving approaches, nevertheless, in order for the resident to make progress, there are procedures to be practiced and followed, goals to be pursued, and feedback to learn from (Pazaratz, 2000a).

RATIONALE OF REINFORCEMENTS

The major premise of behavior therapy is that behaviors are governed by environmental events. Many children and adolescents who experience out-of-home placement can find it to be upsetting and confusing. Even though most staff members in residential placement are skilled and empathic in their interactions, nevertheless, the nature of staff involvement, such as imposing limits, exacting consequences, and applying reinforcements, can be upsetting for some youth. Consequently, avoidance or distancing behaviors will emerge in some youngsters. These defensive reactions can help staff to understand how the resident deals with the pressures of adult relationships, or authority figures; which defenses they employ and the type of coping strategies that could be substituted (Pazaratz, 2000b, 2000c, 2000d). When workers understand how the client (youngster) constructs his or her reality, this knowledge helps to identify the link between the client's (resident's) current problems and the unresolved emotional issues of the past (Rogers, 1951).

Regular staff–youth discussions not only inform the worker of the youth's inner worlds but also provide residents with feedback about their behaviors, or an understanding of the active part of their behaviors that need to be modified. Discussing specific expectations helps replace abstract conceptualizations, or generalities, about inappropriate behaviors with learning-based ideas (Pazaratz, 1993). New behaviors patterns can be acquired through structured learning. A youngster's attitude change is brought about by staff using established procedures in the areas of social learning, so that the skills and behaviors to be learned are presented as steps that can be practiced, memorized, and reinforced. These instructional techniques are the foundation of contingency management principles that need to be articulated clearly and enacted consistently in order for a reinforcement system to be valued. When the resident is made aware of his or her skills deficits without feeling blamed, criticized, or the need to be defensive, then adaptive behaviors can be realized (Pazaratz, 1996a, 1996b).

According to Sterba and Davis (1999), corrective teaching practices show youth how to stop misbehaviors and to learn new positive skills to replace negative behaviors. Proactive teaching as a model utilizes praise and positive discipline to eliminate the need for staff to control behaviors by commands, threats, or consequences. Outbursts of anger or spitefulness toward residents by staff members are inappropriate. Hostility directed at youth causes interactions to escalate into a power struggle, or results in the youth's compliance due to fearing the worker's ire or threats (Pazaratz, 2000d). Instead, behavioral problems can be dealt with by the application or withdrawal of reinforcements that are listed in the youngster's treatment contract (Epstein, 1992). Additionally, the application or removal of reinforcements does not risk the nature of the staff–youth relationship. In fact, when staff members employ reinforcements judiciously, they are seen to be "bitching," or complaining, less to the youth and about youth. By systematically altering staff–youth interactional exchanges, the behaviors of both the worker and the resident can be altered toward desired objectives (Dangel, Yu, Slot, & Fashimpar, 1991). With improved communication between staff and youngsters, their relationship remains task oriented (i.e., it is focused on residents acquiring new skills; Meichenbaum, 1977). Staff should be aware that any intervention technique not applied ethically and equitably can be viewed as odious, and will negatively affect the staff–resident relationship.

A theory has to have the implication that if it is followed, it will allow the practitioner to accomplish what it is purported to do. In a study conducted by Pazaratz (1999), it was determined that a modifying economy, such as the one detailed here, helped staff in a residential facility for adolescents with severe behavioral disorders to tailor programming to individual residents. This qualitative investigation took into consideration differences in terms of each youngster's age, cognitive ability, and emotional development. The modifying reinforcement system provided a standardized treatment approach for a disparate group of youth with divergent problems. Charting of behaviors was facilitative as it offered quick feedback to residents. Consequently, before residents were too far off course, they were brought back to the task at hand. When any intervention was deemed ineffective, it was quickly identified and restructured. Because the reinforcement program included four levels, staff noted that the level system caused residents to approach interpersonal conflicts more reasonably. Fearing being demoted a level (or possibly being demoted to the first level), the resident would avoid escalating conflicts and was more prone to use negotiation or conflict resolution procedures. During difficult or conflictual times, residents were reminded of their previous accomplishments and that they had made progress on the level system, and they were encouraged not to give up. When residents are counseled to pursue goals and not to ruminate over problems, this is intended to stimulate their motivation, sense of self-determination, and ability to problem solve (Epstein, 1992; Pazaratz, 2000a). Importantly, when residents develop new attitudes, these become the basis for or the beginning of therapeutic change (Meichenbaum, 1977).

CRITICAL FACTORS OF REINFORCEMENTS

In residential treatment, providing structure, consistency, and constancy comprises fundamental aspects of the staff's role. But realistically, to be effective, child and youth workers must have diverse skills, at divergent levels of competence. The modifying system assists all staff to maintain daily program structure and cooperative interactions, and ensures uniformity of expectations. The modifying system requires that staff formulate an accurate conceptualization of each resident's problem(s) (encoding), a careful selection of behavioral targets (goal setting), an identification of valued reinforcements for new target goals (plan), and an assessment of the resident's orientation and motivation for treatment (taking action) (Watson & Tharp, 1972). Nevertheless, there will be residents who are skilled at avoiding or hiding their problems. For these youngsters, it will be difficult to establish an accurate observation and charting of their participation. They achieve high levels of reinforcements without internalizing real or significant change. They display adaptation, superficial cooperation, or mask their true feelings. They do not talk about their real problems. They are able to fool staff! Clearly, this specific behavior therapy system does not reflect general emotional adjustment, nor does it have any predictive value. In fact, it has been argued that this type of behavior therapy treats classes of problems (e.g., conduct disorders and attention deficit hyperactive disorder) and not individual behaviors. It is considered palliative as it attempts to modify cognitions and feelings that are not accessible to direct external observation (Skinner, 1988; Wolpe, 1989). In other words, it would be difficult to determine this system's impact or its efficacy, because this approach relies upon subjective evaluation by staff, who are participant observers and only monitor and rate a youngster's externalized behaviors. Therefore, staff are taught to be aware of the limitations of this approach and not to dehumanize the individual, or to act toward the youngster as a person who needs to be contained and managed (Pazaratz, 1993).

The strength of this modifying economy, however, is that it provides information on problem areas of staff–adolescent interactions, such as conflicts with peers and difficulties a youngster encounters during community use. It identifies a youngster's general proneness to emotional upset and the resultant behavioral problems of open destructiveness, poor reality testing, and impulsiveness. It promotes positive personal and social development in those areas diagnosed as weaknesses. It forces residents to focus on expectations, to develop coping strategies, and to improve negotiation skills. It helps in teaching delay of gratification (dealing with immediacy and low frustration problems). It draws attention to a youth's obsessions (negative and destructive behaviors), the tendency of "fight or flight," or going from temper tantrums and verbally assaultive acts to running away physically from the residence (Pazaratz, 1999). Nevertheless, to understand the source of a youth's problems, such as sleeping difficulties, inability to deal with emotions, and interpersonal conflicts (rejection, devaluation, obstructionism, criticism, etc.), staff are required to be involved with the youth. Careful attention to the youngster's daily behaviors, attitudes, and mood fluctuation informs staff of a youth's emotional space, the nature of frustrations, or problem-solving difficulties (Pazaratz, 2000d).

This modifying economy is effective at providing support to those residents who are socially and personally helpless, undersocialized, or suffering from social anxiety. By systematically altering interactional exchanges, it assists youngsters with noncompliance issues to learn and to attend to chores, routines, activities, and group participation (Butterfield & Cobb, 1994). It encourages the timid youth to experience social awareness and risk taking in interpersonal relationships. For those residents who are devalued by their peers or are immature, charting of unassertive behaviors provides the context for understanding the problem (Pazaratz, 1999). For youngsters diagnosed with attention deficit disorder, there is evidence that attention and concentration levels can be improved through the application of reinforcements (Morris, 1985). With residents who suffer from social, performance, and ego anxiety, or are overly dependent on others for approval, not only can they be encouraged to stay in anxiety-provoking situations by being reinforced to do so, but also with therapy they can learn self-acceptance and a tolerance for anxiety (Ellis, 1994). Thus, when youngsters appear erratic on a charting scale, such a display of changing symptoms suggests a borderline personality disorder (Morris, 1985). Any type of recurring characterological weaknesses, once identified in a similar context, can be dealt with in individual counseling. Finally, a meta-analysis in the treatment of delinquency shows a clear therapeutic advantage with a behavioral approach for conduct disorders (Hollin, Epps, & Kendricks, 1995).

Most intrapsychic and interpersonal behaviors in residential treatment can be analyzed and reduced to a stimulus-response equation (i.e., drives and reinforcements; Freidman et al., 1986). When staff become aware of the specific behavioral patterns of each youth, positive reinforcement can be applied to increase desired behaviors and to decrease negative behaviors (Morris, 1985). However, staff should also be aware that a negative consequence to control a behavior can increase negative behaviors, especially when there is an escape, or avoidance of an aversive event (Skinner, 1938). Negative behaviors such as injurious or self-abusive acts can in and of themselves be quite reinforcing as the resident seeks attention (Pazaratz, 1993). Negative behaviors raise serious behavior control problems, often create tremendous stress for staff, and undermine the development of a staff–resident therapeutic alliance (Pazaratz, 1993, 1998c). This observation is supported by Redl and Wineman (1957a), who have found that when surface behaviors are stopped, this blocking interferes with staff–resident relationships. Walsh (1984) concurred in his observation that some residents will react because they are always being watched and evaluated. They project their anger onto staff because of being controlled (Pazaratz, 1996a). Reinforcements can be utilized as an intervention technique, to overcome hostility toward staff and other youngsters, and to promote motivation, choices, incentives, and opportunities for risk taking and connection with others (Reid et al., 1991).

LIMITATIONS OF BEHAVIOR MANAGEMENT

The reinforcement/level system as a behavior rating scale does not provide a diagnostic label, it is not part of a battery of tests, and it does not indicate any kind of deviancy or direct the observer or rater in the direction of a label. The reinforcement scale is used to chart and reflect responses in the areas of cooperation, accountability, social adjustment, self-care, group interactions, values orientation, level of affect, aggression, withdrawal, social anxiety, and problem-solving skills. Many behaviors charted on the scale are externalized behaviors prone to subjectivity and can, therefore, be misperceived by frontline workers when they incorrectly evaluate the motive of a youth's behavior. To overcome errors, charting is based upon definitions so that each behavior can be understood descriptively and rated on a four-point scale. A specific description of the behavior to be rewarded is given to residents. Behaviors that are in compliance are rewarded or reinforced by staff, as are improvements. Positive behaviors are noted and reinforced as soon as possible after they occur to strengthen them. Importantly, responses that are part of a desired new behavior are also rewarded. When staff members are appropriately trained as raters, a higher interrater reliability can be obtained for scores.

Behaviors that are rewarded must be free of ambiguity. Reinforcements can include praise, attention, additional access to free time, and/or a selection of choices for activities. Undesirable behaviors should be ignored if possible or practical, but not rewarded. Progress is charted twice daily, in day treatment and in the residence. Point scores are tallied daily. Weekly point totals can be exchanged for cash (or other valued items), and are used to determine advancement or regression through four levels. Each level consists of different expectations, restrictions, responsibilities, and choices. Even though a youngster may not earn sufficient points to advance a level, at the end of the week, nevertheless an increase in earned points from one week over the previous week's total can be the rationale for a bonus, if it is a significant increase. Once an individual's requisite behaviors are established, the token system is phased out and replaced by reinforcers most appropriate or available in the natural environment. These social reinforcers are employed to advance the youth's transition to discharge and independence.

Explanation of Levels

1. *Level One*: All residents are initially placed on this level from a 2- to 4-week period, depending on the resident's need for structure. Demotion to this level from any other occurs when a youth violates program rules, so that the youth's safety is in question, or the youth experiences more than three time-outs from reinforcements per day. Privileges at this level are restricted to the residence, and school is compulsory. More restrictions and controls are placed on youth at this level than at any other level, because they are new to the program and just beginning the system, or due to being placed on this level for more support. Some youth on this level will proportionately earn more than youth on a higher level because they are subjected to tighter controls. Nevertheless, when this occurs it means that the youth has benefited from additional structure and support. At this level, youth can earn $20.00 per week, half of which goes into the resident's account.

2. *Level Two*: School is compulsory. Youth are accompanied on activities by staff. Youth are allowed two community activities per week, three calls on the telephone per night, and 15 minutes extra time before bedroom retirement. Curfew is still the same, but community time (CT) is increased one hour per night. A point score of 500–600

is required in order to remain at Level Two. Up to $24.00 can be earned, half of which goes into the resident's account.

3. *Level Three*: Youth can earn a half-hour extension on curfew and may also go on an activity alone. Youth are permitted to supplement earnings with chores, have additional phone privileges per evening, and go on an activity with staff. 700 points are necessary to remain at this level. Eligible earnings are $28.00, half of which goes into the resident's account.

4. *Level Four*: Youth have unlimited community access, depending on their destination. Weekend home visits may be extended until Monday morning. A part-time job is a possibility. CT is extended one hour, provided the youth's whereabouts are known in advance. Eligible earnings are $32.00, half of which goes into the resident's account. Must earn 1,300 points on the reinforcement chart to remain at this category at the end of each week.

Explanation of Credit and Point Scale

Level	Enter	Remain	Advance	Number of Weeks	Monetary Value Before Advance
I	0	400 points		2	$20.00
II	500 points	600 points	700 points	2	$24.00
III	700 points	1,200 points	1,300 points	3	$28.00
IV	1,300 points	2,000 points			$32.00
		2,000 points or over			$40.00

Variable Factors

1. *Daily bonuses*: In an individual token economy, the rates of pay and exchange are different for all youngsters involved in this system. Thus, daily bonuses of $1.00 can be awarded to any resident for being most cooperative, helpful, positive, creative, fun, humorous, etc., or for those who have made the most progress from one week to the next on their reinforcement chart or on any one category. This is a discretionary category and takes into account that staff are contingency managers and every staff member will observe a slightly different perspective on each youngster's behaviors, even though there is an attempt for staff to coordinate and to follow specified procedures closely by observing, recording, and reinforcing target behaviors. Daily bonuses also increase a contingency management system's salience, novelty, and meaningfulness.

2. *Response cost*: This means that residents often complain about fairness or that someone else is being treated or valued more favorably.

Thus, residents are taught that not everyone earns points or checks at the same rate for any particular behavior. Earning reinforcements is similar to earning grades in school. Penalties and fines can be deducted from a youth's account to pay for damages to property, breaking of rules, etc.

3. *Reinforcement scale (see end of chapter)*: This is designed to be laid out as a spreadsheet or by placing weekly charts, side by side, so that the graphing of behaviors can be reviewed over a longer duration. Reinforcements are a way of classifying different kinds of causal events and thinking about the relationship between them. Reinforcements aim to make residents self-directed rather than other directed. Reinforcements provide for movement and growth as per the resident's abilities, and help the youth to deal with commonplace problems. Social values that are emphasized include being fair, respectful, and cooperative with others. Reinforcements are also used to encourage youth to be flexible rather than rigid; to collaborate in groups; to develop commitment to people, things, and ideas; to become ethical, trustworthy, constructive, and socialized; and, ultimately, to give up foolish, self-indulgent, and destructive behaviors. The reinforcement system provides strategies for reimaging (valuing) social skills and for decreasing behavioral problems.

4. *Time-outs*: These are used when it is necessary to remove a youth from any situation that is overly stimulating, or when the youth cannot handle the immediate stress and pressures that are destabilizing. Time-outs are employed for safety purposes, or to deescalate a volatile situation that may get out of control, but time-outs are not punitive or harsh. When youngsters do not respond to a category, that category is reframed, changed to include other criteria, or eliminated.

5. *Contracts*: These are used to elicit an understanding from the resident that some behaviors need to change. A written agreement is made concerning those behaviors. Contracts specify reinforcers or the type of credits that are exchanged for money, privileges, and movement on the level system.

6. *Level system*: A level system assists youngsters to understand and to visualize that their behaviors consist of different degrees of intensity, duration, and frequency. This helps youngsters to comprehend the connection between their feelings and their subsequent respondent behaviors. Residents are also taught that when they are reflective and exercise self-control, they are more likely to become competent at tasks and to experience more fulfilling social relationships.

7. *Target behaviors*: All target behaviors on the reinforcement chart are rated twice daily, in the residence and in the school program, on a

scale from 0 to 4. In each category, the youngster can earn up to 4 credits, which can be exchanged for money, privileges, tokens, etc.

8. *Community restrictions*: Some youngsters, although they advance to the fourth level, may still be subject to community restrictions based upon their treatment needs, their pathology, or the danger that they may pose to themselves or others. This means that a youth placed on "one-to-one" or close staff supervision would have a greater opportunity to advance to Level Four because of tighter controls and greater staff support.

9. *Nonparticipation*: There will be youngsters whose behaviors are so defiant or regressive that they appear not to value any reinforcements, including activities or choices. Some residents will absolutely refuse to participate. For other youth, enforced sampling of activities may increase their reinforcing properties.

DISCUSSION

According to the principles of behavior therapy, all behaviors are learned in response to specific stimuli and reinforcements, or occur as the result of a cause-and-effect equation. Proctor and Dutta (1994) described research findings that show that dysfunctional acquisition of behaviors and psychological disorders are the result of faulty learning experiences. The intent of behavior therapy is for youngsters to understand that the significance of a behavior lies in its consequences. The purpose of contingency management is to help youth to develop life skills, self-control, self-confidence, and skills that enhance group cohesiveness and self-agency. There will be youngsters who will participate in a token economy or a reinforcement system because they are in the program. There will be some who find a token economy and staff positivity comforting, because both provide routine, structure, and a direction to follow. There will be others who will attempt to manipulate staff and any system. They will put in only a minimum effort (Coe, 1975). There will be others who argue over expectations and defy staff, and undermine the efforts of adults. There will be youth who find a reinforcement system stressful. To prevent youngsters from experiencing too much pressure and feeling inadequate, contingency management procedures should be designed and enacted in a positive manner, clearly specifying the desired behaviors as well as problem ones. Staff should emphasize that contingency management is only part of the program, which also includes activities and counseling. Staff demonstrating an interest in youth beyond the system help them to feel safe and connected. Close staff–youth relations help youth overcome antisocial destructive behaviors, which is especially necessary for youth who may be accustomed to distant and uninvolved adults (Pazaratz, 2003).

Children and adolescents will exhibit desired behaviors in return for appropriate and valued rewards (Skinner, 1971). Children and adolescents sometimes condemn or inflict harm on themselves when they fail at tasks, do not get praise, experience delays, or do not get immediate rewards. They may even destroy relationships because they give up or feel the relationship is unfair (Pazaratz, 1993). Destructive behaviors and those that are self-injurious or self-abusive are also reinforcing and can be outside the immediate range of a modifying economy. Nevertheless, staff can intervene in self-harming behaviors and help youth to deal with their shortsightedness or shortcomings. Staff can help residents to find alternative choices in recurring negative situations and to identify choices that are adaptive and less self-defeating. A time-out from reinforcements can be useful, especially for a resident who is too emotionally distraught to respond to expectations. Some residents take any reinforcement system too seriously and may need to be placed on a simplified system so that they experience more success or are more relaxed.

Some staff members will passively accept superficial behavioral change. There are others who will give up on a modifying economy when a resident's behavior is out of control, rationalizing that it is better to give consequences. Although consequences can be applied for extreme behaviors, the effectiveness of behavior therapy is undermined when staff are disjointed in their approach, observations, or charting. Residents will react to staff members or any treatment technique that is not applied consistently (rationally), if staff are viewed as being punitive in their approach, or if residents do not like a particular staff (Pazaratz, 2000c). Intervention strategies must be meaningful, focused, and supportive. Therefore, staff should remember that the rating scale can be skewed or inaccurate even when staff observe the same event and during program transition (i.e., when a resident moves from free time to group programming and back again).

The application of reinforcements should assist residents to become aware of changing expectations and different circumstances. There will be residents who adapt more easily to certain program features, but feel more frustrated with others. Staff should remember that not all residents will respond favorably to adult expectations, to being rated or evaluated, or to reinforcements based upon contingencies. Nevertheless, staff must create living conditions that will help residents to resist contrary influences, and to create conditions for youngsters that allow them to change. A regular review of this treatment methodology is essential in order to ensure that reinforcements are being applied fairly, that the particular needs of each individual are emphasized, and that the level system will be replaced when natural community-based reinforcements or opportunities can be substituted (Pazaratz, 1999).

SUMMARY

Residential treatment is founded on the principle of normalization. This means that the opportunities, expectations, and responsibilities that occur in society (in general) are maintained during placement (Pazaratz, Randall,

Spekkens, Lazor, & Morton, 2000). Although each youngster is unique, nevertheless each youth must comprehend that he or she is also part of the therapeutic community, its reality, and its expectations for normative behaviors. When youth do not cooperate with staff and follow their treatment plan, subsequently their personal freedom and choices are limited. A large part of how youth feel and behave toward staff and expectations is influenced by their background or relationship with family. Some youth are closed and will not discuss their disappointments because they are too angry or too withdrawn. Resocialization and relearning of appropriate reactions can be brought about with the systematic management of observable behaviors, the use of reinforcements, growth-oriented activities, and an emphasis on positive peer and staff relationships (Burt, Resnick, & Novich, 1998).

The modifying economy's ultimate goal is to assist residents to comprehend that those behaviors that caused them to be admitted to treatment are inappropriate, self-defeating, and often regressive, and therefore must be corrected in order for discharge. When the resident is prevented from acting out or being self-defeating, alternative choices and the learning of new behaviors can be presented to the youngster. However, a modifying system is designed to stabilize youth and cannot sustain profound characterological changes. Therefore, such a system should be discontinued in the final treatment stage (Graziano, 1984) or when youngsters can observe themselves and their peer relations, appraise their actions, and determine if they are increasing their own satisfaction, autonomy, and academic performance while minimizing conflicts and problems. In effect, this means that the residents have matured to the point that they are problem centered and talk openly about problems rather than wrapped up in their own emotions and conflicts. They no longer ruminate and become upset about problems because they realize those attitudes tend to interfere with performance and growth (Ellis, 1994).

CONCLUSION

An individual's ability to self-evaluate and to self-correct reflects positive characterological development (Forehand & Wierson, 1993) and healthy adjustment. For Lefcourt (1982), residential treatment must aim to help the resident evolve from needing environmental controls and support to attaining self-control, self-support, and self-direction. Thus, when a youth develops self-control, there is a co-occurring rise in self-confidence and a belief that his or her life has come together instead of being fragmented and incomplete. The youngster also attains an enhanced self-view that arises from acquiring new behaviors. The youth has filled the hole, or emptiness, in her or his life (Gilmor, 1978). The youngster experiences a growth in personality that assists her or him to respond differently, and to learn from environmental pressures (Frankl, 1962). Thus, the youth will no longer need to be looked after or feel like a victim, but will have mobilized her or his own energies and created her or his own excitement and meaning (White, 1965). Subsequently, upon discharge the youngster will continue to monitor her or his progress and will no longer conclude that experiencing problems, or having deficiencies, renders the self inadequate, worthless, or a misfit. Instead, the youngster is capable of monitoring his or her environment to understand changes as they occur and to deal with change and its impact positively, rather than to react. The youngster will have developed the ability to be whatever she or he can be, and learned to maximize the potential of her or his life, to remain autonomous and to sustain a sense of meaning.

Reinforcement Scale

Name: _____ Week of: _____

Category	Fri.		Sat.		Sun.		Mon.		Tues.		Wed.		Thurs.	
	AM	PM	AM	PM	AM	PM	AM	PM	AM	PM	AM	PM	AM	PM
Verbal fighting with peers and staff; such as swearing, taunting, and antagonizing														
Physical aggression to staff and to peers; such as threats, hitting, kicking, biting, and throwing objects														
Physical abuse to self														
Rule breaking or difficulty following directives; such as leaving property, being late, needing to be supervised to complete tasks, and ignoring														
Destruction of property or misuse of utilities and/or personal effects														
Mood changes, anxiety, tension, unable to relax, or chronic general fearfulness														

Category	Fri.		Sat.		Sun.		Mon.		Tues.		Wed.		Thurs.	
	AM	PM	AM	PM	AM	PM	AM	PM	AM	PM	AM	PM	AM	PM
Becoming easily frustrated or poor impulse control, crying, or short tempered														
Inappropriate sexuality: touching oneself in public, touching others without permission in a sexual way, sexual comments, and the like														
Routine refusal or difficulty with routines and chores														
Poor personal hygiene, or not appropriately dressed														
Difficulty with chores, room not tidy, bed not made, becoming too dependent on chores, and having trouble functioning without structure														
Inappropriate attention seeking, difficulty maintaining attention, or easily distracted														
Interfering in others' affairs, not minding one's own business, or criticizing others														

Category	Fri. AM	Fri. PM	Sat. AM	Sat. PM	Sun. AM	Sun. PM	Mon. AM	Mon. PM	Tues. AM	Tues. PM	Wed. AM	Wed. PM	Thurs. AM	Thurs. PM
Falsifying complaints, or complaining of physical ailments or lethargy														
Withdrawn (e.g., isolates self, or secretive) or unable to be alone														
Difficulty accepting advice or criticism, or disobedient														
Chronic liar: makes up stories or deliberately knows something is false														
Boisterousness, rowdiness, hyperactivity, or short attention span														
Unable to relate positively to staff and peers														
Does not express self verbally and/or appropriately, feelings easily hurt, or jealous of attention paid to others														
Stealing or using another person's belongings without permission														
Losing property that belongs to another person or the agency														

Category	Fri. AM	Fri. PM	Sat. AM	Sat. PM	Sun. AM	Sun. PM	Mon. AM	Mon. PM	Tues. AM	Tues. PM	Wed. AM	Wed. PM	Thurs. AM	Thurs. PM
Misuse of food, stealing food, hiding it, destroying it, overeating, starvation, or bingeing on snacks														
Irregular bodily functions, soiling, bedwetting, does not dispose of body waste, spreading feces, or urinating publicly														
Inappropriate affect, speech, mannerisms, or body language: for example, stands too close or spits when talking														
Extreme agitations, head banging, rocking, picking at body, or pulling own hair														
Substance use: cigarettes, drugs, alcohol, using inhalants, or sniffing glue or gasoline														
Does not seek help or additional information appropriately from peers, staff, parents, and so on														
Does not use equipment such as telephone, TV, radios, and the like with care, or does not wait turn														

Category	Fri.		Sat.		Sun.		Mon.		Tues.		Wed.		Thurs.	
	AM	PM	AM	PM	AM	PM	AM	PM	AM	PM	AM	PM	AM	PM
Does not engage in hobbies and interests to occupy self and to fulfill self-interests without pressure														
Late, tardy, not on time, or not where supposed to be														
Elopement, runs away, AWOL, or purposeful absenteeism														
Roughhousing: constantly bumping, tripping, poking, tugging, wrestling, and so on														
Cruelty to animals: deliberately hurts, injures, or maims them														
Bullies, mocks, teases, degrades, insults, or gangs up on others														
Incomplete, quits, or does not participate or sustain efforts, activities, or chores														
Intolerant, negative, angry, demanding, abrupt, or loud speech														
Immediacy: will not wait for turn, budges in front of others, talks over others, or needs staff attention first														

	Fri.		Sat.		Sun.		Mon.		Tues.		Wed.		Thurs.	
Category	AM	PM	AM	PM	AM	PM	AM	PM	AM	PM	AM	PM	AM	PM
Does not notify staff when hurt or injured, when someone else is hurt or injured, or when he or she damages property														
Uses phone or equipment without permission; inappropriate use of phone and computers														
Totals:														
Staff initials:														

POINT SCALE

Reinforcement value and frequency:

4 = Never—behavior did not occur

3 = Seldom—only one occurrence

2 = Occasional—behavior occurred two or three times

1 = Frequent—behavior occurred four to six times

0 = Constant—behavior occurs all the time

Total points:

Present Score _____ /2240

Previous Score _____ /2240

Change _____ /2240

EXPLANATION OF REINFORCEMENT CATEGORIES

1. *Verbal fighting with peers and staff*: This category is defined in the context of the individual youngster, in relation to other youth, within his or her normative age group. If the youngster has a history of outbursts that are highly elevated into a clinical range of concerns, which would suggest severe behavioral adjustment problems. The youth earns reinforcement for not fighting verbally (meaning a personal attack on a peer or staff) with screaming, arguing, threatening, being overly loud, or engaging in temper tantrums. Verbally aggressive behaviors can lead to physical fights, assaults, running away, fire setting, substance abuse, etc.

2. *Physical aggression against staff and peers*: Youngsters can and do attack other residents and staff physically, and with objects. Although it is essential to clearly define rules, policies, and structure as well as provide challenging activities, there still will be acting-out behaviors. This externalizing scale reflects extremely high levels of rule-breaking and aggressive behaviors that create significant behavioral management challenges, in addition to serious concerns for the safety of the youth in question and others. Sometimes, police intervention is necessary because nothing else works.

3. *Physical abuse to self*: There are youngsters who run into the street, climb on roofs, and engage in behaviors without apparent awareness of the potential for serious physical harm, in spite of repeated admonitions not to do so and attempts to provide adequate supervision. Youngsters are reinforced for talking about their feelings and frustrations, and when they count, chart, or note their emotions in a daily journal rather than act them out. They are reinforced for dealing with their anxieties or problems, and for seeking help from staff, peers, or family.

4. *Difficulty following directives*: Deals with the passive-aggressive or passive-avoidant youth, who has an excuse for everything. His or her defense mechanism is denial, projection, and/or intellectualization. Some youth can become passive-dependent, especially if they feel they have been repeatedly let down, or their needs are not met, and their naïve expectations about others can in turn produce resentment. Cooperative and compliant behaviors are emphasized and reinforced.

5. *Inappropriate swearing*: This category requires staff not to overreact to foul language, but to teach youngsters how context affects a word's meaning and to differentiate between appropriate and inappropriate swearing, such as swearing in public or in a place of worship, provoking other youth and staff through insults, or screaming expletives at a neighbor and/or responding in kind. Part of resocializing adolescents is to help them understand that in the real world,

some language can become problematic for others, and we live with other people. Youth are cautioned not to personalize, make fun of a person, or degrade others. Respect for others and assertiveness are emphasized. Residents earn reinforcements when they control disruptive and disrespectful language.

6. *Mood changes, withdrawn, and anxious*: No one is punished for having these symptoms. They are reinforced for talking about them. There are youth who can force their attention away from things that are unpleasant so there is not obsessive worry. There are also youth who ignore issues that they should be concerned about. There are youngsters who purposely get overly boisterous, who will not participate, or who are anxious and do not deal with their feelings appropriately. This would include a high frequency of crying, being afraid, feeling unloved and worthless, being overly self-conscious, worrying, etc.

7. *Becoming easily frustrated*: The functions of staff are to encourage adolescents to reflect on what is going on and to problem solve, so that youngsters earn reinforcements when they cooperate with staff rather than block and avoid solutions, or do not ask for help and do not respond to help; and to help youth to examine what they want and need so that their gratification will be self-determined.

8. *Inappropriate sexuality*: This category does not apply to all residents. It is defined in the context of group living and does require that some residents have careful staff monitoring and redirection. This category includes not only physical acts such as touching one's genitals in public but also making sexual comments, sexually aggressive comments, or degrading utterances toward women or those who have different lifestyle choices. It targets youth who walk around with a pants zipper undone, draw attention to their genitals, objectify women, violate personal boundaries by touching others inappropriately, make sexual gestures, or attempt to engage in sexual activity openly by inviting touch, pornography, etc. Thus, some youth need to work on this problem and their attitude, and they are reinforced when they make changes.

9. *Difficulty with routines and chores (undo dependence)*: Residents are taught what is expected of them. When they choose not to comply with expectations, or they perform tasks, chores, or routines incompletely, they do not earn reinforcements. Some youth display undesirable behavior patterns, lack motivation to change, or show a limited capacity for organization and integration. This is a category that often requires constant monitoring; otherwise, personal responsibilities will not be initiated, completed, or completed properly. There are, in fact, adolescents who tend to forget things they have learned. Staff often feel they are reteaching ideas and concepts.

Reinforcements are a good motivator for improved memory, compliance, and proficiency.

10. *Poor personal hygiene, or not appropriately dressed*: Some youngsters refuse to wash and have terrible hygiene. Their body odor can be intolerable to others. Yet, they will not change their clothes, wash them, or keep themselves clean. Some girls dress revealingly. Reinforcements are used to get youngsters to comply with reasonable grooming habits and to dress appropriately.

11. *Room not tidy, or bed not made*: Many residents do this without reminders. Others resist. Others will do it only with consistent reminders. Because there are usually two residents per room, orderliness improves the atmosphere in shared accommodations.

12. *Inappropriate attention seeking*: This means to engage in behaviors that can be destructive to self, others, and property, and cause serious risk or harm. There are adolescents who injure themselves or others to prove how tough or noncaring they can be. There are also youngsters who need to learn how to wait their turn and not to interfere with others, and still others who cannot interact without being loud or the center of attention.

13. *Interfering in others' affairs*: This means being preoccupied with other people's problems or telling others what to do. This category attempts to prevent a resident from joining in when two residents are talking, or a staff and a resident are discussing an issue, and the bystander who has no involvement in the issue takes sides, thereby triangulating the discussion; or he or she spreads misinformation, reveals privileged information, or tells falsehoods about a peer or staff.

14. *Complaining of physical ailments and lethargy*: There are youngsters who fabricate an illness or tell a story so that they do not have to go to school or on an outing. They falsely claim to suffer from a headache, stomachache, etc. This category also includes the chronic complainer who cannot stand the food, thinks the pool water is too cold or too hot, doesn't like any movie, thinks the activity is always boring, never gets things his or her way, always has to sit in the front seat of the van, thinks the staff are stupid, insists the staff don't like him or her, and claims the staff play favorites. They may also have a history of physical complaints, or be preoccupied with body functioning, illness, and disease. When a youngster is in fact sick, however, he or she must receive immediate medical attention.

15. *Isolates self or unable to be alone*: This category is for the avoidant perceptual style in which the youngster "misses" many details of his or her environment that, if properly perceived and interpreted, would help the adolescent to make better judgments and choices, such as participating or responding to staff overtures for connection. An

avoidant perceptual style will contribute to a higher need for structure, because the youth fails either to perceive important details and nuances, or to interpret accurately those that he or she has observed. Nevertheless, youngsters who prefer to be alone, sad, or melancholy can be motivated to participate.

16. *Difficulty accepting advice or confrontation, and purposefully disobedient*: Some youngsters cannot accept advice no matter how it is phrased, such as in education about sexuality or the dangers of drugs, alcohol, and smoking. Some will not accept any kind of confrontation such as "Your behavior is destructive," or, where the youngster is willfully disobedient, "Stop hitting Billy," or "You'll break the vacuum cleaner if you yank on the cord." For many youngsters, this category does not apply because they stop when asked.

17. *Chronic liar*: This category is a general one for any kind of chronic and pervasive rather than temporary and situational behavior. This usually reflects a serious impairment in reality testing or self-control. This category can also target deviousness and misleading behaviors such as drug use, sexual exploitation, physical threats (intimidation), history of theft and any kind of antisocial or delinquent acts that need to be monitored, and an inability to be open and genuine. It is a category that is elaborated upon specific to some young people and under some circumstances.

18. *Boisterousness, rowdiness, hyperactivity, and short attention span*: Delete the words and ideas that do not apply to the youth's individual style of functioning, or substitute something specific to the individual that does apply. That is the idea of all categories. They are tailored to the individual or to the individual in context.

19. *Unable to relate positively to staff and peers*: This category applies to someone who willfully undermines, subverts, or emotionally harms others by having total disregard for the feelings or rights of others. They go out of their way to hurt, control, and dominate others, or subjugate them, so that the other will lose out on the opportunity for tranquility, pleasure, or success.

20. *Does not express self verbally and/or appropriately*: The youngster's thinking is characterized by an escapist aspect whereby he or she subjugates reality to fantasy. The youngster will tend to imagine how others or fortuitous events will make decisions for him or herself, and this contributes to an unhelpful level of dependence upon others. This makes some youngsters especially prone to being led by those more interpersonally skilled or manipulative. Notwithstanding the individual's proneness to defensiveness, when the youngster is confronted, he or she falsely claims that he or she was taken advantage of rather than acknowledging his or her level of responsibility. An example of this occurs when a youth participates in bullying.

CHAPTER 7

The Role of Direct Care Staff in Residential Treatment

PURPOSE OF POLICIES AND PROCEDURES

Residential treatment as a process is a function of a shared language and a shared reality. Direct care staff are considered the most important clinical component in the residential treatment of youngsters with emotional problems. Children and adolescents placed in group care especially need healthy relationships with adults, so that they can navigate the complex social and peer pressures they will encounter. Best practices in youth work are considered to occur when interventions are not experienced as intrusive, assist in the self-inquiry process, and stimulate the youth's developmental potential (Pazaratz, 2000b, 2000c, 2000d, 2003b). This chapter describes the skills and competencies expected of child and youth care workers in residential treatment. The format that is detailed was developed at the Oshawa/Whitby Crisis Intervention Centre (Pazaratz, 1999c) and can be utilized as a job description, or as the basis of a youth worker's evaluation for promotional opportunities. Although there are many duties expected of front-line staff, the nature of the worker's role evolves as the worker matures and develops the skills necessary to harmonize his or her efforts with the treatment needs of residents (Pazaratz, 2003a).

Residential treatment provides the disturbed youth with the critical support of direct care staff. Youth workers are assisted by the residential supervisor to design and to implement therapeutic parameters that foster each youngster's sense of safety, learning, and growth (Stoltenberg, McNeill, & Delworth,

1998; and see Pazaratz, 2005b). Staff members interpret daily events and create meaning from interactions. Staff members provide youngsters with the stimulation required for emotional growth (Pazaratz, 2000c). Treatment is enacted when staff emphasize the importance or value of relationships. Frontline staff enact everyday solutions for solving the problems of family life (relationships) that are often the main basis for developmental delays and social skills deficits (Ivey, 1986). Workers use the events of daily life to help youth learn from experience, through trial and error, and to improve competencies through skills acquisition (Pazaratz, 2000a).

It is the naturally occurring conditions within the milieu, or shared living environment, that fashion the opportunities and conditions for residents to relearn, resocialize, and work through emotions (Pazaratz, 2000b). Thus, staff assist youth at correcting deficits in these important interpersonal and intrapsychic areas of their lives. Staff offer residents an opportunity to return to earlier experiences, which enables them to not only deal with their problems as these occur in the present but also resolve those issues of the past (Bowlby, 1969) in a safer environment. In other words, the child and youth care worker operates within the youth's "life space" and helps the youngster to process all of his or her feelings in the here and now (Redl & Wineman, 1957a), no matter what the source of those feelings. Thus, in residential treatment and care, staff members concern themselves with helping children and adolescents to understand the entirety of their existence and its interconnectedness (i.e., past, present, and future; Pazaratz, 2003a). Staff emphasize meaning as the central purpose of life, so that, as according to Frankl (1967), healing occurs through experience.

POLICY AND PROCEDURE MANUAL

The policy and procedure manual has become the standard or the basis for operating any type of children's shelter in North America. The first policy and procedures manual ever in use in a North American residential program was developed (invented) by the author in 1975, when he was recruited to convert the Oshawa/Whitby Crisis Intervention Centre, a drug rehabilitation program for young people ages 16 to 25, into a Children's Mental Health Centre (Pazaratz, 1998a). Although the format and scope of a residential program's policy and procedure manual have evolved and become more sophisticated, nevertheless the function of this document has remained the same. The manual's intent is to articulate the operational policies enacted in a residence, and to describe the corresponding procedures that staff must follow to achieve each of the stated objectives. In other words, every jurisdiction that licenses children's residential programs or shelters in North America has mandated practices (which are not necessarily best practices) that are prescribed in legislation and regulations (standards).

The policy and procedure manual is a means by which treatment agencies interpret and enact their mission statement and program philosophy. The manual details and explains group care practices that absolutely must be followed. The manual describes how the licensing criteria or regulations are to be implemented, maintained, and complied with by direct care staff and the agency's administration. The licensing of treatment and care programs requires that staff must be able to demonstrate their knowledge of the rules of the agency and that the agency has enacted the required policies in their record keeping. This means that every youth worker within the agency must be versed in the treatment rationale and care policies and procedures during their interactions with residents, other staff, outside agencies, and the like. The manual focuses on the daily workload, job skills, and record keeping of the agency. The manual is a means for orienting staff to the agency's expectations of them and their roles, and for ongoing instruction, referencing, and training. The manual contains sample forms that are used by staff and establishes procedures to be followed under specific circumstances.

The policy and procedure manual provides staff with a framework for developing their own youth worker conduct within the context of a professional code. In the practical application of the manual, the task for the worker is to manage the group home's daily operation by establishing priorities, workload distribution, and ethical decision making. Workers are required to monitor and maintain inventories, prepare requisitions and orders, purchase foodstuff and supplies, organize and maintain work areas, and supervise use and storage of the home's equipment. Workers are also responsible for the overall upkeep of the kitchen, storage areas, utility spaces, staff office, living and sleeping quarters, and surrounding premises. Workers are expected to complete daily log notes, document behaviors, record statistics, complete tracking forms, and maintain routine office records, incident reports, and clinical summaries.

In adhering to the scope of the policy and procedure manual, the youth worker utilizes formal and informal communication in a professional manner; adheres to proper procedures; follows established lines of authority, or protocol; and works within and around rules. Creating a safe environment is a strict requirement and a best practice that includes such procedures as holding fire drills, being certified in first aid, and being qualified in restraint procedures. Workers understand their individual role, their role as a team member, the purpose of teams, and the daily management of the group home, and can conduct emergency procedures. Staff members often are required to administer medications that have been prescribed by (consulting) physicians and to document dispensing of these (Pazaratz, 2003b). In those programs that utilize a token economy, the worker is able to implement behavior therapy principles, which involve monitoring and coding the frequency, intensity, and duration of behaviors (Pazaratz, 2003c). Workers are responsible for the residents having transportation, as necessary, and/or for coordinating the use of public transportation to ensure that residents attend (community) school(s), are involved in work or volunteer programs, participate in family visits or meetings, can practice their religious beliefs, and attend all appointments (e.g., medical and dental) on time.

The policy and procedure manual identifies the following:

1. The purpose of the residence
2. The program provided in the residence
3. The procedures relating to the admission and to the discharge of residents
4. The practices for planning, monitoring, and evaluating the care provided to residents
5. Procedures for the maintenance of records
6. Practices for maintaining discipline
7. The program provided for the residents (principle)
8. The methods of maintaining security of the residents (procedure)
9. The administrative structure of the residence (procedure)
10. Staff and supervisory procedures to be followed by employees
11. The conduct and discipline of employees (practice)
12. Emergency procedures to be followed
13. Financial practices employed for operation of the residence
14. The practices enacted by employees to encourage residents to participate in community activities
15. Treatment techniques that are prohibited (principle)
16. Protocol by which residents can express their concerns or complaints
17. Procedures governing punishment and isolation methods that may be permitted in the residence

PARENTING SKILLS

Staff are required to model genuineness, responsiveness, attunement, and intellectual and affective sympathy; define behavioral limits and consequences; and provide unconditional positive regard. Youth workers engage in a number of parental functions and responsibilities. The parental role provides for the youth's psychological and physical needs. These are enacted by staff emphasizing social skills and the importance of self-care routines (i.e., hygiene habits, physical appearance, grooming, and wearing clothes that are appropriate, in good repair, and in season). Ultimately, the worker is able to integrate the parental functions of child management with clinical treatment in a unified whole, or in an individual's treatment plan. Assisting youth to fit into the social group is facilitated by creating a homelike atmosphere and by organizing the living space. Staff are abreast of the cooperative interactions of residents and those of fellow staff. Maintaining a positive and harmonious atmosphere is the cornerstone of the care aspects of residential treatment. This principle underscores providing for residents' physical well-being and emotional needs (Pazaratz, 2003b). Creating a facilitating environment is a precondition for coordinating interactions that meet program goals and are basic to good youth care practices. With this purpose in mind, youth workers set and follow rules and establish boundaries that create the predictable environment (Fewster & Garfat, 1998).

Teaching residents the importance of the upkeep of the living environment includes providing instruction in performing chores and completing housekeeping duties, in the home and on the surrounding property. Residents often need to be reminded or shown how to care for their personal possessions, to respect other peoples' property and living space, and to be mindful of the orderly use of furnishings, materials, equipment, and articles that belong to the group home or to peers. This encompasses not misusing items, misplacing items, or using them without permission. This values clarification includes instructing residents to wait their turn; not to monopolize resources such as the TV, DVD player, and radios; and not to use them in such a way that is annoying to others, but to share, cooperate, and show respect for others and their right to enjoyment, privacy, and solitude. Included here is the reality that youngsters come from different backgrounds and have a variety of problems, experiences, styles, and approaches, and understanding of how their actions affect others. Staff are able to help residents to comprehend and tolerate different lifestyles, as well as the diversity and multicultural creeds found among individuals, and embedded in different backgrounds, different religions, and society (Pazaratz, 2000a, 2000b, 2000c, 2000d). There are tremendous social benefits for children and adolescents when they learn to accept peers who may have divergent beliefs and perspectives. Youngsters become empowered when they develop empathy, ask others to treat them with dignity, and in turn demonstrate respect and tolerance.

Staff are often called upon to resolve conflicts between residents. This includes the ability to differentiate between and to deal with normal "sibling rivalry." It is important for youth in a group living environment to develop an awareness of, an appreciation for, and an understanding of social decorum, or to develop restraint in social interactions, as opposed to attention seeking and exhibiting grandiosity. Many residents are undersocialized. They can display behaviors that are too overt, loud, and overbearing. Consequently, they are often noisy or demanding in their speech, and offensive in their manner, becoming intrusive, aggressive, and callous toward other residents, adults, or individuals in the community. Staff are required to assist residents to be aware of and to recognize how their behaviors or style of interaction can irritate, displease, and at times offend others. Refining of social skills includes realizing that one's behaviors can adversely affect relationships with others, yet interacting so that one's behaviors are not disturbing, annoying, or provoking. Learning to respect the rights and boundaries of others helps youth to fit in socially (Pazaratz, 2000a, 2000b, 2000c, 2000d). In essence, youth are taught to focus on self-contentment or tranquility, in order to become self-directed. The acquisition of social and life skills also provides for more successful participation in groups, in "the community," and academically.

A life skills program is the means by which residents learn everyday information that helps them to function independently and to obtain desired resources and reinforcements. The learning of life skills includes essential living skills such as the preparation of nutritious meals, budget planning, knowledge of banking, money management skills, and the use of community resources (Pazaratz, 2000b, 2000c, 2000d). Learning to be autonomous and independent includes the ability to resist impulsive decisions, to understand financial limitations and obligations, and to resist the need or the pressures to please others. This may be best taught by those staff persons who have learned from discharging their own financial obligations and adhering to their limitations.

Youth workers are often required to apply general first aid and home nursing, or to attend to a resident who is ill (for whatever reason), on medication, or rehabilitating from a minor injury. The worker needs to be attuned to the youth's physical problems as well as to his or her emotional needs, and ensures that youngsters are seen by the appropriate health care provider or at a community health resource as necessary. There will be occasions when the youth worker will have to react quickly, or respond to emergencies. Some individual problems can escalate into crises, and if these issues are not well managed, they can directly affect others. Many conflicts, incidents, and occurrences can be preempted by the worker's careful monitoring of individuals and the group. In other words, workers are aware of ongoing treatment and care needs, are thoughtful in programming, and demonstrate attentiveness to the emotional content of communication and the climate of the group. Through careful monitoring of residents and their use of household objects, workers ensure the safe use of equipment. Workers caution residents to be thoughtful during physical interaction in sports, games, activities, and the like. To promote safety and prevent potentially problematic situations (injuries or accusations of physical or sexual abuse), "horseplay," wrestling, and physical aggression are prohibited, whether between residents, between staff and residents, or between staff and staff. In fact, any type of physical touching, including hugging a youngster, can be misinterpreted. Therefore, staff are cautioned to practice defensive youth work (Pazaratz, 2000c).

A child or adolescent's developmental process includes encountering and dealing with individual fears. Child care workers are required (by definition) to help youth deal with stressful situations. There are daily issues that can be problematic, such as physical illness, psychosomatic complaints, practicing good health habits, discipline in eating, and overcoming peer pressure to smoke, use alcohol and drugs, become sexually active, and defy staff. Workers need to know the young person's emotional capacity, intellectual limitations, and physical capabilities. Workers teach basic self-help and survival skills, maintain an orderly group home setting, and teach youth to enjoy themselves in self-sustaining activities. Workers recognize a youth's need for independence by helping the youth plan for it. Group living challenges youth to adjust to others and to identify for themselves a position and a role in the unit or group home, while also maintaining their position in their own family. Promoting normal interactional patterns includes residents experiencing friendship within the home, outside the group, in the community, and at school.

Youth workers are required to provide ongoing monitoring of individuals and the group to ensure that youngsters are adjusting and benefit from their interactions and treatment experiences. Youth workers assist children and adolescents to integrate within, and to participate as a member of, the larger group. This is enacted by teaching the ideals of respect, fairness, and positive peer pressure. There can be contradictory group pressures, or subgroups both within the unit and in the community at large. Residents often need assistance to recognize and to deal with negative peer pressure, anti-adult attitudes, or countercultural values (Carkhuff & Berenson, 1977). Staff support healthy male–female interactions, and promote acceptance of nonstereotypical sex or gender roles. This is underscored when workers model genuineness and tolerance. There will be times when youngsters bond or even overidentify with staff. However, when youth become verbally and physically aggressive toward staff, staff members are required to maintain decorum, calm negative situations, and resolve underlying issues (Pazaratz, 2003b).

Many youngsters who require placement have grown up under circumstances that discouraged honesty and reliability in relationships. Instead, they experienced systematic training in dishonesty and betrayal. Youth workers' interventions aim to liberate youth from the distorting influences of their past and encourage them to look at their interactions with more reflectivity and to seek out authenticity. Nevertheless, instances may arise where children or adolescents make accusations that trigger investigations, which obviously will create tension for staff and youngsters alike. These are extremely stressful occasions when youngsters accuse other youth, staff, and even parents or family members of abuse. Allegations of impropriety will lead to investigations because reporting to social services or to a Children's Aid Society is mandatory. Sometimes, the matter will include police involvement. Such events are not uncommon in group care environments (or foster home placement); therefore, staff should understand the advantages of practicing youth work defensively and avoid inappropriate touching, horseplay, foul language, harsh discipline, or reactions that could be interpreted as punitive, exploitive, degrading, sexual, or child maltreatment or abuse. Following approved restraint procedures is mandatory, and a best practice. And staff should attempt to build a positive, trusting relationship with each resident and with fellow staff, and to accurately document their interactions. When arbitrating or resolving disputes, staff should not be influenced by personal prejudices, biases, or needs (i.e., countertransference; Pazaratz, 2000d).

THEORY AND PRACTICE OF THERAPEUTIC ACTIVITIES

Therapeutic activities are one of the most important parts of a residential program. They are the context by which residents develop skills, experiment with roles, and discover knowledge about themselves and others, a dimension for having fun and an opportunity to enjoy social interactions with others (Pazaratz, 1998a). Life skills learning and stimulation of intellectual capacity also occur in activities, as does the development of self-satisfying and ego-enhancing talents and interests. Activities bolster judgment or reflective thinking, provide stress relief, and offer an opportunity to cultivate fine and gross motor skills. Activities include play situations that create an outlet for the expression of creative feelings.

Drama, art, music, acting, sports, and games are included in this category and are viewed as being of primary importance for engaging a disparate group of children and adolescents who possess unique interests and function at different levels due to age, cognitive capacity, physical abilities, and emotional development (Pazaratz, 1997). A well-developed activities and/or recreational program allows all children and adolescents to participate at their level of development, dexterity, and interest, in spite of uneven talent and dissimilar styles of responding and participating, or due to limitations of language, knowledge, and perspectives. Through self-expression, the insecure, awkward, or unsophisticated young person can be made to feel that his or her ideas, meaning, and way of communicating are understood. Activities that include the concept of play are natural and necessary for the healthy development of all children and adolescents (Pazaratz, 1998a). They provide an avenue to explore boundaries, to challenge oneself, and to compete with others. Thus, activities should be designed to assist residents to build rapport with peers and staff, to acquire self-satisfaction, and to learn about and to use the community; there should be an opportunity to identify and to learn about feelings that occur in social interactions.

Child and youth care workers are expected to participate in activities and to physically keep up with children and adolescents. Workers emphasize the value of fitness through sports and exhibit sportsmanship. The worker teaches rules of games, identifies and obtains required material and equipment, secures the use of community resources, sets realistic levels of competition, selects activities for specific circumstances, integrates youngsters into activities, teaches youth how to get enjoyment out of activities, and distinguishes playful (friendly) behaviors from misbehaviors. Some children and adolescents must be taught how to play, relate to others, and enjoy themselves and stay in the moment. Of especial importance is to provide youngsters with opportunities for silent and relaxation activities, musical programs, and arts and crafts, and to experience nature through camping, hiking, and outdoor adventures (Pazaratz, 1998a).

Specific activities should be tailored or selected for children and adolescents with handicaps, learning or developmental impediments, and coordination difficulties. In other words, no youngster should be overlooked, limited, or prevented from participating fully because of a lower level of skills development or functioning, or because of physical disadvantages. Activities should be designed to assist in building rapport with peers and staff. Activities can expedite the identification of feelings, awareness of others and their interests, and the repairing of ego. Activities can also foster group cohesion and attachment to adults, provide learning in games, assist with acquisition of cognitive and problem-solving skills, stimulate creativity, and advance the development of self-enhancing talents and interests (Karp, Butler, & Bergstram, 1998). The worker must time activities, limit the area to be used, organize the event, establish or explain rules, remind participants of how knowledge gained in activities can be transferred to other events, and abet or direct the individual and the group to handle the transition calmly from the termination of the activity to the next part of the daily schedule. Sometimes, a discussion of the events and processing of intense feelings is necessary to resolve lingering hostilities, or to reflect upon the joy gained from interactions (Pazaratz, 1998b).

INTERVIEWING AND COUNSELING SKILLS

There will be unique counseling opportunities in the course of each day, and the youth worker should take advantage of these. The youth worker will be required to perform structured and unstructured, or "spur of the moment" (life space), counseling (Redl & Wineman, 1957b) concerning interpersonal or intrapsychic conflict. Awareness of these potentially problematic situations means that the worker is prepared and able to select or provide an atmosphere conducive to counseling; utilize information from the moment; be cognizant of each resident's moods, fluctuation in moods, or problems; and show the resident how his or her behaviors are part of a syndrome (referral problems) or cluster of issues. The worker should be able to maintain a focus on the youth's problems and to show the youth how issues from the past are set off in the present. The worker also points out and clarifies the meaning of behaviors while showing a genuine interest in or empathy for the client (i.e., the youth; Rogers, 1951). This includes providing the resident with face-saving opportunities and the security of knowing that the worker is available and will follow through on commitments and promises. The worker understands that counseling sessions are not meant to convince the resident to accept consequences, discipline, or punishment, but are aimed at helping the youth to understand him or herself in the context of interactions with others, the environment, and his or her future (Yalom, 1983).

Counseling sessions include the mutual agreement of goals and the nature of ongoing sessions. In counseling sessions, the youth worker recognizes and develops the therapeutic potential of youngsters, directs and controls sessions, helps youngsters to modify and to change goals, and is able to end sessions in a timely and meaningful fashion. The worker is able to evaluate the progress, or the effect of sessions, and the impact these have on relationships and the youth's subsequent behavior in the group home (Carkhuff & Berenson, 1977). Both formal and informal counseling are enacted to help youth learn to make better choices, have greater flexibility, and maximize the use of relationships and opportunities within the environment and community. The worker is able to articulate his or her areas of expertise and interests, but also to recognize his or her limitations due to training and education (Pazaratz, 2000a, 2000b). When children or adolescents misbehave, even though consequences are applied rationally, the youth may feel that he or she is the victim of external forces. Without the youth understanding the relationship between the consequence and his or her misbehavior, it is unlikely the youth will internalize a locus of control. The youth's dignity becomes compromised unless the youth comprehends that consequences are a result of behaviors, or due to his or her choices, and not because the youth is disliked and being picked on.

There will be occasions when workers will have to change rules or to modify the directions of sessions. There will be an ongoing effort to encourage youngsters to make independent choices. Counseling includes workers dealing with personally sensitive matters, using appropriate probing questions, expressing personal opinions (but not opinions that are countercultural), and communicating in a direct and forthright manner. A professional counseling approach includes the youth worker utilizing eye contact and correct use of language and voice tone, and seeking to clarify information. Developing rapport with each resident, at his or her level of comprehension, helps the youth worker to understand and to be understood. Counseling sessions require the worker to test the effectiveness of communication, or the client's (youngster's) level of understanding (Carkhuff, 1969). It is also necessary for workers to help youth to recognize the range and source of their emotions by labeling them, to understand them in a social context, and to teach them how to change negative emotions (Stark, 1990). This process may include "reframing," which is a technique designed to change the youth's view of the problem, or "relabeling" a specific behavior to help youth to reframe the problem on their own.

Residential treatment is a process that continually shapes and reshapes the youngster through discourse, interactions with others and objects, and the embodied sensations, memory, and personal biography of the youth (Lupton, 1998). Counseling will include active listening, nonverbal cues, empathy, elicitation of feelings, reflecting feelings, use of silence, challenging, exploration, assessing facts to verify accuracy of information, and recognizing and dealing with blocking and other defense mechanisms (Rogers, 1951). Interpretation of issues, labeling of behaviors, and confrontation are also employed judiciously.

On occasion, sessions will result from interactions that have occurred or are occurring with others. The worker will either intervene in such situations or be asked to become involved. The worker observes and is able to process nonverbal cues that reveal a client's (child's) intrapsychic conflict or emotional undercurrent (Carkhuff, 1969). To help a youngster improve his or her reality testing, the worker may have to use a counterdelusional approach, consequences, time-outs, and the addition of limits; redefine boundaries; and reframe issues to deescalate a volatile situation. The youth worker's intervention will be based on and influenced by the conditions, time and setting, or nature of interactions, and the emotional tone of the individual or group. The worker may be forced to make immediate decisions, to take action, and to take control of or contain the youth for his or her safety or that of others. Consequences may become part of the resolution or the restitution process. Knowledge of ending sessions (such as debriefing) and providing follow-up, when necessary, are also integral to counseling.

CHILD CARE WORK METHODOLOGY

There are certain specific skills that are required of the child and youth care worker. The worker must realize that he or she is a model of mature conduct and therefore employs appropriate, language, behavior, problem-solving approaches, values, ideals, judgment of right from wrong, and reality testing. This is especially true while interacting with other professionals or during community outings. Thus, it follows that the worker must establish a positive and meaningful relationship with each youth, but also implement rewards and consequences judiciously, without coercion, while encouraging the youth to vigorously pursue self-enhancing choices and behaviors (Breggin, 1997). These ideas are consistent with focusing on meaning that arises from experiences or learning from interactions, such as understanding relationships and being informed by the environment (Frankl, 1967). In this way, the purpose of group care is to teach the youngster social and negotiation skills, and to develop self-care and self-preservation skills.

It is not always easy for workers to achieve a connection with youth because some youth perceive workers as interfering with their rights, whereas others do not believe or trust staff. But workers will not always be able to reassure youth about their motives or intentions. Thus, workers may be required to deal with a youth's hostility, resentment, or testing or manipulative behaviors. There may be situations in which workers must defend themselves or others from physically aggressive behaviors. Nevertheless, in spite of the resident's threats or negative reactions, the worker is required to outline and follow through on consequences. Interventions include identifying for youth those day-to-day events or interactions that affect the youth. Youngsters often do not see that their behaviors are problematic for others, or that they become engaged in circular conflicts. The youngster may not recognize how other youth influence his or her beliefs and actions, or how he or she is being manipulated. Youngsters are often reluctant to admit that they manipulate others, allow themselves to be followers, or encourage peers to be negative and to act out. Variously, the worker will discourage inappropriate behavior through verbal intervention, choose to ignore certain behaviors, or restate expectations for the individual and/or the group.

Workers are often compelled to intervene in hassles and disputes. Unless the worker knows the issues, circumstances may escalate if the worker jumps to conclusions. The worker may have to redirect youngsters from nonproductive activities or too much inactivity. However, the worker should not moralize because this is viewed as a "break in empathy." Consequences for behaviors may need to be clarified, so that residents understand which choices lead to which consequences, and which behaviors are subject to tangible reinforcers, and residents accept that even though they may not like it, some limits and boundaries have to be enforced (Glasser, 2000b). Behavior improvement occurs when staff employ behavior therapy principles based upon specific goals defined in contracts. This approach requires staff to accurately identify problems, clearly state how the task will be worked on, target achievable short-term goals, and blend these with long-term goals. Goals need to be practical, realistic, and meaningful. In the contracting process, the worker reviews with youth their progress or lack of progress. The information gained from a contract review is used to set new goals that may be more advanced (i.e., the youngster has overcome comprehension difficulties, limitations, or blocks). Occasionally, additional preparatory efforts need to occur before some goals can be pursued or become more realistic (Pazaratz, 2000d). Some youth cannot maintain their focus for prolonged periods of time and are easily distracted. Learning to follow directives is an important aspect of shaping behaviors. Youth workers need to be able to recognize and take advantage of spontaneous teaching situations, and identify and prepare the youth for unfamiliar situations. When workers recognize and address strengths and weaknesses, this information can be used to help youth reach their goals.

Critical to group care is youth workers' ability to interact with individuals in the context of the group. This means the worker can recognize and is able to counsel those issues of the individual that originate in the group, and are sustained by the group or in reaction to the group. Sometimes, a group focus is more efficient, effective, and necessary for dealing with an individual youth. However, discussion of an individual's personal issues in a group format, or openly, should not be permitted if it is counterproductive, or where there is shame or embarrassment that triggers a resident's regression. Nevertheless, in the group format, the worker speaks about the group's reality testing, or the negative effect that countercultural or manipulative behaviors are inflicting upon the entire group, or any one individual, dyad, or subgroup.

In group counseling, the youth worker evaluates the group's readiness to cooperate. Interactions or discussions with individuals, or the group, will not be successful at stimulating reflection or causing consideration if the individual or group is not prepared to entertain alternatives. There are different techniques the youth worker must be familiar with, such as knowing when to ask direct questions or, alternatively, when to be circumspect. There are flooding (satiation) tactics that can be introduced when appropriate; however, the use of reflection is preferable. When dealing with the group in an activity, or in an informal context, familiarity with different counseling approaches (integrative), and being able to use them contextually when not contraindicated, are vital for the daily management of individuals and the group (Nugent, 1994). This includes utilizing positive reinforcers for cooperative and adaptive behaviors, teaching alternative or substitute behaviors, and applying consequences and the removal of reinforcers for negative acts as necessary.

FAMILY WORK

There will be occasions when direct care staff come in contact, or are directly involved, with a resident's family, or maybe only one parent. It is essential that these contacts are helpful, nonjudgmental, empathic, and informative. This means that all youth workers are to act professionally and to demonstrate that they are courteous, nonblaming, and supportive of the family. Parents may enter into a discussion with staff concerning their legal and parental rights. This may mean that the parents are seeking clarification or that they need assistance with understanding their rights or status vis-à-vis the treatment program. Parents may have concerns such as the fear that their child will abandon the family, have questions about parental versus agency responsibility, or merely seek information on the protocol for contacts, method for communication, and the like. To help parents deal with a sense of powerlessness, or feelings of stress, anger, loss, and emptiness, family members may need reassurance and a level of reconnection with their child.

Child care workers are often called upon by family members to discuss child management techniques and intervention strategies employed with their child. This may require the worker to interpret dynamics or behaviors, and to explain the pressures on a youth, the effects of peer influence, staff expectations, the impact of treatment, and the youth's fear of abandonment. Parents may require youth workers to confirm that they are sensitive to the physical and emotional needs of children in care. This communication may help some parents to develop empathy as well. When workers demonstrate that they understand and are tolerant of the youth's misbehaviors, this approach usually has a calming effect on parents and becomes the model that parents should subscribe to in dealings with their child.

Critical to a youth's adjustment to residential placement is that the youngster's place within his or her family is not disrupted. This means that the youth continues to have access to personal possessions, the youth is supported and encouraged to maintain relationships with family members, and the youngster's involvement with the family pet(s) is sustained. A youngster's attachment to and interactions with his or her family is strengthened by encouraging both the youth and family members to continue their relationships with each other and the nature of their roles within the family. Family relationships are crucial and must be restored in order to assist with the youngster's treatment and eventual return home. Family bonding may improve if workers emphasize the value of the family and its strengths, and the meaning that family members have for one another (Madsen, 1999).

Workers clarify for families the protocols that are to be followed, and the types of contacts with the group home and their child that are workable. Establishing procedures for communicating includes defining mutual expectations and the methods for resolving misunderstandings or disputes. Understanding these procedures helps the family to adjust to the scheduling needs of the group home and to accept the staff's supervision and control of their child. There may be occasions when the worker discusses the youngster's progress or lack of progress with the parents, the child's developmental stage, why certain privileges are allowed, or why certain freedoms or choices are not permitted or have been curtailed. Information sharing with families may also include the relaying (updating) of medical or clinical information, or the effects of diet on a youngster's behavior. The family may need to connect directly to outside professionals and agencies to get some information they seek. Keeping parents abreast of ongoing issues helps them in their interactions with their child and the agency; it also helps them to deal with practical problems, economic concerns, and social issues, and to develop their own schedules or plans.

The youth worker may need to help youth and their family deal with separation as well as to educate and involve the extended family in the treatment protocol. At times, the worker will be privy to the youngster's interactions with his or her family, such as telephone discussions, information provided following home visits, or how the youth and parents interact during the parents' visit to the group home. The worker's interpretations of parent–youth interactions is an opportunity to offer feedback to the youth and his or her family, so that they can make the necessary adjustments or improve future contacts. The worker can help the family to establish realistic expectations to lessen conflicts, and to seek alternative ways to communicate or different methods of approaching long-standing problems. The worker may need to show the family how to behave harmoniously in their home and during visits. This includes assisting them to change their focus from the child's problem and to realize that the family has problems and that family members can be helped to resolve their problems. In these situations, the worker acts as a communication channel for the entire family (Minuchin, 1974).

TREATMENT PLANNING (PLAN OF CARE)

To ensure that they are enacting quality care, youth workers demonstrate objective case conceptualization and factual treatment-planning strategies in their notes, in reports, and during supervision (Berman, 1997). In formulating treatment plans, youth workers assist residents to verbalize their needs and long-term goals from their own perspective (Pazaratz, 2000d). This is done in the context of reviewing and using historical information, clinical records, and case materials so that the clinical approach is realistic and practical. Essential to this planning is information presented by other team members. Developing a treatment plan includes the counting, graphing, and recording of a youth's problematic behaviors; identification of the youth's strengths and weaknesses; noting what reinforcements the youth responds to; and detailing the expectations or issues that cause the youngster to react. This approach includes observing and assessing actions by the youth, noting the nature of interactions with others, and identifying how peers and adults respond (or react) to the youth (Doren, 1993). This information helps to specify which behaviors need to be changed and the preferred method to assist the youth to attain self-control in a growth-enhancing direction.

In assessing developmental adjustment and the meaning of behaviors, youth are understood in terms of their age and stage of development. This knowledge leads to prioritizing behaviors that need to be changed, determining how these are to be worked on, and pinpointing specific methods for goal attainment, daily and weekly. Workers must be able to differentiate which goals should be pursued sequentially, recognize changes that youth have made, and know when goals have been reached. Workers assist youth to develop natural skills and to utilize available resources that meet specific needs. There is an ongoing process of involving youth in planning for the fulfillment of needs and to identify changing or new needs. The worker keeps the treatment team informed of recommended changes to the youth's treatment plan, as well as integrates team members' observations and suggestions in planning. Workers are encouraged to use an eclectic approach in planning. This flexibility prevents workers from becoming dogmatic, demanding, or critical. When worker–youth interactions are empathic, this approach improves connection, and minimizes the prospect of the youth becoming institutionalized, alienated, or reacting to limits and controls (Pazaratz, 2000c).

Feedback and discussions with youth require understanding of which specific information should or should not (for safety reasons) be delivered to the youth. In the face of sudden change, or in keeping with the youth's progress or regression, the worker may be required to modify or adjust certain variables, or intervention techniques. Nevertheless, the youngster's treatment plan or program and the worker must fit together in order to accurately promote the individual's needs. If staff focus only on the resident's behaviors and overlook the young person's feelings and ideas, then there is the danger of misunderstanding and mishandling the youth. However, some level of oppositionalism and defiance can be overcome when staff are flexible with youth and adjust or time their expectations to the youth's receptiveness. This does not mean that the worker gives into or appeases the youth, but that the worker allows the youngster to make decisions and to select choices that promote growth and responsibility. Such an approach is necessary when recognizing how successive treatment stages affect youth, and it helps in understanding regression.

THEORY AND PRACTICE OF WORKING WITH GROUPS

Group counseling is the preferred approach for enacting residential treatment. It is a powerful means for changing the behaviors of individuals (Rose, 1998; and see Pazaratz, Randall, Spekkens, Lazor, & Morton, 2000). Youth workers should be capable of co-leading groups and be able to focus on relevant topics of group living, personal issues, community use, and so on. Group process includes helping members to define, implement, and abide by common or agreed upon rules of conduct. Youth workers are expected to assist individuals to improve peer relationships and social competence, and to become part of the group (Yalom, 1983). The worker should also be able to read the mood or tone of the group, to maximize its efforts, and to defuse situations that can become problematic or chaotic. This means that the worker knows how to identify the roles each youth performs in groups; to be aware of manipulation; to recognize role changes, progress, or regression as it occurs; and to help the group deal with program and information processing, transition periods, and differences that arise due to challenges, impasses, and perspectives (Rose, 1998).

The effective youth worker is able to assist youngsters to recognize how their behavior affects the group and how group actions affect the individual and each member. The worker needs to be able to label and provide feedback regarding caring and communication, and to differentiate between appropriate and inappropriate affect. The youth worker encourages the development of cooperation, negotiation, or problem-solving skills, and the use of positive peer pressure (Yalom, 1983). The youth worker redirects the energies of the group and teaches listening skills, awareness, sensitivity, mutual respect, values clarification, and assertiveness by individual members. The worker also explains group functioning such as process, circular causality, negative attention seeking, and maintenance (stabilization) skills, and provides balance or adult perspective. The worker encourages openness, genuineness, creativity, the use of humor, and "stroking" (Berne, 1973). The worker teaches leadership skills, shared decision making, and conflict resolution. The worker, at times, must identify, label, and deal with scapegoating, bullying, or "ganging up." Discussions, information sharing, and negotiations are important methods for dealing with behaviors that are antisocial, countercultural, and inappropriate. The task for the worker is to challenge the influence of negative ideas so that these do not become dominant, and to teach deductive-reasoning skills or problem-solving strategies, which are especially important when youngsters are outside the group home or in the community (Pazaratz, 2000a, 2000b).

At times, groups are very specific in their purpose. This requires youth workers to assemble, organize, and direct task-oriented groups. There will also be value-laden issues that need to be dealt with, as well as relationship and interpersonal problems or conflicts that will affect the group, its mood, and its style of interacting. Youth workers understand that sometimes negative feelings that arise in the formal group setting will carry over into the daily life of residents. Conversely, not all issues that arise outside the formal group, between any two or more residents, can be or should be brought back to be resolved in the formal group. Antisocial and exploitive behaviors will exist to varying degrees in groups, in dyads, or between subgroups, and will not always surface but will remain secretive and toxic. The issues can include sexual exploitation, the use of illegal substances, bullying, coercion, theft, manipulation, and the like. Sometimes, these behaviors are hidden due to unhealthy and deviant alliances, due to intimidation, as a debt owed, or out of fear of reprisals and retaliation, fear of exposure and punishment, enjoyment of deviance, bullying, or risk taking. The youth worker should know the signs that reveal these undercurrents and be able to probe for information and confirmation.

Possibly, the most critical skills the youth worker must develop, in working within a group home and conducting groups, are to teach assertiveness, risk taking, allowing oneself to become vulnerable in a healthy way, and resisting negative influences. These attitudinal changes occur through openness, genuineness, cooperation, sharing, helpfulness, and giving and accepting unconditional positive regard. Prosocial attitudes and behaviors are the result of staff modeling and positive peer pressure. Nevertheless, when youth become accountable to each other for their behaviors, due to peer pressure, this process at times can become overpowering, negative, and destructive, especially if youngsters misuse the concept of positive peer pressure to gang up on each other. The worker cannot allow good efforts to deteriorate, or interactions to become oppressive and hurtful. To develop a balance so that peer pressure deals with real problems while remaining a positive influence, the worker teaches listening skills (being reflective), awareness, empathy, sensitivity, and thoughtfulness. When group members function in the here and now, and deal with issues and each other with respect, then decision making and problem solving can become shared outcomes.

There are limitations to the benefits of any form of therapy (Kazdin, 1984), and this is also true of the group process. The worker realizes his or her limitations and does not delve into issues or problems that he or she is not prepared for by training, education, or experience (American Counseling Association, 2005). Some issues should be referred to the appropriate mental health professional or dealt with by more senior staff. However, this does not mean that in difficult situations or gray areas, the worker cannot induce a certain degree of anxiety or discomfort in order to promote change. This may occur through confrontation by the worker or in concert with peers. Wherever possible, the worker creates situations or interactions that encourage group members to assume leadership roles. The worker may need to teach residents organizational and administrative skills, especially to deal with the daily upkeep and operation of the group home. There will be ongoing change in peer group membership and interactions. There will be youngsters admitted to the group home when others are discharged. The worker is able to integrate new members into the group and to deal with feelings of separation and loss that arise when members are to be discharged from the group. These changes to the group can become destabilizing for some youngsters, can alter loyalties within the group, and may cause a transfer of leadership and loyalties in the peer hierarchy and create new subgroups (Pazaratz, 2000c).

COMMUNITY RESOURCES

An important task for workers is to assist residents to become familiar with and to know how to access various community resources or facilities for emotional support, recreation, education, and medical-health assistance. Residents often need help in developing knowledge to locate these facilities in a general way, so that their specific interests and creative urges can be fulfilled. The worker at times may need to initially attend with the youngster to help the youth to deal with any uncomfortable feelings that he or she may have. Youth workers may be required to assist the community resource worker to understand the youth, or the youngster and his or her family. In this respect, the youth worker is aware of confidentiality issues, and of the resource and its focus, such as its mission statement, the type of programs offered, the level of staff talent and program sophistication within the resource, and its geographic boundaries or community catchment areas. Some resources have unique cultural and sometimes specific political purposes. This information is useful because it may demand certain dress and conduct, and exclude certain practices or behaviors.

Reintegrating residents into the community usually begins with the resident attending a regular or community-based school. Children and adolescents in residential treatment programs will need continuous encouragement and support during their transition to the public school system or to a job (Pazaratz, 2001). The worker deals with the youth's adjustment or progress as well as any complaints that come from the school. The worker may have to help the school or other community agencies understand the youth and to deal with any prejudices that they may have toward the youth, or misinformation about children or adolescents in treatment (Pazaratz, 1998a). Sometimes, the worker may need to provide information to the community resource that will assist in the development and utilization of stabilization strategies. This may also mean that the community agency needs to think in terms of coordinating individual goals for the youngster. To help the youth adjust to a new community experience and to minimize conflicts, the worker may need to spend time with the young person in the resource and to teach specific social, communications, and negotiation skills. This is seen as a parental function by the worker.

ETHICS, STANDARDS, IDENTITY, AND RESPONSIBILITY

The youth worker must be thoroughly versed in the legislation and regulations under which the group home is licensed. All geographical jurisdictions have a children's act that defines the legislation, regulations, and standards to which residential treatment facilities and children's shelters must comply. These are interpreted in the policy and procedure manual of the agency and specify the "do's and don'ts" of working with children-in-care. The agency's manual is a prescriptive approach that focuses on the proper care and case management of children and adolescents, and the daily operation of the facility. By being versed in the agency's philosophy and goals, the worker understands the expectations and limits of his or her roles and responsibilities (American Counseling Association, 2005). Yet, residential treatment of disturbed youth transcends merely implementing the policy and procedure manual. Nevertheless, all licensing regulations must be complied with, exactly and thoroughly, especially to safeguard the rights of the children-in-care, to fulfill the agency's mandate, and to ensure that staff are acknowledged for a job well done (Forester-Miller & Davis, 1996).

There are various duties that the group home worker engages in, such as being a role model, parental figure, and leader in activities. Workers present themselves appropriately for these comprehensive but multifaceted roles. In all interactions, the worker is able to recognize the effect of his or her behavior and self on others, and to understand how residents and staff affect him or her (Pazaratz, 2000c). In this respect, the worker has the ability to evaluate and to be open about his or her strengths and weaknesses, to seek and to accept direction or assistance from other staff or the residential supervisor, and to be responsive to feedback given by residents. This approach to youth work is necessary for professional growth and is an essential aspect of the team-building process. This may mean the worker learns to accept criticism from fellow employees as well as to live with and to overcome rejection by residents. In other words, the worker is able to recognize his or her own limitations on the job, or job role; to be open about mistakes; and to be willing to learn from mistakes. The worker can also enjoy a relationship with and develop the respect of residents and other staff, without imposing his or her will, beliefs, values, or perspective (Pazaratz, 2000b).

In any discussion of cases and youngsters, the worker does not jeopardize confidentiality. This means the worker cannot use any information against the resident, or share it openly with other residents. Any direct knowledge about youth is privileged information to be used only to assist the resident. The worker functions professionally and does not overidentify with youth or their issues (Nugent, 1994). In effect, the worker practices mental and emotional self-preservation. Youth workers are required not to react but to understand the clinical basis of (although never accept) inappropriate behavior and to overcome any personal dislikes they may develop for youth. Ultimately, the worker has learned to control his or her own needs and does not engage in power struggles with residents. Undoubtedly, workers will experience both negative and positive feelings toward residents, and these should be discussed with their supervisor. Youth workers may even be perplexed when trying to differentiate between a youth's genuine emotions and phoney or imitated emotions. The worker must be able to offer constructive criticism whenever possible and is reflective before responding to misbehaviors (Pazaratz, 2000a).

In working within a team, the youth worker tolerates different styles, paces, and philosophies of work as encountered. This does not mean that youth workers overlook destructive or abusive behaviors, or avoid compromises and cooperative solutions. Team building requires that each youth worker conducts him or herself professionally, communicates factual and accurate information, and shares in workload and day-to-day responsibilities. At times, the worker may have to act independently and to make immediate decisions. The worker documents these actions and keeps other team members informed. Acting independently may include enforcing rules or boundaries to ensure the safety of an individual, other children, or the worker him or herself, or the well-being of the agency. This means that (wherever possible) the worker attempts to safely transfer responsibility from the self to the youth. The worker should be able to critically appraise the emotional makeup of individuals and the group at large. The worker is also able to utilize suggestions by consultants and other team members, is diligent in his or her duties, and acts with good conscience or probity and genuineness (Pazaratz, 1998a, 2000a, 2000b, 2000c, 2000d).

COMMUNICATION SKILLS

Communication skills are vital for information processing, storage, retrieval, transmission, and treatment intervention. Without careful attention to the importance of gathering accurate data and utilizing precise communication, misunderstanding is likely to result (Nugent, 1994). The worker demonstrates a professional manner in telephone use, with youngsters, and in public. Good grammar and clarity of ideas are essential for oral reports and written treatment progress reports. Report writing and log notes allow workers on the team to compare another's perceptions with their own. The worker is able to convey ideas and factual information in reports and daily logs and is able to summarize important issues with details. In practice, the worker is able to communicate accurately, logically, clinically, and dispassionately. Attention to details and thoroughness in information processing and sharing are essential youth worker skills (Pazaratz, 2000c).

Any actions that elucidate a youngster's problems and his or her effect on established treatment goals should be recorded in the agency's log notes on the date they occurred. These notes are to be reviewed and initialled by staff during staff changeover, and discussed during staff meetings and supervision. These notes inform all staff whether the resident's treatment plan is being followed and those corrections, adjustments, changes, or deletions that need to take place in keeping with the youth's progress or lack thereof. The use of specific techniques is to be monitored and evaluated regularly, to ensure their appropriateness and efficacy, in relation to individual residents achieving specific treatment goals. Any treatment approach should be stopped if it is not producing beneficial results. Regularly scheduled team meetings are the format for reviewing individual treatment plans and a youth's progress.

INTERPERSONAL SKILLS

All workers should make every effort to attend staff meetings fully prepared to contribute to the discussions. This requires youth workers to interact and communicate with personal observations, factual information, and interpretations based upon clinical reasoning. The worker sets personal goals for growth, is abreast of the latest professional theories and changes in terms or usage, keeps up with current information and activities of his or her own agency, forms an open but work-related relationship with his or her supervisor, and has realistic expectations of his or her supervisor and other staff. The worker is reasonable and accountable in dealing with other professionals and problems that arise in interactions (Pazaratz, 2000b).

UNIT FUNCTIONING

The daily management of a group home is a shared staff responsibility. Although the team leader defines the direction of work, distributes labor, and sets workloads, individual staff members cooperate and support team members in their efforts. This means that staff communicate around tasks in a problem-solving manner without laying blame or passing off responsibility to someone else. Interpersonal problems should not interfere with professional conduct toward others. When confronting difficult interpersonal problems, these are sometimes best resolved by a third party, such as the team leader. Ultimately, every worker must realize that their attitude and efforts affect every other person in the group home. Thus, staff show an awareness of the total unit and how their attitudes and work ethic affect others (Pazaratz, 2000b).

JOB RESPONSIBILITIES

Treatment integrity occurs when workers actually do in treatment what they say they are doing, and there is a reliability of data collection (American Counseling Association, 2005). Workers must provide written documentation in a timely fashion, and all reports must be comprehensive. Thus, log notes are to be completed before workers leave their shift, and written reports must be completed on time. A high level of motivation and cooperation by staff can be seen with minimal use of sick time, being punctual for work and/or meetings, and not slacking off during their shift or sneaking off early. Direct care staff will experience work difficulties if they do not realize that their personal needs are not the basis of the employment relationship (Lowman, 1993). It is especially helpful to the team when all staff members do more than what is expected, rather than merely make a minimal effort. Staff who relate positively to their team members and supervisors, and who follow all policies and procedures, demonstrate their job commitment and leadership potential. Although there can be a certain level of paperwork, these duties are to be completed regularly, thoroughly, accurately, and on time in order to minimize client risk and to ensure agency compliance. Some duties for front-line staff include maintaining a clean, neat, safe, and therapeutic environment. Because staff are often responsible for meal preparation, all purchases of foodstuff are to be purposeful in order to maintain a high quality of meals in regard to taste, nutrition, and appearance. Staff should be mindful of medical-, cultural-, or religious-based diets that are necessary for some individual residents.

TEAMWORK

In residential treatment, front-line staff are organized and operate in teams. In their efforts, staff members need to be cooperative, seek consensus to make decisions or to resolve divergent points of view in order to enact program-ming, and follow up from one shift to the next or across time and space. Staff should be able to understand and verbalize treatment rationales, or explain the reason for the implementation of intervention strategies (Fewster, 1990), and to know and to adhere to best practices and mandated practices. Effective team functioning has been correlated to positive outcome (Fulcher, 1991). Without good team work, the group home will be in chaos, and the residents will not make progress. To avoid communication breakdowns and to mini-mize problems with residents, staff know and use good lines of communica-tion. This means that while on shift, staff deal with each other cooperatively and interact as would parents, sharing responsibility and decision making. Workers must be able to examine their own work (behavior and ideas) and personal relationships, with other team members, on a face-to-face and regu-lar basis. Cooperative interactions will not develop if workers are defensive, secretive, and dishonest with team members or attack each other. Developing harmony and understanding requires workers to explain and to defend (as needed) their child care work and child care practices to other team members. It is also reasonable and necessary, at times, for workers to confront other team members. This means identifying the specific work-related issues or problems as they occur with other workers and not discussing differences, misunderstandings, or one's personal issues arising with any one worker with another team member (Pazaratz, 2000b).

According to Lowman (1993), it is the employees and not organizations that suffer when conflicts occur between goals. Therefore, direct care staff are required to follow staff schedules and obtain permission if they wish to deviate from, or to not follow, the scheduled shifts. Direct care staff must attempt to resolve conflicts with colleagues or employee–employer disputes at the time these arise, with the view of being supportive, equitable, and professional. All staff are required to be prepared for staff meetings, support fellow and new staff, and conscientiously enact tasks that have been assigned to them. When job expectations are not clear, or when job expectations create conflicts in terms of the worker being away from the residence attending appointments, then the front-line worker ensures that a "double" booking in his or her schedule does not lead to insufficient staff coverage. Staff must keep residents safe and free of harm, and of inflicting harm on others. When there are transgressions by youth or serious incidents, these are dealt with rationally and documented factually. All staff are required to follow the group home's home budget guidelines, but to seek prior spending approval as necessary, and to provide receipts for all expenditures.

TREATMENT PLANNING

A written treatment plan for each youth and his or her family should be made available and known to all staff. The plan of care is consistent in scope with the task-centered contract introduced at the Oshawa/Whitby Crisis Intervention Centre, a Four Phase Re-Entry Program, in 1975 (Pazaratz, 1998a).

The plan should include the following:

1. Formulation of the problem as identified by youth, parents, and workers.
2. Treatment approach: This includes short- and long-term goals, and the resources and supports that are available.
3. A school, educational, or work plan that identifies the youth's needs and details his or her specific difficulties.
4. The method of working on goals, or tasks to be performed. The method should identify the focus, and clarify the role of the resident and that of staff.
5. Specific indicators or means of monitoring progress toward goals should be described.

6. A timely review of the plan must be identified that will include an analysis of the factors that have contributed to the creation and maintenance of the problem, and an indication of which areas need to be modified.
7. The discharge plan (and its anticipation) helps youth to evaluate their accomplishments, the meaning of those actions, and the way in which the information the youth has learned can be used in ongoing problem solving.

SUMMARY

The Role of Youth Workers

1. To implement policies and procedures that provide for a youth's safety and care, and carry on those tasks that maintain stability and are necessary for the group home's operation
2. To plan and carry out therapeutic activities
3. To explore and to understand the emotional and cognitive abilities and limitations of each youth, based upon background and current information
4. To interrupt and to control disruptive and dangerous behaviors in the least intrusive and restrictive manner
5. To counsel and to use reinforcements for the goals and objectives established for each youth
6. To participate in treatment planning and implementation of care, and to monitor progress or regression
7. To develop social group cohesion
8. To teach the use of community resources for recreational purposes and skills acquisition
9. To participate with team members in the daily management of the group home unit
10. To utilize space and location for normal routines, and to support developmental patterns in each youngster such as decreasing dependency, developing interdependency, and eventually increasing independence or autonomy
11. To relate in a positive and professional manner with parents, neighbors, colleagues, and community agencies

Group Home Management

The youth worker engages in the following:

1. *Limit setting*: This assists residents to learn how to modify behaviors and to deal with their difficulties more rationally. Limits also provide safety for individual youth, provide security for the group, and protect the rights and feelings of others.

2. *Normalization*: As a fundamental principle of group care, it is the basis for establishing daily programming and staff–youth interactional patterns. Programming is to replicate as close as possible the everyday conditions and opportunities provided to children or adolescents not in treatment or living at home. Even though each individual group home has its unique environment and group dynamics, nevertheless, when the group home is part of a treatment facility, then objectives (mission statement) of the larger treatment facility must also be complied with.

3. *Individualization*: This has the purpose of meeting the needs of an individual. It takes into account the normal as well as the special physical, psychological, developmental, and environmental needs of each youth.

4. *Acceptance*: Children and adolescents are accepted as they are in the totality of their uniqueness, goals, gender, sexuality, religious beliefs, preferences, culture, worldview, strengths, weaknesses, and feelings.

5. *Self-determination*: Each youth has the right to choices and decisions, and these are to be promoted within the context of each youth's treatment plan, but carefully balanced with respect to keeping the youth, other individuals, and the community safe.

6. *Empathy*: Staff demonstrate the ability to communicate warmth, acceptance, and understanding of each youngster as a unique individual.

7. *Therapeutic activities*: Staff demonstrate through participation a genuine interest in daily activities and recreational periods.

8. *Positive reinforcements*: Staff have the ability to use themselves, treatment decisions, and the milieu to reinforce the goals and the objectives established for residents.

9. *Responsiveness*: Staff are available to all youth equally and understand the importance of preplanned and spontaneous activities.

10. *Work ethic*: Staff demonstrate reliability and a sense of responsibility, i.e., they are diligent, ethical, genuine, and professional. They follow agency protocol and document all interactions as these occur.

11. *Maintenance of the unit*: Staff create and promote an orderly structure, which includes the proper use and storage of equipment and the mindful upkeep of the group home, surrounding property, as well as agency vehicles and equipment.

12. *Efficient and effective in report writing*: Staff are thorough and precise, and provide meaningful data and information.

13. *Knowledge and use of community resources*: Staff demonstrate an ability to use community resources in such a fashion that it becomes a positive learning experience for youngsters.
14. *Executive skills*: Staff show leadership qualities and behave professionally with residents, with fellow staff, and in the community.

CHAPTER 8

Positive Discipline

CAUSES OF MALADAPTIVE BEHAVIOR

In the behavior management of children and adolescents, the most frequently asked question by parents and practitioners is "What are the causes of oppositional, defiant, and aggressive behavior?"

1. *Failure to reward or acknowledge compliant and positive behavior*: Without recognition, praise, and reinforcement (reward) for cooperative and compliant behaviors, there is little reason for some youngsters to display positive acts or to comply with expectations. Many youth in treatment have experienced their parent's angry response to inappropriate acts. This punishment has reinforced their oppositional, defiant, and aggressive behaviors, and therefore becomes the way in which these youth get attention, approval, and their sense of self (Larsen & Dehle, 2007).
2. *Failure to respond appropriately to misbehavior*: Youngsters who act out have typically received few rewards for compliant behaviors, too many severe consequences for poor choices, and at other times no consequences for misbehaviors. Some youngsters never have any of their actions monitored, redirected, or challenged; therefore, their oppositional and defiant acts have become part of their developing personality. Ultimately, inconsistent child management increases the potential for at-risk antisocial behaviors to develop in adolescents (Wachtel, 2004). Thus, during placement, the issues of morality and

right versus wrong are initially imposed from outside by the youth worker until this understanding emerges from within the youngster.

3. *Overreliance on punishment*: Excessive use of punishment will aggravate behavior problems. Youth become immune to a barrage of punishment because they get used to it or they have no escape from such treatment. Thus, when youth are abused, they react in kind. To avoid punishment, some youth will engage in sneaky behaviors. They can become fearful of their parents and actually avoid them. Punishment may curtail oppositional behaviors initially, but it does not modify the youngster's future acts, because it does not change the youth's motivation for misbehaving. Fear-based approaches to child management weaken a caregiver's control, and threats turn youngsters against the caregiver and cause youth to rebel. Ultimately, youth recognize those acts that are abusive and unfair and will not tolerate them, and threats break down the lines of communication (Cameron & Pierce, 1994).

4. *Consistency*: Child management, when inconsistent, can make the youth's behaviors worse over time. Ineffective monitoring and enforcement of rules cause the youth to believe that he or she can get away with things. Noncompliant behaviors that receive intermittent or periodic censure will increase in frequency. Behaviors become resistant to change when consequenced intermittently. The youth's oppositional behaviors become strengthened when the youth worker does not follow through on rules, incentives, and consequences or penalties (Deci, 1972).

5. *Individual temperament*: Each youngster is an individual and has his or her own unique characteristics and temperament. Some youth are social, engaging, flexible, and cooperative. Youngsters in placement are typically difficult, rigid, and demanding, and can be aggressive. The youngster's attitude or temperament is an indicator of how he or she will react to rules and expectations. Nevertheless, the key is to reinforce each youth's strengths and to acknowledge those efforts to be compliant. Each youth needs recognition for his or her individual ideas, beliefs, feelings, hopes, and preferences. Ultimately, the youth worker should allow the youth to discover, appreciate, and develop his or her unique inner potential and purpose (Deci, Vallerand, Pelletier, & Ryan, 1991).

6. *Ability to tolerate stress*: Developmental changes and challenges create a great deal of stress in youth. Social activities and academic challenges can cause many youngsters to react with irritation and to be uncooperative. Therefore, youth need help to identify and resolve stressors. Stress can be passed from one youth to another or from one staff member to a youngster, and this will only exacerbate a youth's lack of adjustment. Inflexible or inconsistent responses by staff can

also be stressful and lead to oppositionalism (Ellio & Devine, 1994). Therefore, youth should be allowed to exercise their own goals and to define a true and positive sense of self. The aim of residential placement is to develop a willingness to cooperate and to be guided by the youth worker. The youth worker must learn to manage the youth's resistive side and to stay in control while giving youth increased choices and freedoms.

7. *Poor impulse control and deficient problem-solving skills*: Misbehaving youth display both irrational (self-harming) attitudes and poor problem-solving skills. They also display self-defeating efforts and ineffective problem-solving skills at coping with frustration. Youth should be encouraged to want more opportunities in order to develop a sense of what they deserve and the ability to delay gratification. Even though they want more, they can also learn to be happy with what they have.

8. *Rewarding misbehaviors*: Inappropriate or disruptive behavior can be strengthened when staff respond with laughter, too much attention, or minimizing. Disobedient behavior or acting out can be strengthened and rewarded if the youth worker backs off and does not challenge the youth. Some youth are able to get staff to overlook misdeeds by whining, complaining, or protesting that they are being treated unfairly. The youth learns that compliance and cooperation can be avoided through enough resistance or protest. At times, however, some youth should be allowed to make errors or mistakes in order to learn to self-correct. They can learn from mistakes and achieve greater success (as per a reinforcement or contingency management system). Youth should also be permitted to express negative emotions appropriately so that they learn to manage their emotions and develop a feeling of awareness (Eisenberger & Cameron, 1996).

9. *Bizarre symptoms*: Some youngsters have a vivid imagination and fantasy life, and can visualize themselves inflicting harm on others or even cutting, mutilating, or killing the self. These youth need careful and constant monitoring. Some youth will find these intrusive thoughts disturbing and try to suppress them. But the more they try to suppress them, the more they occur (Kandel, 2005). These obsessive thoughts need to be reported immediately and dealt with by a psychiatrist or psychologist.

CONFRONTATION VERSUS CONTROL

When residents learn to accept staff members for who they are, they often conclude that front-line staff are helpful, fun, and interesting to be with. However, some youth frequently experience staff as intrusive or bossy, and therefore they do not listen to them. There are also youngsters who overreact no matter how staff approach them, justifying their negative attitude by claiming that staff are interfering or have no right to raise any issues. These youth not only react to the message and its content, but also to the idea that staff are telling them what to do. There are also youth who are disinterested in staff. They draw a blank when requested to cooperate. They do not listen on any level to staff. Sometimes, the youngster does not hear the message, or does not understand what was said. There are youth who do not remember or who fail to do what is required of them. A youngster's oppositionalism, defiance, or indifference can cause some staff to be upset. They become frustrated when youth are not responsive and do not follow through with expectations. Staff frustrations can be compounded when youngsters give "attitude" when confronted.

How are staff members to understand and to deal with the noncompliant resident? Youngsters in placement often are easily frustrated and disagreeable. Some have a profound learning disability or attention deficit. Others lack continuity or meaning in their lives. They live between conflict and fragmentation. They engage in a kind of dance, whereby they purposefully distance staff and sometime later draw them back. When the distance is too great, this may mean that the youth is experiencing regression, has a developmental delay, or is being defensive. In effect, the youth is unable to focus on his or her thoughts, is confused by what is said, or is easily distracted. When staff become too close, or too involved for too long, some youth will feel overwhelmed and smothered. The youth's consciousness is distracted, and the reflective awareness of self is diminished, nonexistent, or overly acute. When this occurs, staff should deal with the youth's avoidance, distancing, or sudden shift to attachment and clinging as an internal struggle. This form of noncompliance occurs because the youth has difficulty in maintaining a balance in the relationship with staff and the self at the same time (Brodie, 2007).

CONFRONTATION AS AN ENCOUNTER

The widespread use of confrontation was devised and developed in encounter groups. The main emphasis of confrontation is to get the individual to deal with his or her feelings in the here and now (Yalom, 1983). However, confrontation during daily interactions between peers can be quite uncomfortable. If peer confrontations are not handled skillfully, the fundamental requirement to show caring for each other will likely be overlooked. Caring is an essential part of the confrontation process. Unless residents learn to confront appropriately, in an assertive but nonhostile fashion, they cannot convince each other that they do care. Without appropriate confrontation, youth cannot really begin to understand how their behavior affects others. The main difficulty with unfocused venting, or retaliatory confrontation, is that these behaviors can quickly degenerate into a power struggle, escalate into a battle of wills, or diffuse into petty bickering.

Confrontation is an active intervention targeting behaviors and attitudes that are intense and disruptive. Confrontation by staff members can be effective when it is reality based and used to penetrate such defenses as denial, intellectualization, projection, and reaction formation. Unbreaking of a common defense, such as intellectualization, through temporary "disorganization" or confrontation may lead to a new self-understanding (Bellak, Hurvich, & Gediman, 1973). Opening up of an individual to new levels of awareness occurs when confrontation is interpretative. Confrontation stirs up strong passions because it is anxiety provoking. Confrontation can trigger anger when youth believe they are devalued, they are being treated unfairly, or their actions are justifiable.

Confrontation by staff members can become the basis for change when hope is emphasized. It is effective when the youth worker shifts the approach from discussing poor reality testing to dealing with the youth's potential and strengths. This involves pointing to the good choices the youth has made previously. Confrontation as a process should include the reminder that responsible behaviors lead to fewer controls and more privileges. Confrontation is guided by standards of fairness and respect, and is enacted as an intervention when youth are not fair and/or respectful. The youth worker addresses negative emotions that are the basis for self-serving or hurtful behaviors. This includes any kind of poor reality testing whereby the youth is not living in the here and now, or is not being future oriented.

With youngsters who are substance users, sexual perpetrators, aggressive, poorly socialized, or somewhat psychotic, heavy confrontation can be necessary (Hollin, Epps, & Kendricks, 1995). Even though many residents often react negatively to any confrontation, nevertheless destructive behaviors need to be limited. Staff members also need to reaffirm positive leadership and that they are in control. Confrontation assures and advances the supportive nature of the worker–youth relationship. Confrontation should be timed to occur when the youth is receptive, but it may have to be enacted even though the youth feels provoked or reacts as if threatened. However, confrontation is not an aggressive intervention or intended to be provocative. As a counterdelusional technique, it is designed to have the youth deal with reality, and to cut through manipulation or game playing, for example where the youth fails to accept responsibility for behaviors, or exhibits phoney (confused) symptoms. For some youth, confrontation is necessary in order for them to realize how they reinforce their own isolation and fearfulness of social interactions. When confrontation is used in conjunction with support and caring, staff members take on the parental role. The youth worker's intervention has shifted from verbal, or a question-oriented approach, to a more reflective, nonquestioning, and even imaginative interaction (Pazaratz, 2000b, 2000c, 2000d).

SUPPORTIVE CONFRONTATION

The behaviors that are most frequently confronted are those that arise due to social and interpersonal ineptness. Inept behaviors, and oppositional and defiant attitudes that need to be confronted, are those that create legal, personal, and social problems for youth. For the poorly socialized youth, there is a repetitive nature to their self-defeating or self-destructive behaviors (Hollin et al., 1995). Sometimes, confrontation includes reminding youth about their past dysfunctional behaviors, or that their current behaviors are similar to the reasons for their placement. For youth to grow, they must resolve those issues that led to their placement. Learning to deal with issues calmly and in the moment, especially when feeling attacked, without attacking or blaming others, is a new experience for most youth, as per these examples:

1. Poor reality testing occurs where youth are unable to recognize their own grief, anger, or longing for connection. They behave in detached or avoidant ways. The practitioner get youth to become aware that they are being passive-aggressive or internalizing. The worker makes the recognition of these behaviors an explicit objective in a noncritical way (Brodie, 2007).

2. Inability to give up behaviors occurs even though youngsters become aware of problematic behaviors and the reason for them. They are not always motivated to give them up as they may be experiencing cognitive dissonance. This impasse could leave workers frustrated or evolve into a power struggle. There are reinforcements to negative behaviors and the fear of change. Staff get youth to focus on their self-talk in order to help them understand that awfulizing and ruminating about the problem prevent solutioning.

3. Lack of emotional perspective can cause some youth to have severe mood swings or inappropriate emotional responses. This occurs in some youth due to cognitive distortions or an inability to identify basic issues, short- and long-term goals, and how to get there. Thus, they are unable to adapt to daily challenges. They need to know how to limit excessive behaviors, deal with stressors and losses, self-soothe, and protect themselves. They must learn to ask for, not demand or give up on, what they want and not overreact; also, they must be able to say when they do not want something. It requires the youth to deal with conflicts between what they want and what others expect of them so that the youth overcomes his or her confusion, avoidance, or fight-or-flight tendencies (Redl & Wineman, 1957b). Thus, youth can avoid or defend against conflict-laden stimuli like thoughts, feelings, or images by learning to experience conflict but linking it to an adaptive emotion.

4. Expression of interpersonal affect occurs when youth use it appropriately in their daily lives and by restoring a connection to significant others (Fewster & Garfat, 1998).

5. Emotional disorders are the result of a pervading negative self-view and the negative manner in which one views and is viewed by others. These maladaptive representations of self and others are the focus of developing self-acceptance and the focus of healing through meaning. This occurs as the youngster improves his or her intellectual and experiential sense of self and others. This creates an opportunity to shift the negative sense of self and maladaptive view of others. In changing self–other representation, the focus by staff is on defenses, unconscious affect, and conscious affect in order to build a more adaptive perception of self and others (Brodie, 2007). There may need to be social skills building, such as assertiveness or problem solving, in order to shift the youth's sense of self and that of others.

6. During formal counseling, the youngster will go through stages of awareness and internalization of information. These stages can occur simultaneously with later stages. Sometimes, the youth will experience a back-and-forth movement through the stages and a complex interaction among stages, and these interactions with other people can undo, intensify, and interrupt movement (Kohut, 1977). The stages of awareness and internalization are as follows:

   A. In the denial stage, there is denial or deception of vulnerability. This includes avoidance, minimizing, discounting, and rejection that the youth did anything wrong. This can mean that there have been pain-killing or mood-altering behaviors that need confronting.

   B. The second stage consists of anger and withdrawal. The youth blames others for his or her emotions, problems, and behaviors. The youth often justifies his or her anger toward others for the hurt he or she feels and for being treated unfairly. Typically, the youth reacts to confrontation by being argumentative, being silent, engaging in self-pity or passivity, devaluing others, and displaying obsessiveness and even poor reality testing.

   C. The third stage is termed *resistive* and is characterized by oppositionalism. The youth controls interactions with others by setting up conditions for the relationship, cooperation, or interactions. However, there is some recognition of how he or she created the problem and that there is a part of the self that needs to be changed. When staff react to the youth's resistance with counter-resistance, this will often lead to a power struggle.

   D. In the fourth stage, there is a reprocessing that occurs and an inner realization of information. The youth begins to understand how he or she overreacted or misunderstood, and how this intensified the issue. Some youth even recognize the depth of their hatred and envy. They feel shame, guilt, and depression. They realize they must let go of these.

E. In the final stage, there is resolution and acceptance. The hurt and anger are resolved. The youth wants to move on and is committed to a positive path. There are recovery and overcoming where the youth accepts the self and others, including negative aspects of both (Kohut, 1984).

STRATEGIES FOR EMOTIONAL INTERVENTIONS

The emphasis by front-line staff should be to treat children and adolescents fairly and with respect; to help them acquire knowledge of themselves, others, and the world around them; and to help them develop a personal identity (Pazaratz, 2003b). Youth workers will differ in their feelings and reactions to youth, or to the same youth. This is to be expected! Workers typically bring their own way of viewing the world and a unique interactional style. If workers recognize and understand their personal preferences, this awareness may prevent them from reacting to youth (or other staff) when they do not agree with them. Workers who have self-understanding and self-acceptance are more capable of dealing with intense feelings in others. However, all workers are fully human and fallible. But they are cautioned not to bring their particular biases, or to allow their subjective experiences to negatively influence their views or the way in which they perform their duties. They must especially avoid control by coercion or by force. By definition, youth workers are required to develop treatment skills and the perspective of a benign caregiver. When they concentrate on persevering through difficult moments, residents will believe that staff members are genuine and that they care.

Because social interactions are the major source of anxiety in group living, the quality of staff–youth relationships will determine happiness or disappointment. Yet, if any one element is underestimated by individuals entering the field of youth work, it is the amount of hostility and defiance they will encounter. Youth workers are often upset, if not shaken, by the extent of animosity and lack of cooperation they face. Unprovoked verbal hostility from youth and even parents can be intellectually perplexing and emotionally draining for youth workers, as well as social workers and adjunct professionals. Despite the youth worker's best efforts to develop a close supportive relationship, the resident may still verbally degrade the worker, make false accusations of assault or sordid improprieties, and even physically attack the worker. Nevertheless, the youth worker must remember that even unprovoked rage and mistruths are symptoms of the youth having a larger problem, and that the high-risk youth needs empathic attunement by caregivers. In spite of personal attacks, the youth worker needs to be goal oriented and methodical in problem solving.

To foster a sense of bonding and to be fully understanding, the youth worker maintains a positive attitude with residents. The youth worker provides guidance and control, and bears in mind the long-term view of behavior change. The youth worker aims to teach youth to be self-reflective and self-controlled. An effective youth worker is also a realist. The worker understands that not all youth are receptive to working on goals. And youngsters will not always follow the worker's time frame or respond to the worker's sincere efforts. Yet, youth workers should not blame themselves because a resident does not make progress. Instead, the youth worker should continually review the resident's treatment plan, realize that change requires many intermediate steps, and accept that the youth may experience regressive episodes. Processing daily interactions and seeking feedback allow the youth worker to learn from experience and are essential for skills acquisition and skills development (Pazaratz, 2000b, 2000c, 2000d). Nevertheless, the youth worker will undoubtedly experience feelings of self-doubt and confusion. The worker's learning process is never ending. Learning includes continuing education (CE), staff training, individual and group supervision, and feedback from colleagues, residents, and residents' families.

When the youth worker convinces youth to cooperate, or to give as well as take, the youth in effect has accepted and internalized the nature, order, and purpose of group living. This acceptance helps residents to deal with feelings of meaninglessness, a sense of being different, or maybe feeling defective. Youngsters in care need to feel that they belong, are accepted, and matter and that they can develop a meaningful life. In fact, residential treatment is informed by attachment theory, and the humanistic values of unconditional positive regard or acceptance. When the youth worker is a good object for identification and a positive role model, the interactional style enhances the development of both attachment and meaning. When the youth experiences bonding, the youth's inner world (sense of self) evolves (Maier, 1987). However, identification with the youth worker and the group home occurs gradually, as do growth in self-esteem and the capacity for self-control or self-soothing.

COUNSELING STRATEGIES (PSYCHOTHERAPY)

Effective counseling requires that the practitioner's manner is genuine and reflective. The worker listens and probes respectfully, and conveys understanding (Rogers, 1951). The youth worker is actively involved in the youth's life and day-to-day issues, and is not merely an authority figure, or a detached observer accumulating data and recording notes about the youth's behaviors or views on life. The youth worker conducts informal counseling sessions. The social worker engages youth in psychotherapy or formal sessions. Both the social worker and the youth worker ask questions about the different areas of the youth's life and want to know the sorts of things that have happened, how these were experienced, or their meaning (the youth's personal narrative).

This does not mean that either practitioner should interact with the youth as a confidant, respond to questions concerning personal issues, or present any values, ideas, and opinions that are counter to the agency's policies or to the youngster's worldview, religious beliefs, and treatment plan. The focus of therapy sessions is on the youth and the nature of his or her problems. The practitioner aims to teach youth how to solve problems, or at least to live with them, in the here and now, and to plan for the future.

During daily interactions, youth workers must not vent personal anger. They should not be domineering or overly controlling. Major control issues occur when obedience is emphasized. When youth workers use authority intrusively or injudiciously, residents will become resentful. They will inevitably find ways of fighting back with passive-aggressive behavior, active rebellion, defiance, protracted power struggles, or false accusations. This means youth workers must become sensitive to what causes youth to react. They must not degrade youth or treat them harshly and punitively (Polsky & Berger, 2003). But, at times, youth workers must understand that their experiences with youth are very human, even though they may feel irritable, abrupt, impatient, unfocused, demanding, and angry toward the youth. This in turn may cause some youth to be uncooperative or to retaliate. Some youngsters may attempt to manipulate (or con) the worker, or further provoke the worker, because they view the worker's anger as entertainment. Some youth may become frightened or scared because the worker's behavior may remind them of parental anger, rejection, or some sort of abuse and shaming.

Because youth workers and social workers act as role models, they need to be conscious that their behaviors and attitudes can assist youth to make either self-enhancing or self-defeating choices (Williams & Luthans, 1992). Thus, practitioners should be conscious that they model the behaviors and attitudes that they want youth to develop. Workers' behaviors should match stated expectations and rules so that they are not sending mixed messages. Youth generally pay more attention to workers' behavior than their words. They know when workers are hypercritical or insincere. But some youth workers use mixed messages as a trap. This is dishonest! It sets up youth for failure in order to punish them. This occurs when the youth worker (metaphorically) smiles at a youth, all the while daring the youth to defy the worker. In other words, the youth worker is looking for an excuse to retaliate, to engage in a holding session, to give consequences, or to revoke some privilege. This is termed *counterresistance*.

When social workers and youth workers demonstrate hopefulness and optimism about youth and to youth, they are underscoring the belief that youth have the potential to do better, and that improvement will occur in time. Encouraging youth toward self-direction assists youth to live up to the positive vision of their future (Rogers, 1951). However, when treatment staff convey that they are frustrated by the youth's slowness or lack of progress, they may create unnecessary conflict with youth. But youth will eventually make progress in areas that are important to them, yet seemingly inconsequential to the worker. This means that youth workers should have tolerance for minor infractions, but not overlook the youth's tendency to get involved in other people's affairs or to stir up conflict. Some inappropriate behaviors may only mean that the youth needs to be redirected. At other times, the youth may benefit from consequences, or a short time-out from the stress of the program. Firmness, consistency, following up on rules, and restating expectations by all staff eliminate potential resentment from colleagues, who may view some team members as too casual, indifferent, rigid, or harsh.

Playfulness and humor are important during therapy, to the mental health needs of both youth and staff (Ellis, 1994), and to the overall emotional tone of the home. Youth workers should have an awareness of what each youth is thinking and feeling, but youngster's moods can change rapidly. Some youth are quite good at masking their true feelings or saying what is necessary to get by. With some youth, it is quite risky to assume that outward signs of calmness reflect the youth's actual thinking state and mood. Some high-risk youth are especially adept at pretending that everything is okay and "cool," yet they are actually feeling the opposite; they may be planning to retaliate in some way, contemplating some self-destructive act, or on the verge of running away.

Oppositionalism to staff is exhibited either directly or indirectly, by emotions of anxiety, anger, irritability, passive-aggressiveness, and distraction. These feelings occur because the youth is not willing to deal with requests for compliance (seriously, openly, or honestly). But this negativity can and does occur in the context of other issues. Oppositionalism can be triggered by a number of factors, such as the way in which a practitioner confronts, when significant material surfaces, or when youth are faced with the dilemma that they must admit that their symptoms, or acting-out behaviors, were ways of avoiding underlying issues (Anderson & Stewart, 1983). Sometimes, youth are unable to identify the problems they have avoided with negative behaviors or defense mechanisms. However, when specific issues are made conscious, or labeled by staff, this assists the youth to see the problem and its solution. Yet, in spite of staff clarifying issues, some youth literally believe they cannot live without negative behaviors. They continue to use illegal substances, avoidance strategies, and addictive habits. Some youth cooperate with staff in order to get the worker to leave them alone. There are times when youth "bottom out" and cooperate out of desperation because they do not know how to deal with pressure, fear, or worries. But the youth may not necessarily want to get better. The youth is merely complying at the moment due to too much pressure, confusion, lack of an escape plan, or feeling trapped emotionally.

During staff–resident interactions, any angry, defensive, or overly warm feelings on the part of treatment staff toward youth indicate countertransference. Treatment staff may also find themselves imposing themselves upon a somewhat unwilling youth. Whenever workers are angry, punitive, or unavailable (remove themselves, distance. or reject the youth) for any reason, these negative feelings toward youth can become overpowering and obstruct the youth's positive connection (Borum & Verhaagen, 2006). If the practitioner's negative emotions cannot be quickly and fairly resolved by examining one's motives, then these countertransference feelings should be discussed with a supervisor. During interactions, if treatment staff are extreme, excessive, or harsh, and do not deal objectively with their issues, then treatment staff are replaying something from their past. This means treatment staff need to put their feelings in perspective (be aware of them intellectually), so that they are not threatened or overly stimulated by them (Wexler, 1991).

THE GROUP HOME ENVIRONMENT

In the group living environment, youth often engage in power struggles with staff and/or peers. Power struggles frustrate staff and impede treatment. But when workers overreact, this can create additional problems in worker–youth dynamics. A poor connection and bad feelings may be the reasons why the youth is testing the worker. Confident workers do not buy into a youth's obvious challenges. Instead, the worker maintains structure and enforces limits, or the worker has anticipated the volatile situation and was prepared. But there are workers who have difficulty maintaining cooperative interactions. They discount and/or overlook the value of reinforcing a youth's positive responses. This could be because the worker is too detached, or has missed critical aspects of a youth's progress. Some staff get into conflicts with youth when they are too focused on their own emotions, take themselves and their work too seriously, escalate power struggles, and get caught up in chasing after a youth in order to win (Borum & Verhaagen, 2006). Unfortunately, there is no prescriptive approach for gauging how to respond to different youth during conflictual situations. It is when workers realize that they cannot absolutely control youth, or do all the youth's problem solving, that they are positioned more realistically in their efforts (Pazaratz, 2000b, 2000c, 2000d).

Youngsters who have features that include suicidal ideation, instability, primitiveness, mood swings, extreme learning disabilities, or a tendency to be hyperactive require a higher degree of structure (Pazaratz, Randall, Spekkens, Lazor, & Morton, 2000). Staff must also impose a realistic structure for those youth who defy limits and rules more frequently. But the method that staff employ to create and implement structure is critical to stabilizing youth and for getting them to cooperate and respond. Staff are required to focus on creating a congenial atmosphere in order to undertake their various roles such as authority figure, friend, teacher, and parent more functionally. When youngsters' specific needs are targeted, they benefit from adult relationships. However, most troubled youth do not know how to respond and interact in the give and take of relationships, so they may even require encouragement to participate in fun activities and to be with staff.

Some youth workers are better at developing structure for youngsters. Others prefer a more casual relationship whereby they can associate freely with residents. But, although these different approaches are important, staff members need to be able to tailor their interventions to the demand of the situation. But there will always be some youth who do not respond even to the least intrusive approach. With some youth, no single approach or style works. They do not allow workers to get close. This blocking or distancing of staff is due to the type of pathology (problems) that they are experiencing, or the fluctuation of the youth's moods from day to day. The worker, understandably, will feel disappointed at the lack of progress. Staff should not feel defeated, incompetent, or unsuited for the role of youth worker or social worker because a youth or a number of youth do not respond positively, or trust them and reveal their innermost feelings. It is important for workers to persevere and remain open to new possibilities, ideas, and approaches. However, with a closed, detached, or secretive youngster, the worker monitors the youth's behavior, and ensures that the youngster is safe and follows programming expectations. But when a worker realizes that he or she is reacting to a youth's oppositionalism, defiance, or purposeful distancing, the worker should change the focus from the youth's attitude to the youth operating within acceptable boundaries (Borum & Verhaagen, 2006). In effect, the worker has not invested in any one intervention strategy, but remains open to dealing with the youth in the context of the situation.

THE INTEGRATIVE PRACTITIONER

The integrative practitioner commands working knowledge of child and adolescent pathology, demonstrates tolerance and patience during interactions, is flexible with interventions, and remains positive with youth in spite of a youth's level of disturbance or nature of behavioral characteristics. The worker above all else is professional and does not become angered, or disgusted, by a youth's bizarre behaviors, instability, or regression. The worker is aware that unstable youth are often volatile, and that they can quickly shift from being cooperative, reasonable, and even thoughtful to aggressive, demanding, or self-destructive, or even run away for no apparent reason. They can often switch from being a perpetrator to acting the victim, complaining about other youngsters or the worker or blaming the worker, or even become a blatant liar or cunning deceiver. An emotionally out-of-control youth can suddenly change from wild outbursts to sullenness, or withdrawal and depression. Extreme mood swings and volatile behaviors can undermine a worker–youth relationship, leaving a negative impact on both the staff member and young person.

Even when a youth has consolidated some treatment gains and has been stable for a while, the individual can quickly take on a more regressive posture and be temporarily destabilized. Youth who have been reasonable and pleasant for a period of time can also become suspicious and nontrusting (appear paranoid), ungrateful and uncooperative, anxious, depressed, agitated, and angry. These mood changes can indicate regression, decompensation (deterioration), possible drug use, that the youth is being abused in the residence (on home visits) or in the community, or that he or she is merely under too much pressure. There may be issues from the past triggered in the present. The youth worker must be ready to respond accordingly and meet the needs of each youth in the moment. This may mean that the worker has to become more active and involved with the youth, or to back off (changing or adapting limits), especially if the youth is feeling too much pressure. Ultimately, the worker needs to be aware of any cognitive distortions or reasoning error that may have caused an overreaction or misunderstanding. When thinking disorders or irrational beliefs are the cause of behaviors, the worker helps the youth to understand the issues. Ultimately, treatment staff teach youth to recognize that thoughts are neither good nor bad, but just thoughts. They are often inaccurate and limiting.

As a result of an ongoing diagnostic reading of youth, youth workers and social workers should be able to modify their intervention techniques to respond to a youth's changing emotions and level of functioning. With this in mind, the worker comprehends the youngster's ongoing reason for moods, the youngster's change in mood, the type and level of defensiveness, the degree and nature of ego functioning, the capacity to deal with distress, awareness of time and place, and the context of the youth's problem (e.g,, as perpetrator, victim, superior, or inferior). In spite of practitioners' best efforts and diligence, they will miss cues that indicate youth are stressed. Workers will invariably overlook the obvious or misperceive information because they are focused on other issues and demands. The worker's abilities are especially challenged when youth are venting or explosive. It is during these moments of one or more youth erupting, and the worker being confronted with defiance or hostility, that the worker will be pressed to remain calm and focused. It is the worker's own sense of self, or value system, and awareness of job responsibilities and how to enact them that ultimately create treatment, or the holding environment, and the youth's safety (Pazaratz, 2003b).

Treatment staff's capacities to deal objectively with issues and to make the youth feel safe and secure stem from their ability to resist the urge to personalize issues or to moralize. When workers maintain a balanced sense of personal and professional identity, they are demonstrating a realistic perspective on their role as a care provider. It is essential for workers to recognize their own limitations and to accept oppositionalism or defiance as undercurrents to the youth's pathology. It is impossible for any practitioner (or their supervisor) to have all the answers for any youth. In some situations, there may not be an absolute or a right answer, only choices, some of which may not work, and some of which could work if only the youth would allow them to work. It is also realistic that there are limits to what any given worker can or is willing to tolerate regarding negative behaviors. This is especially a factor when treating the more psychotic, primitive, regressed, or extremely violent youth. It is difficult for any treatment program to handle too many psychotic, or conduct-disordered, youth in an open setting at any one time (Pazaratz et al., 2000). There are certain character disorders that pose a higher risk in community settings, and youth with these disorders are especially effective at pulling workers out of therapeutic roles and forcing workers to be more controlling. Treatment staff should be alert to this manipulation and to the danger of feeling overwhelming anger and not being empathic.

PREVENTING DETERIORATION

There are many factors that influence the forming of relationships and the nature of communication patterns in the group home. For example, any object or even relationship (peer, staff, etc.) can become an object of attachment, fixation, or identification (Bowlby, 1969). Humans attach to and become obsessed with, even addicted to, food, drugs, alcohol, sex, gambling, money, TV, computer games, the Internet, sports, movies, rock stars, other people, and so on. There are youth who relate more passionately to inanimate (material) objects than to people or relationships. Some youth who are detached and cannot respond or relate to others see other people only as something to manipulate and to use. These youth usually have backgrounds of being ignored, rejected, or harshly treated by parents or parental figures. Their attachment disorders are the result of a lack of a positive connection in the parent–child bonding process (Ainsworth, 1985). Treatment staff want to find a way to stop the youth from using others as objects, or from becoming addicted to material objects. To do this, practitioners must be able to insert themselves as the new attachment object or role model by being sustaining and caring. Sometimes, the group home itself becomes the primary, idealized object of attachment. This can occur if the youth perceives the group living situation as being able to provide a substitute or symbolic family and a sense of meaning.

An immense advantage that group home placement has over that of a foster home is that when youth live in a group home, they do not have to be intimate, close, or emotionally connected to others. They are allowed to have more emotional and intellectual space in a group home. A group home environment is especially beneficial for youth who come from families that have not been emotionally close, families where family members are disengaged, or families with rigid boundaries and role confusion. Many youngsters in placement guard against revealing themselves by distancing or blocking adult efforts to uncover what is hidden. Thus, a foster home placement will be contraindicated for youth who defend, intellectualize, or react impulsively against intimacy or self-disclosure; have a reactive attachment disorder or conduct disorder; or are histrionic. The youth's true self is hidden or protected with a veneer of anger, severe depression, or extreme anxiety (Pazaratz, 1993, 1996a).

Why do some youth persist in self-destructive behaviors even though they are aware that their behaviors cause them more problems? Often, they do not know how to do anything else or to feel and to behave any differently (Perls, 1969a). They are unable to imagine an alternative to being the way they are, and if they do realize there is something wrong with themselves, they are unsure of what to do to make changes in their behaviors. The way youth feel and see the world forces them to develop certain communication styles and interactional patterns (Pazaratz, 1993). These dynamics often create additional problems or lead to disapproval by others (Ellis, 1994). This means that because they have not learned to deal with the world unemotionally, it is the thinking style and pattern of relating that have to change in order not to provoke others. These youngsters need new ways of understanding themselves, and to develop new knowledge in areas of connecting, emoting, acting, experiencing, and so on. In other words, they have to learn new ways of interacting to replace the old ways that have never worked, but often made matters worse. They must also become aware of how their behaviors cause other people to react to them (Winnicott, 1984).

All individuals learn and grow through experience. Disturbed youth have not learned sufficiently from their experiences to fit together with others unemotionally. There are unconscious forces at work so that these youth oppose change. These forces include defenses, oppositionalism, resistance, buying into negative behaviors, identifying with subgroups (Redl & Wineman, 1957a), or the erroneous belief that changing is too hard and stressful (Ellis, 1994). Some youth conclude that they cannot be successful at anything. They do not put in the effort. For others, the idea of change would not be rewarding. They would have to give up on fun and excitement. Emotional growth requires cognitive adjustments or changing one's thinking process and philosophical view of the world (Ellis & Dryden, 1987). Changing means to give up immature, rationalizing, negative, self-absorbed, selfish behaviors for the rest of one's life. This cannot occur until youth are prepared to make substantial changes in how they live their emotional lives and how they relate to others.

All humans have adaptive and maladaptive emotions. To change maladaptive behaviors, youth are required to work on the psychological forces that lie behind these patterns that act as reinforcers (Bandura, 1986). When youth pay attention to experiences (activating events) and the interpretation (or belief) of these stimuli, they can see how their reactions (emotional responses) are a function of their self-talk (Ellis & Dryden, 1987). When maladaptive emotions are discussed by staff members, alternative ways of self-talk are proposed and can be practiced. New ways of viewing experiences can arise from altered cognitions and from learning rational self-talk. This process of increased awareness and emotional flexibility helps create new models of self in-the-world (Elson, 1986).

THE NATURE OF CONFLICTS

Residential treatment is interactional, placing great emphasis on youngsters developing cooperative dependence on the youth workers. But some staff members have particular difficulty in working with certain kinds of youth. It is essential for treatment staff to be aware that their feelings about a youth may become the basis for creating or aggravating a conflict, shunning youth, and being overly intrusive or controlling of youth. Some staff members project strong feelings onto youth (Pazaratz, 2000b, 2000c, 2000d). This may mean that they deal with youngsters as if they are lazy, stupid, uncoordinated, different, or not fitting in. There are indeed workers who become too emotionally involved with youth. This overidentification is inappropriate. Any projection or intense feelings by staff onto a youngster can become part of that youth's own self-representation. This means that there are youth who will incorporate or internalize the staff's view of them as they have with their parents. To avoid contributing to the youth's negative self-view, staff should look for the youth's uniqueness and attempts at adaptiveness. In addition, staff should realize that careful interpretation of behaviors (insincerity, manipulative, etc.) can assist youth to process material that was inaccessible because of their own insecurity, trust issues, fears of closeness, and the like (Brodie, 2007).

Unresolved developmental issues are the focal points of therapeutic interventions. These should be identified in the youth's treatment plan. The youth must resolve and master such major developmental tasks as trust, autonomy, sexual identification, and separation–individuation. Negative beliefs from early developmental experiences become part of a disturbed youngster's self-view. A youth's self-concept will be revealed in the way the youth interacts with others. For example, a youth who has a history of chronic abuse may misinterpret people's comments as criticism and shaming, and then react defensively and defiantly (Wozner, 1991). Due to developmental deficits or disturbed perception, or because of rigid rules that govern interpersonal behavior, some youth will have inaccurate beliefs about, or views of, others. These primitive responses interfere with successful experiences and satisfactory relationships.

Some youth experiencing psychiatric disorders are stabilized on psychotropic medications. Other youth with symptoms of mood disorders may also benefit from drug therapy. A youth's outlook, however, can be modified by corrective interpersonal experience, positive role models, and insight, and by changing negative self-talk (Bernstein, 1996). A corrective interpersonal experience means that treatment staff function as a new object of identification or role model for the youth (Kohut & Wolf, 1978). When workers are valued, then they are permitted to make observations and interpretations that can have a powerful impact on youth. Therefore, staff members should be careful not to equate a youth with his or her behaviors. Staff should help youth to express their feeling states by teaching them to differentiate what other people have said about them from their self-view (Wexler, 1991). To assist youngsters to achieve more mature functioning, staff provide them with the intellectual and emotional assistance they did not receive from their parents. Staff learn to comprehend the finer nuances of a youth's feelings that are directed at staff. Staff understand a youth's motives by looking at induced feelings during interactions. When staff listen, are reflective, and are empathic, this approach to worker–youth interactions leads to ego building, strengthens identity, overcomes unresolved developmental issues, helps youth to develop a more cohesive sense of self (self-knowledge), and leads to behaviors that better suit the youth's current reality (Rogers, 1951).

Counseling techniques will vary according to each youth's temperament or mood. However, in spite of careful, comprehensive plans and preparation by treatment staff, youngsters do not always respond. They may operate at a slower pace. Therefore, daily routines may not always unfold on time. Youngsters' inattentiveness is often a major reason why schedules go astray. Another reason is staff's lack of anticipation. Conflict over trivial issues can be frustrating for staff. It is the unexpected outcomes of oppositionalism, defiance, and escalating negative behaviors that can shake up staff or create uncertainty. Emotionally charged responses make daily interactions tedious and can test staff's self-control or emotional strength. In spite of staff trying to remain in control of conditions and to keep youngsters focused, there will be times when staff members overreact or develop anxiety, confusion, self-doubt, disorientation, fear, anger, a sense of unreality, and so on (Borum & Verhaagen, 2006). But these complex moments also offer staff a teaching opportunity, whereby they can help youth to problem solve. This occurs by staff members asking youngsters to look at what is happening to them emotionally, what they let others do to them, and what they are doing to others (Pazaratz, 2000b, 2000c, 2000d).

COUNSELING IN THE HERE AND NOW (CONTEXTUALLY)

Conflicts in residential placement are the result of reactive emotional interactions. When individuals feel offended, treated unfairly, or mistreated, they can be known to ruminate and dwell on their anger. The internal conflict can be viewed as painful and troublesome. The resident begins to feel anxious or angry, and then engages in fight-or-flight behavior(s) (Redl & Wineman, 1957b). Most interpersonal problems result from cognitive miscues, or erroneous beliefs, that lead to exaggerated or intense emotions (Ellis, 1994). Counseling involves altering cognitive distortions. The youth is taught how to reappraise irrational or negative beliefs and how to practice appropriate emotional responses. Residents are continually shaped and reshaped via discourse, experiences, and interactions with others. When workers emphasize rational beliefs, this process helps youth to get in touch with concepts of the self and to experience life for what it is. In this way, the youth improves reasoning skills or access to the self, experiences the world with tolerance, and accepts disappointments in life.

Counseling aims to assist youth to be more competent in evaluating what troubles them so that they can learn to react appropriately to their problems. Counseling sessions can be informal or formal. Informal sessions occur in the life space and deal with issues in the moment. Formal sessions are preplanned and ongoing, and follow a treatment plan. Both types of counseling focus on the youth's inner difficulties that interfere with the youngster's ability to cope with internal and external pressure. In the context of a session, how does the worker accomplish this? The worker wants to hear and to understand what the youth has to say. The worker summarizes what has been said. This enables youth to feel understood and helps the youth to separate his or her feelings from the issue. When the youngster understands the stressor, the worker can present alternatives or choices so that the youth can take corrective action (Glasser, 1998). Counseling aims to help youngsters to no longer feel help-lessly caught up in their anxieties, feel overwhelmed by circumstances, and ruminate about their problem.

Counseling itself is the process through which a youth learns and devel-ops new methods and skills to manage life in a more realistic way that is less distorted and less burdened by repressed emotions (Boszormenyi-Nagy, 1987). Both the worker and youth bring their own personalities and past experiences to each session. Sessions can occur at any time in the group home or during community use, or they can be more formal and scheduled at a spe-cific time. Counseling sessions provide an opportunity for staff–youth positiv-ity, sharing, enacting a healthy reliance upon others, stabilizing interactions, and increasing trust. Ultimately, all forms of counseling have the purpose that something of positive value and constructive usefulness can be transmitted to youngsters. Counseling can provide the following benefits:

1. It is based on the relevant facts of a youth's life and their effect on the current situation, or the here and now.
2. It assists youth to enhance their relationships by learning to understand others, to understand their points of view, and to be understood.
3. It enables youth to achieve their goals more quickly as they learn problem solving.
4. It is supportive, reducing the likelihood of youth getting into sig-nificant trouble with staff, peers, family members, etc. Youth learn to understand themselves in the context of relationships and the demands of others.
5. It teaches youth how to deescalate and to eliminate significant per-sonal and emotional conflict through relaxation techniques and cognitive restructuring.

6. It is based upon a contract that helps youth to become aware of who they are and what they want to accomplish.
7. It helps them overcome peer pressure and/or attachment issues.

During counseling, youth are encouraged to replace personal troubles (negative views) with new problem-solving skills (positive views). By using active listening and teaching youth to be an active listener and reflective, workers help youth to develop a less troubled approach and view of inter-actions. When residents practice using active-listening techniques, they feel more in control and interpersonally aware. The worker attempts to teach the youth to develop greater give and take in his or her interactions. However, the worker is not an expert on the youth's problems, nor does the worker necessarily know more about the youth's problems than does the youth. But, by encouraging youth to be genuine and open, this provides the worker with details. When a worker learns about the issues that affect a youth, this infor-mation can be used to organize the problem and to indicate a solution. This flexible approach provides youth with choices and perspectives on their lives and their problems (Glasser, 1998).

Some formulations (problem definitions) are more likely to lead to solu-tions than others. Staff can teach youth to understand their problems non-emotionally and to develop practical strategies that make goals achievable. The worker can ask youth to think of solutions. When staff talk about prob-lem resolution, they speak of compromise and change (Epstein, 1992). After asking the youth to discuss solutions, the worker can shift back to the prob-lem so that the youth now rethinks the problem. By using interactional and interpretive methods, workers are elaborating on change in the moment and in the youth's life. However, when youth are not responsive to staff efforts, workers talk about the youngster's previous positive efforts, how the youth has already changed, and the changes that have occurred in the social system; provide positive interpretations of a youth's motives; offer the belief that the youth can continue to make positive choices and changes; and construct new problems for youth to work on in the future.

SUMMARY

In staff–youth interactions, youngsters are not necessarily aware of the source of their negative feelings, how their behaviors affect others, or how others affect them. Yet, treatment staff want youth to become aware of their think-ing and self-talk and to understand how they construct their belief system, even if these appear inexplicable (Ellis, 1994). A lack of awareness of nega-tive emotions arises from a lack of self-observation. Successful relationship building causes youth to become more attuned to themselves and others, to diminish negative interactions, to increase assertive interactions, to improve group cooperation, and to engage in active discussions with workers. More discussions and positive worker–youth interactions will prevent future troubles from occurring while helping to repair and to restore the youth's relationship with other authority figures.

CHAPTER 9

Therapeutic Programming

TREATMENT COMPONENTS

Residential treatment consists of various therapeutic activities that fall under the rubric of programming. Therapeutic programming is a core principle of residential treatment and care, and includes such categories as activities, life skills, community use, games, and sports. Therapeutic programming assists youngsters with their integration into treatment and transition from placement. Therapeutic programming helps youth to deal with unconscious material and to relieve tension. It also enlarges the youth's interests. Therapeutic programming consists of structured and unstructured activities (Pazaratz, 1998b) Sometimes, staff members are highly involved in the planning of as well as participation in activities, which allow different emphases and meet the unique needs and interests of individual youth. Some activities do not include staff and can also be an individual effort. Activities can include or stimulate a range of skills and effort. They have the purpose of connecting youth to themselves and others to learn from experience (Swann & Pittman, 1977). This chapter explains the rationale and method of therapeutic activities and their connection to integrative practice.

ACTIVITIES PROGRAM

Activities are considered to be one of the more enjoyable and fun parts of group home life. Most youth in placement do not enter into treatment voluntarily and are not comfortable talking about and revealing their thoughts and feelings. Activities are very useful in enticing participation, shaping behavior, and building relationships. Activities help the passive and dependent youth to become active and involved with other youth and to develop satisfaction from social interactions. Activities, which are related to each youth's individual treatment plan, focus on the behaviors targeted for change and skills to be learned. Integrating specific activities, or recreational experiences, into daily programming contributes to personality development, reduces defensiveness, increases cooperative group interactions, and helps participants to learn and to gain enjoyment from social experiences (Crenshaw & Mordock, 2005b). Activities serve as a "safe haven" when anxieties mount and the youth needs to retreat from ruminating about his or her life. Activities help youth to express their anxieties and conflicts through interactions, in the context of safe (staff member) relationships (Swann & Pittman, 1977).

An activities program includes both group participation and individual pursuits. An activities program that includes the participation of youth workers gives treatment a purpose, direction for change, meaning, and value. Activities are designed to encourage youth to develop talents, pleasures, and attachments in the area of sports, games, and hobbies. Creative activities, and the development of hobbies, helps youth to behave beyond their age and above their daily behaviors, and to deal with emotional turmoil, self-awareness, self-esteem, and concentration difficulties. They assist with the verbalization of feelings (Elkind, 2007b). Not only do residents learn to process feelings and to control aggressive impulses (through sublimation), but also they learn how to build friendships and use opportunities to anticipate or to experience future roles. Activities assist with diagnostic understanding and help to establish treatment relationships. Activities provide the mechanism for working through defenses and handling anxieties.

LIFE SKILLS PROGRAM

Not all youngsters are stimulated by the traditional school setting or make progress in special education and treatment classes. Therefore, not all will learn adequately in academic or vocational environments. For those youth who have learning or academic difficulties, their developmental delays and deficits may make them additionally disadvantaged by preventing them from obtaining gainful employment. Due to a combination of cognitive impairment, ineffective learning style, emotional difficulties, and work skill deficiencies, an alternative intensive learning experience is necessary. Life skills as a structured program can be geared to a youth's real-life problem. Life skills focus on social-emotional adjustment, and the acquisition of work and living skills. Skills are achieved through ongoing, practical, real-life experiences and work projects. Youngsters also acquire skills by encountering and practicing a variety of problem-solving techniques in a wide range of life situations. For example, instruction is provided in lessons that cover such topics as self-awareness in the nature of leisure, the family, and work; the use of the community and its resources; as well as learning to adjust to the ever changing world at large and the advances in technology.

Life skills provide youth with an emotionally congruent, systematic, and adaptive way to learn to interact in relationships and deal with daily problems. Life skills training is founded on the principle of living and functioning in the real world. Life skills emphasize the acquisition of practical information and the benefits of negotiation skills to minimize conflict. Acquiring life skills includes living skills that enable youth to live alone and on one's own, and with others, and to enhance personal satisfaction and meaning. Skills acquisition includes the very practical recognition that youth must learn cooperative transactions while relying on their own resources. Futures-oriented attitudes are essential life skills for every youth's treatment plan. Life skills aim to prepare youth for discharge by offering real experiences in basic aspects of independent living. A life skills curriculum inculcates youngsters with current and applicable information on shopping, cooking, finding a place to live, securing and keeping a job, using public transit, budgeting (banking), planning and using leisure time, taking care of personal health, and knowing which community resources are available for which needs.

THEORY OF THERAPEUTIC ACTIVITIES

Play is basic to the lives of children. Play helps to develop the mental capacity to visualize conditions or obstacles, to generate multiple action plans or options toward goal-directed behavior, and to select those that are most likely to be successful. Interactive play becomes more important as the youngster matures into adolescence. Through participation in play-based activities, youngsters create new ideas about the world and new responses to the world (Elkind, 2007b). Therefore, it is important that child and youth care workers promote play-based activities that stimulate sensory-motor development, gamesmanship, and sublimation. Internalization of play produces novel combinations of speech or actions, and entirely new messages or behavior sequences. Activities and play offer an array of change mechanisms or therapeutic powers, so that visual imaging and private language are developed. Participation in play stimulates self-expression and motivation for advancing to more socially sophisticated activities. Interactive experiences provide a concrete form for the youngster's inner world. Within activities, the youth uses and manipulates objects, learns by rote and through abstraction, develops an understanding of cooperation and competition, and has a healthy forum to display feelings, to reflect upon the self, and to contemplate the change process. Threatening attitudes and feelings can be more safely discharged in activities as they are harmlessly projected onto an object. Activities become therapeutic when staff members assist youngsters to relive emotional distress through the symbolic communication of the event (Pazaratz, 1998b).

SOCIAL SKILLS DEVELOPMENT

Social skills are acquired through formal instruction, in peer group inter-actions, and during activities. Activities provide youth with learning expe-riences and social skill interactions that help them to be unafraid of staff members wanting to know how to understand them as people. During staff–youth interactions, the youth acquires a more comprehensive awareness of the self and others, and a better understanding of his or her abilities in rela-tion to the demands of his or her environment. Activities become therapeutic because they create the context to form secure relationships or an emotional connection to others. Activities offer the opportunity for youth to express themselves in their own terms, in the moment, in their own way, and on their own time (Pazaratz, 1998b). Activities emphasize learning derived from expe-rience, and these thinking strategies can be transposed to other situations (Crenshaw & Mordock, 2005a).

Positive interactions with peers and the utilization of the peer group as a resource are essential social skills that must be learned by each resident. The ability to communicate effectively within a group and to learn from others is a primary focus of social skills training. Although the treatment milieu continually employs the interplay between members of the group as a means for discovery and change, there are also structured group interac-tions (group sessions) and less formal group activities. Regular group meet-ings allow youth to resolve the important issues that arise in day-to-day relationships. The group process is a controlled, safe venue for problem solving. It provides feedback and understanding of different points of view. Besides focusing on interpersonal relationships, the therapeutic group offers many occasions to explore larger issues such as "being aware" and becom-ing empowered to negate the pressure of peers in terms of drugs, sexuality, gang activity, and the like (Gibbs, Potter, & Goldstein, 1995). Participation in community-based support groups is also beneficial to those residents involved in discharge planning.

GROUP ACTIVITIES AND COMMUNITY USE

The purpose of life is the enjoyment of living, doing, being, becoming, dis-covering, experimenting, asserting, thinking, believing, hoping, dreaming, loving, expressing, and emerging. There are enormous benefits for youth to focus on living life, developing tolerance for others, and acquiring self-under-standing and self-acceptance, rather than being dependent on the need for love, approval, and validation of others, or even trying to be what others think they should be (Ellis, 1994). There are a number of therapeutic techniques that can be utilized to help youth to discover who they are. Group activity is that part of the treatment program in which youth participate in pleasurable or challenging pursuits with other youth, staff, or adults. Group activities promote the self-discovery process and stimulate the youngster's interest in forming relationships with others. Group activities are designed to teach youth to think about opportunities and to take advantage of them as they become available, rather than to ruminate over missed possibilities or actual losses.

Social and emotional growth occurs when youth are involved in the group process of planning and carrying out activities. Within a comprehensive group activity program, youth can learn physical skills, enhance problem-solving strategies, and develop psychological satisfaction. Group activities prevent youngsters from sitting around and getting bored. Group activities can be designed to provide youth with stimulating experiences of life in the real world. Group activities allow both youth and staff to look at and to understand the nature of the youth's referral problems, in the context of natural interactions and structured expectation. Group activities emphasize relationship and social skills development. Games, therapeutic play, and pastime events assist the uncommunicative youth to feel connected by creating conditions for interactions with peers. For youth who suppress feelings, group activities help them to be risk takers, to be more talkative, to learn to follow instructions, and to develop confidence in communication. Group activities draw out the withdrawn and easily frustrated youngster. Group activities help to alter the perception of youth who are sad and have a need to please, or must have the feeling of success and self-fulfillment. For youth who are insecure and timid, group activities enable them to interact on a less formal level. Group activities provide residents with an opportunity to give and receive support and to experience warm and friendly interactions with peers and adults. Group activities offer a variety of reinforcing events and enhance both personal and group goals (Gruber, 1986).

A range of pleasurable activities for the group removes the necessity of coming up with one activity that is of value to all youngsters. Group activities can consist of sports or recreational interests. Group and individual activities provide a practical way of stimulating personality development. Sport as an activity helps to develop physical maturation, dexterity, perseverance, and problem-solving skills. Recreational activities offers entertainment, foster passions, and can be the context to inculcate organizational and social skills. Activities that provide entertainment and social interactions help youth to fit in, enhance the youth's sense of self, and stimulate abilities and interests. For youngsters who have difficulty with relationships, group activities are an indirect and less stressful way to fit in. When youth are resistant to treatment and counseling, group activities can provide a less threatening context for dealing with conflicts or interpersonal issues that similarly arise in activities. By participating in an activity, the event is often less demanding, more tangible, and more fun than the youth had imagined. Group activities help to develop the youth's potential in social experiences (Pazaratz, 1998b). Gains made on an interpersonal level can be used to augment a youngster's treatment goals.

Informal, spontaneous, or unstructured group interactions are an essential context for the development of social skills and the forming of peer relationships (Beaumeister & Leary, 1995). The difference between formal and informal group activities includes the nature of staff involvement, the resident's level of required participation, the degree of structure, and the amount of directed learning. Studies have shown that dependent youth are significantly less inclined to engage in risk-taking activities, thus doing themselves the additional disservice of missing out on new challenges and new contacts (Elkind, 2007b). With inhibited youth, persistent encouragement to participate in group activities is necessary. Informal group activities are as important as formal or structured activities. It is when group dynamics are incorporated with treatment goals that the activity or experience becomes therapeutic. Critically, group activities also help with the relearning of tasks and resocialization of youth. Treatment is enhanced when group activities are structured and staff provide coaching and feedback.

STRUCTURED ACTIVITIES

As an assessment tool, group activities help direct care staff to understand the kinds of problems each youth has, such as low frustration tolerance; poor impulse control; degree of perseverance; aggressiveness; low self-esteem; degree of passivity; whether the youth is a follower; leadership qualities; degree of age-appropriateness (or maturity); degree of difficulty and comfort with concepts or abstractions; type of problem-solving strategies; level of skills development and coordination; ability to utilize concepts of time, space, resources, research, and relationships; and the ability to ask for assistance, accept feedback, habituate, generalize knowledge to other situations, and learn from trial and error. During group activities, youth also reveal their cognitive and social skills levels, and language proficiency (ability to express and to comprehend concepts about the activity; Gruber, 1986).

Group activities can be instructive when they provide workers and youngsters with information on problem areas to be worked on. When youth remain in a constantly shifting event that is emotionally challenging, they internalize a sense of accomplishment. Behavioral changes can be made when youth experience satisfaction during interactions with peers, adults, or the demands of the activity. Friendly competition can reinforce the youngster's desire to work even harder to achieve success. However, when a youth is not successful at an activity, this becomes an opportunity for the youth to seek feedback, acquire information, learn from mistakes, and focus more on enjoyment than performance (Elkind, 2007b).

Group activities should be designed so that each youth can develop a sense of belonging, friendship, and good feelings. Youngsters benefit when they learn how to increase cooperation and communication skills. Youth discover that involvement with or belonging to a group can provide them with some recognition, an enhanced sense of self-worth, and meaningful connection to others (Beaumeister & Leary, 1995). As youth become more skilled at an activity and the accompanying social interactions, they typically feel better about themselves. In turn, they look forward to that activity, engage in different activities, and become more comfortable in social interactions.

It is through involvement and discussion about activities, games, and sports, that youngsters learn about themselves. They learn how to understand and to relate to others, and to refine reasoning, social, and communication skills. As they become aware or reflective, this discovery of another's frame of reference enables them to get closer to other youth and adults. As they compete and cooperate with others, they also learn from and teach one another (Burton, 1993). They can learn to respect their adversaries and to develop fellowship. This process is considered to be the active and programmed resocialization of youth within their treatment plan. These interactive experiences make youngsters better attuned to different possibilities in the real world.

Social learning in an activity is more important than the activity, or the outcome of the event. To maximize the potential for positive outcome and to minimize problems, staff plan community activities and games. Youth left to their own devices do not always have enough experience to anticipate all the variables involved in organizing community activities. However, youth should be involved in planning so that outings are not the result of happenstance. Staff should also provide youth with suggestions or ideas that help in decision making. Staff should be cognizant of the emotional, intellectual, and developmental capabilities of each youth. Staff should not plan or approve of activities that are too difficult, too easy, or potentially dangerous. Instead, activities should stimulate and sustain the interests of all residents. As youth acquire the ability to assume a leadership role, plan, cooperate, and have good judgment, the worker's therapeutic role changes from being a participant observer to that of a detached observer. When youngsters are involved in weighing different options, they learn to deal with conflicts, develop flexibility, consider other people's interests, and allow themselves to be fallible (Crenshaw & Mordock, 2005b).

Community activities begin by staff members outlining the events and the rules to be followed. Staff discuss the degree of emotional risk taking (especially of concern for loners), the nature of the youth's interaction with others, the level of comprehension needed, and the type of skills required. Individuals are encouraged to discuss their feelings concerning the scheduled activity. It is quite important that staff be involved in activities because their participation will encourage youngsters to be more active, and youth are more likely to openly discuss their experiences afterward if it is a shared experience. It is always easier for youth to relate to real-life experiences in the moment or contextually than to talk of abstractions. After the event, the group is given an opportunity to discuss the experience, and to share their observations and their view (feedback) of the activity. Individual gains are noted from self-statements. Thus, the goal of therapeutic group activities for youngsters is to do the following:

1. Learn to identify and to share their feelings.
2. Develop feelings of self-accomplishment and self-confidence (Swann & Pittman, 1977).
3. Learn to conceptualize a task, and to develop interactional or problem-solving strategies.
4. Learn to deal with conflicts and competition in a group or between individuals, and to resolve differences.
5. Learn from the efforts and accomplishments of others (Bandura, 1977).
6. Learn unconditional self- and other acceptance (Bandura, 1986).
7. Learn to follow rules, and to develop good sportsmanship and fellowship.
8. Enjoy oneself, and build a repertoire of leisure interests and skills.

SUSTAINING INTEREST

Formal group participation can be challenging and anxiety inducing. Therefore, group participation is not always an easy task for many children and adolescents. Although there is a degree of gratification when activities go well, inevitably there can be a degree of disappointment when personal expectations are unmet, or conflict when individual interests are overlooked. But, by establishing and pursuing collective goals, youngsters can feel connected and develop critical knowledge that can be generalized to other social situations. In group activities, youth are directed to pursue ventures that stimulate social growth and personality development (frustration tolerance and delay of gratification). However, the more challenging the activity, the greater the likelihood that some youth will experience considerable difficulty and may even develop feelings of inadequacy. But challenging activities should not be avoided!

Group activities that capture a youngster's imagination or creativity, and sustain interest, will assist youngsters to become involved with others. Staff members can be powerful role models. During games and community outings, staff need to epitomize enthusiasm and sportsmanship. When youth workers show youth how to learn from experience, the activity is a valued addition to the treatment process. Group activities help residents to structure, manage, and maximize the use of time. Group activities stimulate and enhance psychological, intellectual, and physical development. Deriving pleasure from group activities can often be the motive for attempting new activities. Learning from activities is aided by insight, feedback from others, and an increased awareness of one's experience. Through trial and error, or repetition, hopefully, each resident will become more skilled so that activities become sustaining and reinforcing (Danish & Nellen, 1997).

GAMES AND SPORT

Games are viewed as providing pleasure, are an ideal method for morale building, enhance individual talents and skills, and teach problem-solving strategies. Games offer youth a different way of perceiving and being perceived. Games increase memory (i.e., sequencing and tracking information, processing it, and retrieving it). Games help foster leadership skills, as well as cognitive strategies to formulate and reevaluate assumptions, and stimulate verbal skills with participants when they discuss interactions. The structured use of games teaches youth to interact more reasonably in social situations and requires youth to develop impulse control and attain gratification appropriately through sublimation. Games (which can include sport) are usually viewed as occurring in or at the residence, whereas group activities are regarded as occurring in the community, or on outings, such as trips to the zoo or museum. Sport can also be an activity, and a variety of sport can occur at the residence or in the community.

Games and sport offer a safe medium to experience a range of emotions and to work them through. The impermanence of the game situation as a metaphor can help youth to understand how conditions in life are affected by many variables. Youth do not always have enough verbal skills and vocabulary to explain their feelings and thoughts or to talk about dynamics. Games and sport offer natural and developmentally appropriate ways for those youth who cannot always express themselves through language to convey their feelings through movement or action (Danish & Nellen, 1997). Games and sport have repetitive actions that can be calming for some individuals. For some youth, physical exertion and contact with objects such as bats, hockey pucks, balls, and rackets allow for the sublimation of aggression. Games and sport also require participants to think abstractly and to realize that they cannot control the outcome of events. Games and sport allow youth to participate at their developmental level or operational stage, for example emotionally, linguistically, socially, physically, and cognitively. Games and sport provide a communal connection to others. During games and sport, it would be unrealistic and unfair to expect youth to function at a level beyond their developmental abilities (Burton, 1993).

THERAPEUTIC EFFECTS OF ACTIVITIES

The most important part of stabilizing youth is through the formation of a therapeutic alliance with staff members. During activities, the youngster deals with stress by the release of repressed feelings and thereby attains cognitive mastery. The youngster moves from feeling overwhelmed by his or her emotions, which leads to freezing or becoming out of control. Activities provide a goal, direction, and opportunity to control the discharge of emotions. Youngsters will often reenact relationship issues during interactive activities (Elkind, 2007b).

Often, youngsters in placement have not acquired sufficient coping strategies and typically have lacked sufficient familial support in order to deal with their experiences of abuse, neglect, and illness in the family, or community violence and their own developmental pressure. Youngsters may not be able to communicate their needs verbally, compounding the problem of feeling emotionally and intellectually isolated. Therefore, therapeutic activities as a nonverbal communication method can help to establish trust in relationships and help the withdrawn youth to talk. Sometimes, activities are the primary intervention or connection with youngsters. Activities are more potent when they are used in conjunction with other program features. Activities can become a preventative or time-efficient intervention with youth facing difficult issues. During activities, youngsters can express and work through emotional conflicts. Activities provide relief to clinical symptoms and act to remove impediments to the youth's emotional maturation and development, so that the prospects for the youth's future growth are enhanced.

The dual therapy goals of activities are symptom relief and removing obstacles in the youth's growth. Many youth do not possess the command of language that can convey the infinite subtleties that are found in interactions. Thus, social interactions can be complex because they are both verbal and behavioral. Activities can help youth to compensate and overcome defeats, suffering, and frustrations, especially as a result of language limitations. Among the therapeutic effects of activities, self-expression occurs as a concrete form of the inner life of the youth. During activities and the use of objects, youth show how they feel about themselves, others, and the events in their lives. Their feelings and attitudes, which may be too threatening to express directly, can be safely projected onto objects (Elson, 1986). Thus, symbolic communication of activities occurs when staff members seek to relieve the youth's emotional distress through the symbolic experience of activities. Staff can help youth to identify self-soothing activities such as play. Play is fundamental to the lives of youngsters. They develop, communicate, and relate best through play. This includes individual and group, sensory motor, team sports, and solitary play. It is vital that staff members have working knowledge of the opportunities within various activities. The thoughts and techniques of group interaction are important. Inherent in activities is a wide array of change mechanisms and therapeutic powers.

SUMMARY

As a youngster matures, the later the youth acquires social skills, the greater the anxiety he or she will experience because these skills become more complex and more difficult to master as youth get older. The rejection and humiliations a youth suffers because of poorly developed social skills can create fears of additional rejection that will lead to avoidance of appropriate peer social contacts. Thus, socially immature youngsters present a difficult therapeutic obstacle and challenge. However, therapeutic programming in the form of group activities, games, and sport provides another opportunity for staff to connect with youth, and to reach those youth with whom it is difficult to establish or maintain a treatment alliance. Group activities, games, and sport also help staff to engage those youngsters who do not benefit from direct counseling techniques. Therapeutic programming is considered a best practice and a safe way for many youth to allow adults and direct care staff into their lives. Most youth do improve in residential treatment when programming offers a variety and richness of therapeutic activities (Pazaratz, 1998b, 1999).

In order for a youth to resume a normal life after discharge from placement, there are many challenges, adjustments, and transitions that the youth must make psychosocially. The youth must be able to live (sometimes alone) and function in the community, to interact communally with others, and to engage in tasks that require the skillful use of limited resources. Youngsters must be able to rely on their own resources that enable them to function without continuous adult support. They must also be in sufficient control of their emotional responses in order to resist a host of destructive temptations while seeking good relationships. In effect, youngsters have to be able to deal with issues of loneliness, relate to authority figures, overcome feeling inadequate socially, develop some self-confidence in their academic and vocational opportunities, be able to make proself and prosocial choices, know how to distinguish reality from what is illusory, and have an understanding of the cause and effect of behaviors. These life and social skills are necessary in order to make a successful transition from placement.

In summary, group activities, sport, and games are how youngsters spend their leisure time and discharge their emotions appropriately. Activities, sport, and games can consist of the formal, structured use of leisure time either individually or in groups. Activities, sport, and games can also be informal, yet instructive (preplanned) for the group or for the individual. Appropriate activities, sport, and games include, but are not limited to, playing football, hockey, basketball, or lacrosse; exercising; enjoying one's hobbies; rollerblading; bike riding; skate boarding; shooting snooker; camping; boating; snowboarding; skiing; horseback riding; fishing; shopping or browsing; seeing movies; visiting arcades or amusement parks; attending religious practices, such as going to church; visiting museums and galleries; touring factories and businesses; performing volunteer work (such as picking up garbage in parks or planting trees); joining sports teams; pursuing education, such as taking courses beyond the regular formal school setting; participating in the arts; engaging in spectator sport; jogging; hiking; watching live theatre;

attending rock concerts; dancing; playing bingo; attending an opera; hearing a symphony performance; making crafts; and going to garage sales. In the residence, activities consist of the pursuit of interests and hobbies, and these include watching TV, surfing the Internet, listening to the radio, socializing, reading, playing musical instruments, painting, or writing.

Games, sport, and activities become therapeutic or a clinical technique when they provide the following:

1. A diagnostic assessment tool of the individual youngster, during individual pursuits and in group interactions.
2. A context in which growth and development are enhanced, such as through emotional and/or intellectual stimulation.
3. A useful behavior management strategy that also offers an opportunity for developmental growth.
4. An opportunity to practice social skills in group situations, to experiment with new roles, and to develop problem-solving strategies and engage in friendships.
5. A learning situation for the mastery of skills, the release of aggression, the enjoyment of relationships, learning conflict resolution, assuming a leadership role, and developing organizational skills.
6. An enhanced ability to engage in a task and sustain oneself at it until completion (the benefit of sublimation).
7. An opportunity to learn from discovery or to access one's own motives in the immediacy of live interactions, and to learn to analyze disparate information and to work toward congruence of divergent viewpoints, or to accept that not all viewpoints can be synthesized or resolved.
8. Opportunities for risk taking in new challenges and new contacts offer the growth and pleasurable experiences of normal life (including art, music, crafts, theatre, etc.). Some youth have missed out on the growth and pleasure associated with normal life, because they have a history of being loners, scapegoats, ostracized by peers, and fighters. Activities can assist these youngsters in transcending their self-imposed barriers and motivate them to change.
9. Help for youth to develop strengths, expressiveness, and tolerance for uncertainty. They also help youth to accept their weaknesses and misfortunes as well as to be tolerant of other's weaknesses, differences, or idiosyncrasies. Youth can also learn that there is not always a best course of action and that some circumstances are unfulfilling.
10. An opportunity for the worker to understand what the youth experiences, learns, or does not learn as it happens in the moment. The worker's participation helps the youth to overcome the struggle of fitting in, and to deal with the uncertainty of what to do or not to do.

11. An enhanced discussion about constructive living and healthy choices; they ultimately provide, upon discharge home or to independent living, a means for overcoming a depriving environment.
12. Moments of good experiences and feelings in youngster's daily lives, so that they are not sulking or ruminating about what is bad.
13. Many opportunities to give help to, and to seek help from, peers and staff.
14. Healing potential in relationships so that youth no longer conceal themselves from others and do not fear social connection. In other words, youngsters who have not developed social skills, do not enjoy being with their peers, do not have friends, and do not learn from peer interactions have greater difficulty overcoming delays because those social skills and adaptive behaviors were not learned at an earlier age.

CONCLUSION

In conclusion, therapeutic activities demonstrate the healing power found in supportive relationships. Therapeutic activities allow a youngster to choose the communication medium that he or she feels comfortable with at the moment to express him or herself and to deal with issues of hurt and anger. Painful experiences can enter into a youngster's fantasy life (Crenshaw & Murdock, 2005b). Activities such as sport allow youth to deal with pain in a safer place, instead of acting out. In games, youth can make effective use of fantasy to gain mastery over situations that he or she was not in control of. The youth works through personal pain by shifting roles from aggressor to victim and back again. The youth also can make sense of other people's motives, regain some of his or her lost dignity, and even understand and forgive the parent who failed him or her. If the youth replays the conflict again and again, eventually it may work itself through as the youth has tried different solutions.

Therapeutic activities in and of themselves are not sufficient to resolve painful events. It is also probable that a youngster will still question why negative experiences happened, and still see his or her life as unfair—and full of punishment. The process of playing through a painful situation is important because it enables the youth to place a situation in a meaningful context. When youngsters process a painful memory, the youth is no longer a passive victim of what can be viewed as adult cruelty or abandonment (Crenshaw & Mordock, 2005b). Talk is still essential—to debrief conflicts in the present and to help with the reality of the youth's perception and memories of previous conflicts.

CHAPTER 10

The Role of Education in Residential Treatment

Generally, the purpose of formal education is similar to the aim of residential treatment. It emphasizes learning or relearning. As a socializing agent, formal education requires that young people take control of their behaviors, formulate goals, and become industrious. Because children and adolescents placed in residential treatment have emotional problems to deal with, they become doubly disadvantaged if they fall too far behind academically. Therefore, in order to maximize a youngster's emotional-cognitive potential, formal education is considered an integral part of the treatment process. In this effort, many residential programs have established treatment classes as an adjunct to their treatment facilities. This special education model, at first known as day treatment, originated in the Four Phase System and is expanded upon in this chapter. This chapter also provides an overview of the various influences on the youth-in-placement educational experiences such as the nature of the public school system, relationships with other students and teachers, how the youth fits in or does not fit in academically, and knowledge of how special education and treatment classes operate within the overall educational system. Finally, this chapter locates the "residential" treatment class on the educational continuum and details the youth worker's and teacher's roles.

THE PUBLIC SYSTEM OF EDUCATION

As the main socializing institution of youth outside the family, schools aim to maintain the status quo. Education as an industry is complex and expensive. There is a wide range of social, cultural, psychological, and pedagogical knowledge that educators must possess in effective and transformative practice (Kincheloe, Hayes, Rose, & Anderson, 2006). Traditionally focused educators believe that parents want their children inculcated with specific values, beliefs, and skills that will enable them to participate successfully in social interactions (Campbell, 1999). Thus, they argue that schools should focus mainly on educational goals and that these are best attained by making students more accountable (Fernandez & Underwood, 1993). However, there are reform-minded academics who believe that in order to accommodate and balance the demands of divergent parenting groups, education should be more relevant, and they emphasize student adjustment, attitude improvement, and interactional skills. They also believe the range of curriculum options should be expanded with more electives and less emphasis on the core curriculum. There are also some academics within the reform movement who espouse a comprehensive, integrated program of social and emotional education that can help students meet parental demands of fitting into society (Elias et al., 1997).

Many parents believe that the innovative teaching methods have gone too far and are too radical and ineffective, because testing and grading practices are nonpunitive. They feel there are too many peripheral school activities and affective educational techniques that interfere with and take the place of substantive learning (Jacobs & Jacobs-Spencer, 2001). Some of these parents want schools to teach their children the literacy skills necessary to gain employment, to hang onto a job, and to achieve at that job. They also want more than mere unskilled labor opportunities for their children. They demand that the curriculum at the secondary school level develop those literacy skills essential for access to secure, well-paying jobs. They believe that the curriculum should be rich, meaningful, current, and abreast of the employment conditions of the real world, so that upon matriculation (graduation from high school) their child can fit into it (Littky, 2004). In this respect, these parents believe that academic programs that cannot present data to justify their existence and document their effectiveness should be redesigned or eliminated (Rye & Sparks, 1998). But there are educators who believe that successful school reform begins from the inside out with teachers and administrators, not with external mandates or standards (Elmore, 2004).

There are convincing arguments that advance each side of the debate. Yet, both the reformers and the traditionalists blame the other for the failure of schools to ensure the important maturational needs of youth, which include the development of autonomy and self-esteem (Cohen & Fish, 1993). Each side accuses the other of failing to create an effective learning climate, arguing that many students have not acquired functional literacy and basic arithmetic skills (Rye & Sparks, 1998). Each group believes that their approach does more to stimulate students with intrinsic motivation, broaden their interests, and increase learning from direct experience. Unanswered in this debate is whether it is more important for students to learn on their own or to merely imitate others (Elias et al., 1997). However, because schools are a social environment where students in fact have interactions and interdependence with fellow students, and learn for themselves and with others, then this part of the argument appears moot. What, then, are the real reasons for the so-called educational shortcomings that both the reform group and traditionalists have identified?

Although educators of either stripe and conviction have tried to make the public school system more relevant, the stability and structure of the family unit have undergone enormous changes that also affect youngsters and their school-related difficulties. Family cohesion has been affected by postmodern society, bringing about the family's isolation and interfering with parents' ability to respond to their children's maturational and learning needs (Pazaratz & Morton, 2000). The ever increasing divorce rate and higher incidence of single-parent families have translated into less parental monitoring of their children and lower parental expectations (Jeynes, 2002). Some parents feel overwhelmed by the changes in moral standards that influence children's lives, which they do not fully understand or feel capable of dealing with. Other parents are too lax and do not emphasize the importance of social decorum, healthy lifestyle attitudes, and children being personally responsible. Increased discipline problems have also arisen due to the concurrent backing away of authority figures (in institutions) from their traditional socializing roles (Pazaratz & Morton, 2000). There has been an enormous growth in the crime rate that is complicated and disconcerting, leaving parents frustrated at dealing with the deviant forces that affect children. There has also been an increase in the glorification of sex, drugs, and violence in television, music, and pop culture, all of which influence children and adolescents' attitudes and behaviors (Cottle, 2001). There are also a growing number of youth essentially on their own who seek peer models or adults who will accept them on the streets (Kipnis, 2002).

Davis (1999) believed that youth are caught up in a crisis state, or conditions of chaos and confusion, brought about by social upheaval, violence, political cynicism, educational decline, and a decrease in compassion. Abbott and Ryan (2001) added that the so-called crisis in education is really a crisis in childhood and that the unit of change is not the school, but rather the larger community. They believe that family disorganization and too much mobility have deprived many youngsters of roots. Frequent school changes have subjected numerous children and adolescents to a conflicting sequence of instructional methods and contents that manifest as school difficulties and adjustment problems. In an attempt to make up for the deficiencies in the home, most often schools, rather than acting as an extension of the family, provide services in place of the family. Thus, schools are forced to deal with

negative attitudes and acting-out behaviors by neglected youth toward authority figures, but with reduced powers and less support to correct misbehaviors.
As a result of the failure of traditional disciplinary practices, principals, teachers, and school counselors have embraced zero tolerance for school-related
violence (Macciomei & Ruben, 1999).

There are no easy answers to whether the traditionalists or the reform-
minded educators are correct in their understanding of how to improve the
educational system. There are teens who have developed a "school kid" identity that enables them to succeed in school (no matter what the scholastic
doctrine), whereas other youth develop a "street kid" identity and drop out
(Flores-Gonzalez, 2002). There are students who are frustrated with rapid
changes in curriculum, innovative teaching techniques, open classrooms, the
extreme use of the elective system, independent study, and nonpunitive grading. There are students who do better when there is an emphasis on structure,
clear rules, teaching of fundamental skills of reading and writing, and cognitive rather than affective learning (Egan, 1997). Therefore, the problem with
education is not necessarily limited to the permissive didactic model, or the
traditional conservative approach, but to the fact that some youngsters do not
have the capacity, or psychosocial dimensions, to benefit from either educational model. There are also large numbers of students who do quite well
no matter what the academic format. This means that the educational model
could be balanced so that academic innovations are introduced gradually and
carefully, and limited to those situations and for those students with mature
judgment and learning abilities, or who are sufficiently versed in the basics so
that some modification in academics would be stimulating (Rathvon, 1999).

It has also been argued that schools have failed to get students to question their acceptance of institutional values and beliefs (Hopkins, 1994). It has
been postulated that if democratic societies are to survive as true democra-
cies, they need citizens who are informed, concerned, and active (Sherrod,
Flanagan, Kassimir, & Syvesten, 2006). But encouraging students to challenge the school's bureaucratic responsibilities could be counterproductive for
schools, especially because educators already compensate for the lack of stable
homes and parental involvement, and for rapid social changes. Learning from
a structured curriculum and keeping schools safe are inextricably connected
to the development of character and conduct (Stein, Richin, Banyon, Banyon,
& Stein, 2000). Therefore, promoting challenges to a school's somewhat conservative doctrine of maintaining the status quo could become problematic.
Nevertheless, the question remains, "To what degree should students be permitted to identify their needs, or should academics be at the total control of
educators?" Deal and Peterson (1999) believed this dilemma can be resolved
when teachers harness the power of the school culture to build a lively cooperative spirit and a sense of school identity. Gershman (2004) believed school
reforms should recognize the challenge of getting students to engage in their
school by seeking to make the curriculum more interesting and energizing.

Rodriguez and Bellanca (2007) asserted that students' achievement begins with the classroom teacher's expectations.

EDUCATIONAL OPTIONS

Current models of education are based on ideas about learning from the industrial age and thus, according to Abbott and Ryan (2001), cannot bring out the full potential of all children and adolescents. However, according to Erikson (1968), the majority of high school students are cognitively capable of comprehending philosophical ideas and thinking abstractly about themselves and their future. This means that a well-rounded student can evolve when the fundamentals of learning are stressed in the area of basic scientific and mathematical knowledge, traditional reading, writing, and research skills. Therefore, it is when the foundation and structure of learning or the core content areas have been omitted, in favor of relevance and "presentism," that many students experience academic difficulties. The results of various studies would suggest that cognitive learning, or the lecture–discussion method of teaching, cannot be totally replaced by affective learning (Egan, 1997). But, once the average and even less than average student has been grounded in well-organized and moderately paced lecture material, instruction can be broadened to include teaching machines, computer instructional materials, audiovisual resources, independent study, and the like (Healy, 1998).

High schools, as socializing institutions, have an enormous task to accomplish. This includes instilling the norms and standards of the community, dealing with the developmental-intellectual changes of childhood into and through adolescence, and preparing adolescents for adulthood. Thus, the high school teacher's task is complex. But, the teacher's academic agenda is better fulfilled when he or she is cognizant of the student's social, maturational, and personality development (that is, by understanding that students have varying economic, family, and social backgrounds that affect concentration and learning; Fukuzawa & Letendre, 2001). This means that teachers need to be aware of how adolescents cope with their rapid stage of development and social obligations, or the conflicts they encounter between the ideal of group harmony and individual competition, and how these issues affect the youth's academics. Therefore, high schools need to offer an atmosphere and structure that reflect community conditions, but do not deprive youth of the stability and sameness they require in order to develop into adulthood (Child, 1997).

Education takes place on two levels: the factual knowledge presented by teachers, and the socialization process within education. The student's school life is shaped by teachers' attitudes, temperament, instructional style, and life philosophy, and their interests in developing relationships (Rogers, 1969). The youth's life is also influenced by the way a school develops its atmosphere and organizes its tasks. It may be difficult for some teachers to keep up with the community's demands for enacting a balanced approach in the classroom, especially because there has been an enormous increase in the sheer volume of social and technological change in society and the workplace. Teachers have had to shift from the instruction of established fact to the instruction of the learning process per se, because it has become realistically impossible to keep up with the explosion of knowledge. With the unpredictability of future demands, it is difficult not only for the adolescent but also for the teacher to speculate accurately upon the kind of preparation that is in fact the optimum (Healy, 1998).

In the past 20 years, there have been dramatic changes to high schools as institutions and an enormous increase in the size of high schools. This growth is due to the population increase. This means that high schools built for a capacity of around 600 students are now accommodating several thousand. In any given grade, there are anywhere between 150 and several hundred students. Given the adolescent's need for personal attachment and group formation, it is obvious that in a large high school, the youth may feel alone and unconnected. Yet, with the multiplicity of functions that high schools are expected to undertake, large schools do present economic and administrative efficiency (Cohen & Fish, 1993). This means that students are sorted or streamed into various instructional experiences based upon individual differences, and, therefore, not everyone is expected to succeed in the public school system (Milofsky, 1984).

For the less socialized, more timid youth, larger high schools compound their social angst and increase their isolation (Pazaratz, 2004). The diversity of the high school's population can also lead to victimized and marginalized students (Darling-Hammond, French, & Garcia-Lopez, 2000). Because students do not necessarily take courses sequentially, or by grade level, students often find themselves with a different age group in about every course. Courses are usually taken because they fit into a timetable. There are no longer small cohesive classes or communities, in the traditional sense, to which teens belong and with which they advance through high school. The grouping that exists among students is mostly that of cliques. Students who fit into cliques or form groups are athletes, outstanding students, individuals with special interests, or those of a given ethnic background. For the vast majority of high school students in any one grade, the class grouping is too large to be meaningful or to provide lasting contact. The cliques that exist are often quite exclusionary in terms of membership. For some youngsters, because of their social differences or individual problems, they are often isolated and in some instances bullied. The more serious conflicts with peers can evolve into psychological stress that can often lead to additional academic, behavioral, or social dysfunction (Pierangelo & Giuliani, 2000; and see Pazaratz, 2004). Therefore, to help integrate the student into the school's community, groups are needed that permit unification on the one side and definition by contrast on the other. The optimum class size for this grouping to facilitate interaction and assimilation has been shown not to exceed 20 to 40 students (Glasser, 1975).

BEHAVIOR CONTROL OF STUDENTS

Educators and the general public have concluded that discipline is the primary problem in schools today. It is believed that the violence and vandalism that are prevalent in our society are outgrowths of the lack of discipline in schools and at home (Macciomei & Ruben, 1999). Many adults believe that much of what is wrong in North American society could and should be corrected in the schools. However, rather than being a force for change, schools often function more as an extension of society. As society has become more permissive and lax toward norms of behavior, schools tend to reflect these beliefs. Nevertheless, schools are required to maintain a reasonable level of structure and order to promote learning and safety, and thus the intent of discipline is to control student behaviors (Phillips, 1998). The dilemma schools face is to define and apply a realistic and workable concept of discipline (Campbell, 1999; Macciomei & Ruben, 1999).

It is believed that children and adolescents do not behave randomly, but act to meet some need, such as to gain attention, attain power, seek revenge, or display inadequacy (Dreikurs, Grunwald, & Pepper, 1982). Discipline is used to deal with these behaviors when they become problematic. Discipline is enforced at the discretion of principals, superintendents, and school boards. The effectiveness of disciplinary measures such as punishment has generated concerns regarding its use for behavioral control. The central issue is whether aversion techniques that are the basis for discipline are preferable to positive reinforcements that inculcate appropriate behaviors. Most behaviorists are in agreement that both approaches will work (Allyon & Azrin, 1968; Wicka-Nelson & Israel, 1991). However, Glasser (1975) believed that when students are punished, it can generate negative consequences, whereby students do not assume responsibility for their behaviors. For example, some students prefer to be disciplined for classroom disruption than to be embarrassed by failing the course. Other students will suppress their participation, withdraw emotionally and intellectually, and seek situations in which punishment does not occur rather than make the constructive change for which punishment was intended.

Undoubtedly, there are students who fear punishment and can be controlled by it. However, to avoid punishment, some students may pursue a course of dysfunctional behavior, making it increasingly difficult for teachers to apply behavior controls for rules that punishment was intended to enforce (Campbell, 1999). For those students who seek negative attention, or do not know how to attain positive attention, punishment will not necessarily lead to extinction of inappropriate acts. At times, punishment seems to work because it temporarily induces a negative emotion. But a defensive reaction is also aroused in students when they are harshly disciplined (Pazaratz, 2003b), and this can impede the development of desired positive behaviors. Some youngsters will "act out" more when punished, as receiving and enduring punishment reinforces their image of being tough (Phillips, 1998).

Traditionally, schools try to control students' behaviors and to shape attitudes. The common method for dealing with students displaying adjustment problems, and overtly acting out, has been through punishment such as detentions, suspensions, or even failure. For some students labeled *at risk*, no amount of discipline seems to work. As teachers escalate control, these students escalate their behaviors (Thomas, 2006). Because they do not have goals or future plans, think that they have nothing to lose, and do not care about consequences, they can win any power struggle. Control becomes counterproductive as these youth spiral downward (Phillips, 1998). When these approaches do not correct or remediate the student's misbehaviors, an extended school suspension is enacted. Punishment may simply make it easier for some adolescents to "turn off," "tune out," and "drop out." The act of escaping is what is ultimately reinforced. The escape may climax with the youth becoming alienated toward any type of education or upgrading (Thomas). The youth who becomes alienated by teachers and school will quickly find a peer group with similar negative experiences. Then the student's misbehavior and subcultural affiliation are what are reinforced in the school environment as the youth receives more scrutiny from teachers for negative conduct than for doing the right things at school (Campbell, 1999).

Personal difficulties are often overlooked in misbehaving students. For example, emotionally withdrawn or reserved students are often viewed as misfits, or underachievers. Consequently, both the acting-out and the seriously withdrawn youngster are either alienated by or lost to the school system as they are encouraged to leave school and get a job. Whatever the basis for poor high school adjustment, the result is that many youth become "dropouts" and socially marginalized (Brodie, 2007). Ultimately, the "at-risk" student needs to feel accepted and understood and become goal directed. It is more pleasant for them to tune into a reward system as opposed to punishment, especially if they come from a home where they are yelled at or physically abused. When youth are shown that their misbehavior or withdrawal is a matter of concern, they become more responsive to reason than to an adversarial system (Campbell, 1999). A school's discipline policy that focuses on the goals and dilemmas of students in effect encourages students to be self-directed. Youngsters are more likely to become accepting and responsive to expectations when teachers work cooperatively with students instead of against them (Phillips, 1998). Thus, educators are better positioned to connect with students when they establish and enforce reasonable rules, monitor student progress, and provide positive reinforcements (Campbell, 1999).

In various studies, it has been shown that there is a direct correlation between a student's academic achievement and social reinforcements or positive discipline given by significant adults (Macciomei & Ruben, 1999). Teachers ease hostility by not reacting to or rejecting a student, are nonconditional in their acceptance, and remain available to students (Rathvon, 1999). Thus, it is more likely that students will comply with classroom rules and show an improved effort at learning when teachers are supportive, firm, and fair (Durrant, 1995). In addition, when teachers concentrate on present behaviors and avoid criticism rather than resurrecting previous discipline issues, they create an environment where students can be successful (Glasser, 1975). This reflective approach by teachers is the impetus that assists youngsters to develop an internal locus of control, and increases their belief that achievement occurs through their inner resources of skill, competence, and intellect. In contrast, low academic achievement is correlated with the need for an external locus of control, or a belief that one's fate or destiny is determined by outside sources, such as chance, luck, or the actions of significant others. Therefore, more monitoring is required of students who do not believe they are in control of their behaviors, especially for those who have lower self-esteem, do not display confidence in themselves and their ideas, or are followers. These students are also less likely to interact with others for fear of attracting negative reactions (Gullotta & Blau, 2008).

PARENTAL INFLUENCE ON LEARNING

It has been demonstrated that bright students who achieve significantly below their predicted level of measured abilities generally have fewer favorable personality characteristics than academic achievers. Academic achievers' personality profiles reveal them to be more self-assured, independent, organized, and optimistic, and to have internalized more realistic life goals and values, in comparison with underachievers. Uniformly, underachievers are stuck in self-defeating beliefs and negative self-evaluations, or identifications formed earlier in their development. They do not continue to examine, clarify, and reformulate their own values. Additionally, they lack the formation of a mature and cohesive identity that is realized by high achievers (Rothstein & Glenn, 1999). For the most part, the underachievers are too self-absorbed, are preoccupied with their own thoughts, and display little initiative (Phillips, 1998).

There is little doubt that the connection between school achievement and self-esteem is complex. Perhaps many of the educational difficulties that students experience are directly due to youngsters trying to behave in a manner that is consistent with the way they view themselves and the way they believe others perceive them. Consequently, youth will experience either growth or difficulties according to their self-concept as a learner. Youth who regard themselves negatively, such as being insignificant, unworthy, unacceptable, and/or even disturbed, are unlikely to develop the level of self-esteem that is necessary to function as a learner (Rothstein & Glenn, 1999). Therefore, it is evident that the development of self-esteem is directly related to school success, so that whatever happens in one area (self-esteem or school success) will affect and feed into the other.

Elias et al. (1997) have demonstrated that there is a direct relationship between an adolescent's successful involvement with school and his or her self-perception. Conversely, this means that school failures engender a negative self-evaluation among adolescents who suffer repeated school failures. These youths do not have the confidence and skills to face new tasks. As a result of their self-doubt and the fear of being judged by others, they avoid any potential source of negative evaluation, or any interaction that might become a negative experience. In other words, the fear of failure has become a self-fulfilling prophecy. It is easier to accept failure than to try a new task and still fail. Consequently, school alienation and socially unacceptable behaviors are common features of students unable to achieve academic success (Jacobs & Jacobs-Spencer, 2001).

Some youngsters encounter academic problems because their parents have unrealistic expectations for educational achievement. Others experience conflict with their parents to increase proportionately with the frequency of school contacts over lack of academic progress or adjustment. This means that there would be fewer academic and school-related issues for some youngsters if their parents only desired and did not demand that their child fulfill his or her academic potential. It is when parents elevate this worthwhile goal into an absolute standard and demand success that they create too much pressure for children. But there are also parents who do not hold their child accountable for academic difficulties or any discipline-related issues. They displace their anxiety over their child's school problems by finding fault, or some cause for the problem(s). Thus, these parents blame the school administration, teachers, or guidance personnel when counselors contact them as their child's problems increase. They believe that their youngster would be doing fine if it had not been for the school official who does not like their child, treats their child unfairly, or has not taught their child properly (Cohen & Fish, 1993).

Parents do have a significant influence on their child's attitude toward school and the value of education. But it is not helpful to allow children or adolescents too much latitude for making choices, or for parents to be rigid, overcontrolling, inconsistent, or vague, or to have undefined expectations. These attitudes will lead to a youngster's confusion, insecurity, and low self-esteem. Inflexible expectations or impossible academic standards can lead to rebellion. Parents are more inspirational when their expectations for academic achievement are reasonable, realistic, and supportive. Negotiations will foster a child's development of self-esteem and pro-self attitudes. Cooperative conduct on the part of a daughter or son should be stressed by parents. This interaction includes parent–child discussions on appropriate conduct in order to set realistic expectations. Parents should also state their concerns on such topics as curfews, homework, chores, drugs, and the like, and then encourage their child to express his or her feelings on the positions held by the parents. Ultimately, parents should decide which expectations are firm and nonnegotiable and make their position clear. It is also necessary for parents to understand their child's point of view by being flexible in those areas where the youngster's judgment and sense of responsibility can be demonstrated (Cohen & Fish, 1993).

A student's school performance is positively correlated to the presence of appropriate models within her or his home. This means that parents should convey the appropriate expectation or standard by prioritizing academics, and by creating an environment where the youth's behaviors are directed toward academic attainment. Parental involvement in their child's academics is essential, as are parental modeling, support, and caring. Parents should also convey that there are real advantages for their children attaining good grades, but they should not equate their child's success, or lack thereof, with the youngster's worth. When children and adolescents are made to feel good and secure within themselves, they feel prepared to cope with life and its challenges. Some children and teens need to be given the opportunity to pursue less academically based courses without being judged or labeled. They will then discover their unique abilities and competencies, accept themselves relative to others, and learn how to interact with others in a positive or prosocial manner (Durrant, 1995).

School discipline policies and teachers' attitudes can either obstruct or advance the emerging youngster's development and quest for exercising personal autonomy. Inclusiveness emerges in youth when they understand how society works, how to effect change, and how to enact positive choices that are consistent with the evolving self. Youngsters can be taught to deal with social problems through debating, cooperative efforts, competitiveness, conflict resolution, negotiations, and compromising. This occurs by discussing their lives and the understanding of their experiences. Through a reflective exercise, youngsters will develop thinking strategies and learn to deal with their emotions, understand others, comprehend cause and effect, and imagine the implications of several strategies, perspectives, or alternate choices (Stein et al., 2000). In taking on a social identity, there is experimenting with different roles and synthesizing them into a coherent self-definition (Erikson, 1968). Role taking occurs through practicing responsibility and choices (Glasser, 2000). If the youngster has excessive confusion about the self and about his or her values, and an unrealistic method for dealing with society, then identity diffusion occurs. Therefore, educators should encourage adolescents to examine those elements of their existence that help to define the self, affect the direction of one's development, and increase good judgment (Phillips, 1998).

THE NEED FOR SPECIAL EDUCATION

Children or adolescents who have been labeled *exceptional* are those who either excel at academics or, alternatively, have a complexity of developmental and/or unique learning needs. The developmentally delayed adolescent, like the youngster with emotional problems, has experienced social maladjustment, has severe learning disabilities, can be afflicted with physical maladies, or has mental health problems. In order to provide the resources that match the learning needs of the academically delayed exceptional student, most North American state and provincial governments have set aside additional funding and resources for these students. In fact, many educational regulations require local school districts to establish a means for identifying and placing exceptional students in special education classes. The special education class provides the academically challenged student with social supports that are geared to improve learning, behavior, and social skills (Rathvon, 1999).

The exceptional student, experiencing academic difficulties, is initially identified by his or her teacher. The student's academic deficits are then reviewed by the school's principal. As needed, the student is referred to the school district's psychological services. Yet there are some academically at-risk youngsters, with learning-based problems, who are not identified. There are teachers who view poor achievement as a lack of motivation. These teachers gear their efforts only to motivated students and overlook the underachieving student. Some district school boards' psychological services operate apart from schools; others are narrow in defining academic problems as primarily a behavioral matter and not learning based. Consequently, a number of students are overlooked for remediation because of systemic failures. But once a student is identified as having academic-related problems, placement is made in a remedial or special education class for those youth who need support beyond mere curriculum adjustment.

Special education is sometimes referred to as teaching the "mildly disturbed," or geared to those who are at risk for school failure and in need of remedial help (Wang, Reynolds, & Walberg, 1995). This means that students who are admitted to special education classes because of learning difficulties often also display behavioral problems. The common profile of the at-risk student is one who has a learning disability, has difficulty staying on task, is easily distracted, is quickly frustrated, and is often oppositional and sometimes even defiant of authority and rules. Early disturbances in development or personality impairment have prevented the learning-disabled student or the youngster with social adjustment difficulties from benefiting from the kind of learning and socialization that most children acquire in their homes before they commenced school. Thus, the emphasis on traditional educational goals of cognitive operations and mental acquisition has not had a significant impact on these children.

The learning-disabled and undersocialized student also displays a pattern of characterological difficulties. Central to their learning-based difficulties is a deficiency in cognitive processing skills. Learning-disabled students often make proportionately more academic errors that interfere with meaning and understanding. They have difficulty at identifying and self-correcting mistakes. Thus, their errors take on a different meaning, which perpetuates and compounds their confusion. Learning-disabled students especially require immediate feedback for error correction. Due to ongoing academic difficulties, the learning-disabled student develops a poor self-concept (as does the undersocialized youth) and exhibits low frustration tolerance, short attention span, and depression (overlaid with guilt and anxiety). They can become withdrawn when they feel overwhelmed and display little interaction with their peers, poor effort in their homework, a preoccupation with themselves, a difficult home life, and conflict with peers. Most notably, during the course of a school day, these students also present themselves as being intellectually deficient, socially inhibited, or excessively shy, and their class participation is poor (Glasser, 1975).

The learning-disabled student exhibits many of the social and academic characteristics as identified in the learned helplessness model. Learned helplessness occurs when an individual believes that he or she is unable to achieve and receive contingent, positive reinforcement. Over a period of time, learned helplessness emerges into a pattern, or prior expectation, that there will not be positive feedback from significant others for self-caring activities. Therefore, the individual no longer enters into these activities. The individual lacks confidence to deal with and to control his or her environment, to gain desired reinforcements, or to influence others. For the atypical learning style of the learning-disabled student, the curriculum may be too complex so that school becomes a negative experience. According to Durrant (1995), by age 9, learning-disabled students believe that their failures are insurmountable and their limited successes are due to chance, not effort. Consequently, they display and engage in learned helplessness characteristics.

The learned helplessness pattern becomes compounded when students expect and accept failure. The youngster prefers not to attempt tasks that might be well within his or her academic ability. Instead, the youth engages in self-defeating, maladaptive, avoidance behaviors. The youth, fearing being viewed as dumb or stupid, develops a preference to be viewed as not caring, tough, or crazy. Consequently, the youth falls behind grade level. With this syndrome in mind, it is easy to understand why many learning-disabled adolescents lack motivation, function poorly in groups, are fearful of responsibility, are not willing to become involved in activities, have uncertain directions or goals, cannot follow directives, disobey rules, cannot work independently, do not participate in school activities, and are in need of constant, close, and direct supervision (Hopkins, 1994).

TREATMENT CLASSES

When a modified academic program in a regular or a special education class cannot meet a student's educational, emotional, and behavioral needs, a treatment class may be appropriate. Treatment classes are in many ways similar to special education classes. Each provides targeted intervention for students who are struggling academically and in need of a supportive school environment (Irvin, Meltzer, & Dukes, 2007). In both environments, the class size and remedial focus are designed to meet the at-risk student's exceptionality. Students benefit from individualized education plans (IEPs) designed for their learning disabilities and needs (Pierangelo & Giuliani, 2007). There is an emphasis on teaching interpersonal skills, skills of continued learning, and life and vocational skills. In the special education class, the student's parents are required to assume greater responsibility and involvement for their child's behavior. However, the treatment class differs in that it is an integral unit of a residential treatment facility, or a therapeutic group home, wherein youngsters are placed to receive treatment and care, and to be physically safe. Youngsters placed in treatment programs are unable to attend a regular school because their primary need is treatment. They require intense individual support. The problems experienced by children and adolescents admitted to a treatment class are deeply rooted, and they need more structure, controls, and feedback than can be provided in a special education class.

Children and teenagers placed in treatment facilities typically have difficulty adapting to normal school routines, due to a variety of personal problems such as school phobia, dangerous behaviors toward others and toward self, inability to deal with and to stay in reality, socially incompatible behaviors, poor locus of control, and inability to understand the cause and effect of their behaviors (Pazaratz, 1998c). When the treatment facility operates a treatment class, the treatment center's director, and not the principal, is mandated to determine standards for admission and defines the priority of objectives. This includes criteria for ongoing assessment, care and treatment practices, and rationale for discharge from the class (Pazaratz, 2001). In effect, education becomes the secondary goal. However, cooperative planning with education and joint supervision are essential in order to meet the ongoing clinical and academic needs of each child or adolescent. In the youth's academic plan, education is blended with the youth's psychosocial needs, so that the curriculum and instruction methods are continually adjusted to the youth's abilities or developmental level. Additionally, some youngsters who are not placed in residential treatment but reside at home can be more adequately serviced in a treatment class (operated by a residential treatment facility) than in a special education class (Pazaratz, 1998a).

Treatment classes are designed to provide a comprehensive, therapeutic, and socializing climate that enables youngsters to develop to the point where they will be able to return to the community school system or enter the workforce, or, for the more disturbed and mildly retarded, learn to function without being institutionalized. Thus, in a treatment class youngsters with specific limitations are directed to activities that are designed to develop the capacities they have (Pazaratz, 1998c). This may mean that some youngsters need help to face their shortcomings. But it also means that youngsters can pursue their own interests and progress according to their abilities. They are taught to deal with rules and expectations in order to bring about a change in attitudes and behaviors, or beliefs about themselves and others, and eventually to be mainstreamed. Positive socialization is promoted as an essential principle of treatment classes. Importantly, education is an integral part of the treatment class, and the class has the same standards, expectations, and opportunities as are found within a community school setting (Pazaratz, 2001). Munger (2005) made the case that a school setting that provides care, offers interesting and challenging activities, and has adult mentors makes a big difference in helping children to become motivated, competent, and compassionate.

According to Harmain (2006), to transform classrooms into communities of active responsible learners, it is essential for teachers to focus on mutual respect, collaboration, commitment to learning, and the dignity of all. In a treatment class, the unique and special needs of the individual youngster are the focus of intervention so that institutionalization or creating a patient is avoided. This means that the care, treatment, and education of the emotionally disturbed child or adolescent require the cooperation of various professionals who comprise the multidisciplinary team. The team can include a psychiatrist, medical doctor, nurse, psychologist, psychometrist, teachers, social workers, and child care workers. Thus, there are numerous views that are accommodated in the development of each individual's treatment plan. Education becomes interwoven with treatment and care. Both child management and the academic curriculum are tailored to the youth's abilities and are incorporated into the program's treatment focus (Pazaratz, 1998c, 2001).

In the treatment class, education and treatment are combined to focus on the common factors in the change process. The treatment class model, with its highly structured intervention techniques, assists the student by providing for the following:

1. Emotionally fulfilling and trusting relationships with staff (teacher and youth workers) that help to build connection, competence, and skills, and are the prerequisites and conditions to stimulate learning and for experiencing success
2. A safe and simplified setting that offers structure, stability, and constancy
3. A systematic schema and diagnostic approach for identifying both academic difficulties and behavioral problems, and a plan for remediation and adaptation
4. A supportive, interactive, and participatory environment for practicing new skills and strategies for improving interpersonal interactions

WHAT TYPES OF YOUNGSTERS REQUIRE A TREATMENT CLASS?

The type of youngster most appropriate for a treatment class is the youth who is emotionally disturbed, behaviorally disordered, or mentally ill. The youngster usually has a co-occurring learning disability, but there are exceptions.

The emotionally disturbed youth with a learning disability is handicapped both socially and academically. The defense mechanisms, or the methods for coping, employed by the emotionally disturbed youngster include undersocialized behaviors that are aggressive, passive-aggressive, or oppositional defiant. Both the emotionally disturbed and the learning-disabled youngsters rate their self-concept lower than does the same-aged nondisabled peer. Learning-disabled and emotionally disturbed children and adolescents are even rated less popular and more socially unattractive by their peers. They also feel less acceptance and approval from their teachers, display more discouragement than their peers, and avoid academic discussions. The aggressive behaviors of the emotionally disturbed child or adolescent tend to have a detrimental effect on their relationships with their peers and their teachers, as they create a hostile environment for themselves (Pazaratz, 1998c).

The disturbed child or adolescent tends to be more hyperactive than the average youngster. They engage in behaviors that are the cause of, or exacerbate, serious problems. Academic proficiency and inculcation of knowledge require students to concentrate for extended periods of time on tasks and for sorting through information. But the disordered youth has profound difficulty in these areas because of ineffective learning patterns and maladaptive behaviors, which are reinforced and maintained in the present by a reality the youngster has helped to create. Their overt negative behaviors interfere with and diminish the amount of learning that occurs. For example, the emotionally disturbed adolescent tends to be absent from school more often, due to psychosomatic complaints that are the result of negative experiences such as teasing from peers, exasperation of their teachers, and their own sense of inadequacy. This negative feedback from others also contributes to reactive or aggressive behaviors as the youth experiences new hurt, and more academic difficulties. They also display poor social judgment and distorted perceptions, auditory and visual confusion, and misinterpretation of social cues, gestures, affective states, and verbal messages (Rothstein & Glenn, 1999). Disturbed youngsters are ultimately set apart from their peers because of their dysfunctional behaviors that are reflective of younger children, such as silliness, attention seeking, engaging in power struggles, moodiness, and emotional outbursts.

It is difficult for the disturbed child or adolescent to develop a positive self-image, because the self-view that emerges is that of a marginal person who is not part of society in general, is often rejected by peers, and does not fit into school academically or socially. Compounding the youngster's problem can be peer bullying. Additionally, the parents of disturbed youth find their child to be more impulsive, anxious, hostile, depressed, insecure, and dependent when matched to control groups or to siblings. Parents also describe their own feelings of self-blame and guilt, for causing or contributing to their child's learning and emotional difficulties. Without sufficient practical information on learning disabilities and emotional disturbance, parents experience frustration and a sense of hopelessness. Siblings also report that they feel increased anxiety, fear, and/or depression due to having a disturbed sibling. The family as a system often experiences more parental separation and/or divorce (Rose, 1998).

As the disturbed youth encounters more difficulties at home and in school, this greater stress leads to more severe, indiscriminant, and habitual acting-out behaviors. Hostility arises in a person out of fear of betrayal or further harm; thus, the alienated youngster will often seek out a bad relationship even when a good one is offered. The child or adolescent's poor self-concept is also directly related to an unhealthy or dysfunctional relationship with his or her parents, which may cause the youth to become depressed and/or rebellious. In school, the teacher will bear the brunt of the hostility that originated in the home, and then the emotionally disturbed youngster is identified either by the school district's psychology services or by child protective services, whereby the youth enters the social service system (Kipnis, 2002).

CURRICULUM DESIGN OF THE TREATMENT CENTER CLASS

The treatment class is a secure, responsive, and participatory environment sensitive to the developmental needs of emotionally disturbed children and adolescents. Both the youth's internal reality and external precipitating events must be understood to stabilize the young person. Youth workers and teachers focus on a treatment method, educational plan, and intervention approach based on the emotional and learning needs of the youth. Treatment class staff promote an atmosphere conducive to open discussion and participation. Staff encourage students to exercise some choices in their academics. Behavioral techniques are employed that will alter and improve interpersonal patterns to motivate, to develop cooperation, and to manage powerful or debilitating affects (Pazaratz, 2003b). There is a heavy emphasis on discussing feelings, dealing with conflict, and developing problem-solving strategies. Refining social skills enhances the youth's self-image; increases reflexivity, or the understanding of others; and improves academic performance. The combination of affective education and social skills training provides an in-depth integrated approach, which is more effective than the structure of a regular class, where the focus is on learning and the social interactions are beyond the ability of the disturbed youngster to comprehend them (Pazaratz, 2001).

As a restrictive environment, the treatment class frees the youngster from the stress of coping with the complex demands that occur in the public school system. The instructional model is based upon individual objectives and not on the class progressing as one unit, or until all students have mastered the same material. This allows each student to proceed and advance at his or her own rate without feeling embarrassed about not keeping abreast of the class. The smaller class size makes participation less threatening. Youngsters learn to develop competencies, meet challenges, and establish close cooperation with peers. Students with special academic needs respond more favorably to learning in this environment, as the immediate teacher availability reduces conflicting expectations and inconsistent rule enforcement, and diminishes curriculum confusion and subsequent behavioral problems (Pazaratz, 1998c). It is also harder for youth with personality disorders or impulse control problems to be in class rotation, with different teachers and different expectations, than to be accountable to one teacher and responsible for learning one set of behavioral expectations (Pazaratz, 2001). Therefore, the constancy of the classroom and familiarity with academic requirements provide certainty and relief.

ACADEMIC ASSESSMENT

A complete physical and sometimes neurological examination may become the starting point of any assessment for the individual experiencing problems with learning. However, for most youth entering a treatment class, an overall assessment that establishes the areas of weakness and the areas of functional strength is usually the first step in determining the academic supports the youth needs. The teacher evaluates the student by giving the child or adolescent an opportunity to describe him or herself and his or her own level of self-awareness. This allows the youth to provide a personal narrative and to reveal the style and nature of his or her interactions. This is then compared with formal testing and a behavioral analysis. The diagnostic results specify the academic levels of functioning and observable skills, and provide a description of the youngster's learning style (Gronlund, 1985). The teacher makes distinctions among such concepts as developmental lag, learning problems, and diagnosis of learning disorders, learning difficulties, and learning disabilities. Not all learning disabilities derive from conflict because they can be neuropsychologically based (Rothstein & Glenn, 1999). The diagnostic evaluation of the child's or adolescent's learning and behavioral patterns works if it is ongoing and open and seeks to understand how the student learns. The assessment reflects the student's adjustment so that academic goals can be modified according to the student's progress or lack of response.

By understanding the student in the context of his or her interactions with the total environment, the teacher is able to break down barriers to academic success and to be eclectic in tailoring the curriculum to the student's needs (Deshler & Schumaker, 2006). It is also essential to assess a youth as to the age appropriateness of behaviors, and his or her functional grade level in each subject, in order to construct a total program for the adolescent. When the aim is to understand why a youth organizes her or himself in the way that she or he does, the youth is not viewed as being dysfunctional. This approach is important for understanding the particular learning style and potential of the student. This method is a practical approach that recognizes the immense importance of the basics in any subject matter as building tools. The student's knowledge in any area is not taken for granted or inferred. The teaching direction is based upon mutually definable and attainable goals in the student's entire curriculum. The student is taught to approach all aspects of learning and behaving systematically even for unrelated tasks. This instructional approach works because of the interrelation of the curriculum with the student's skills (Meyer, 1987).

It should be noted that although weak areas or real problem areas are not avoided, individual weaknesses are remediated or worked on secondarily. The academic emphasis is on the building of individual strengths and existing competency skills that youth require in any new learning situation. This includes developing problem solving-strategies and competency skills and not merely mastery of subject matter (Rathvon, 1999). Competency as an educational goal means that in order to acquire new skills necessary for the attainment of prescribed goals, the skills already present must be optimized. Thus, the design and utility of any curriculum can be made so much more flexible with competency as the central focus. Because the treatment class is carefully structured to be responsive to the functional strength of an individual's learning style, the class is in effect a comprehensive learning environment, where social skills development and the treatment objective are harmonized (Pazaratz, 2001).

In the assessment process, the teacher evaluates the student's academic strengths and weaknesses in order to develop teaching strategies needed to augment strengths and to overcome weaknesses. In the implementation or application of the assessment, the teacher avoids concluding that the cause of a learning problem is the result of difficulty in any one area of development. In this effort, the teacher must be attuned to individual differences, which are revealed in interactions within the student's curriculum and in the classroom environment. Competition is initially taken out of learning and achieving. Each child or adolescent works at his or her own program, at his or her own pace. There is an emphasis on basic skills building so that information is presented in a structured fashion and innovative teaching styles are "atypical." There is a blend and proper mix of traditional educational methods with limited and proven innovative concepts. For the emotionally disturbed learning-delayed youth, this approach yields far better results than using too many innovations (Rothstein & Glenn, 1999).

Understanding individual learning styles is a practical approach to academic assessments and a starting place for mutually agreed upon goals for achieving competence (Glasser, 1975). Competency and skills building in a modified curriculum are emphasized primarily, and individual weaknesses are remediated secondarily. Any curriculum is made more useful with competency emphasized to optimize those skills already present while simultaneously increasing the acquisition of new skills needed to achieve prescribed goals. Thus, in the therapeutic learning environment the student needs are matched to curriculum goals. The academic curriculum is directed at concrete educational goals, and the teacher is cautious about nonspecific and esoteric objectives. When the academic focus is on how to learn and not what to learn, and on the value of commitment rather than what the youngster should be committed to, this philosophy is deemed to be more effective (Hyson, 1994).

The educational objective in a treatment class is to provide the student with the acquisition of basic academic skills in reading, language arts, and arithmetic. This means building the curriculum around those areas in which the student already possesses an aptitude. The curriculum is designed to give the student an understanding of the purpose of a particular lesson, the required skills, and how to employ them in specific circumstances. The student is given plenty of time to complete his or her academics and to learn a body of knowledge. It is important to give the emotionally disturbed youth an opportunity for success and the image of success. This prevents lowering standards for success. Written agreements, or learning contracts, establish a commitment between the youth and the teacher regarding the particular amount of work to be accomplished, which is consistent with treatment contracting (Pazaratz, 2000a). This gives the student a sense of control over his or her program, stimulates motivation, and allows for increased creativity. Grading policies and practices are initially nonpunitive, as discussed in Glasser (1975).

The main difficulty in creating remedial programs is that most academics, learning of tasks, and relearning of information are not stimulating for the emotionally disturbed adolescent. Thus, in order for the academic curriculum to be more interesting, it should be clearly connected and continuous, so that all aspects of the youth's life, from the process of growth to maturation, changing, making friends, playing games, and dealing with emotions, can be interrelated to general learning of reading, writing, and the like. In effect, each task, or part of the curriculum, is not foreign, unique, and totally new. Tasks are altered so that new information is more naturally reinforcing, or an old task is paired to another event that has a higher probability of being reinforcing. It is especially beneficial to "hook" an adolescent on special activities that will stimulate an interest in school (Rathvon, 1999). This means the learning of remediation skills is integrated with coping and compensation techniques. The development of compensatory strategies helps to minimize a specific disability or even failure, while optimizing accomplishment and success. Gradually, grading is introduced to acknowledge progress, distinguish among students, and motivate them. Grades are an appropriate symbol that reflect the way in which work can be improved and help students to improve their efforts.

After the basic skills in reading, language, and mathematics have been identified, the student receives training in problem-solving strategies and critical-thinking skills. These occur in the context of group discussions where classroom issues and real-world events are topics. Social roles and behaviors are realized in groups, as are the student's sense of identity and feeling of commitment (Deal & Peterson, 1999). Child care workers teach students how to solve problems, express opinions orally, and get involved in their own progress, and encourage youth to engage in classroom management. The learning of debating strategies fosters moral development and critical-reasoning skills (Rose, 1998). Role playing allows youth to see positions held by others. This awareness helps to reconcile interpersonal conflicts. Activities are an important context for social skills development; act as a resource in young peoples' lives; help emotional development; reduce violence by bridging racial, gender, or class inequalities; and improve intergroup relations (Gatz, Messner, & Ball-Rokeach, 2002). Activities such as sport, games, music, theatre, and arts also address and teach improved social perception.

THE ROLE OF THE TREATMENT CLASS TEACHER

Resilient students are considered to be those youth who are able to "beat the odds" in learning even though their life situation shows much adversity. It has been found that students who experience academic problems because of emotional or behavioral difficulties, and learners with severe intellectual disabilities or with language impairment, manifest certain recognizable traits and characteristics. In other words, a correlation exists between a youth's problematic characteristics and his or her school failures. The most critical and pronounced of these characteristics that are common to academic impediments are social and interpersonal. These include the youngster's inability to get along with his or her family, peer group rejection, being a follower of inappropriate peer models, and engaging in discipline problems. These children and teenagers also lack motivation, have poor study habits, are disinterested in developing postsecondary plans, and have an inability to see the relevance of school to future goals (Wang et al., 1995). These youngsters also experience more punishment, correction, criticism, and censure from teachers and school personnel than do other youth (Barkley, Fischer, Edelbrock, & Smallish, 1990).

In the therapeutic environment of the treatment classroom, it is important for the child care workers and teachers to understand the precise nature of each youngster's emotional difficulties and learning problems. This evaluative process includes information derived from monitoring and observing interactions of the individual. This means that treatment staff should disregard labels, not stereotype a youth, and refrain from making judgments about the child's or adolescent's potential. It is important for all youngsters to experience interactions with adults that are positive and create the feeling of being accepted. Stabilizing youth and making youth feel safe allow the treatment team time to analyze observable behaviors and to formulate goals. Including the youth in goal setting has the purpose of encouraging the youngster to attempt new behaviors (Durrant, 1995). The youngster's responses, along with old methods of coping, are the criteria used in the ongoing clinical-educational evaluation and program adjustment.

It has been demonstrated that students respond positively when teachers create a participatory environment. In practice, this means that teachers develop a connection with students when they do not take themselves and their roles too seriously, but express an interest in individual students beyond the narrow subject matter (Hopkins, 1994). When teachers are approachable, patient, sensitive, and sincere, rather than authoritarian and judgmental, students become more cooperative and positive, because they believe that the teacher cares about them (Durrant, 1995). Obviously, it is rather naïve to expect that teachers should respond to students only on a personal level. However, in the treatment class, teacher–student relations are more informal, and this approach also tends to diffuse oppositionalism and defiance and lessen student–teacher power struggles. Importantly, the treatment class teacher has a more realistic appraisal of students and their potential, and thus encourages students to believe in their strengths, not just brood about their weaknesses. The teacher stimulates the student's organizational capabilities by instruction, modeling, rehearsal, role playing, assisting with transitions, and understanding divergent perspectives (Hyson, 1994). Ultimately, the teacher challenges students to learn from experience and to set new goals, so that each student's cognitive development is central.

The main reason that youngsters with emotional, behavioral, and learning difficulties are more successful when placed in a treatment class is because of the tighter structure and controls, frequent feedback, and emphasis on counseling. Treatment classes are developed as secure environments, but with informal interactions. Staff members also emphasize clear and consistent expectations and sensitivity to each youngster and his or her feelings (Pazaratz, 2001). The management of the teaching–learning milieu is also considered as important as what is being taught. There is an emphasis on the personal nature of student–teacher interactions, and better understanding and trust in relations with teachers. Educational goals that are based on passing and discipline are not paramount (Redl, 1966). There is also the recognition that changes (transitions) in the social structure are difficult if not confusing for youngsters with learning difficulties and emotional problems. Treatment classes take into account that students learn from routines and rituals, especially about matters of character. This means that youngsters respond intellectually, meet educational goals, and develop their own agency when adults believe in them (Sizer & Sizer, 1999), which is emphasized by treatment staff.

The treatment class teacher's duties include the following:

1. Emphasizing basic academic skills by good delivery techniques and by presenting lessons in a way that maintains interest.
2. Managing the class and using class time efficiently. Monitoring and handling behavioral patterns with minimal disturbance to the rest of the class.

3. Teaching improved communication skills by eliciting positive responses.
4. Teaching beyond basic skills development. Teaching critical-thinking and problem-solving skills, such as presenting conflicts or dilemmas for students to resolve, that are useful outside the classroom.
5. Developing appropriate values, enhancing intact personality structure, and improving students' self-concept.
6. Evaluating progress and providing constructive feedback. Determining and developing career and vocational skills through diagnostic testing and screening.
7. Using structure to curb impulsivity.
8. Demonstrating sensitivity and supporting developmental differences. There is a relationship between teacher empathy and student growth. When teachers are empathic, students develop a positive attitude toward self, and they also tend to make greater efforts.

DISCUSSION

Socialization is a complex and cumulative process, and the maturing child or teenager is not necessarily aware of it. It can be viewed as the continuous task of acquiring values, opinions, and competencies that enable the individual to optimize his or her involvement in social interactions. The socialization process and experience take place within groups. This interaction occurs on many levels with significant others and cannot be totally controlled, stimulated, enhanced, or shaped. Outside the home, school is the most important source of influence and socialization for young people.

Adolescence can be viewed as that developmental period where the beginnings of the adult emerge. The teenager experiences tremendous physical change and sexual development. The youth undergoes intellectual maturation, which is centered on the emergence of moral reasoning and the realization of identity (Erikson, 1968). During adolescence, the individual gains the ability to think about him or herself and to organize his or her role relative to other people and their roles. The young person is in a position intellectually to understand how he or she is valued and the expectations that significant others have of him or her, such as family members, authority figures, the peer group, and society at large (Pazaratz & Morton, 2000). This realization is central to the process of socialization. The adolescent's moral judgment derives from role taking and legitimately perceived expectations (Bandura, 1977). Importantly, the adolescent's abilities to apply reason and to formulate abstractions are signs of a moral capacity (Cottle, 2001), and an indication of maturation.

Successful integration of the adolescent into groups and into institutions requires the youth to conform to the group's and institution's expectations, norms, and social order. For some adolescents, as they struggle for adult privileges and freedoms, their parents block desires for liberty, fearing that their child's aspirations may get him or her into trouble, or that the young-ster might disregard his or her responsibilities (Lerner & Hultsch, 1983). Nevertheless, most adolescents are able to successfully resolve this stage as they balance their desire for independence with their need for adult support. They are aware of their parents' concerns that their judgment is consistent with their ability to handle the risks that they engage in (Erikson, 1968). However, there are adolescents who must have independence and individual-ity above all else. For them, nothing else is of consequence as they pursue this course. Their judgment is wanting. They do not comply with school rules or follow societal norms, and generally, they seem to have a steadfast objection to learning anything from anybody and do not reassure their parents (Pazaratz & Morton, 2000).

The stated intention of education is to develop skills of continued learn-ing and the use of organized knowledge. Educational achievement and suc-cess are not necessarily related to, or ensure, successful integration into society. Nevertheless, there seems to have been an overemphasis on select human traits and characteristics that enable the adolescent to fit into the pub-lic school system. However, merely concentrating on academic competence without explicitly teaching personal development and interpersonal skills misses the psychosocial needs of ever-evolving children and adolescents. Many educators believe that schools should be at the vanguard of encourag-ing positions favorable to social change, rather than presenting the value of maintaining the social order (Davis, 1999). But too often, school socialization is seen as being conservative and traditionalistic, intent on preserving the status quo (Sizer & Sizer, 1999).

In the school itself, teachers are the most important variable in the social-ization process. They present the normative view of socialization or societal values. Teachers are role models. They reinforce life attitudes and goals that are generally middle class. As a total environment, the school is a complex sys-tem that not only teaches youth how to communicate but also arranges tasks whereby the youngster receives gratification, learns cooperative and group sharing behaviors, acquires social skills, and seeks other people's approval and validation. It is within the school setting that youngsters formulate an awareness of self and of others (Fukuzawa & Letendre, 2001).

In the regular school system, teachers often control and correct behaviors by intensifying punishment for breaches of existing rules or by adding new rules. Some teachers rely on sarcasm and embarrassment to punish or con-trol students. This approach to discipline and control is a means to an end. It is questionable whether these reactive tactics attain the results the teacher desires in dealing with problematic students, especially because relatively few students cause most of the discipline problems. Also, when a teacher's attempts to curtail negative behavioral patterns fail, and the teacher's disap-pointment is sensed by the students, some students will then deliberately "act out" even more (Phillips, 1998). Therefore, it can be concluded that too much time and energy are devoted to behavior control. Likewise, enforcing and/or adding rules in an arbitrary and rigid manner is unfair, is inefficient, and alienates a great deal of the student body.

There are students who correctly perceive that many discipline problems by their peers arise because teachers are ill prepared, or as a result of teacher incompetence. It would be a valid argument that student boredom and teacher disrespect are part of the reason why students act out. It is, therefore, important for teachers to design learning activities that are challenging, stimulating, and inclusive in order to maintain student interest. Educators can also avoid a negative atmosphere by emphasizing the value of education, improving dialogue and interactions with students, being more flexible, negotiating discipline, providing a variety in the choice of curricula, modernizing facilities, and offering job or vocational counseling. As students demonstrate responsibility, it is incumbent that they are allowed increased independence, autonomy, decision making, and choices in curricula and vocational goals (Durrant, 1995).

SUMMARY

All treatment programs focus on resocializing youngsters by strengthening the individual's self-image and self-control (Pazaratz et al., 2000). Treatment classes aim to accomplish this task by offering highly structured settings utilizing a multidisciplinary approach to provide care, counseling, socialization, and education through the combined efforts of educators and clinicians. Treatment classes are based on sociological theories, mental health techniques, reeducational models, or, more usually, a combination of all these approaches. Treatment classes utilize different intervention strategies (integrative) such as behavior therapy, psychodynamic theory, and milieu therapy. Treatment classes focus on enhancing the youth's self-concept, which is the basis for stimulating change in other areas (Pazaratz, 2001). Education is interwoven with treatment and care, so that curriculum and child management meet each youngster's academic and emotional needs (Pazaratz, 1998c).

In the treatment class, mental health professionals such as social workers, psychologists, and youth workers are available to support troubled students. They have more time and expertise in dealing with a youth's emotional problems than do educators in a public school. Additionally, the youngster's socioeconomic background or differences are not a negative factor. There is also greater staff monitoring of a youth's happiness and purposefulness. Students are taught to interact with their environment in a positive fashion, or to "rock the boat" when this approach is needed (Cartledge & Milburn, 1996). In other words, they are encouraged to influence the attitudes of their teachers, the classroom youth workers, and their peers in order to attain their needs with fewer hassles (Pazaratz, 2001). In the treatment class, child care workers provide immediate support during crises, regular contact with collateral agencies, and feedback and advice to parents, and they teach child management techniques. Child care workers act as the go-between with police and the justice system, as needed; counsel school phobia; resolve peer and adult difficulties; and ultimately reduce the amount of acting out and school suspensions. Reintegration into the public school system occurs when youngsters have sufficiently modified their inappropriate behaviors, so that their attitudes toward school and life have become more positive, enabling them to continue their progression in overall adjustment (Pazaratz, 1998c).

CONCLUSION

In combining treatment with education, the question that must be addressed is "How are the disparate factors of two distinct disciplines coordinated and synthesized?" There are clear differences in roles, duties, background, training, and job emphasis for teachers and youth care workers. However, there are also common elements such as focusing on youngsters and relationships, creating conditions for learning and discovery, and blending program rationales, rituals, and protocols. This means that when these two different approaches are combined, the limits of each discipline seemingly make up for the shortfall of the other. In other words, the parameter or scope of either discipline, and the nature of the teacher's and youth worker's involvement with students, does not prevent an overlap. It is when one approach is insufficient in depth or perspective that the other will compensate with greater clarity; then, utility, purpose, and direction will be found in the other. In practice, the youth worker's approach in language and interactions will be neutral in order to foster transference, whereas the teacher is didactic in order to convey ideas and to instruct. Even though the contexts for the educator and counselor are different, nevertheless, each discipline supports the other. The student benefits from the educational knowledge and training of the teacher. The emotional needs of the youth are addressed by the counseling skills of the youth worker.

Classroom Behavior Scale

Student:
Date:

	Never	Very Infrequently	Infrequently	Moderately	Frequently	Very Frequently	Always
	1	2	3	4	5	6	7

I. Academic Behaviors

  A. Tasks

1. Starts each task promptly.							
2. Stays on task.							
3. Follows instructions.							
4. Completes assignments.							
5. Corrects identified errors.							

35

  B. Attitude

1. Pays attention.							
2. Talks in turn.							
3. Asks permission to go off-task.							
4. Deals appropriately with delays.							
5. Deals appropriately with task change.							

35

II. Peer Interaction

1. Works cooperatively in groups.							
2. Participates in discussion.							
3. Shows respect for peers.							
4. Deals with peers equitably.							
5. Makes responsible decisions.							

35

III. Teacher Interaction

1. Obeys requests, rules, and instructions.							
2. Asks for help when necessary.							
3. Deals cooperatively with teacher.							
4. Accepts error correction.							
5. Manifests a friendly manner toward teacher.							

35

Comments on Behavior:

Total Points:
Present Score_____/140
Previous Score _____/140
Change _____/140

Student Progress Report

Student: _____ Date: _____

Facility: _____ Teacher: _____

A. Academic Performance

Code: Achievement: P = Passing (50%); F = Failing; NA = Not Applicable
       Effort: S = Satisfactory; NS = Not Satisfactory

| | | | Achievement | | |
Subject	Code or Grade Level	Credit Value	Past	Present	Effort

B. Learning Skills Development

Code: 1: Strong; 2: Satisfactory; 3: Improving; and 4: Needs Improvement

				Past	Present
Understanding of materials—visual					
Understanding of materials—oral					
Note making					
Research skills					
Participation					
Work completion					
Organization of daily work					
Presentation of daily work					
Overall achievement					
Overall effort					

C. General Comments

This report covers the school period from _____ to _____ .

Number of days absent: _____ Number of times late: _____

Teacher: _____ Principal: _____

CHAPTER 11

Residential Treatment of a Disturbed Adolescent
A Case Study

Children and adolescents labeled conduct disordered (CD) are the most frequently diagnosed referral to residential treatment. Conduct-disordered youth do not trust adults. They have difficulty with impulse control, reality testing, and emotional decoding. Most have never experienced affection and stable family relations. They are disturbed and disturbing because they disregard the rights of others and societal norms. They also display antisocial behaviors, such as aggressiveness, lying, stealing, manipulation, and callousness. Attention deficit hyperactive disorder is a common comorbidity (Conduct Problems Prevention Research Group, 1992). This chapter is based upon the data collected by using the Psychosocial Assessment profile as outlined in Chapter 3. This case study explicitly describes the integrative residential treatment techniques utilized to stabilize and treat a teenage male whose presenting problems are quite representative of the conduct-disordered youngster.

Conduct disorder (also abbreviated CD) in adolescents is characterized by constant conflict with others, especially parents, teachers, and peer groups. Adolescents diagnosed as CD do not see the world as a place of manageable contingencies (Short & Shapiro, 1993). They are often easily provoked, overreact, and enjoy creating chaos. Conduct-disordered adolescents have difficulty controlling their impulses. They are unable to postpone or delay gratification. They are manipulative. They attempt to use, or do use, physical force or threats to get what they want (Eppright, Kashani, Robinson, & Reid, 1993). Due to social skill deficits, they have trouble forming genuine friendships. Although conduct-disordered teens have chronic relationship problems, come from unstable homes, and have educational deficits, they are identified only after they violate the rights of others and engage in assault, theft, or property damage (Conduct Problems Prevention Research Group, 1992).

The inability of the conduct-disordered youth to learn (cause and effect) from his or her behaviors is viewed by Offerd, Boyle, and Racine (1991) as an indicator of a learning disability, and by Pazaratz (1996b) as a manifestation of poor reality testing. Such youths' incapacity to develop appropriate positive social bonds relegates the CD adolescent to interact with similarly behaviorally disordered peers, as they are shunned by their normative age group. According to Bernstein (1996), CD adolescents are the most difficult of all youth who enter treatment. Chescheir and Shulz (1989) supported this observation, stating that there is little prognosis for change in conduct-disordered adolescents because they seem to lack the capacity to care for or relate to others; thus, they do not learn from relationships. Their inability to feel anxious and to have insight limits their aptness to change. In other words, they are unaware that they have problems, and when these are pointed out, they do not want to overcome them. These shortcomings hinder the likelihood of successful treatment outcome (Pazaratz, 1996b). Nevertheless, because the majority of male adolescents admitted to residential treatment are diagnosed as CD, it is important for treatment staff to understand the nature of the young person's conduct problems, within social, cultural, situational, and gender contexts, as this material informs treatment (Feital, Margetson, Chamas, & Lipman, 1992).

FAMILY DYNAMICS

Winnicott (1998) believes that an individual cannot be seen in isolation from the (m)other. He believes the way in which all of us relate to each other and the world at large comes from our experience of being born into context. Children also develop their sense of self from interactions with important others: parents, siblings, relatives, teachers, and so on. Children especially long for sustaining (supportive and involved) relations with their parents. The nature of these relationships, or the quality of attachments, shapes most of their social and emotional actions (Kohut, 1977). As children mature, they internalize images of objects (parents), which are not really present (Speltz, DeKlyen, Greenberg, & Dryden, 1998). But parent–child bonding can be damaged when parents react to their child's shortcomings over expectations or the like, and when the parent's style of discipline is excessively harsh or indifferent. Many parents are unaware that their interactions, such as exerting too much control, being too emotionally or physically distant (withholding of affection), or their spousal conflicts, affect their child. Tragically, some parents believe their child is the cause of all the family's problems, as they overlook or do not recognize that their child does not adapt easily to changes and new stimuli. There are parents who have difficulty coping with the various challenges and pressures their child struggles with during maturation (Kazdin, 1995). Nevertheless, their child is expressly aware of his or her vulnerability and dependence on the goodwill and reasonableness of his or her parents. Consequently, some children develop anxious attachments to their parents (Farber & Egeland, 1987).

In examining the influence of family dynamics on children, Laing and Esterson (1970) found that disordered thinking patterns and irrational behaviors are created, exacerbated, or alleviated by the family. Mallinckrodt (1992) supported these conclusions, and Mollerstrom, Patchner, and Milner (1992) added that both high family conflict and low family cohesion are significantly associated with an elevated potential for abuse. Walters-Leeper, Wright, and Mack (1994) have found that children who experience an abusive or chaotic environment will become bitter with diminished relational capacity. They will not have the ability to meet parental expectations. They will not develop self-worth or trust adults. They will often frustrate adults with their noncompliance and hostility. As a result, a cyclical interactive pattern emerges whereby parents retaliate and mistreat, or are neglectful of, their child, causing additional negative reactive behaviors from their child (Pazaratz, 2004). This is supported by Feital et al. (1992), who have determined that in response to physical or sexual abuse within the family, child and adolescent misconduct will occur at extremely high rates.

Personality development also occurs in the context of cultural influences that are conveyed to the individual in the course of various interpersonal dynamics. Transmitted in these interactions are the unique cultural ways of dealing with stress. Children who experience too much failure, too early in life, are exquisitely vulnerable to a wide variety of emotional complications. These include developing a negative outlook (mood), poor self-esteem, and an inability to regulate feelings (Pazaratz & Morton, 2000). Unstable or absent family ties and impoverished social bonds at school increase the likelihood for delinquency (Sampson & Laub, 1993). Consequently, emotional, conduct, and learning problems also emerge. Learning problems will lead to additional school difficulties and impaired relationships with peers and family members (Kelly, 1999). Maintaining positive relationships becomes tedious for CD youngsters because of language and reasoning disabilities. Young persons diagnosed with CD have difficulty asserting themselves, tend to blame others for their behaviors, and do not develop the ability to feel or care for others because they are emotionally detached (Chescheir & Shulz, 1989). Their inability to talk and express ideas leads to frustration and even violence. Language and comprehension disorders are the basis of the chronic emotional problems manifest in juvenile delinquency (Cohen, Davine, & Meloche-Kelly, 1998).

RESIDENTIAL TREATMENT

The Haydon Youth Services treatment program is located in Oshawa, Ontario, Canada. It consists of seven therapeutic group homes for 55 emotionally disturbed and behaviorally disordered males and females, ages 12 to 18. The clinical program utilizes the integrative treatment model. Haydon subscribes to the principle of containment (safety), or the capacity of staff members to provide treatment and to maintain control. The aim of the program is to enable children and adolescents to tolerate separation and loss, and to generate profound change (reunion). Child and youth care workers are employed to teach residents those social skills that are necessary so that they can deal competently with the outside world and the people in it. These skills are developed through mediated learning experiences (i.e., the young person is shown how to interpret and understand interactions and communication). Youth workers utilize a diversity of perspectives in order to enter into the individual's internal experience and comprehend the youth's particular perception (Berman, 1997). Ultimately, the youth is taught that cooperating with staff (the hated object) is not as bad as the youngster feared. Staff members emphasize that the youth cannot get better without facing certain painful realities, such as intense feelings of emptiness and guilt (Pazaratz, 1996a).

Because the emotionally disturbed young person has experienced severe disruptions to important relationships, the treatment focus is on dealing with the youth's emotional pain (hurt and anger) and the youngster's sense of abandonment, or emptiness and nothingness. Exploration of each resident's coping style, such as his or her strengths, weaknesses, and ability to learn from experience, is fundamental to treatment planning at Haydon. When residents react or become conflictual, staff members attempt to make youth aware of what they are unaware of, and face those issues that must be resolved in order for youngsters to move on. Clarification of problem areas and the monitoring of a youngster's progress are coded or graphed on a level/reinforcement scale (Pazaratz, 2003b). This assists the resident in focusing on specific recurring difficulties, demystifying the causes and effects of behaviors, and creating a sense of meaning and purpose. In counseling terms, this means the front-line worker asks youth to examine how they create their own emotions through their belief system and self-talk (Ellis & Dryden, 1987). Kazdin (1995) believed that unless negative emotions and disruptive behaviors are treated in children and adolescents, dysfunctional attitudes will become entrenched as antisocial behavior in adulthood.

TREATMENT ISSUES

A majority of male adolescents admitted to Haydon Youth Services, since it was established in 1980, have been diagnosed as conduct disordered. There has also been a high incidence of comorbidity in these youth (Pazaratz, 1999). This observation of co-occurrence in CD youth is supported in clinical research (Harrington, 1993). Additionally, the conduct-disordered adolescent is often heavily into substance abuse (Wetzer & Sanderson, 1997). In designing interventions, comorbid disorders such as ADHD, substance abuse, and/or sexual aberrations are dealt with separately (Bernstein, 1996). These problems are unlikely to improve with interventions that target symptoms alone. Therefore, it is preferred that treatment is multifaceted in order to deal with the pervasive and chronic nature of emotional disorders, and to address the behavioral, academic, and psychogenic needs of the youth. Clark (1998) added that understanding defense mechanisms is essential in stabilizing children and adolescents in treatment. According to Fonagy and Target (1995), the therapeutic task is to alter the CD youth's sense of self by providing a therapeutic relationship in which the adolescent can experience him or herself as different from the negative projections he or she has received in his or her family and from peers. This requires managing the youngster's resistance to incorporating new information by clarifying conflicted behaviors, engendering more adaptive functioning, and providing positive experiences. This means that during interventions, youth workers are required to be sensitive to the cognitive, social, and emotional demands of each major developmental stage.

As reported by Pazaratz (1993), conduct-disordered children and adolescents exhibit developmental disorders. They have poor ego strength or inhibiting functions and display difficulty organizing themselves. They also demonstrate a profound inability to understand the role they played in creating relational problems. They avoid taking personal responsibility for their behaviors, and they have difficulty letting go of old disturbances or anger (Loeber, Lahey, & Thomas, 1991). To improve frustration tolerance and to acquire adaptive social skills, the CD youngster needs to develop the ability to become self-observant, to become aware of and empathic to others, and to utilize critical-thinking strategies (Frankel, Myatt, & Cantwell, 1995). Because CD youngsters are also anxious and mistrustful, they often misperceive communication and display oversensitivity, falsely believing they are being challenged and blamed. Fearing criticism and unable to trust or be trusted, CD youngsters challenge and resist adults, defy rules, and violate boundaries. Conduct-disordered youngsters need specific feedback, such as describing how their emotional and behavioral reactions are connected to their problems (Pazaratz, 1996b). Information that unravels interactional sequences also helps them to understand the reasons for other people's feelings of anger and rejection, and to comprehend the nature of social systems (e.g., family and educational) and their present and future connections with them (Hanna, Hanna, & Keys, 1999).

GROUP INTERACTIONS

According to a meta-analysis of studies by Rose (1998), the cognitive-behavioral framework is among the most effective means for working with this population. This means youth who fit this *Diagnostic and Statistical Manual of Mental Disorders* (*DSM-IV-TR*; American Psychiatric Association, 2000) category will comprise a heterogeneous population in terms of abilities and liabilities. Therefore, the group format offers a powerful clinical context for changing the behavior of CD youngsters. At Haydon Youth Services, groups are an integral feature of programming. Within the group format, the youth worker's objective is to assist the resident to reveal or express his or her thinking and action patterns, and to utilize staff's interpretation effectively in the change process. It is when staff inculcate values during interactions with residents and through modeling that each youth and group member learns to entertain new ways of thinking and doing (i.e., to admit that his or her behaviors are self-defeating and self-harming). This coincides with the process of group work, which includes improving peer relationships, social competence, and problem-solving strategies. Understanding the problems of substance abuse, improving school performance, and learning about family interactions are discussion topics. Conduct-disordered adolescents can become adaptive in these areas when staff assist them to decipher emotional content embedded in communication (encoding and decoding), develop self-regulation of emotions, and acquire a sense of meaning or purpose (Camras, Gow, & Ribordy, 1983).

In group sessions, the youth worker reassures residents that not having all the answers, and not knowing how to express oneself, is just as acceptable as having insight and knowing. When adolescents experience the group setting as a safe place, they are more likely to express what they really think and feel (Proctor & Dutta, 1994). This means that upon feeling secure and trusting, the youth will risk revealing his or her shortcomings and mistakes. Staff also teach residents that clear, nonemotional, and direct communication is the basis for problem resolution, and that behaviors can be reshaped by constructive problem solving. Staff also emphasize that the ability to describe behavioral events with words is essential for both communicating well and acquiring self-control. When residents learn to be less impulsive and develop a more reflective style, new skills and increased frustration tolerance emerge. As the locus of control becomes internalized, youngsters gain a sense of confidence and their self-esteem improves. The correlation between having self-control and experiencing self-esteem is significant, because working in one area can bring change in another (Pazaratz, 1996b). It is when youngsters need fewer external controls that they feel better about themselves.

CASE STUDY

James is a 15-year-old boy who is small for his age. He has a history of being physically abused and neglected. He also has a background of theft, truancy, drug use, arson, vandalism, assault, promiscuity, and intensely physical behavior characterized by recklessness and destructiveness. He holds many negative feelings about his past, due to the difficult relationship he had with his parents. James' parents had "short fuses" and low tolerance for frustration. Tension within the family was high, and communication patterns were indirect, chaotic, and disturbed. Anger was a common emotion in this disengaged family, as were blaming and shaming.

James' parents could become overinvolved, critical, and intrusive, so that none of his behaviors went unnoticed. James' behaviors were elicited by a family system that caused behaviors to occur (Wachtel, 1993). This lack of temperamental fit between James and his parents led to them labeling him a "weasel." When they were questioned as to what they meant, they referred to him as a sneak, a liar, and a thief. He could never be trusted or believed. For Perls (1969c), the client (James) is doing what he has learned to do in order to survive. By the age of 10, James had been in and out of numerous foster homes. Garmezy and Rutter (1983) stated that multiple placements of children comprise another indicator of instability, which predicts antisocial behavior. Upon admission, James displayed extremely low self-esteem and weak verbal skills (he lacked ideas and problem-solving strategies). He was continually in conflict with all the other adolescents in the home. His interactions were based upon manipulation, exploitation, and violence. Because James' parents had forbidden him to discuss his difficulties and feelings with anybody outside the family, the youth workers found it difficult to get close to James. The youth workers described James as superficial, manipulative, a liar, and verbally aggressive.

James suppressed and denied all emotions (shameful rage) and concealed information (hypervigilant), which only led to increased tension. When his tensions became unbearable (discomfort anxiety), his behaviors would escalate. James, being small for his age, often expected to be hurt, but nevertheless he would still provoke others. He seemed to be constantly in fights. He followed the rule that when you are bigger than other people, it is okay to hurt them. James bullied and was cruel to children who entered the residence subsequent to his arrival, especially taking advantage of their vulnerability of being new. He learned how to force others to back him up, and this power added to his aggressiveness. James seemed incapable of empathizing with his victims or comprehending the meaning of terrorizing another individual. These bullying behaviors and acceptance of being hurt, stated Johnson (1997), are the key components central to an abused child's thinking and behavior. Kivel and Creighton (1997) added that the imbalance of power and disrespect is at the heart of violence.

The youth workers tried to create a positive climate for change, consisting of brief but focused discussions on the benefits of openness. They challenged James to find new solutions to recurring problems, worked with him to improve his listening and communication skills, showed him how to calm himself down, and requested that he practice emotional honesty. Staff focused on James' shame and its pervasive negative effect on his relationships, and on the healing of shame through open, supportive discussion. In group and individual sessions, James was confronted with his manipulative and aggressive behaviors. Corder (1994) stated that highly structured groups are especially useful for adolescents with limited verbal skills. James had a difficult time revealing himself in groups for fear of being ridiculed. To counter this fear of embarrassment, staff tried to get James to discover the value of his own life. He must be able to value himself even though he felt ashamed of being abused and abandoned. He needed to learn to tolerate anger and loneliness, especially when others disagreed with him or shunned him. When James became upset, his acting out consisted of doing considerable damage to the group home. He had developed a remarkable but costly trick of kicking doors off their hinges. James also used drugs to help him deal with his problems and to resist staff controlling him. Walters-Leeper et al. (1994) viewed habitual drug use as a maladaptive response to existential fear in young males.

A youngster's lack of progress in residential treatment can be caused by the way in which intervention is approached by staff, or because of unsuccessful solutions being implemented in treatment planning. Clearly, some youth workers found James frustrating and difficult to work with. Ross (1996) stated that conduct-disordered youth are frequently deceitful and have become sophisticated at lying and manipulating others. Some staff described James as uncooperative and unwilling to change. Even though there were staff who imposed themselves on James, which led to power struggles, they remained nonthreatening and nonpunitive. It is the ability to manage countertransference that sets apart the superior from the mediocre worker (Van Wagner, Gelso, Huges, & Diemer, 1991). A few countertransference issues were dealt with in supervision, whereby staff were reminded not to personalize James' behavior. Instead, when James "acted out," there was to be a subsequent loss of privileges, and more restrictions were to be placed on him.

Consequences were employed as a clinical tool to teach James to learn from experience and to control behaviors. James was informed that the only way he could escape control was by giving up the behavior that was being controlled. James was taught that concealing (suppressing) personal information or feelings (as per his parents' rules) usually triggered his negative moods and surly attitude, whereas confiding in someone served as an emotional release. Staff also pointed out that when his thinking and behavior were controlled by his emotional state, he became hyperactive, so that he needed to become reflective. When staff clarified conflictual communication, this helped James to understand and to carefully think through his responses. The development of reflexivity, self-awareness, and agency within self-awareness, or through person-centered counseling that was employed with James, was detailed by Rennie (1998).

James did not allow staff easy access to his thoughts, causing some staff to view him as primitive and narcissistic. Other staff argued that his narcissism was a defense or control of staff by keeping them at a distance. Staff stressed to James that treatment offered him security, even though he was not interested in change. He often ignored staff, played confused or dumb, scorned staff, and viewed them as people he could manipulate. Not all staff reacted to his put-downs, defiance, and hostility. Some calmly confronted James' main defense of rationalization, which he used to justify his behaviors. Some of James' resistance was directed against his dependent needs. Izzo and Ross (1990), in a meta-analysis of delinquents, concluded that understanding the offender's thinking style is as significant as how the youngster thinks and feels. James acted out more, especially when consequenced, and this was interpreted as projective identification whereby he exhibited attitudes and feelings that confirmed staff interpretations (Goldstein, 1995). Unfortunately, some staff attempted to change circumstances, or the situation, by reasoning or appealing to him. James was quick to realize he had the upper hand, and he enjoyed the power he exercised and the ability to put these staff in a predicament.

Even though James was unable to identify any problems he had solved through his oppositional attitude, he literally believed he could not survive without his defiant behaviors. At times, to get staff to leave him alone, James cooperated with them. Other times, he responded out of desperation. He did not know what else to do, or how to deal with his fears and worries. However, he did not necessarily want to change. It was when staff repeatedly made specific unconscious problems conscious, and were consistent in applying consequences, that James became capable of seeing a more practical solution to interpersonal conflicts. James eventually began to relate quite positively to a couple of energetic staff and their focus on fun in sport. They questioned his idealized beliefs (as per rational emotive behavior therapy) that he was entitled to always have his way and that not having it was unbearable (Ellis & Dryden, 1987). Learning to dispute his irrational self-talk helped him to give up his hostility and negative way of experiencing others. James was shown that self-esteem and positive regard for others flow from the development of self-control and are essential for psychological well-being (Pazaratz, 1993).

Family sessions focused on childhood developmental stage problems, problems in the parental relationship, and positive resolution of conflicts, which Vetere (1993) believed help parents of conduct-disordered adolescents to develop balanced parenting styles. Family counseling also attempted to create a positive climate for change consisting of brief but focused discussions on home atmosphere, communication skills, patience, and the child's self-esteem (as per Hurrelmann & Hamilton, 1996). Even though James made progress, his parents had a difficult time accepting any kind of information on parenting styles or being responsible for James, arguing that they were being blamed. They also resisted discussing fundamental issues of family functioning and the parental relationship. The family worker reported that James' parents were unwilling to trust and that they reacted to the worker, claiming that she did not understand the nature of their relationship with James. James' dad even refused to discuss his own childhood and his relationship with his father, stating that that information was highly personal.

After four sessions, James' parents declined to attend any additional sessions. Roberts (1989) has noted that parental resistance to being involved in their child's problems impedes effective intervention. Nevertheless, after 14 months at Haydon, James no longer needed staff assistance to deal with the bulk of his emotional problems. He learned to calmly discuss issues and stopped exploiting others. The parents agreed with the discharge plan that James would be sent to a foster home instead of returning to their home. James responded to the laidback but consistent approach of the foster parents. James also benefited from residing in a different community and interacting with different peers. Since he moved to the foster home 5 months ago, he has not experienced any serious problems. He has also experienced significant academic progress, based upon an accelerated remediation curriculum developed at Haydon's Treatment Class.

FORMULATION

In his background history, James was described as fixated at an early level of childhood development. James had not learned socially acceptable behavioral controls and lacked awareness of personal and other people's boundaries. James' antisocial behaviors emerged as a reaction to negative, critical, inflexible, and nonaffectionate parenting. James' parents, although keen at enforcing some trivial expectations for James, nevertheless were unavailable for his emotional and daily needs. His parents exerted power and dominance with minimal amounts of affection, support, praise, or friendship. They also did not communicate calmly, nor did they articulate the prosocial values required for James to internalize a sense of personal safety and meaning. These negative and primitive interactional patterns undermined the parent–child attachment and limited James' ability to develop competent social skills, as discussed in Cicchetti, Lynch, Shonk, and Manly (1992). The lack of appropriate parental monitoring of and involvement in James' activities caused James to seek acceptance and meaning with his peers, who were also at odds with society's values. Doherty (1995) supported this interpretation, stating that morality is socially constructed, and where and how individuals find a basis for morality are critical to their socialization.

Because James was not emotionally connected to his family, he developed an identity and displayed behaviors that were more closely linked with those of his antisocial peers. James repressed his personal identity for group membership. He also acted as the most important person in the world, and this grandiosity became the basis for all his distortions. The deviant peer group became a training ground for delinquent acts and risk taking, such as drug usage, petty theft, bullying, and extortion. The deviant group provided unmet identity and image needs, a sense of belonging and purpose, and an outlet for stored anger, hurt, and frustration. Group membership offered a safe place for James to hide his shame, low self-esteem, and anxieties in the bravado and excitement of delinquent activity. Intimacy was not demanded with his group (gang), only loyalty. Rules and rituals defined the solidarity of the group. Values got twisted when James was praised for getting away with antisocial and deviant acts. James believed he was omnipotent and smarter than others. James' distorted belief system and contempt for others perpetuated additional antisocial behaviors.

DISCUSSION

Upon admission to Haydon Youth Services, James did not have sufficient verbal skills to articulate feelings and interpret dynamics. Residential treatment allowed James to express all his emotions, and sometimes these emerged in physical rage. Youth workers attempted to get James to understand the source of his conflict, to revise his belief system, and to change his destructive habits. This was accomplished by helping James to be aware of his unique developmental style that led to certain difficulties (i.e., cognitive, emotional, social, and linguistic). In individual and group sessions, youth workers showed James how to work on these developmental delays and consequential frustration. Staff recognized the pattern of James' mood swings and learned to anticipate those situations under which his frustration would burst forth. Unlike James' parents, who would incite James' frustrations, staff became adept at defusing his emotions. Staff helped James to understand that he became violent when he could not talk, or express his ideas and thinking in words. Staff and some higher-functioning peers helped James to understand that his feelings of shame and rage were a normal response to his history of physical abuse, but his angry outbursts and retaliation when frustrated were not acceptable. He learned that his peers were not always trying to do him in, as he had erroneously believed. On most occasions, they were merely putting themselves first, or looking after themselves, and were probably indifferent to others, including James. James was asked to counsel a peer with similar anger problems and to develop interests and activities for pleasure.

James' treatment plan was multimodal. Insight was used to give James an awareness of his inner conflicts and to help him to understand his anger. Relationship building occurred by staff displaying warmth and empathy. Natural and logical consequences were employed to change James' behaviors and attitudes. But fundamentally, staff emphasized that all interactions are based upon communication and its impact. Staff focused on providing James (and all residents) with a new way of interpreting dynamics rather than reacting with old patterns or defensiveness. In utilizing a solution-focused approach to James' problems, staff attempted to have James put problem-solving strategies (anger management and frustration tolerance) into practice. James was taught to change his focus, shifting problems or activating events into goals and tackling those goals through understanding past successful and unsuccessful solutions (Pazaratz, 2000b). The relationship between the problem (his expectations of others) and the maladaptive interactional patterns (James demanding to have his way) was repeatedly pointed out to James. Eventually, he learned to recognize the connection between the symptomatic problem (shame and anger) and ineffective problem solving (physically acting out to get his way) (Klinger, 1982).

Some children and adolescents demonstrate progress while in residential placement but regress to preintervention behavior levels after discharge because they are easily drawn into a deviant peer group (Pazaratz, 1998a). Harris (1999) supported this particular interpretation of the power and impact of group socialization and concluded that all children, but especially teenagers, are primarily influenced by peers and community experiences and not by their family. In every youngster's discharge plans from Haydon, staff take into account Lymann and Campbell's (1996) position that when treatment programs emphasize predischarge and postdischarge planning, they are more effective at reintegrating adolescents into the community, especially if the person is helped to establish a new social network. This was enacted with James. Yet, James had mixed feelings about moving to a foster home in a different community some distance from his friends. He had wanted to move home or even close to home. James spent three weekends on preplacement visits. Finally, he decided that even if he moved to a foster home, he could still have contact with his parents and friends via the phone and on some visits.

CONCLUSION

This case study of James supports Gibbs, Potter, and Goldstein's (1995) findings that some conduct-disordered adolescents can help one another effectively when motivated through a positive group context where they are equipped with specific skills for giving mutual help. Additionally, in individual sessions, the treatment approach with James included teaching mature moral judgment, teaching strategies or skills to manage anger, correcting thinking errors, and practicing social skills. This type of intervention is supported by Hanna et al. (1999). Staff implemented what Kazdin (1995) and Dodge (1993) have also shown: that conduct-disordered adolescents should be handled by staff facilitating clear communication, altering the child's interactional pattern, utilizing cognitive problem-solving skills training, and encouraging and developing acute interpretation of cues, social problem solving, and the anticipation of consequences.

The case study of James demonstrates the utility of the implementation of the Psychosocial Assessment model. The case study also provides some specific implications in the residential treatment of conduct-disordered children and adolescents. These include taking the individual and his or her needs into account when utilizing multidimensional and integrative interventions, such as preventing aggressive behaviors, teaching youngsters conflict resolution skills, and helping them to build self-esteem, social competence, and self-regulating skills. According to Zoccolillo, Tremblay, and Vitario (1996), long-term solutions include identifying oppositional and defiant and aggressive children at an early age to prevent maladaptive behaviors from escalating to a more intense level, giving children and their families psychological support, and teaching families positive interactional skills, which help them to provide a supportive environment to overcome a youth's negative behaviors.

CHAPTER 12

Afterword

This afterword reviews and summarizes the main empirically supported practices employed in the residential treatment of emotionally disturbed children and adolescents utilizing an integrative treatment model. It has been shown that the key to harmonizing the tenets of treatment with the concepts of the social environment is the manner by which direct care workers enact relationships. However, it is when an integrative framework is utilized in a logical, focused format that child and youth care workers make group care principles comprehensible and accessible. It has also been shown that it is the variety of clinical strategies, specific suggestions, and treatment rationales that makes residents feel safe and deeply understood. Finally, this chapter concludes with the observation that the integrative therapeutic model creates an ideal balance between theory (literature) and practice.

INTRODUCTION

Integrative treatment recognizes that no single orientation can resolve the vast range of problems and issues that define the needs of disturbed youth in residential placement. Integrative therapy instructs and teaches direct care staff to comprehend youth and treatment from many perspectives. The integrative approach seeks to ascertain those strategies that can be learned from other ways of thinking about behavior change (Lazarus, 1989). It draws a connection between different theories so that these can be blended into coherent practice. In its contributions to the field of group care, integrative therapy hopes to provide something original and realistic. There is an emphasis on staff developing a clinical framework, knowing the experiences of youngsters in the context of group living, and being flexible when employing intervention techniques to manage disruptive behaviors. Integrative therapy also addresses the complex family system and its vital link to youth in care. The youngster's treatment needs cannot be grasped realistically without knowing the nature of the youth's relationship with his or her entire ecosystem of family, peers, school, and cultural-religious beliefs and practices. In other words, each youth lives within and is connected to a system of relationships that influence identity and behaviors (Bronfenbrenner, 1979). Residential treatment cannot be effective unless youngsters are viewed in this context, and there are various clinical tools in the integrative model that assist treatment staff in this effort.

THE FOUR PHASE SYSTEM

The integrative approach to residential treatment originated in 1973 with the inception of the Four Phase System in Metropolitan Toronto, Ontario, Canada (Pazaratz, Randall, Spekkens, Lazor, & Morton, 2000). The system, as a continuum of treatment, demonstrated that a number of agencies located in various community settings, utilizing therapeutic models from divergent clinical perspectives, could be integrated into a system of care. Although all programs worked from the same material (referral information and treatment plan), each developed its own unique model or therapeutic method. This meant that every facility and its staff implemented their own realism and clinical coherence. Various clinical theories (multimodal) were enacted as interventions so that individual treatment centers offered novel approaches but concepts that would complement each other. For example, common to all Phases Three and Four was the use of the milieu to organize and to shape interpersonal interactions. The social system or culture was structured to enact positive peer relationships so that the individual was not additionally pathologized by negative peer or subgroup attitudes. These clinical standards were basic to every agency in the system and ensured the smooth transfer of youngsters between agencies and phases. Thus, all Four Phase agencies adhered to the philosophy that effective residential care must not be harsh or too superficial, but had to have relevance and to be goal oriented.

The Four Phase System's genesis was to deinstitutionalize adolescents (i.e., provide an alternative to hospitalization or training school placement). This plan was realized with the system developing highly resourced community-based residential programs to divert adolescents. The system's goal was to provide the appropriate level of intervention to maintain the adolescent safely in the community. As a continuum of care, the Four Phase System was structured to stabilize any disorder or pathology, but also for the adolescent to benefit from the intervention. Thus, to meet the treatment and developmental needs of high-risk adolescents, the system acknowledged the inadequacy of any one treatment rationale and advocated the potential benefit of others. The limitations of the Four Phase System were reflected by the system's search for solutions outside itself or its paradigm when youth were placed in programs not part of the system. However, the real strength of the system was highlighted by Phase One's home care–aftercare program, which was flexible enough to treat and support adolescents by placing workers in their homes to prevent family breakdown or to foster reconnection upon discharge. Ultimately, the system aimed to increase the family's ability to interact functionally and to obviate the youth's need to enter into care in the first place, and to prevent recidivism when adolescents were placed.

The integrative approach of the Four Phase System was, in reality, the only design that could have worked. Given the number of adolescents with a multiplicity of disorders, problems, and needs, it was improbable that any one therapy could have been sufficient. The integrative model, also known as eclecticism, convergence, or rapprochement (Goldfried, Castonguay, & Sanfran, 1992), enabled the system to be all-inclusive, comprehensive, and encompassing, with the ultimate purpose of maximizing its applicability and efficacy. The concept of the model had to be realistic and pragmatic in order for the system to work, and it did for 17 years. The system's legacy, relevance, and impact are immeasurable and profoundly important as it demonstrated that high-risk adolescents did not have to be institutionalized, not all disturbed and disordered adolescents had to be treated outside their home, and most adolescents who needed residential placement could be handled safely in the community. Importantly, the Four Phase System's policies and practices have evolved into standardized operational regulations and clinical methodology, and as a model for enacting residential treatment facilities.

INTEGRATIVE TREATMENT

According to most North American children's shelters licensing legislation, treatment programs are required to define precisely those interventions that can and cannot be imposed and how these will be delivered. In practice, this means that treatment staff are expected to maintain a structured environment, monitor a range of behaviors, follow a clearly defined treatment model, and establish positive relationships (Pazaratz, 2000b, 2000c, 2000d). These principles are meant to be enacted by a team of staff who are responsible for fostering a treatment culture that is empathic, is relevant, provides dignity, and is goal oriented. Staff are also expected to help youngsters to grow developmentally, to assist them to understand how issues from their past affect their current attitudes, and to teach them how they can develop new views. This rationale enables staff to be theoretically consistent while technically eclectic (Dryden, 1987). In effect, staff can use any counseling technique that enables youth to attain their treatment goals consistent with their ability to process these.

The Four Phase System supported the view espoused by Winnicott (1965) that residential treatment's main focus is that of a "holding environment," where youngsters' feelings and defenses are dealt with by staff. In addition, according to evidence-based research, treatment progresses more smoothly with integrative practices that provide a balanced approach to working with children and adolescents (Kazdin & Weisz, 2003). Integrative therapy allows for the best possible treatment plans for individual youth because different therapies such as behavioral, cognitive, psychodynamic, constructionism–solutions-oriented, and transtheoretical techniques can be employed (Shapiro, Freiberg, & Bandstein, 2006). When these treatment concepts are part of the milieu, it becomes a reinforcing environment that can aid in stabilizing youngsters, enhancing their self-concept, improving their reactions to challenges and stress, and increasing their ability to get along with others (Bettelheim, 1960). Importantly, the integrative treatment approach allows staff to employ techniques from various theoretical disciplines that optimize the youth worker's style and improve the worker's flexibility in dealing with combined disorders. According to Drake and Mueser (2000), integrative treatment is the preferred approach for clients experiencing severe mental illness, with better engagement and adherence rates and improved clinical outcome.

In examining models of care for dual disorders, Minkoff and Drake (1991) have found that the integrative treatment model is generally viewed as the most appropriate. The overarching benefit of staff utilizing the integrative model is that it acknowledges the strengths and limitations of all therapies. It emphasizes those approaches that are not offered by only one therapy or theoretical construct. Employing more than one therapy enhances the possibilities of others and the options available to connect with the client. Milieu therapy, for example, emphasizes resocialization and relearning by creating conditions to learn about life and relationships, and to live in the here and now. It seeks to help youth to develop a stable sense of self so that they can deal with significant distress. When social process (psychodynamics) and behaviorism are combined with clear concrete problem definitions, this combination provides beneficial results (Sheldon, 1987). Social process includes integrating the findings of the Psychosocial Assessment with task-centered contracts and a level/reinforcement system. Combining all these elements is the basis for collecting background information, identifying current problems in interpersonal and intrapersonal behaviors, and structuring individual and family interventions. Thus, integrative therapy specifies treatment goals within social relationships or the group context, develops an explicit collaboration between youth workers and residents, informs the treatment plan, and provides new opportunities in the milieu and beyond (Pazaratz, 2003b).

PSYCHOSOCIAL ASSESSMENT OVERVIEW

The Psychosocial Assessment is a coordinated profile that was first implemented in 1975 at the Oshawa/Whitby Crisis Intervention Centre, a Four Phase reentry program located in Oshawa, Ontario. The Psychosocial Assessment is based on an evaluation of the life history of the young person; the nature of his or her relationship with family, adults, and peers; and the impact these people have had on the youth. The diagnostic strategy of the Psychosocial Assessment is to build upon the findings and recommendations of a psychological or psychiatric assessment by evaluating the youngster's personality traits, family history, living environment, style of interactions, nature of community behaviors, support outside the family, school achievement, self-understanding, self-esteem, previous history of problems, and stress responses, and the influence of these on the child or adolescent. The assessment process enables staff members and other practitioners to understand the youth's pattern of interactions, the relationship among the client's constitutional factors, to others and life events (Sullivan, 1953). The Psychosocial Assessment provides an understanding of risk issues (protective or buffering factors) and identifies the youth's resiliency and vulnerabilities. By evaluating both at-risk issues and resiliency factors, during residential placement, interventions can be planned that will either protect the resident or activate coping as a response to stress, crises, or problem solving. This information is used to determine treatment planning, the nature of family contacts, school enrollment, employment as an alternative, and the issues surrounding discharge.

The Psychosocial Assessment looks at both symptomology and the youth's position on a developmental scale with regard to drive, ego, superego, personality structure, primary versus secondary thought processes, age adequacy, and level of emotional development. The assessment informs staff of the youth's pattern of interactions, his or her relation to others and life events, and what support system the youth uses. When youth workers incorporate assessment data in their intervention strategies, this convergence of information can be used to recognize the degree of dysfunctionality, help to define an appropriate level of dependence, and provide information that will assist the resident to become more resourceful, competent, and resilient. The Psychosocial Assessment, like the mental status exam or psychological assessment, also requires subjective opinions, which means that staff are asked to interpret the quality of a resident's interactions with peers, family, and staff. Cooperation with others, or resistance to directives and a reluctance to participate in programming or activities, helps staff to understand the youth's conflicts (fears) that are revealed in behaviors or identified by others.

This assessment profile does not view behavioral or emotional disorders as fixed entities or from a structural viewpoint. But it is a descriptive behavioristic phenomenological type of a nosological system that takes into account that children and adolescents are viewed as still developing. The assessment categorizes areas of ego strength as well as weaknesses. The classification of strengths and special skills or development is as valid descriptively as are classifications of their counterpart deficiencies (Pazaratz, 1997). Exceptionally advanced areas of functioning may and often do coexist with unmotivated (laziness, learned helplessness, etc.) or deficient areas of development relative to age appropriateness (Pazaratz & Morton, 2000). Social norms are used as reference points for adaptive behaviors in adolescence such as social skills (emotional intelligence), school adjustment, and the like. Behavioral constellation in latency-aged youth is assessed from the standpoint of the developmental level at which the behavior appears.

When implementing a Psychosocial Assessment, youth workers should have comprehensive knowledge of the developmental stage of the child or adolescent operationally (i.e., cognitively, emotionally, linguistically, and physically). Critically, the youngster's adaptive capacity is a vital variable for this nosological system. It takes into account maturational and developmental events, or the concept of phases so that development is viewed as age appropriate, not yet developed, or regressed. There is also developmental unevenness that can be seen in discerning between speech, mobility, and the sensory mode. Youth workers are cautioned that if they are uncertain of normative functioning and appropriate developmental levels, they do not overestimate a youth's internalized conflict. It is impossible and destructive to expect youth to function at a level beyond their growth and developmental potential (at any moment in time). Activities and group interactions should be designed that are developmentally realistic and enable youngsters to express themselves safely (Pazaratz, 1998b).

REINFORCEMENTS

Residential treatment's main function is to create a secure environment or a safe place for youngsters to experience emotions and work them through (Winnicott, 1965). The nature of the environment and staff–youth relationships allow residents to express and repeatedly revise emotions. Most child and adolescent behaviors are shaped and defined by anxiety, (anger) rebellion, depression, withdrawal, and overconnection (Driekurs, Grunwald, & Pepper, 1982). However, youngsters are also affected by their fears or those factors beyond their understanding or control. These include the unknown (unfamiliar), being alone, rapid change in their bodies, disapproval or rejection, and inadequacy (self-blame). These insecurities arise from within a youth and from his or her environment, and are reinforced during social interactions. Thus, youngsters cannot immediately accept an unknown worker before basic trust is established, even though the worker is supportive. Youth tend to relate to staff when they feel safe and understood.

Many children and adolescents in treatment function at a concrete level so that abstract social issues and emotional dynamics are beyond their level of comprehension. Some regressed youngsters are also more sensory and kinesthetic. Their use of language is not well developed, and they do not have the ideas to express themselves. A behavioral intervention model such as the level/reinforcement system is designed to stabilize youth, to assist youngsters to make their environment and interactions predictable, and to help youth to understand both concrete and abstract issues (Pazaratz, 2000a). According to Franks (1982), combining the precepts of behavior therapy with systems theory creates facilitating conditions, or (in this instance) the rationale for the level/reinforcement system as described in Chapter 6.

The level/reinforcement system is a dimensional classification method that emphasizes quantitative assessment measures by employing behavior rating scales (Kamphaus & Campbell, 2006). It utilizes staff members' observations to monitor behavior change, a baseline for staff feedback, and a measure of a youth's behaviors in terms of adaptation and competencies. It utilizes positive reinforcers and response cost, transfer of stimulus control and stimulus fading, shaping, modeling, and desensitization. It aims to make structure and programming familiar and supportive. It is a detailed systematic approach to behavior management because it enables youth workers to analyze those issues that interfere with the youth being adaptive, being cooperative, and advancing developmentally. It helps staff identify learned patterns of behavior and how these are maintained in the environment. It illustrates how the youth evolves or regresses in treatment, and this informs the Psychosocial Assessment and the treatment plan or contract. When staff apply or remove reinforcements, adaptive behaviors can be increased, and negative attitudes extinguished. In effect, as the relationship between the resident's behaviors and the stimulus (environmental factors) is changed, this sequence results in adaptive behaviors and minimizes issues of control and staff–youth conflict (Pazaratz, 1998b).

The rating scale of the level/reinforcement system begins with an evaluation of a youth's behaviors that are problematic. Staff generate a list of behaviors that need to be worked on. Daily charting or graphing is based on observation and coding of a youth's behaviors by staff. The scale is divided into general categories of self-management of emotions and tasks that need to be performed. The scale is used to rate the youth's level of adherence to these identified areas. Staff use the information obtained from observation and charting of behaviors to teach improved peer relations, self-control, assertiveness, empathy, cooperation, responsibility, and treatment compliance. When youngsters advance from one reinforcement level to another, they exhibit different symptoms at the new one. This may mean that they appear more problematic when they progress up the scale or ladder. However, it should be remembered that behaviors at the higher level require more refined skills and create more difficult management problems. Staff do not always agree that the new behaviors reflect growth or adaptation to challenges (as per James in Chapter 11), because some staff members see these behavior changes are a sign of regression (Rosenfield, Frankel, & Esman, 1969).

The reinforcement chart is used to show youngsters the causal chain of events linked to their behaviors. These data can indicate probability and predictability, or help to unravel complex issues so that youth understand cause and effect. The emphasis of the reinforcement system is on the choices that youngsters make. Poor choices are the result of self-defeating reasoning that is influenced by strong emotions. The worker is mindful that sometimes choices are a result of a youth's value system or cultural beliefs (Pazaratz, 2005b). It is also probable that the youth's behaviors, preferences, and learning do not completely reflect past experiences, or past histories of reinforcements.

To develop a better understanding of underlying issues and to become aware of a youth's thinking and reasoning patterns, the worker engages youth directly in discussions and explores for any misunderstanding (Stadden, 2001). Sometimes, the youth's self-talk needs to be modified. Staff also remind youth of previous successful behaviors and deemphasize those areas that the youth is getting upset about. Staff convey that they are interested in knowing the youth and not just focusing on undesirable characteristics or behaviors. The youth worker demonstrates an acceptance and understanding of youth and who they are (Cartledge & Milburn, 1996). This affirms or validates youth by seeing the purpose, or intention, of their actions. When staff recognize and reinforce the youth's efforts verbally and on the level/reinforcement system, this cultivates attitudes of acceptance. Ultimately, when youth learn self-management skills, this reduces their dependence on external factors, such as group home reinforcements and staff intervention.

HOW EVALUATION INFORMS BEHAVIOR MANAGEMENT

The milieu as a treatment model becomes predictive when behavior therapy and solutions-oriented contracting (task-centered casework) are integrated as clinical instruments (Pazaratz, 2000a). Unless the youth worker understands normal as well as pathological functioning, the conceptual fit or integration of these theories may be lost or random. Staff become better at comprehending youth and their needs by the use of the Psychosocial Assessment model (as described in Chapter 3) or by utilizing a similar schema for understanding developmental issues. The Psychosocial Assessment is a categorical classification method that emphasizes qualitative assessment measures such as history taking and observations and interpretation of behaviors (Kamphaus & Campbell, 2006). In the Psychosocial Assessment model, youngsters are viewed and understood from diverse theories such as ego psychological theory, attachment theory, systems theory, social learning theory, psychodynamic theory, behaviorism theory, and the like. Staff observations are subjective, as are their theoretical ideas, interpretations, and conclusions (Lazarus, 1989). However, the assessment also attempts to explain the youth's emotions and behaviors that occur in the milieu and are affected by its social order. The assessment provides youth workers with information that helps them to understand the idiosyncrasies and vagaries of a youth's actions and personality.

Youngsters in residential treatment are admitted because they present with an internal or external crisis. They are often overwhelmed by the nature of their problems. They experience debilitating affect flooding that leads to clinically significant distress. When they are overwhelmed by their emotions, they project their internal struggle onto others. The Psychosocial Assessment model is structured to identify deficits in communication, problem solving, and anger management, as well as areas of distress. The Psychosocial Assessment improves staff members' and collateral professionals' understanding of how youth are to be engaged, the problems or progress that results from being engaged, types of adjustment to the treatment plan that are needed, and the youth's experience with placement.

The Psychosocial Assessment facilitates the integration of historical and current events with emotional issues and offers a means for exploring the youth's potential and interests. The Psychosocial Assessment, through detailed data collection, integrates all aspects of the youth's life and points the way to change or how to modify the youth's needs with a realistic treatment plan. The Psychosocial Assessment seeks to identify impairment in cognitive processing, interpersonal relations, and emotional balance. Variously, workers elicit the emotions that are problematic. At other times, youth workers are compelled to deal with some dysfunctional emotions until the appropriate ones surface. Upon identifying the nature of a youngster's needs, there are preferred techniques that direct care staff can employ such as providing a supportive nonjudgmental intervention and engaging residents intellectually so that they become reflective, reasoned, and aware of choices. Most importantly, the assessment challenges staff to make the milieu experience meaningful for youth.

The systematic use of reinforcements is also an assessment instrument that not only preserves the fundamental nature and vitality of staff–youth relationships, but also offers youth a self-measure of progress and a direction for change. The use of behavior therapy techniques such as a level/reinforcement system can make the issues that have been identified on referral, during placement, and on contracts more visible in the milieu, or more practical and accessible to both youth and staff. For example, change and growth are toward some criteria relative to symptoms such as disordered thinking, self-esteem, emotional control, or the youth's capacity to balance inner and outer worlds (Kazdin, 1995). Understanding of a youth's cognitive process is central to assessing a youngster's development, ideas, and attitudes. A youth's cognitive style can be a shared experience and an opportunity for staff–youth relationships to have meaning. Staff can manage observable behaviors through reinforcements and simultaneously implement a didactic or a teaching approach to modulate destructive impulses and behaviors that are triggered by faulty problem solving (Winnicott, 1984). Teaching and reinforcing self-soothing techniques make a resident's impulsive and incorrigible behaviors less severe.

The quality of staff–youth relationships is the key component that provides for the youth's sense of safety and successful group interactions. Staff connection with youth enables youth to tolerate the intensity and uncertainty of treatment and the complex social system (Pazaratz, 2000a, 2000b, 2000c). However, different staff will often approach youth or the group from different points of view. Any intervention may or may not fit, or work, for any one youth or even all youth. Nevertheless, it is critical for staff to deal with basic programming issues from clinical perspectives that can be predictive or explanatory, and remain efficacious even when the context, meaning, and protocols are changed. In other words, the techniques employed by staff should be informed by the Psychosocial Assessment and the level/reinforcement system. Youth workers' feedback should assist the youth to function more successfully in the group home and the real world. Effective youth work means to choose an intervention approach, or method, based on the current situation and issues, and the future needs of youth or a group of youth (Redl & Wineman, 1957b). Employing empathetic intervention techniques builds and supports a therapeutic alliance with youngsters, who uniformly possess a fragile sense of self. This client-centered practice is pragmatic and emphasizes the youth's experiences in care. Staff reflections and observations are used to challenge youth to face and to change attitudes and behaviors that are destructive (Phelan, 2001).

OPPOSITIONALISM AND DEFIANCE

The therapeutic task of residential treatment is to replace the chaos in youngsters' lives with order and safety. The milieu is designed to stabilize and to resocialize youth who display minimal impulse control and poor judgment. This is accomplished when youngsters rely upon staff to teach them to anticipate problem situations, not overact, and not fight or run away when negotiation fails or conditions become intolerable. Self-control or being able to disengage from conflict develops when an individual can differentiate other people's feelings from his or her own and take care of his or her own needs without imposing upon others (Maier, 1987). Behavior modification techniques can be combined with ego-supportive or psychodynamic models to provide youth with social awareness. Meaningful rewards for competency, in social skills and self-management, are central to an effective reinforcement system. A system of rewards and positive feedback also seeks to ensure that developmental attainment goes beyond symptom improvement to impulse control that is sustained when the reinforcement system is removed.

Acting-out behaviors can be perplexing. Workers often wonder why residents do things that create additional problems that lead to conflict, embarrassment, and consequences. However, acting-out behaviors have multiple meanings and functions. They can be a coping strategy, a defense, or a source of gratification (Pazaratz, 1999). Acting out can occur due to a buildup of emotions that require a release where something had to be done physically. Acting out can be a search for something in the self, or a striving for the lost part of the self. It can be an attempt to make a connection to the self, or due to a core identity problem such as a loss of self (Perls, 1969b). It may occur because of a deep-seated or hidden problem. It can arise to reaffirm an identity and connection with a youngster's family; thus, the youth refuses to give in to staff because to change would mean to renounce the self (Pazaratz, 1996a). Acting out can reflect improper handling by staff, or a misunderstanding by youth of staff's true intentions (Pearce & Pezzot-Pearce, 1997). It can be reflective of a treatment crisis (Pazaratz, 1996b). It can be based on anxiety, or because the youth feels unsafe (Pazaratz, 1996a). Acting out may escalate when a youth seeks to be in control of interactions with staff or due to a refusal to engage in certain aspects of programming. Acting out can be habitual, insincere, or manipulative (Pazaratz, 1993). It can arise because of the child's or adolescent's difficulty at expressing ideas and being understood. It can reflect the issues and ideas that cannot be articulated with language (Pazaratz, 1996b). It may occur because the youth is overwhelmed with transitions or changes in the group. It can be due to anger, depression, stress, or decompensation, or merely to have fun. Sometimes, it is a sign of substance use, due to guilt or a need to be punished. It can mean the youth is being molested or abused by other residents, staff, or family members, or in the community. It can mark the progression from the honeymoon phase to exhibiting the true self. Unless there is careful listening, a nonjudgmental and nonpunitive approach, and an awareness of the youth as an individual, youth workers may miss the underlying causes or reinforce a youth's negative view of adults (Fewster & Garfat, 1999).

There will be times when the youth worker will need the capacity to entertain multiple perspectives about a youth, or a group of youth, without arriving at an understanding, or when no time resolution is immediately foreseen, available, or ultimately possible (Ghent, 1992). There will also be situations where no intervention by the youth worker is productive. Some behavior problems are beyond the resident's awareness (as in James). Such residents do not realize that others have personal boundaries, or they are unaware that their behaviors are intruding upon another's private or physical space. Yet, curiously, these same youth overreact when they are intruded upon (Winnicott, 1984). Some youth have difficulty locating a sense of self. They come from chaotic families where there are unhealthy boundaries, or the youth did not feel safe and could not get his or her needs met. However, through staff feedback and positive peer pressure, residents can learn to accept the idea that good boundaries make good relationships and interpersonal endeavors can be enjoyable (Polsky, 1962). Ultimately, youth need to regulate what comes into their personal space and to respect what others allow or disallow. This requires communicating how much closeness and distance are acceptable. Boundary awareness is the basis for creating good relationships and fulfilling individual needs, and helps with differentiation of self, as well as connectedness (Polsky & Berger, 2003).

THE TREATMENT CLASS

For some youth, school-related problems are often linked to a lack of parental interest early in a child's school life. This often means that the parents did not believe there is pleasure in school. The Academic Assessment is an essential resource for identifying skills, talents, and interests in order to plan for programs and interactions that will maximize the youth's strengths and help them overcome their weaknesses. By articulating a different set of possibilities, teachers serve an important educative function. For some youth, their problems with education require different choices. These may be determined by answering the following questions: Can youth conform to expectations in a general way, but still develop their individual interests and talents? Do they ultimately see education as an access to opportunity, or do they feel that they are stuck on a path determined and controlled by others? By means of values clarification, staff can help youth answer these questions and overcome their dilemmas and uncertainties. Staff also assist youth to negotiate a role in groups, to develop knowledge of others, and to learn how to interact so that youth believe they belong. When staff convey that satisfaction and pleasure in academics are real possibilities, this message can have a therapeutic effect.

The Treatment Class is designed as a simplified environment that provides a resource-rich social system. Youngsters who are admitted are viewed as having many unique characteristics such as learning styles, background experiences, characterological development, and intellectual capacities (Pazaratz, 1998c). There is no attempt in a Treatment Class to homogenize students, as would occur in the public school system (Glasser, 1975). Careful monitoring of behaviors by treatment staff ensures a high level of individual attention to meet specific emotional needs. Meanwhile, teaching staff focus on the individual's academic strengths and weaknesses (Pazaratz, 2001). For youngsters with long histories of academic difficulties and whose emotional problems have disrupted their learning potential, this approach is practical, realistic, and therapeutic. The remediation of learning disabilities enables youth to catch up academically and to find their potential. To ensure that education and treatment interconnect and overlap (are integrative), youth workers and teachers coordinate their efforts. Youth workers and teachers develop a partnership where both contribute equally, form a cooperative alliance, and create a facilitating environment. They also approach subject matter and daily issues guided by their disciplines, as well as from their life experiences and personal outlook.

Selectivity within the environment is important. The Treatment Class emphasizes that students have choices in academics, sport, activities, and the like. To overcome the youth's deficits in achievement, the teacher facilitates the development of skills. The teacher implements an academic program for each student. The teacher begins by reviewing or teaching basic academic skills. Core subjects are structured to meet each individual's particular learning style. What works for one student may not be of value for another. In terms of interpersonal issues, positive peer pressure and staff counseling are utilized to resolve disagreements and to build consensus. In group sessions, the discussions aim to improve negotiation skills and self-confidence. It is through the team approach of educators and youth workers providing close monitoring and immediate feedback that students are assisted in adjusting and achieving their full potential (Pazaratz, 2001). The combination of teachers and youth workers enriches the classroom environment by bringing the best each discipline can offer. Youth workers focus on emotional issues in order to stabilize youngsters and assist with developmental growth. Teachers promote habits so that youth can manage academics, develop study skills, and learn to handle those subjects that were difficult for them.

A core area for intervention in social skills acquisition and academic proficiency is the enhancement of basic language skills. Learning to use language accurately, or literacy (which is defined as reading, writing, speaking, listening, and viewing), is extremely important. Language can be used in a ritualized way to express concerns and to establish rapport. Speech is used to develop shared understanding based on a common meaning structure. The idea is for teachers to incorporate rich literacy-based learning experiences into the classroom with the goal of helping students to learn to think across the curriculum (Ivey & Fisher, 2006). When teachers and students arrive at a shared language or an academic work plan, this describes what the youth is good at and what the youth ascribes to (e.g., [re]integration into a public school, a job, a trade, and the like). Acknowledging goals begins to define the parameters of the student's self-expression in academics and social interactions.

Skills are the foundation and building blocks of educational excellence (Glasser, 1975). Competency as a goal is needed in subjects of basic mathematics and life skills. This is achieved by focusing on reading, writing, spelling, grammar, speaking, negotiating, and learning problem resolution skills. In a student's progress toward proficiency and mastery, the youth passes through stages of internalization. At each learning stage, harmonization of knowledge and skills is reinforced. In every subject matter, youth are assisted to develop, strengthen, and practice analytical and creative-thinking strategies (Pazaratz, 2001). However, core skills, talents, and interests may not gain expression in any one subject, but may guide the progression in a particular direction. Academic instruction that focuses on the learning process can also elicit progress or even support the student during difficulties or setbacks. Feelings of shame, frustration, and anger can be dealt with by emphasizing that performance on any one task or project is best understood as part of a learning process. Interpersonal skills are learned like any other through specific interactions. Staff emphasize the importance of effort, the value of assertiveness, and the benefits of risk taking and changing in order to experience the passion for learning. It is a youth's rigidity, fear of failure, lack of confidence, and need for control that must be overcome. To assist with challenges and to offset self-doubts, direct care workers allay the youth's fears of failure. Without denying the real disappointment in failure, the youth is encouraged to use the opportunity for learning that emerges from all situations, conditions, and experiences. Ultimately, unless youth develop self-control and an enthusiasm for learning, the treatment class is ineffective (Pazaratz, 1998c).

ACTIVITIES

Structured and informal activities are considered an important assessment instrument and a powerful management technique. In activities, there are rules to be followed, proper strategies to be implemented, and skills to be utilized in order to overcome obstacles and to meet challenges (Crenshaw & Mordock, 2005b). Activities help to resocialize youth by teaching, modeling, and structuring. Activities enable youth to get in touch with their feelings, to participate with others, to risk, to explore, to become self-learners, to give and to receive, to share, to develop an individual style of problem solving and mastery, and to be fully alive, creative, and reflective (Pazaratz, 1998b). Activities promote flexibility, concentration, and critical-thinking strategies. They help youth to relax, understand and express feelings, and improve interpersonal relationships. Activities demonstrate the order and purposefulness that can be found in experiences. They increase the youth's experience of living in the moment. In activities, games, and sport, problems occur naturally. Participating in activities reveals a youth's ability or inability to work within limits, to deal with destructive or obtrusive behaviors, and to enact distancing and displacement through playful actions. Thus, behaviors in activities can comprise an indicator of the youth's level of self-discipline.

Activities enhance the youth workers' observation and evaluative skills and guide access to the inner world of youngsters. During activities, direct observation by workers determines how well the youth handled problems (i.e., defenses and calming skills), whether the correct strategies were employed to deal with the situation, whether the activity was too easy or too hard, the youth's physical fitness level, whether the youth has developmental delays, and the types of resources and anxiety engendered, as well as identify the areas the youth enjoys or excels in. Nevertheless, youth are expected to demonstrate sportsmanship during activities. Lack of cooperative efforts is an indicator of poor problem-solving strategies and low frustration tolerance.

Youth workers want to ascertain whether youth are eager participants or are passively involved. Workers also want to determine how to teach youngsters to transfer learning from any one activity to others and to generalize from experience. Although youth develop skills and have agendas different from those of adults, nevertheless, they also learn from staff and each other. Yet, in activities they can also be who they are, free to express their talents and interests and to share in their excitement or disappointment. This occurs by staff emphasizing empathy, teaching the language of feelings, facilitating language expression and moderation, and helping youth to resolve disappointment or loss (Crenshaw & Mordock, 2005a).

THE CHILD AND YOUTH CARE WORKER'S ROLE

Child and youth care workers have a wide range of tasks that require them to alternate or shift in their roles from being detached observers to participant observers. At times, youth workers are teachers or didactic in their interactions. They are also required to understand their status as role models and to be very aware that they can stimulate emotions or foster transference. Unless staff deal with youngsters empathetically and from a clinical perspective, youth will often express an overreaction to staff or strong passion about the issue of fairness. Thus, central to the youth worker's role and use of techniques is the ability to predict problems that arise from sequences of interactions, to practice defensive youth work, and to be reflective or reasoned. When youth workers are not consistent in their approach or methodology and do not work within team parameters, residents may feel that workers do not understand or do not care, or that the resident can play staff off each other. When staff appear indifferent to any youth, this may result in damage to the worker–youth relationship and disrupt treatment. Some residents will be disinterested in forming a relationship with any staff who cannot comprehend the youth's problem, are inarticulate, or have difficulty communicating ideas clearly, logically, and unemotionally. Youth may feel unsafe, or even confused, if staff limited in their abilities to understand and unravel issues, or are unnecessarily dispassionate (Pazaratz, 2003a).

Youngsters who are diagnosed as needing treatment mainly suffer from disruptions in thought processes (comprehending content), so that they often misunderstand the affect involved in communication (metacommunication). What, then, are the techniques that workers can use to assist these youth? Treatment plans emphasize goals and strategies for helping youth to organize their problems and to develop solutions. Implementing treatment plans in effect ensures a continuity or an approach for all staff to adhere to and to comply with. Even when youth follow their treatment plan, change is a slow process and can be stressful, especially if youngsters feel overwhelmed and isolated, and have difficulty understanding and being understood. However, even when youth follow their treatment plan and obey rules, they can still regress and display disturbed behaviors. Disruptive behaviors provide an area where youngsters can remain in control. Acting out can arise when staff are viewed as inflexible, emotionally volatile, or excessively withdrawn. Staff's lack of insight or awareness into underlying issues may cause some youth to feel deprived or unsafe, especially if the worker cannot manage the youth's or the group's intensity without being overly permissive or unusually removed (Pazaratz, 1999). Thus, residential care is a process that helps youngsters to release and to contain affect, or acting-out behaviors, and to feel connected and understood.

Placement can also stir up strong emotions in youth who are unable to contain stress. Treatment resistance that is manifest in the form of a delinquent ego (defiance of staff) protects the child's or adolescent's self-concept (Redl & Wineman, 1957a). When youth maintain this sense of self, or rigidly adhere to their problematic behaviors, this becomes the central hindrance to treatment adherence and behavioral change. For some youngsters, removal from their home and family confirms for them that they are not as bright, talented, or normal as their peers. Thus, many youngsters avoid dealing with new ideas or new situations that might cause them to feel below average in abilities or intelligence. Oppositionalism and regression may arise at other times because it is easier for youngsters to revert to previous maladaptive behaviors (Pearce & Pezzot Pearce, 1997). Nevertheless, even though staff support and encourage youth to face or confront the problems that led to placement, residents often react as if they are not strong enough to deal with those issues. They resist staff and act out even more, believing that separation from family will become permanent. The youth feels rejected and abandoned. The fear of permanent separation arouses anxiety, guilt, and self-downing. The youth feels responsible for behaviors that led to the family being upset and the youth being placed. Separation anxiety can then be an additional factor in acting out. Unless separation anxiety is resolved, it is unlikely that the youth will ever fully accept placement or identify with staff and treatment goals.

Most youngsters will avoid dealing with what they did to cause placement. They often blame child protective services or the court system (Philion, 2002). Most deny that placement means that their family has abandoned them (even though many youngsters secretly believe this to be the case). In effect, they are reluctant to admit their fears and to change any existing beliefs, behaviors, or symptoms (as described in the case study of James). In dealing with separation and the fear of abandonment, youth workers should be aware that youth will attempt to maintain family relationships as they existed prior to placement. Ironically, as the youth tries to remain connected to his or her family by employing old or familiar behavior patterns, the youth does not realize that it is these behaviors that got the youth removed from the family and sent into treatment. Thus, the youngster's fear of change becomes an obstacle to therapeutic progress. The youth avoids change, erroneously believing that change may mean the permanent loss of family. When direct care staff recognize this dynamic, they can help the youth to confront these beliefs at a comfortable pace. Knowing how to integrate a systematic understanding in observations, interpretations, and assessments is a critical clinical skill for front-line staff. With exploration that does not panic youth, staff can assist youth to develop options for maintaining family involvement, which will serve to lessen the effects of separation anxiety and the fear of change (Pazaratz, 2003a).

An ongoing task for youth workers is to maintain cooperation, treatment adherence, and positive group interactions. Many youngsters are oppositional toward staff because they do not believe that adults accept or respect them. They also view staff as insincere and do not view staff as really caring what residents think and want. Residents become mistrustful and jaded because of their experiences of having to repeatedly talk about their problems (Fewster & Garfat, 1998). Thus, some interactions with staff do contribute to the youth's self-doubts and lack of confidence in their ideas and cognitive skills. Fears of being inadequate have also been reinforced by the youngster's experiences with the educational system and a society where competence is demanded (e.g., being bright, sophisticated, and a beautiful person).

Some youth who believe they are (intellectually) inferior or even mediocre in their talents, looks, and so on develop fears of being humiliated or rejected as they are compared to peers, especially in the form of grades or popularity. They evaluate and rate themselves, too! When they do not measure up or do not advance as rapidly as their peers, they become depressed; develop a poor self-image; have lower self-confidence, diminished levels of motivation, and weak concentration; and do not acquire good cognitive strategies (Pazaratz & Morton, 2000). However, when these same youngsters are faced with new or unknown situations and challenges, workers can help them to manage their doubts, uncertainties, fears, vulnerabilities, and weaknesses by identifying the specific issues that create these beliefs (Pazaratz, 2000d).

Many youth wear masks and play roles. They have lost touch with their real selves, and do not know who they are and how to fit in. Real healing and change occur when a youngster's relationship with family and/or significant others improves. Healing in the context of relationships aims to bring about pervasive change in the youth's personality and a reduction in symptoms. Thus, youth workers must establish rapport with all youngsters! The worker's job includes being a good role model and demonstrating a commitment and a genuine interest in all residents. When workers develop positivity, interactions flow more smoothly and improve the youngster's relationships with others (peers, adults, and family; Fewster, 1990). Youth workers teach youngsters how to obtain what they need in relationships with people in their lives, so that ultimately the staff and the residential facility are no longer necessary to sustain them. In essence, this focus means that relationship conflicts in a youngster's life must be overcome, so that youth can reconnect with their families, and in some cases the youngster will have to accept that not all issues are immediately resolvable (Pazaratz, 2003a). But, when there are improvements or more positivity in family relationships, the youth's cognitive functioning, self-control, and sensitivity or awareness toward others increase. The child and youth care worker ultimately creates a conceptual bridge from residential treatment goals to the youth's experience, or a focus on care and the normalization of relationships (Pazaratz, 2003b).

FAMILY COUNSELING

Family solidarity is necessary for its survival. However, in some families, the nature of the relationships and interactions does not sustain the family's cohesiveness. Sometimes, the parents and/or children view other family members as obstacles rather than resources. They settle into interactions that inhibit growth. For example, the family can become stuck between the need to protect their current situation (roles and organization) and the need for change (Bell, 1963). Thus, when a child is identified as unmanageable, delinquent, or psychotic and placed in treatment, parents can be relieved because the youth takes on the ownership for the family's problems, which protects their interactional patterns or secrets (Boszormenyi-Nagy & Spark, 1984). In the course of residential placement, when parents participate in family sessions, their child(ren)'s behaviors are understood in context (Kwantes, 1992). Parental involvement and support of their child's treatment are among the strongest factors that determine adherence (Rowe, Cain, Hundleby, & Keane, 1984).

In family sessions, the social worker gains information that assists with treatment planning, advancing interpretations of the youth's behaviors, and understanding parenting style (i.e., the degree of attachment or disengagement, and the methods used to resolve disagreements or problems). The social worker's task is to assist families to shed their old ways of manipulating or attacking each other (Boyd-Webb, 2003). Central to family counseling and the youth developing treatment adherence is the resolution of the parent–child conflict. This cannot occur unless the family worker knows how to operate within the family's rules and cultivates a relationship with every family member (Minuchin, 1974; Taibbi, 2007). To achieve this goal, the family worker must be aware of and sensitive to the family's struggles, stress, culture, patterns, and rhythms (Kruger, 1991). The family worker must also be skilled at resolving issues of anger, guilt, sibling rivalry, and relationship conflicts, and at teaching child management techniques. The family worker wants family members to see beyond the dysfunctional patterns to the potential healing power of growth through relationships. The family worker aims to make parents more attuned and better emotional and intellectual resources for their children. The family worker challenges the family to change self-defeating attitudes and behaviors by experiencing competence in the moment or connection and reflecting upon it (Phelan, 1999). Ultimately, the family worker teaches family members that harmonious relationships are maintained through acceptance, respect, involvement, and honesty (Boszormenyi-Nagy, 1987).

Ongoing concerns in family sessions are fixed entanglements and the nature of any changes in relationship dynamics. The family worker focuses on deficits in communication, problem-solving strategies, anger management skills, and relational attitudes. Unrealistic standards and unfair consequences are also explored, and new approaches are discussed. The family worker promotes interactions that foster the unique needs and strengths of each family member (Maier, 1987; Taibbi, 2007). The family worker organizes the youth and his or her family's formless array of problems with a coherent set of tasks. The family worker encourages communication between parents and their child as a search for mutual reality, or a common ground where they can understand each other (Garfat, 2003). The family worker wants to increase and substitute positives, and rewards, for punishing behaviors (Minuchin, 1974). Increasing positivity breaks the cycle of parent–child distress (Minuchin & Fishman, 1981). This means that the youth is able to be him or herself and to disagree without being emotionally shrill. Similarly, the parents are able to agree without fear of losing control or authority (as in the case of James). Success in child–parent interactions teaches the youth to make better use of the available relationships in the group home.

When the level of risk for reactivation of family problems has been reduced, discharge home can be planned. However, upon discharge, when a return home is not possible, it is the skills and resources that youth have developed in treatment that then become central to transition directly to independence. Most youth are aroused by the prospect for discharge, whether to their own home or onto independence. Their stress and anxiety can often become overwhelming. Many youngsters are uncertain about their future; therefore, they project their internal struggle onto staff or peers. Some manufacture antagonism to push themselves out on a bad note and to bolster a sense of self. For others, a kind of grandiosity is displayed that takes the form of "See how wonderful I was, am, and will be," both in a positive sense and as a denial of their corresponding fears. Discharge from residential treatment is an interpersonal event that should be shared, giving the youth a chance to speak of his or her feelings. Residents deal best with transition issues when they prepare for them and can adjust to the anticipation (Whittaker, 1979). When youth are exposed to community programs, this assists them with transition to the outside world. They develop a sense of familiarity and acquire an understanding of the resources and supports that they can rely upon.

SUMMARY

The search for residential treatment and care strategies that are effective with emotionally disturbed or disordered children and adolescents is both pressing and controversial. Yet, as has been described, the integrative treatment model of the Four Phase System of Metropolitan Toronto was the first and arguably the most influential continuum of treatment and care of adolescents. But it begs the question as to whether there is a universal model that fits the demands and parameters for children and adolescents deemed "high risk," "hard to place," and/or "hard to serve" today. Practitioners cannot know precisely why some youth develop emotional disturbance but other youngsters who have similar experiences and backgrounds do not. For that matter, it may be difficult to predict which factors converged that enable youth, such as James, to change and to give up self-defeating and destructive behaviors. It is by having a comprehensive understanding of a youth's background and current experiences that enables staff to work more realistically. This means that if residential treatment is not conceptualized and articulated rationally, or when it fails to follow a structured model, as a process it can become chaotic for staff and residents alike, and deflate the morale of all (Polsky & Berger, 2003). Therefore, when a treatment program includes other possibilities, not only do workers enhance their observation and evaluative skills, but they also have clearer treatment strategies.

Youth do not always communicate clearly or openly. They do not always acknowledge when staff have helped them because they are afraid it might be used against them. Nevertheless, some staff need direct feedback and positivity, not just anger and defiance. They do not realize that some resistance or acting out by residents is unconscious and habitual. Some resistance that staff encounter from youth is based on the fear of them being in the situation or faced with the dilemmas that they have avoided by means of their symptoms. Some youth will not agree that the staff's solution to their problems is better. Thus, they demand to be left alone. But, there are youth who will largely cooperate with staff. However, it is the virtual nature of a residential program that causes youth workers and residents to interact, communicate, and continually influence each other. But, unless youth take up the challenge to do the bulk of the work on their own, treatment is not effective.

It is the core issues of understanding and empathy that are the hallmarks of good parenting and the best youth worker practice (Winnicott, 1984). The great advantage of employing youth workers occurs when they connect with youth and interpret the complex experiences that youth encounter. This includes understanding each youth's developmental level along with selecting the right tasks or activities needed to stimulate growth. Youth workers are often continually confronted with oppositional and defiant youngsters who do not make significant treatment gains. Yet, as the case study of James has demonstrated, youngsters in treatment as well as child and youth care workers can encounter sharp turns in their experiences and thoughts about each other and the milieu in general. This means that high-risk youngsters have similar profiles that make working with them tedious, but when staff employ an integrative intervention, this can assist them to be flexible and to appeal to a youth's uniqueness and differences.

There will always be children and adolescents in residential placement who are unwilling to accept any responsibility for their behaviors, as well as parents who shirk their roles and cannot benefit from any form or experience of counseling. They remain bitterly opposed to social workers, probation officers, and the courts intruding upon their lives (Philion, 2002). Nevertheless, when children and adolescents need placement, residential treatment is selected because it provides the best possible alternative or least intrusive form of care. However, no form of residential treatment (as we have seen in the Four Phase System) can offer a vision and a hope for healing to all youngsters requiring placement. Also, residential treatment cannot help all youngsters or provide any youngster with all the answers (Pazaratz et al., 2000). But when youngsters encounter their fears and problems while living with a group of peers who have similar difficulties, residential treatment can create an opportunity for change (Polsky, 1962). It can also help most youngsters to reclaim or develop a theme for their lives.

CONCLUSION

This book has not attempted to describe the entire residential treatment process. Instead, it offers a supplement to the practitioner's knowledge and insight. There are many ways to treat emotional disturbance in youth successfully. Yet, it is unlikely that there is an optimal technique based upon an abstract theory not devised from clinical expertise or evidence-based studies. Theoretical and technical approaches that can be validated clinically offer the best hope for dealing with the complexity of disturbing behaviors, even though some adolescents may not respond. Different theories or models create flexible alternatives and increase the likelihood of being meaningful. They help the youth worker to understand normal as well as abnormal adjustment, and explain maladaptive development and problematic behaviors in children and adolescents.

Understanding youth from a variety of perspectives provides a more realistic framework for intervention. Knowledge of different strategies helps direct care staff to fulfill the developmental needs of a variety of youth. When basing treatment on a range of strategies, the workers' efforts are more likely to succeed. This is especially true when children and adolescents are provided with opportunities that help them to adjust, learn, and grow at a rate consistent with their emotional and intellectual abilities. In other words, because integrative therapy combines diverse disciplines or overlaps rationale and practices, it offers staff the use of techniques that work and allows them to discard those that do not. For clients with dual disorders, Drake and Mueser (2000) found consistent effectiveness of integrated treatment, so that clients showed better engagement and adherence rates and improved clinical outcome compared to those in nonintegrative treatment. In conclusion, this book on integrative treatment principles and practices ultimately wants to teach the practitioner how to help youngsters to understand the world as it is in order for them to be able to function more competently and with a greater degree of self-sustaining satisfaction upon discharge.

References

Abbott, J., & Ryan. T. (2001). *The unfinished revolution: Learning, human behaviour, community and political paradox*. Alexandria, VA: Association for Supervision and Curriculum Development.

Achenbach, T. M. (1980). DMS-III in light of empirical research on the classification of child psychopathology. *Journal of American Academy of Child Psychiatry, 19*, 395–412.

Adler, A. (1938). *Social interest: A challenge to mankind*. London: Farber & Farber.

Ainsworth, F. (1997). *Family-centered group care: Model building*. Aldershot, UK: Ashgate.

Ainsworth, M. D. S. (1985). Patterns of infant-mother attachment: II, attachment across the lifespan. *Bulletin of the New York Academy of Medicine, 61*, 771–812.

Ainsworth, M. D. S., Blehar, M. C., Waters, E., & Wall, S. (1978). *Patterns of attachment: A psychological study of the strange situation*. Hillsdale, NJ: Erlbaum.

Ainsworth, F., Maluccio, A. N., & Small, R. W. (1996). A framework for family centered care practice: Guiding principles and practice applications. In D. J. Braziel (Ed.), *Family-focused practice in out-of-home care* (pp. 35–45). Washington, DC: Child Welfare League of America.

Aldridge, M., & Wood, J. (1998). *Interviewing children: A guide for child care and forensic practitioners*. Chichester, UK: Wiley.

Algozzine, R. (1985). *Problem behavior management: Educator's resource services*. Rockville, MD: Aspens Systems.

Allyon, T., & Azrin, N. H. (1968). *The token economy: A motivation system for therapy and rehabilitation*. New York: Appleton-Century Crofts.

American Counseling Association. (2005). *Code of ethics and standards of practice*. Alexandria, VA: Author.

American Psychiatric Association. (2000). *Diagnostic and statistical manual of mental disorders (DSM-IV-TM*; 4th ed., Text Rev.). Washington, DC: Author.

Anderson, C., & Stewart, S. (1983). *Mastering resistance: A practical guide to family therapy*. New York: Guilford.

Anderson, J. A. (2000). The need for interagency collaboration for children with emotional and behavioural disabilities and their families. *Families in Society: The Journal of Contemporary Human Services, 81*, 484–493.

Anderson, J. A., Kooreman, H., Mohr, W. K., Wright, E. R., & Russel, L. (2002). The Dawn Project: How it works, who it serves and how it evaluated. In C. Liberton, C. Newman, K. Kutash, & R. Freidman (Eds.), *The 12th annual research conference proceedings: A system of care for children's mental health: Expanding the research base* (pp. 50–62). Tampa: University of South Florida.

Andreasen, N. C. (1979). The clinical assessment of thought, language and communication disorders. *Archives of General Psychiatry, 36*, 1315–1321.

Andrews, J. (1989). Integrating visions of reality: Interpersonal diagnosis and the existential vision. *American Psychologist, 44*, 803–817.

Arches, J. (1991). Social structure, burnout, and job satisfaction. *Social Work, 36*(3), 202–206.

Ariel, M. (1997). *The occupational experience of residential child and youth care workers.* New York: Haworth.

Axline, V. M. (1998). *Child psychotherapy: Practice and theory.* New York: Guilford.

Bandura, A. (1977). *Social learning theory.* Englewood Cliffs, NJ: Prentice Hall.

Bandura, A. (1986). *Social foundations of thought and action.* Englewood Cliffs, NJ: Prentice Hall.

Bardach, E. (1977). *The implementation game: What happens after a bill becomes law.* Cambridge, MA: MIT Press.

Barkley, R. A. (1997). *Defiant children: A clinician's manual for assessment and parent training* (2nd ed.). New York: Guilford.

Barkley, R. A., Fischer, M., Edelbrock, C. S., & Smallish, L. (1990). The adolescent outcome of hyperactive children diagnosed by research criteria: I, an 8 year perspective fellowship study. *Journal of the American Academy of Child and Adolescent Psychiatry, 29*, 546–557.

Barton, W. H. (2006). Incorporating the strength's perspective into intensive juvenile aftercare. *Western Criminology Review, 7*(2), 48–61.

Beaumeister, R. F., & Leary, M. R. (1995). The need to belong: Desire for interpersonal attachments as a fundamental human motivation. *Psychology Bulletin, 117*, 497–529.

Beker, J., & Feuerstein, R. (1991). The modifying environment and other environmental perspectives in group care: A conceptual contrast and integration. *Residential Treatment for Children and Youth, 8*(3), 21–37.

Bell, J. E. (1963). A theoretical position for family group therapy. *Family Process, 2*, 1–14.

Bellak, L., Hurvich, M., & Gediman, H. K. (1973). *Ego functions in schizophrenics, neurotics, and normals: A systematic study of conceptual, diagnostics and therapeutic aspects.* New York: Wiley.

Benjamin, M. P., & Isaacs-Shockley, M. (1996). Culturally competent service approaches. In B. Stroul (Ed.), *Children's mental health: Creating systems of care in a changing society* (pp. 475–491). Baltimore: Paul H. Brookes.

Berman, P. S. (1997). *Case conceptualization and treatment planning.* Thousand Oaks, CA: Sage.

Berne, E. (1973). *What do you say after you say hello?* New York: Grove.

Bernheim, K. (1982). Supportive family counselling. *Schizophrenic Bulletin, 8*, 634–641.

Bernstein, N. (1996). *Treating the unmanageable adolescent: A guide to oppositional defiant and conduct disorders.* Northvale, NJ: Aronson.

Berry, M. (1997). *The family at risk: Issues and trends in family preservation services.* Columbia: University of South Carolina Press.

Bertolino, B., & Thompson, K. (1999). *The residential youth care worker in action: A collaborative competency-based approach.* New York: Haworth.

Bettelheim, B. (1960). *The informed heart: Autonomy in massage.* New York: Free Press.

Bettelheim, B. (1974). *A home for the heart.* New York: Knopf.

Bleiberg, E. (2001). *Treating personality disorders in children and adolescents: A relational approach.* New York: Guilford.

Borum, R., & Verhaagen, D. (2006). *Assessing and managing violent risk in juveniles*. New York: Guilford.

Boszormenyi-Nagy, I. (1987). *Foundations of contextual therapy: Collected papers of Ivan Boszomenyi-Nagy, MD*. New York: Brunner/Mazel.

Boszormenyi-Nagy, J., & Spark, G. (1984). *Invisible loyalties*. New York: Brunner/Mazel.

Bowen, M. (1978). *Family therapy in clinical practice*. Northvale, NJ: Jason Aronson.

Bowlby, J. (1969). *Attachment and loss: Vol. 1. Attachment*. New York: Basic Books.

Boyd-Franklin, N., & Bry, B. H. (2000). *Reaching out in family therapy: Home-based, school and community interventions*. New York: Guilford.

Boyd-Webb, N. (2003). *Social work practice with children* (2nd ed.). New York: Guilford.

Breggin, P. R. (1997). Coercion of voluntary patients in an open hospital. In R. B. Edwards (Ed.), *Ethics of psychiatry: Insanity, rational autonomy, and mental health care* (pp. 423–436). Amherst, NY: Prometheus.

Brendtro, L., & Shahbazian, M. (2004). *Troubled children and youth: Turning problems into opportunities*. Champaing, IL: Research Press.

Brodie, B. R. (2007). *Adolescence and delinquency: An object relations theory approach*. Lanham, MD: Jason Aronson.

Bromfield, R. (2005). *Teens in therapy: Making it their own*. New York: Norton.

Bronfenbrenner, U. (1979). *The ecology of the human development*. Cambridge, MA: Harvard University Press.

Bronfenbrenner, U. (1986). *Childhood: Great expectations* [Cassette recording, Tape 1]. New York: Ambrose Video.

Burt, M. R., Resnick, G., & Novich, E. (1998). *Building supportive communities for at-risk adolescents: It takes more than services*. Washington, DC: American Psychological Association.

Burton, D. (1993). Goal setting in sport. In R. N. Singer, M. Murphy, & L. K. Tennant (Eds.), *The handbook of research on sport psychology*. New York: MacMillan.

Butterfield, W. H., & Cobb, N. H. (1994). Cognitive behavioural treatment of children and adolescents. In D. K. Granwald (Ed.), *Cognitive and behavioural treatment: Methods and applications* (pp. 32–62). Pacific Grove, CA: Brooks/Cole.

Cameron, J. & Pierce, W. D. (1994). Reinforcement, reward and intrinsic motivation: A meta-analysis. *Review of Educational Research, 64*, 363–423.

Campbell, J. (1999). *Student discipline and classroom management: Preventing and managing discipline problems in the classroom*. Springfield, IL: Thomas.

Camras, L. A., Gow, J. G., & Ribordy, S. C. (1983). Recognition of emotional expression by abused children. *Journal of Clinical Child Psychology, 12*, 328–328.

Cantwell, D. P., & Baker, L. (1985). Interrelationship of communication, learning and psychiatric disorders in children. In C. S. Simon (Ed.), *Communication skills and classroom success* (pp. 43–61). San Diego, CA: College Hill Press.

Carkhuff, R. R. (1969). *Helping and human relations* (Vols. 1 and 2). New York: Holt, Rinehart and Winston.

Carkhuff, R. R., & Berenson, B. G. (1977). *Beyond counselling and therapy* (2nd ed.). New York: Holt, Rinehart and Winston.

Cartledge, G., & Milburn, J. F. (1996). *Cultural diversity and social skills instruction: Understanding ethnic and gender differences*. New York: Harper & Row.

Chandler, S. M. (1991). Current efforts in the development of public mental health policy. In C. G. Hudson & A. J. Cox (Eds.), *Dimensions of state mental health policy*. New York: Praeger.

Chescheir, M., & Shulz, K. (1989). The development of a capacity for in antisocial children: Winnicott's concept of human relatedness. *Clinical Social Work Journal, 17*, 24–39.

Child, D. (1997). *Psychology and the teacher* (6th ed.). Washington, DC: Cassell.

Christopherson, E. R., & Finney, J. W. (1993). Conduct disorder. In R. Ammerman & M. Hersen (Eds.), *Handbook of behaviour therapy with children and adults: A developmental and longitudinal perspective* (pp. 251–262). Boston: Allyn & Bacon.

Cicchetti, D., Lynch, M., Shonk, S., & Manly, J. T. (1992). An organizational perspective on peer relations in maltreated children. In R. D. Parke & G. Ladd (Eds.), *Family-peer relationships: Modes of linkage* (pp. 345–383). Hillsdale, NJ: Erlbaum.

Clark, A. J. (1998). *Defence mechanisms in the counselling process.* Thousand Oaks, CA: Sage.

Clausen, J. (1975). The social meaning of different physical and sexual maturation. In S. Dragaslin & G. Elder (Eds.), *Adolescence in the life-cycle* (pp. 25–47). New York: Wiley.

Coe, W. (1975). Token economies: A description. In J. G. Cull & R. E. Hardy (Eds.), *Behaviour modification in rehabilitative settings* (pp. 18–45). New York: MacMillan.

Cohen, J. J., & Fish, M. C. (1993). *Handbook of school-based interventions: Resolving student problems and providing healthy educational environments.* San Francisco: Jossey-Bass.

Cohen, N. J., Davine, M., & Meloche-Kelly, M. (1989). Prevalence of unsuspected language disorders in a child psychiatric population. *Journal of the American Academy of Child and Adolescent Psychiatry, 28*, 107–111.

Cohen, P., & Cohen, J. (1996). *Life values and adolescent mental health.* Mahwah, NJ: Erlbaum.

Cohen, R., & Cohen, J. (2000). *Chiselled in sand: Perception on change in human services organizations.* Belmont, CA: Wadsworth.

Condrell, K. N. (2006). *The unhappy child: What every parents needs to know.* Amherst, NY: Prometheus.

Conduct Problems Prevention Research Group. (1992). A developmental and clinical model for prevention of conduct disorder: The fast track program. *Developmental Psychology, 4*, 509–527.

Constantino, G., Dana, R. H., & Malgady, R. G. (2007). *Assessment in multicultural societies.* Mahwah, NJ: Erlbaum.

Corder, B. F. (1994). *Structured adolescent groups.* Sarasota, FL: Professional Resources Press.

Cottle, T. J. (2001). *Adolescent consciousness in culture of distinction.* New York: Peter Lang.

Cotton, N. S. (1993). *Lessons from the lions den: Therapeutic management of children in psychoactive hospitals and treatment centers.* San Francisco: Jossey-Bass.

Crain, W. (1993). *Theories of development: Concepts and applications* (3rd ed.). Englewood Cliffs, NJ: Prentice Hall.

Crenshaw, D. A., & Hardy, K. V. (2005). Understanding and treating aggression in out-of-home care. In N. Boyd-Webb (Ed.), *Working with traumatized youth in child welfare* (pp. 171–195). New York: Guilford.

Crenshaw, D. A., & Mordock, J. B. (2005a). *Understanding and testing the aggression of children: Fawns in gorilla suits?* Lanham, MD: Jason Aronson.

Crenshaw, D. A., & Mordock, J. B. (2005b). *A handbook of play therapy with aggressive children.* Lanham, MD: Jason Aronson.

Curry, J. F. (1991). Outcome research on residential treatment: Implication and suggested directions. *American Journal of Orthopsychiatry, 61*, 348–357.

Daley, D. C., & Thase, M. E. (2000). *Dual disorder recovery counseling: Integrative treatment for substance use and mental health disorders* (2nd ed.). Independence, MO: Independence Press.

Dangel, R. F., Yu, M., Slot, N. W., & Fashimpar, G. (1991). Behaviour parent training. In D. K. Granwold (Ed.), *Cognitive and behavioural treatment: Methods and applications* (pp. 108–122). Pacific Grove, CA: Brooks/Cole.

Danish, S. J., & Nellen, V. (1997). New roles for sports psychologists: Teaching life skills through sport to at-risk youth. *Quest, 49*, 100–113.

Darling-Hammond, L., French, J., & Garcia-Lopez, S. P. (Eds.). (2000). *Learning to teach for social justice*. New York: Teachers College Press.

Davidson-Methot, D. (2004). Calibrating the compass: Using qualitative improvement data for outcome evaluation, cost control and creating quality organizational cultures. *Residential Treatment for Children and Youth, 21*(3), 45–68.

Davis, G. L., Hoffman, R. G., & Quigley, R. (1988). Self-concept change and positive peer culture in adjudicated delinquents. *Journal of Child and Youth Care Forum, 17*(3), 137–145.

Davis, N. J. (1999). *Youth crisis: Growing up in the high-risk society*. Westport, CT: Praeger.

Deal, T. E., & Peterson, K. D. (1999). *Shaping school culture: The heart of leadership*. San Francisco: Jossey-Bass.

Deci, E. L. (1972). The effects of contingent and non-contingent rewards and controls of intrinsic motivation. *Organizational Behaviours and Human Performance, 8*, 217–229.

Deci, E. L., Vallerand, R. J., Pelletier, L. G., & Ryan, R. M. (1991). Motivation and education: The self-determination perspective. *Educational Psychology, 26*, 325–346.

deShazer, S. (1985). *Keys to solutions in brief therapy*. New York: Norton.

Deshler, D. D., & Schumaker, J. B. (2006). *Teaching adolescents with disabilities: Accessing the general education curriculum*. Thousand Oaks, CA: Crown.

Dinkmeyer, D., & McKay, G. (1989). *Systematic training for effective parenting: The parents' handbook* (3rd ed.). Circle Pines, MN: American Guidance Service.

Dodge, K. A. (1993). The future research on the treatment of conduct disorder: Toward a developmental perspective on conduct disorder. *Development and Psychopathology, 5*, 311–319.

Doherty, W. J. (1995). *Soul searching: Why psychotherapy must promote moral responsibility*. New York: Basic Books.

Donovan, D., & McIntyre, D. (1991). *Healing the hurt child: A developmental-contextual approach*. New York: Norton.

Doren, D. M. (1993). Antisocial personality disorder. In R. Ammerman & M. Hersen (Eds.), *Handbook of behaviour therapy with children and adults: A developmental and longitudinal perspective* (pp. 263–276). Boston: Allyn & Bacon.

Drake, R. E., & Mueser, K. T. (2000). Psychosocial approaches to dual diagnosis. *Schizophrenic Bulletin, 26*, 1005–1118.

Dreikurs, R. (1972). The individual psychological approach. In B. B. Wolman (Ed.), *Handbook of child psychoanalysis: Research, theory, and practice* (pp. 415–461). New York: Van Nostrand Reinhold.

Dreikurs, R. B., Grunwald, B., & Pepper, F. (1982). *Maintaining sanity in the classroom: Classroom management techniques* (2nd ed.). New York: Harper & Row.

Dror, Y. (Ed.). (2002). *Innovative approaches in working with children and youth: New lessons from the Kibbortz*. Binghamton, NY: Haworth.

Dryden, W. (1987). Theoretical consistent eclecticism: Humanizing a computer "addict."
        In J. C. Norcross (Ed.), *Casebook of eclectic psychology* (pp. 221–237). New York:
        Brunner/Mazel.

Dryden, W. (1996). *Research in counselling and psychotherapy: Practical applications.*
        Thousand Oaks, CA: Sage.

Dumphrey, D. (1978). Phases, roles and myths in self-analytic groups. In G. Gobbard,
        S. Hartmann, & F. Mann (Eds.), *Analysis of groups.* San Francisco: Jossey-Bass.

Dunst, C., Trivette, C., & Deol, A. (1988). *Enabling and empowering families: Principles
        and guidelines for practice.* Cambridge, MA: Brookline.

Durrant, M. (1993). *Residential treatment: A cooperative competency based approach to
        therapy and program design.* New York: Norton.

Durrant, M. (1995). *Creative strategies for school problems: Solutions for psychologists and
        teachers.* New York: Norton.

Dyer, C. (2006). **Research in psychology**: *A practical guide to methods and statistics.*
        Malden, MA: Blackwell.

Egan, K. (1997). *The educated mind: How cognitive tools shape our understanding.* Chicago:
        University of Chicago Press.

Eisenberger, R., & Cameron, J. (1996). Detrimental effects of reward: Reality or myth?
        American Psychologists, 51, 1153–1166.

Elias, M. J., Zins, J. E. Weisber, R. P., Frey, K. S., Greenberg, M. T., Haynes, N. M.,
        et al. (1997). *Promoting social and emotional learning: Guidelines for education.*
        Alexandria, VA: Association for Supervisors and Curriculum Development.

Elkind, D. (2007a). *The hurried child: Growing up too fast too soon* (3rd ed.). Cambridge,
        MA: DaCapo Lifelong.

Elkind, D. (2007b). *The power of play: How spontaneous, imaginative activities lead to hap-
        pier, healthier children.* Cambridge, MA: DaCapo Press.

Elliot, A. J., & Devine, P. G. (1994). On the motivational nature of cognitive disso-
        nance: Dissonance as psychological discomfort. *Journal of Personality and Social
        Psychology, 67,* 382–394.

Ellis, A. (1977). *How to live with and without anger.* New York: Crowell.

Ellis, A. (1985). *Overcoming resistance: Rational-emotive therapy with difficult clients.* New
        York: Springer.

Ellis, A. (1994). *Reason and emotion in psychotherapy* (Rev. ed.). Secaucus, NJ: Birch Lane.

Ellis, A., & Dryden, W. (1987). *The practice of rational emotive therapy.* New York:
        Springer.

Elmore, R. F. (2004). *School reform from the inside out: Policy, practice and performance.*
        Cambridge, MA: Harvard Educational Press.

Elson, M. (1986). *Self psychology in clinical social work.* New York: Norton.

England, M. J., & Cole, R. E. (1992). Building systems of care for youth illness. *Hospital
        and Community Psychiatry, 43,* 630–632.

Eppright, T., Kashani, J., Robinson, B., & Reid, J. (1993). Comorbidity of conduct dis-
        order and personality disorder in an incarcerated juvenile population. *American
        Journal of Psychiatry, 150,* 1233–1236.

Epstein, L. (1992). *Brief treatment and a new look at the task-centered approach.* New York:
        Macmillan.

Erikson, E. (1959). Identity and the life cycle. *Psychological Issues, 1,* 50–100.

Erikson, E. H. (1963). *Childhood and society* (2nd ed.). New York: Norton.

Erikson, E. (1968). *Identity: Youth and crisis.* New York: Norton.

Erker, G. J., Searight, H. R., Amanat, E., & White, P. D. (1993). Residential versus day treatment for children: A long-term follow up study. *Child Psychology and Human Development, 24*, 31–39.

Erwin, E. (1978). *Behaviour therapy: Scientific philosophical and moral foundations.* Cambridge: Cambridge University Press.

Farber, E. A., & Egeland, B. (1987). Invulnerability among abused and neglected children. In E. J. Anthony & B. J. Cohler (Eds.), *The invulnerable child* (pp. 253–288). New York: Guilford.

Farrington, D. P. (2004). Conduct disorder, aggression and delinquency. In R. Lerner & L. Steinberg (Eds.), *The handbook of adolescent psychology* (pp. 627–664). New York: Wiley.

Fausel, D. F. (1998). Collaborative conversations for change: A solutions focused approach to family-centered practice. *Family Preservation Journal, 3*, 59–74.

Feital, B., Margetson, N., Chamas, J., & Lipman, C. (1992). Psychosocial background and behavioural and emotional disorders of homeless and runaway youth. *Hospital and Community Psychiatry, 43*, 155–159.

Feldman, L. B. (1992). *Integrating individual and family therapy.* New York: Brunner/Mazel.

Ferguson, E. D. (1968). Alderian concepts in contemporary psychology: The changing scene. *Journal of Individual Psychology, 24*, 151–156.

Fernandez, J. A., & Underwood, J. (1993). *Tales out of school.* New York: Little, Brown.

Feuerstein, R., Rand, Y., & Rynders, J. E. (1988). *Don't accept me as I am: Helping "retarded" people to excel.* New York: Plenum.

Fewster, G. (1990). *Being in child care: A journey into self.* New York: Haworth.

Fewster, G., & Garfat, T. (Eds.). (1998). The effective child and youth care intervention: A phenomenological inquiry [Monograph]. *Journal of Child and Youth Care, 12*(1–2), 1–178.

Fewster, G., & Garfat, T. (Eds.). (2001). Self-evidence: Selected writings of Gerry Fewster [Monograph]. *Journal of Child and Youth Care, 15*(4), 1–179.

Finch, J. H., & Hewling, D. G. (1978). Organizations and training for the task of treatment in the prison services. In E. Miller (Ed.), *Task and organization.* New York: Wiley.

Finlay, D., & Randall, D. (1975). Treating the "untreatable" adolescent. *Canada's Mental Health, 23*, 3–7.

Fitzgerald, A. J. (2005). *Animal abuse and family violence: Researching the interrelationship of abusive power.* Lewiston, NY: Mellon.

Flaherty, L. T., & Horowitz, H. A. (1997). *Adolescent psychiatry: Developmental and clinical studies* (Vol. 21). Hillsdale, NJ: Analytic Press.

Flores-Gonzalez, N. (2002). *School kids/street kids: Identity development in Latino students.* New York: Teachers College Press.

Fonagy, P., & Target, M. (1995). Understanding the violent patient: The use of the body and the role of the father. *International Journal of Psychoanalysis, 76*, 487–502.

Fonagy, P., & Target, M. (1997). Attachment and reflective functions: Their role in self-organization. *Development and Psychopathology, 9*, 679–700.

Forehand, R., & Wierson, M. (1993). The role of developmental factors in planning behavioural interventions for children: Disruptive behaviour as an example. *Behaviour Therapy, 24*, 117–141.

Forester-Miller, H., & Davis, T. E. (1996). *A practitioner's guide to ethical decision making.* Alexandria, VA: American Counselling Association.

France, K. (1993). *Basic psychological skills for frontline staff of residential youth facilities.* Springfield, IL: Thomas.

Frankel, F., Myatt, R., & Cantwell, D. P. (1995). Training outpatient boys to conform with the social ecology of popular peers: Effects on parent and teacher ratings. *Journal of Clinical Child Psychology, 24*, 300–310.

Frankl, V. (1962). *Man's search for meaning: An introduction to logotherapy*. Boston: Beacon.

Frankl, V. (1967). *Psychotherapy and existentialism: Selected papers on logotherapy*. New York: Washington Square Press.

Franks, C. M. (1982). Behaviour therapy: An overview. In C. M. Franks, G. T. Wilson, P. C. Kendall, & K. D. Brownell (Eds.), *Annual review of behaviour therapy and practice* (Vol 8, pp. 1–78). New York: Guilford.

Freeman, A., & Reinecke, M. A. (Eds.). (2007). *Personality disorders in childhood and adolescence*. Hoboken, NJ: Wiley.

Freidman, R., Goorich, W., & Fullerton, C. S. (1986). Locus of control and severe psychiatric illness in the residential treatment of adolescents. *Residential Group Care and Treatment, 3*(2), 3–15.

Freud, S. (1975). *The psychopathology of every day life*. London: Penguin.

Fukuzawa, R. E., & Letendre, G. K. (2001). *Intense years: How Japanese adolescents balance school, family and friends*. New York: Routledge Falmer.

Fulcher, L. C. (1991). Teamwork in residential care. In J. Beker & Z. Eisikovits (Eds.), *Knowledge utilization in residential child and youth care practice* (pp. 213–236). Washington, DC: Child Welfare League.

Fuller, F., & Hill, C. E. (1985). Counselor and helpee perceptions of counsellor intentions in relation to outcome in a single counselling session. *Journal of Counselor Psychology, 32*, 329–338.

Gagnon, L. H., & Coleman, M. (2004). *Stepfamily relationships: Development, dynamics and interventions*. New York: Kluwer Academic.

Garbarino, J. (1999). *Lost boys: Why our sons turn violent and how we can help them*. New York: Anchor.

Garfat, T. (Ed.). (2003). *A child and youth care approach to working with families*. Binghamton, NY: Haworth.

Garmezy, N., & Rutter, M. (1983). *Stress, coping and development in children*. New York: McGraw-Hill.

Gatz, M., Messner, M. A., & Ball-Rokeach, S. J. (Eds.). (2002). *Paradoxes of youth and sport*. Albany: State University of New York Press.

Ge, X., Conger, R. D., Loreng, F. O., Shanahan, M., & Elder, G. H. (1995). Mutual influences in parent and adolescent psychological distress. *Developmental Psychology, 31*, 406–419.

Germain, C. B. (1991). *Human behaviour in the social environment: An ecological view*. New York: Columbia University Press.

Gershman, K. W. (2004). *They always test us on things we haven't read: Teen laments and lessons learned*. Lanham, MD: Hamilton.

Ghent, E. (1992). Paradox and process. *Psychoanalytic Dialogue, 8*, 149–182.

Ghurman, H. S., & Sarles, R. M. (Eds.). (2004). *Handbook of adolescent inpatient psychiatric treatment*. Philadelphia: Brunner/Mazel.

Gibbs, J. C., Potter, G. B., & Goldstein, A. P. (1995). *The Equip Program: Teaching youth to think and act responsibly through peer-helping*. New York: Haworth.

Gilmor, T. M. (1978). Locus of control as a mediator of adaptive behaviour in children and adolescents. *Canadian Psychological Review, 19*, 1–26.

Glasser, W. (1965). *Reality therapy: A new approach to psychiatry*. New York: Harper & Row.

Glasser, W. (1975). *Schools without failure*. New York: Harper & Row.

Glasser, W. (1998). *Choice theory: A new psychology of personal freedom*. New York: Harper Perennial.

Glasser, W. (2000a). *Counselling with choice theory: The new reality therapy*. New York: Harper Collins.

Glasser, W. (2000b). *Choice therapy*. New York: Free Press.

Goldfried, M. R., Castonguay, L. G., & Sanfran, J. D. (1992). Core issues and future directions in psychotherapy integration. In J. C. Norcross & M. R. Goldfried (Eds.), *Handbook of psychotherapy integration*. New York: Basic Books.

Goldstein, E. G. (1995). *Ego psychology and social work practice* (2nd ed.). New York: Free Press.

Goldstein, E. G. (2002). *Object relations theory and self-psychology in social work practice*. New York: Free Press.

Gottman, J., Gonso, J., & Rasmussen, B. (1975). Social interaction, social competence and friendship in children. *Child Development, 46*, 709–718.

Gottman, J. M., Fainsibler, L., & Hoover, C. (1997). *Meta-emotion: How families communicate emotionally*. Mahwah, NJ: Erlbaum.

Graziano, A. (1984). *Children and behaviour therapy*. New York: Aldine.

Green, W. H. (1991). *Child and adolescent clinical psychopharmacology*. Baltimore: Williams & Wilkins.

Gronlund, N. E. (1985). *Measurement and evaluation in teaching* (5th ed.). New York: MacMillan.

Gruber, J. J. (1986). Physical activity and self-esteem development in children: A meta-analysis. In G. Staff & H. Eckert (Eds.), *Effects of physical activity on children*. Champaign, IL: Human Kinetics and American Academy of Physical Education.

Grych, J. H., & Fincham, F. D. (1990). Marital conflicts and children's adjustment: A cognitive-contextual framework. *Psychological Bulletin, 108*, 267–290.

Gullotta, T. P., & Blau, G. M. (Eds.). (2008). *Handbook of childhood behavioural issues: Evidence-based approaches to prevention and treatment*. New York: Routledge.

Haley, J. (1979). *Leaving home: Therapy with disturbed young people*. New York: McGraw-Hill.

Hanna, F. J., Hanna, C. A., & Keys, S. G. (1999). Fifty strategies for counselling defiant, aggressive adolescents: Reaching acceptance and relating. *Journal of Counselling and Development, 77*, 395–404.

Hardy, K. V., & Laszloffy, T. (2005). *Teens who hurt: Clinical interventions to break the cycle of adolescent violence*. New York: Guilford.

Hardy, L. (1991). *The fabrics of this world*. Grand Rapids, MI: Eerdmanns.

Hargrove, E. (1975). *The missing link: The study of the implementation of social policy*. Washington, DC: Urban Institute.

Harmain, M. (2006). *Inspiring active learning: A complete handbook for today's teachers* (2nd ed.). Alexandria, VA: Supervision and Curriculum Development.

Harrington, R. (1993). *Depressive disorders in childhood and adolescence*. New York: Wiley.

Harris, J. D. (1999). *The nature assumption: Why children turn out the way they do*. New York: Harper & Row.

Hayden, D. C. (1987). Counselor and client responses to hypothesis: Testing strategies. *Journal of Counselling Psychology, 34*, 149–156.

Healy, M. (1998). *Failure to connect: How computers affect our children's minds—for better and worse*. New York: Simon & Schuster.

Hebb, D. O. (1980). *Essays on mind*. Hillsdale, NJ: Erlbaum.

Helgerson, J., Martinovich, Z., Durkin, E., & Lyons, J. (2005). Differences in outcome trajectories of children in residential treatment. *Residential Treatment for Children and Youth, 4*, 67–70.

Hodges, S., Nesman, T., & Hermandez, M. (1999). Promising practices: Building collaboration in systems of care. In *Systems of care: Promising practices in children's mental health, 1998 series* (Vol. 6). Washington, DC: Center for Effective Collaboration and Practice, American Institute for Research.

Hodges, V. G. (1994). Home-based behavioural interventions with children and families. In D. K. Granvold (Ed.), *Cognitive and behavioural treatment: Methods and applications* (pp. 90–107). Pacific Grove, CA: Brooks/Cole.

Hoffman, L. (1981). *Foundations of family therapy*. New York: Basic Books.

Hoge, R. D. (1999). *Assessing adolescents in educational, counselling and other settings*. Mahwah, NJ: Erlbaum.

Hollin, C. R., Epps, K. J., & Kendricks, D. J. (1995). *Managing behavioural treatment: Policy and practice with delinquents*. New York: Plenum.

Hollis, S., & Woods, M. E. (1981). *Casework: A psychosocial therapy* (3rd ed.). New York: Random House.

Honig, A. (1985). Compliance, control, and discipline. In N. Lauter-Klatell (Ed.), *Readings in child development* (pp. 56–61). San Francisco: Mayfield.

Hooper, S. R., Murphy, J., Devaney, A., & Hultman, J. (2000). Ecological outcomes of adolescents in a psychoanalytic residential treatment facility. *American Journal of Orthopsychiatry, 70*, 491–500.

Hopkins, R. L. (1994). *Narrative schooling: Experimental learning and the transformation of American education*. New York: Teacher's College Press.

Horner, R. H., Sugai, G., Todd, A. W., & Lewis-Palmer, T. (2000). Elements of behaviour support plans: A technical brief. *Exceptionality, 8*(3), 205–215.

Hughes, D. A. (2007). *Attachment-focused family therapy*. New York: Norton.

Hurrelmann, K., & Hamilton, S. F. (Eds). (1996). *Social problems and social contents in adolescence: Perspectives across boundaries*. New York: Aldine de Gruyter.

Husain, S., & Cantwell, D. (1992). *Fundamentals of child and adolescent behavior*. Washington, DC: American Psychiatric Press.

Hyson, M. C. (1994). *The emotional development of young children: Building an emotional centered curriculum*. New York: Teacher's College Press.

Irvin, J. L., Meltzer, J., & Dukes, M. (2007). *Taking action on learners*. Alexandria, VA: Association for Supervision & Curriculum Development.

Ivey, A. E. (1986). *Developmental therapy*. San Francisco: Jossey-Bass.

Ivey, G., & Fisher, D. (2006). *Creating literacy-rich schools for adolescents*. Alexandria, VA: Association for Supervision and Curriculum Development.

Izzo, R. L. Y., & Ross, R. R. (1990). Meta-analysis of rehabilitation programs for juvenile delinquents: A brief report. *Criminal Justice and Behaviour, 17*, 134–142.

Jacobs, D. T., & Jacobs-Spencer, J. (2001). *Teaching virtues: Building character across the curriculum*. Lanham, MD: Scarecrow Press.

Jeynes, W. (2002). *Divorce, family structure and the academic success of children*. New York: Haworth.

Jeziorski, R. M. (1994). *The importance of school sports in American education and socialization*. Lanham, MD: University Press of America.

Johnson, J. H., Rasbury, W. C., & Siegel, L. J. (1997). *Approaches to child treatment: Introduction to theory, research and practice* (2nd ed.). Needham Heights, MA: Allyn & Bacon.

Johnson, T. C. (1997). *Sexual, physical and emotional abuse in out-of-home care: Prevention skills for at-risk children.* Binghamton, NY: Haworth.

Jordan, C., & Franklin, C. (1995). *Clinical assessment for social workers: Quantative and qualitative methods.* Chicago: Lyceum Bas.

Kagan, J., & Klein, R. E. (1973). Cross-cultural perspectives on early development. *American Psychology, 28,* 947–961.

Kagan, R. (1996). *Turmoil to turning points: Building hope for children in crisis placements.* New York: Norton.

Kagan, R. (2004). *Rebuilding attachments with traumatized children: Healing from losses, violence, abuse, and neglect.* New York: Haworth.

Kagan, R., & Scholosberg, S. (1989). *Families in perpetual crisis.* New York: Norton.

Kamphaus, R. W., & Campbell, J. M. (Eds.). (2006). *Psychodiagmetric assessment of children: Dimensional and categorical approaches.* Hoboken, NJ: Wiley.

Kandel, E. R. (2005). *Psychiatry, psychoanalysis, and the new biology of the mind.* Washington, DC: American Psychiatric Publishing.

Karp, C. L., Butler, T. L., & Bergstram, S. C. (1998). *Treatment strategies for abused adolescents from victim to survivor.* Thousand Oaks, CA: Sage.

Kashubeck, S., Pottenbaun, S. M., & Read, N. O. (1994). Predicting elopement from residential treatment centers. *American Journal of Orthopsychiatry, 64*(1), 126–135.

Kazdin, A. E. (1980). Acceptability of alternative treatments for deviant child behaviour. *Journal of Applied Behaviour Analysis, 13,* 259–273.

Kazdin, A. E. (1984). *Behavior modification in applied settings* (3rd ed.). Homewood, IL: Dorsey Press.

Kazdin, A. E. (1990). Conduct disorders. In A. Bellack, M. Herson, & A. Kazdin (Eds.), *International handbook of behaviour modification and therapy* (pp. 669–706). New York: Plenum.

Kazdin, A. E. (1995). *Conduct disorders in childhood and adolescence* (2nd ed.). London: Sage.

Kazdin, A. E., & Weisz, J. R. (Eds.). (2003). *Evidence-based psychotherapies for children and adolescents.* New York: Guilford.

Kegan, R. (1982). *The evolving self: Problem and process in human development.* Cambridge, MA: Harvard University Press.

Kelly, F. D. (1999). *The psychological assessment of abused and traumatized children.* Mahwah, NJ: Erlbaum.

Kendall, P., Reber, M., McLeer, S., Epps, J., & Ronan, K. (1990). Cognitive-behavioural treatment of conduct disordered children. *Cognitive Therapy Research, 22,* 279–297.

Kernberg, O. (1984). *Severe personality disorders: Psychotherapeutic strategies.* New Haven, CT: Yale University Press.

Kettler, J. A. (2001). *Learning group leadership: An experimental approach.* Needham Heights, MA: Brunner-Routledge.

Kincheloe, J. L., Hayes, K., Rose, K., & Anderson, P. M. (Eds.). (2006). *The Praeger handbook of urban education* (2 vols.). Westport, CT: Praeger.

Kingery, P. M., McCoy-Simandle, L., & Clayton, R. (1997). Risk factors for adolescent violence: The importance of vulnerability. *School Psychology International, 18,* 49–60.

Kipnis, A. (2002). *Angry young men: How parents, teachers and counsellors can help "bad boys" become good men.* San Francisco: Jossey-Bass.

Kiraly, M. (2003). *Residential child care staff selection: Choose with care.* Binghamton, NY: Haworth.

Kitchener, R. F. (1991). The ethical foundations of behaviour therapy. *Ethics and Behaviour, 1*, 221–238.

Kivel, P., & Creighton, A. (1997). *A fifteen-session violence prevention program for young people*. Alameda, CA: Hunter House.

Klein, M. (1957). *Envy and gratitude*. New York: Basic Books.

Klein, M. W. (1995). *The American street gang: Its nature, prevalence, and control*. New York: Oxford University Press.

Klinger, E. (1982). On self-management of mood, affect and attention. In P. Karoly & F. H. Kanter (Eds.), *Self-management and behaviour change: From theory to practice* (pp. 129–164). New York: Pergamon.

Kohlberg, L. (1969). Stage and sequence: The cognitive developmental approach to socialization. In. D. Goslin (Ed.), *Handbook of socialization theory and research* (pp. 347–480). New York: Rand McNally.

Kohlberg, L. (1981). *Essays on moral development: The philosophy of moral development* (Vol. 1). New York: Harper & Row.

Kohlberg, L., & Meyer, R. (1972). Development as the aim of education. *Harvard Educational Review, 43*, 449–496.

Kohut, H. (1977). *The restoration of the self*. New York: International Universities Press.

Kohut, H. (1984). *How does analysis care?* Chicago: University of Chicago Press.

Kohut, H., & Wolf, E. (1978). The disorders of the self and their treatment: An outline. *International Journal of Psychoanalysis, 89*, 413–425.

Kreisher, K. (2002). *Burnout*. Washington, DC: Child Welfare League of America.

Kronenberger, W. G., & Meyer, R. G. (2001). *The child clinician's handbook* (2nd ed.). Needham Heights, MA: Allyn & Bacon.

Krugen, M. V. (Ed.). (2004). *Themes and stories in youth work practice*. Binghamtom, NY: Haworth.

Kruger, M. (1986). *Job satisfaction for child and youth workers*. Washington, DC: Child Welfare League.

Kruger, M. A. (1991). Coming from your center, being there, meeting them where they're at, interacting together, counselling, on the go, creating circles of caring, this covering and using self and caring for another. *Central Themes in Professional Child and Youth Care, 15*, 43–51.

Kurdek, L. A., Fine, M. A., & Sinclair, R. J. (1995). School adjustment in sixth graders: Parenting transitions, family climate, and peer norm effect. *Child Development, 66*, 430–445.

Kwantes, C. (1992). Rethinking residential care: Working systematically within the constraints of residential treatment. *Journal of Child and Youth Care, 7*, 33–44.

Laborde, P. R., & Seligman, M. (1983). Individual counselling with parents of handicapped children: Rationale and strategies. In M. Seligman (Ed.), *The family with a handicapped child: Understanding and treatment* (pp. 261–284). New York: Grune and Stratton.

Laing, R. D. (1965). Mystification, confusion and conflict. In I. Boszormengi-Nagy & J. Framo (Eds.), *Intensive family therapy* (pp. 343–364). New York: Harper & Row.

Laing, R. D., & Esterson, A. (1970). *Sanity, madness and the family*. New York: Basic Books.

LaPointe, J. M., & Legault, F. (2004). Solving group discipline problems without coercion: An approach based on attribution retraining. *Journal of Classroom Interaction, 39*(1), 1–10.

Larsen, D., & Dehle, C. (2007). Rural adolescent aggression and parental emotional support. *Adolescence, 42*(165), 25–50.

Laursen, E. K. (2000). Strength-based practice with children. *Reclaiming Children and Youth, 9*(2), 70–89.

Lazarus, A. A. (1989). *The practice of multimodal therapy.* Baltimore: John Hopkins University Press.

Lee, M. Y., & Gaucher, R. (2000). Group treatment for dually diagnosed adolescents: An empowerment-based approach. *Social Work with Groups, 23*(2), 55–78.

Lee, R. E. (1996). FIRO-B scores and success in positive peer-culture residential treatment program. *Psychology Reports, 78*(1), 215–220.

Lefcourt, H. M. (1982). *Locus of control: Current trends in theory and research* (2nd ed.). Hillsdale, NJ: Erlbaum.

Lerner, R. M., & Hultsch, D. P. (1983). *Human development: A life-span perspective.* New York: McGraw-Hill.

Levy, T. M., & Orlans, M. (1998). *Attachment, trauma, and healing; Understanding and treating attachment disorder in children and families.* Washington, DC: Child Welfare League of America.

Lilberman, M. A., Yalom, I. D., & Miles, M. B. (1973). *Encounter groups: First facts.* New York: Basic Books.

Littky, D. (2004). *The big picture: Education is everyone's business.* Alexandria, VA: Association for Supervision and Curriculum Development.

Loeber, R., Lahey, B. B., & Thomas, C. (1991). Diagnostic conundrum of oppositional defiant disorder and conduct disorder. *Journal of Abnormal Psychology, 100,* 379–390.

London, P. (1977). *Behaviour control.* New York: New American Library.

Lowman, R. (1993). *Counselling and psychotherapy of work dysfunctions.* Washington, DC: American Psychological Association.

Luborsky, L. (1984). *Principles of psychoanalytic psychotherapy: A manual for supportive-expressive treatment.* New York: Basic Books.

Ludburg, A. M. (1972). Hysteria: A neurobiological theory. *Archives of General Psychology, 27,* 771–777.

Lupton, D. (1998). *The emotional self: A sociological exploration.* Thousand Oaks, CA: Sage.

Lymann, R. D., & Campbell, N. R. (1996). *Treating children and adolescents in residential and inpatient settings.* London: Sage.

Macciomei, N. R., & Ruben, D. H. (Eds.). (1999). *Behavioural management in the public schools: An urban approach.* Westport, CT: Praeger.

MacKinnon, R. A., & Michaels, R. (1971). *The psychotic interview in clinical practice.* Philadelphia: Saunders.

Madanes, C. (1984). *Behind the one-way mirror.* San Francisco: Jossey-Bass.

Madanes, C., Kein, J. P., & Smelser, D. (1995). *The violence of men: New techniques for working with abusive families: A therapy of social action.* San Francisco: Jossey-Bass.

Madsen, W. C. (1999). *Collaborative therapy with multi-stressed families: From old problems to new futures.* New York: Guilford.

Mahler, M. S. (1979). *Selected papers of Margaret S. Mahler, M.D.: Vol. 2. Separation-individuation.* New York: Aronson.

Maier, H. W. (1979). The core of care: Essential ingredients for the development of children at home and away from home. *Child Care Quarterly, 8,* 161–173.

Maier, H. W. (1987). *Development group care of children and youth: Concepts and practices.* New York: Haworth.

Malan, D. (1976). *The frontier of brief psychotherapy.* Cambridge, MA: Harvard University Press.

Mallinckrodt, B. (1992). Childhood emotional bonds with parents, development of adult social competencies and availability of social support. *Journal of Counselling Psychology, 39,* 453–461.

Manguel, A. (Ed.). (2000). *On lying in bed and other essays of G. K. Chesterton.* Toronto, ON: Arts.

Mann, J. (1991). Time-limited psychotherapy. In P. Crits-Christoph & J. P. Barber (Eds.), *Handbook of short-term dynamic psychotherapy* (pp. 17–41). New York: Basic Books.

Maslow, A. H. (1968). *Toward a psychology of being* (2nd ed.). Princeton, NJ: Van Nostrand.

Masterson, J., & Costello, J. (1980). *From borderline adolescent to functioning adult: The test of time.* New York: Brunner/Mazel.

McDermott, J. F., & Char, W. F. (1974). The undeclared war between child and family therapy. *Journal of the American Academy of Child Psychiatry, 13,* 422–426.

McLeod, J. (1998). *Narrative and psychotherapy.* Thousand Oaks, CA: Sage.

Meichenbaum, D. (1977). *Cognitive behaviour modification: An integrative approach.* New York: Plenum.

Menzies, I. (1979). Staff support systems: Task and anti-task in adolescent institutions. In R. Hinshelwood & W. Manning (Eds.), *Therapeutic communities.* London: Routledge and Kegan Paul.

Meyer, R. E. (1987). *Educational psychology: A cognitive approach.* Boston: Little, Brown.

Milofsky, C. (1984). *Testers and testing: The sociology of school.* New Brunswick, NJ: Rutgers University Press.

Minkoff, K., & Drake, R. E. (Eds.). (1991). *Dual diagnosis of major mental illness and substance disorders.* San Francisco: Jossey-Bass.

Minuchin, S. (1974). *Families and family therapy.* Cambridge, MA: Harvard University Press.

Minuchin, S. (1995). Foreword. In P. Adams & K. Nelson (Eds.), *Reinventing of human services.* Hawthorne, NY: Aldine de Gruyter.

Minuchin, S., & Fishman, C. (1981). *Family therapy techniques.* Cambridge, MA: Harvard University Press.

Mollerstrom, W., Patchner, M. A., & Milner, J. J. (1992). Family functioning and child abuse potential. *Journal of Clinical Psychology, 48,* 445–454.

Monk, G., Winslade, J., Crocket, K., & Epston, D. (Eds.). (1997). *Narrative therapy in practice: The archaeology of hope.* San Francisco: Jossey-Bass.

Moody, E., & Lupton-Smith, H. (2002). Interventions with juvenile offenders: Strategies to prevent acting out behaviour. *Journal of Addictions & Offender counselling, 20*(1), 2–14.

Morris, R. J. (1985). *Behaviour modification with exceptional children: Principles and practices.* Glenview, IL: Scott, Foreman.

Moss, R. H. (1974). *Evaluating treatment environments.* New York: Wiley.

Munger, R. L. (2005). *Changing children's behaviours by changing the people, places and activities in their lives.* Boys Town, NE: Boys Town Press.

Newman, B. M., & Newman, P. R. (2001). Group identity and alienation: Giving the WE its due. *Journal of Youth and Adolescence, 30,* 515–538.

Nichols, M., & Shwartz, R. (1991). *Family therapy, concepts and methods.* Needham Heights, MA: Allyn & Bacon.

Noshpitz, J. D. (1993). The child care worker and the youth with character disorder. *Residential Treatment for Children and Youth, 10,* 49–67.

Nugent, F. A. (1994). *An introduction to the profession of counselling* (2nd ed.). New York: Merrill.

Nurmi, J. (1991). *The development of future-orientation in a life-span context.* Helsinki: University of Helsinki Press.

Offerd, D. R., Boyle, M. C., & Racine, Y. S. (1991). The episdemology of anti-social behaviour in childhood and adolescence. In D. J. Repler & K. H. Rubin (Eds.), *The development and treatment of childhood aggression* (pp. 31–54). Hillsdale, NJ: Erlbaum.

Ogden, T. H. (1986). *The matrix of the mind: Object relations and the psychoanalytic dialogue.* Northvale, NJ: Jason Aronson.

Olson, D. H., Portner, J., & Lavee, Y. (1985). *Faces III.* St. Paul: University of Minnesota.

Olson, D., Russell, C., & Sprenkle, E. (1979). Circumflex model of marital and family systems II: Empirical studies and clinical interventions. In J. P. Vincent (Ed.), *Advances in family intervention assessment and theory* (pp. 128–176). Greenwich, CT: JAI.

Ontario Government. (1967). *White Paper tabled by the Honourable Matthew Dymond, minister of health.* Toronto: Author.

Page, R. C., Campbell, L., & Wilder, D. C. (1994). Role of the leader in therapy groups conducted with illicit drug abusers: How directive does the leader have to be. *Journal of Addiction & Offender Counselling, 14*(2), 57–67.

Patterson, G. R., & Stouthamer-Loeber, M. (1984). The correlation of family management practices and development. *Child Development, 55*, 1299–1307.

Patterson, L. E., & Welfel, E. R. (1994). *The counselling process* (4th ed.). Pacific Grove, CA: Brooks/Cole.

Pazaratz, D. (1993). The nature of communicative relationships within a residential milieu. *Journal of Child and Youth Care, 8*(3), 51–58.

Pazaratz, D. (1996a). Teaching a young woman to understand the nature and consequences of her behaviours. *Residential Treatment for Children and Youth, 14*, 25–35.

Pazaratz, D. (1996b). Intervention strategies with a behaviour-disordered male. *Journal of Child and Youth Care, 11*, 37–45.

Pazaratz, D. (1997). Children's art: An assessment instrument. *Context: Journal of the American College of Counsellors, 11*, 72–80.

Pazaratz, D. (1998a). The establishment and growth of a mental health center. *Residential Treatment for Children and Youth, 15*, 11–23.

Pazaratz, D. (1998b). Therapeutic application of play. *Journal of Child and Youth Care, 12*, 27–38.

Pazaratz, D. (1998c). The counselling role of the child and youth care worker in a treatment classroom. *Adolescence, 33*, 725–734.

Pazaratz, D. (1999). An impressionistic evaluation of the efficacy of a residential treatment facility for emotionally disturbed youth. *Residential Treatment for Children and Youth, 16*, 15–35.

Pazaratz, D. (2000a). Task-centered child & youth care practice in residential treatment. *Residential Treatment for Children and Youth, 17*, 1–16.

Pazaratz, D. (2000b). Training youth workers in residential treatment. *Residential Treatment for Children and Youth, 18*, 35–56.

Pazaratz, D. (2000c). Youth worker job description and self-evaluation compendium, *Residential Treatment for Children and Youth, 18*, 57–74.

Pazaratz, D. (2000d). Defining and describing the child and youth care worker's role in residential treatment. *Journal of Child and Youth Care, 14*, 47–78.

Pazaratz, D. (2001). Theory and structure of a day treatment program for adolescents. *Residential Treatment for Children and Youth, 19*, 29–43.

Pazaratz, D. (2003a). Therapy with a child experiencing a reactive attachment disorder. *Context: Journal of the American College of Counsellors, 9*, 9–23.

Pazaratz, D. (2003b). Skills training for managing disturbed adolescents in a residential treatment program. *Clinical Child Psychology and Psychiatry, 8*, 119–130.

Pazaratz, D. (2003c). The application of a reinforcement/level system in the residential treatment of adolescents. *Residential Treatment for Children and Youth, 21*, 17–32.

Pazaratz, D. (2004). An at-risk student and school retaliation. *Journal of School Violence, 3*, 111–121.

Pazaratz, D. (2005a). Compendium model for residential supervisors self-evaluation. *Residential Treatment for Children and Youth, 22*(3), 319–337.

Pazaratz, D. (2005b). Maintaining cultural integrity in residential treatment. *Residential Treatment for Children and Youth, 24*(4), 15–30.

Pazaratz, D. (2005c). Assessment and counselling of the adolescent substance user. *Context: Journal of the American College of Counsellors, 13*(1), 7–16.

Pazaratz, D. (2005d). Concepts in structural family therapy: A case study. *Context: Journal of the American College of Counsellors, 12*(1), 44–54.

Pazaratz, D., & Morton, W. J. (2000). The postmodern adolescent: Counselling issues. *Alabama Counselling Association, 26*, 41–51.

Pazaratz, D., & Morton, W. J. (2002). Intervention strategies for occupational stress. *Global Visions for Counseling Professionals, the Official Journal of the Tennessee Counseling Association, 4*, 69–77.

Pazaratz, D., & Morton, W. J. (2003). A psychosocial model for the evaluation of children and adolescents. *Context: Journal of the American College of Counsellors, 9*, 38–54.

Pazaratz, D., Randall, D., Spekkens, J. F., Lazor, A., & Morton, W. J. (2000). The Four Phase System: A multi-agency coordinated service for very disturbed adolescents *Residential Treatment for Children and Youth, 17*, 31–48.

Pearce, J. W., & Pezzot-Pearce, T. D. (1997). *Psychotherapy of abused and neglected children*. New York: Guilford.

Pecora, P. J., Whittaker, J. K., & Maluccio, A. N. (1992). *The child welfare challenge: Policy, practice and research*. New York: Aldine de Gruyter.

Penn, P. (1982). Circular questioning. *Family Process, 21*, 267–281.

Pennell, J., & Anderson, G. (Eds.). (2006). *Widening the circle: The practice and evaluation of family group conferencing with children, youth and their families*. Washington, DC: National Association of Social Workers Press.

Perlman, H. H. (1979). *Relationships: The heart of helping people*. Chicago: University of Chicago Press.

Perls, F. S. (1969a). *In and out the garbage pail*. Toronto, ON: Bantam.

Perls, F. S. (1969b). *Gestalt therapy verbation*. Lafayette, CA: Real People Press.

Perls, F. (1969c). *Ego, hunger and aggression*. New York: Vintage.

Phelan, J. (1999). Experiments with experience. *Journal of Child and Youth Care Work, 14*, 25–28.

Phelan, J. (2001). Experiential counselling and the child and youth care. *Journal of Child and Youth Care Work, 15–16*, 256–263.

Philion, C. A. (2002). A legacy for the millennium: Two hundred years of systematic abuse of children in substitute care. *Journal of Child and Youth Care, 15*, 33–41.

Phillips, V. (1998). *Empowering discipline: An approach that works with at-risk students*. Carmel Valley, CA: Personal Development.

Piaget, J. (1974). *The origins of intelligence in children*. New York: Prentice Hall.

Piaget, J. (1975). *The equilibrium of cognitive structures: The central problem of intellectual development* (T. Brown & J. Tampy, Trans.). Chicago: University of Chicago Press.

Pierangelo, R., & Guiliani, G. A. (2000). *Why your students do what they do and what to do when they do it: A practical guide for understanding classroom behaviour (grade 6–12)*. Champaign, IL: Research Press.

Pierangelo, R., & Giuliani, G. (2007). *Understanding, developing and writing effective IEP's: A step-by-step guide for education*. Thousand Oaks, CA: Crown.

Pike, D. R., Millspauch, C. M., & DeSalvator, G. (2005). Controlling behaviour or reclaiming youth? Creating a behaviour management system based on the circle of courage. *Reclaiming Children and Youth, 13*, 213–217.

Pinsof, W. M. (1981). Symptom/patient defocusing in family therapy. In A. S. Gurman (Ed.), *Questions and answers in the practice of family therapy*. New York: Brunner/Mazel.

Polsky, H. W. (1962). *Cottage six*. New York: Russell Sage Foundation.

Polsky, H. W., & Berger, R. (2003). *From custodialism to community: A theory-based manual for transforming institutions*. Lanham, MD: University Press of America.

Powell, M., & Oei, T. (1991). Cognitive processes underlying the behaviour change in cognitive behaviour therapy with childhood disorders: A review of experimental evidence. *Behaviour and Cognitive Psychology, 19*, 247–265.

Preston, D., & Murphy, S. (1997). Motivating treatment-resistant clients in therapy, *Forum, 9*, 39–43.

Prochaska, J., & Norcross, J. (1994). *Systems of psychotherapy: A transtheoretical analysis* (3rd ed.). Pacific Grove, CA: Brooks/Cole.

Proctor, R. W., & Dutta, A. (1994). *Skill acquisition and human performance*. Thousand Oaks, CA: Sage.

Putman, F. (1991). Dissociative disorders in children and adolescents: A developmental perspective, *Psychiatry Clinics of North America, 14*, 519–531.

Rapp, C. A. (1998). *The strengths model: Case management for people suffering from severe and persistent mental illness*. New York: Oxford University Press.

Rappaport, J. (1981). In praise of paradox: The social policy of employment over prevention. *American Journal of Community Psychiatry, 9*, 1–25.

Rathvon, N. (1999). *Effective school interventions: Strategies for enhancing achievement and social competence*. New York: Guilford.

Redl, F. (1966). *When we deal with children*. New York: Free Press.

Redl, F., & Wineman, D. (1957a). *Controls from within*. New York: Free Press.

Redl, F., & Wineman, D. (1957b). *Children who hate*. New York: Free Press.

Reid, D., Parsons, M., Green, C., & Schepis, M. (1991). Evaluation of components of residential treatment by Medicaid ICF-MR Survey: A validity assessment. *Journal of Applied Behaviour Analysis, 22*, 143–156.

Reid, W. J. (1996). Task centered social work. In F. J. Turner (Ed.), *Social work treatment: Interlocking theoretical approaches* (4th ed., pp. 601–616). New York: Free Press.

Reiser, M. F. (1988). Are psychiatric educators "losing the minds"? *American Journal Psychiatry, 145*, 148–153.

Reiss, D. (1991). *The family's construction of reality*. Cambridge, MA: Harvard University Press.

Rennie, D. L. (1998). *Person-centered counselling: An experiential approach*. Thousand Oaks, CA: Sage.

Riegel, K. (1975). Toward a dialectical theory of development. *Human Development, 18*, 50–64.

Rippel, L. (1964). *Motivation, capacity, and opportunity: Studies in case work theory and practice*. Chicago: University of Chicago Press.

Robbins, S. P. (1992). *Essential of organizational behaviour*. New York: Simon & Schuster.

Roberts, A. R. (1989). Family treatment. In A. R. Roberts (Ed.), *Juvenile justice: Policies, programs and services* (pp. 219–244). Pacific Grove, CA: Brooks/Cole.

Robin, A., & Foster, S. (1989). *Negotiating parent-adolescent conflict: A behavioural family systems approach*. New York: Guilford.

Rodriguez, E. R., & Bellanca, J. (2007). *What is it about me you can't teach? An instructional guide for the urban educator* (2nd ed.). Thousand Oaks, CA: Corwin.

Rogers, C. R. (1951). *Client-centered therapy*. Boston: Houghton-Miffin.

Rogers, C. R. (1969). *Freedom to learn*. Columbus, OH: Merrill.

Rose, R. L., Beardon, W. O., & Teel, J. E. (1992). An attributional analysis of resistance to group pressure regarding illicit drug and alcohol consumption. *Journal of Consumer Research, 19*, 1–13.

Rose, S. D. (1998). *Group work with children and adolescents: Prevention and intervention in school and community systems*. Thousand Oaks, CA: Sage.

Rosenfield, E., Frankel, N. R., & Esman, A. H. (1969). A social model of criteria for evaluating progress in children undergoing psychosis. *Journal of American Academy of Childhood Psychiatry, 18*, 193–228.

Ross, D. M. (1996). *Childhood bullying and teasing*. Alexandria, VA: American Counselling Association.

Rothstein, A., & Glenn, J. (1999). *Learning disabilities and psychic conflict: A psychoanalytic casebook*. Madison, CT: International Universities Press.

Rowe, J., Cain, H., Hundleby, N., & Keane, A. (1984). *Long-term foster care*. London: Batsford Academic and Educational.

Rye, D. R., & Sparks, R. (1998). *Strengthening K–12 school counselling programs: A support system* (2nd ed.). Philadelphia: Accelerated Development.

Sampson, R. J., & Laub, J. H. (1993). *Crime in the making: Pathways and turning points through life*. Cambridge, MA: Harvard University Press.

Satir, V. (1964). *Conjoint family therapy*. Palo Alto, CA: Science and Behaviour Books.

Sattler, J. M. (1988). *Assessment of children* (3rd ed.). San Diego, CA: Sattler.

Scherer, M. (1985). How many ways is a child intelligent? An interview with Howard Gardner. In N. Lauter-Klatell (Ed.), *Readings in child development* (pp. 21–25). San Francisco: Mayfield.

Schoenberg, S. (1994). *Making it happen: A guide to program development for services to children and adolescents who are experiencing a severe emotional disturbance and their families*. Washington, DC: Substance Abuse and Mental Health Services Administration.

Scull, A. (1993). *The most solitary of afflictions: Madness and society in Britain, 1700–1900*. New Haven, CT: Yale University Press.

Serin, R., & Brown, S. (1996). Strategies for enhancing the treatment of violent offenders. *Forum, 8*, 45–48.

Seruya, B. B. (1997). *Empathic brief psychotherapy*. Northvale, NJ: Jason Aronson.

Severe, S. (2000). *How to behave so your child will too*. New York: Viking.

Shafir, M., & Shafir, S. (1992). *Clinical guide to depression and childhood*. Washington, DC: American Psychiatric Press.

Shapiro, J. P., Freiberg, R. D., & Bandstein, K. K. (2006). *Child and adolescent therapy: Science and art*. New York: Wiley.

Sheldon, B. (1987). Implementing findings from social work effectiveness research. *British Journal of Social Work, 17*, 573–586.

Sherradan, M. (1992). *Community-based youth services in international perspective.* Washington, DC: Carnegie Corporation.

Sherrod, L. R., Flanagan, C. A., Kassimir, R., & Syvesten, A. M. (Eds.). (2006). *Youth activism: An international encyclopaedia* (Vols. 1 and 2). Westport, CT: Greenwood.

Shervin, H., & Shectman, F. (1973). The diagnostic process in psychiatric evaluations. *Bulletin Menniger Clinic, 37,* 451–494.

Shiller, V. M. (2003). *Rewards for kids: Ready to use charts and activities for positive parenting.* Washington, DC: American Psychological Association.

Shirk, S., & Phillips, J. (1991). Child therapy training: Closing gaps with research and practice. *Journal of Consulting and Child Psychology, 59,* 766–776.

Short, R., & Shapiro, S. (1993). Conduct disorders: A framework for understanding and intervention in schools and communities. *School Psychology Review, 22,* 362–375.

Shulman, I. (1957). Modifications in group psychotherapy with antisocial adolescents. *International Journal of Group Psychotherapy, 3,* 310–317.

Siegler, A. L. (2000). *The essential guide to the new adolescent: How to raise an emotionally healthy teenager.* New York: Dutton.

Silver, A. A. (1984). Children in classes for the severely emotionally handicapped. *Journal of Developmental and Behavioural Paediatrics, 5,* 49–54.

Silverberg, S. B., & Gondoli, D. M. (1996). Autonomy in adolescence: A contextualized perspective. In G. R. Adams, R. Mortemayor, & T. P. Gulotta (Eds.), *Psychological development during adolescence: Progress in developmental contextualism* (pp. 12–61). Newburg Park, CA: Sage.

Sizer, T. R., & Sizer, N. F. (1999). *The students are watching: Schools and the moral contract.* Boston: Beacon.

Skinner, B. F. (1938). *The behaviour of organisms.* New York: Appleton-Century-Crofts.

Skinner, B. F. (1971). *Beyond freedom and dignity.* New York: Knopf.

Skinner, B. F. (1988). The operant side of behavioural therapy. *Journal of Behaviour Therapy & Experimental Psychiatry, 19,* 171–179.

Skinner, H. A., & Blaskfield, R. K. (1983). Increasing the impact of cluster analysis research: The case of psychiatric classification, *Journal of Consulting and Clinical Psychiatry, 50,* 727–735.

Smith, D. G. (1991). *Parents guide to raising kids in a changing world: Preschool through teen years.* New York: Prentice Hall.

Sparrow, S. S., Fletcher, J. M., & Cicchetti, D. V. (1985). Psychological assessment of children. In R. Michels, J. O. Cavenar, & H. K. Brodie (Eds.), *Psychiatry* (pp. 1–12). Philadelphia: Lippincott.

Speltz, M. L., DeKlyen, M., Greenberg, M. T., & Dryden, M. (1998). Clinical referral for oppositional defiant disorder: Relative significance of attachment and behavioural variables. *Journal of Abnormal Psychology, 23,* 487–506.

Springer, D. (2006). Substance abuse treatment for juvenile delinquents: Promising and not-so-promising practices in the U.S. *Social Perspectives, 8*(1), 23–52.

Stadden, J. (2001). *The new behaviourism: Mind, mechanism, and society.* Philadelphia: Psychology Press.

Stark, K. (1990). *Childhood depression: School-based interventions.* New York: Guilford.

Stein, J. A. (1995). *Residential treatment of adolescents and children: Issues, principles and techniques.* Chicago: Nelson.

Stein, R., Richin, R., Banyon, R., Banyon, F., & Stein, M. (2000). *Connecting character to conduct: Helping students do the right things.* Alexandria, VA: Association for Supervision and Curriculum Development.

Steinberg, L., Fletcher, A., & Darling, N. (1994). Parental monitoring and peer influence on adolescent substance use. *Pediatrics, 93,* 1060–1064.

Steinberg, L., & Silverberg, S. B. (1986). The vicissitudes of autonomy in early childhood. *Child Development, 57,* 841–851.

Sterba, M., & Davis, J. (1999). *Dangerous kids: Boys Towns' approach for helping caregivers treat aggressive and violent youth.* Boys Town, NE: Boys Town Press.

Stierlin, H. (1977). *Psychoanalysis and family therapy.* Northvale, NJ: Jason Aronson.

Stoltenberg, C. D., McNeill, B., & Delworth, U. (1998). *IDM supervision: An integrated developmental model for supervising counsellors and therapists.* San Francisco: Jossey-Bass.

Stoner, R. J. (1985). *Presentations of gender.* New Haven, CT: Yale University Press.

Stroul, B. A., & Friedman, R. M. (1986). *A system of care for children and youth with extreme emotional disturbances* (Rev. ed.). Washington, DC: Georgetown University.

Sullivan, H. S. (1953). *The interpersonal theory of psychiatry.* New York: Norton.

Swann, W. B., & Pittman, T. S. (1977). Initiating play activity in children: The moderating influence of verbal cue on intrinsic motivations. *Child Development, 48,* 1128–1132.

Taibbi, R. (2007). *Doing family therapy: Craft and creativity in clinical practice* (2nd ed.). New York: Guilford.

Tannehill, R. L. (1987). Employing a modified positive-peer culture in a state youth center. *Journal of Offender Counselling, Services and Rehabilitation, 12,* 113–129.

Tannen, D., Kendall, S., & Gordon, C. (Eds.). (2007). *Family talk: Discussions and identity in four American families.* New York: Oxford University Press.

Taylor, D., & Alpert, S. (1973). *Continuity and support following residential treatment.* New York: Child Welfare League of America.

Thatcher, R. W. (1994). Cyclic cortical reorganization: Origins of human cognitive development. In G. Dawson & K. W. Fischner (Eds.), *Human behaviour and the developing brain* (pp. 232–266). New York: Guilford.

Thomas, G., Farrell, M. P., & Barnes, G. M. (1994). The effects of single mother families and non-resident fathers on delinquency and substance abuse in black and white adolescents. *Journal of Marriage and the Family, 58*(4), 884–894.

Thomas, R. M. (2006). *Violence in America's schools: Understanding, prevention and responses.* Westport, CT: Praeger.

Thorton, S. (1995). *Children solving problems.* Cambridge, MA: Harvard University Press.

Tichy, N., & Ulrich, D. (1984). Revitalizing organizations: The leadership role. In J. Kimberly & R. Quinn (Eds.), *Managing organizational transitions.* Homewood, IL: Irwin.

Tomm, K. (1988). Interventive interviewing: Part III. Intending to ask circular, strategic or reflexive questions? *Family Process, 26,* 3–15.

Tremblay, R. E., Hartup, W. W., & Archer, J. (2005). *Developmental origins of aggression.* New York: Guilford.

Tuma, J. (1989). Mental health services for children. *American Psychologist, 44,* 188–199.

Turnell, A., & Edwards, S. (1999). *Signs of safety: A solution and safety oriented approach to child protection case work.* New York: Norton.

Urberg, K. A. (1992). Locus of peer influence: Social crowd and best friend. *Journal of Youth and Adolescence, 21,* 439–456.

Van Lieshout, C. F., & Heymans, P. G. (Eds.). (2000). *Developing talent across the life span.* Philadelphia: Psychology Press.

Van Wagner, S. L., Gelso, C. L., Huges, J. A., & Diemer, R. A. (1991). Countertransference and the reputedly excellent therapist. *Psychotherapy, 28*, 411–421.

Vernon, A. (1996). *Counseling children and adolescents*. Denver, CO: Lone.

Vetere, A. (1993). Using family therapy in services for people with learning disabilities. In J. Carpenter & A. Treacher (Eds.), *Using family therapy in the 90's*. Oxford: Blackwell.

Vorath, H. H., & Brendtro, L. K. (1985). *Positive peer culture*. New York: Aldrine de Gryter.

Wachtel, E. F. (1992). An integrative approach to working with children and their families. *Journal of Psychotherapy Integration, 2*, 207–224.

Wachtel, E. F. (2004). *Treating troubled children and their families*. New York: Guilford.

Waller, C. (Ed). (1996). *Contributions to residential treatment 1996*. Alexandria, VA: American Association of Children's Residential Centers.

Walsh, J. M. (1984). Considerations in the implementation of a behavioural system within a residential treatment center. *Residential Group Care and Treatment, 2*(4), 51–67.

Walters-Leeper, G., Wright, N., & Mack, A. (1994). Language disabilities of anti-social boys in residential treatment. *Behavioural Disorders, 19*, 159–169.

Wang, M. C., Reynolds, M. C., & Walberg, H. J. (Eds.). (1995). *Handbook of special and remedial education: Research and practice* (2nd ed.). Oxford: Pergamon.

Watson, D. L., & Tharp, R. G. (1972). *Self-directed behaviour: Self-modification for personal adjustment*. Monterey, CA: Brooks/Cole.

Watson, J. B. (1919). *Psychology from the standpoint of a behaviourist*. Philadelphia: Lippincott.

Webb, W. (1999). *Solutioning: Solution-focused intervention for counsellors*. Philadelphia: Accelerated Developmental.

Well, K. (1991). Placement of emotionally disturbed children in residential treatment: A review of placement criteria. *American Journal of Orthopsychiatry, 61*, 339–347.

Wetzer, S., & Sanderson, W. C. (Eds.). (1997). *Treatment strategies for patients with psychiatric comorbidity*. New York: Wiley.

Wexler, D. B. (1991). *The adolescent self: Strategies for self-management, self-soothing and self-esteem in adolescents*. New York: Norton.

White, R. W. (1965). The experience of efficacy in schizophrenia. *Psychiatric Journal for the Study of Interpersonal Processes, 28*, 199–211.

Whittaker, J. K. (1979). *Caring for troubled youth*. San Francisco: Jossey-Bass.

Whittaker, J. K., & Pfeiffer, S. I. (1994). Research priorities for residential group child care. *Child Welfare, 73*, 583–601.

Wicka-Nelson, R., & Israel, A. (1991). *Behavioural disorders of children*. Englewood Cliffs, NJ: Prentice Hall.

Williams, A., & Thurow, C. (Eds.). (2005). *Talking adolescence: Perspectives on communication in the teenage years*. New York: Peter Larry.

Williams, S., & Luthans, F. (1992). The impact of choice of rewards and feedback on task performance. *Journal of Organizational Behaviour, 13*, 653–666.

Winnicott, D. W. (1965). *The maturational process and the facilitating environment*. New York: International Universities Press.

Winnicott, D. W. (1984). *The child, the family and the outside world*. London: Penguin.

Winnicott, D. W. (1998). *Thinking about children*. Toronto: Harper Collins.

Wolfensberger, W. C. (1971). *The principle of normalization in human services*. Toronto: York University, Downsview, National Institute on Mental Retardation.

Wolpe, J. (1989). The derailment of behaviour therapy: A tale of conceptual misdirection. *Journal of Behaviour Therapy and Experimental Psychiatry, 20*, 3–15.

Woods, M. E., & Robinson, H. (1996). Psychosocial theory and social work treatment. In F. J. Turner (Ed.), *Social work treatment: Interlocking theoretical approaches* (4th ed., pp. 555–580). New York: Free Press.

Wozner, Y. (1991). *People care in institutions: A conceptual schema and its application.* New York: Haworth.

Yalom, I. D. (1983). *In patient group psychotherapy.* New York: Basic Books.

Yalom, I. D. (1985). *The theory and practice of group psychotherapy* (3rd ed.). New York: Basic Books.

Yalom, I. D., & Rand, K. (1966). Compatibility and cohesiveness in therapy groups. *Archives of General Psychiatry, 15*(3), 267–275.

Ysseldyke, J. E., & Christenson, S. L. (1987). *The Instructional Environment Scale.* Austin, TX: Pro-Ed.

Zoccolillo, M., Tremblay, R., & Vitario, F. (1996). DSM-III-R and DSM-IV criteria for conduct disorder in preadolescent girls: Specific but intensive. *Journal of the American Academy of Child and Adolescent Psychiatry, 35,* 461–470.

Index

A

Abbott, J., 229, 231
Abstract reasoning skills, 44
Abuse
    and bullying, 263
    family dynamics, 119, 259
    and personality development, 259
    staff–youth relationship building,
        94–95
Abusive behaviors
    causes of maladaptive behavior, 192
    family work, 131
Academic Assessment, 244–247, 282
Academic functioning
    parental monitoring and, 115
    psychosocial assessments, 83–84
Academic remediation, 12; *See also*
        Education, role in residential
        treatment
Acceptance
    behavior disturbances and, 37
    counseling stages, 198
    group activity goals, 220
    staff role, 189
    treatment principles, 18
    unconditional positive regard, 199
Acceptance of reality
    defense system assessment, 85
    integrative counseling, 101
    treatment practices, 21
Accountability
    psychosocial assessments, 75
    reinforcements and, 140
Accusations, false, 170, 171, 198, 200
Achenbach, T. M., 88
Acting out, 120
    activities and, 225

    anger directed at youth workers, 55
    attitudes toward placement and, 123
    behavior modification, 154, 161
    classroom behavior, 230, 234, 243,
        252
    conduct disordered adolescent study,
        264, 268
    confrontation, 47
    contextual management, 54
    as coping strategy, 118, 281
    family dynamics, 118, 123
    function/purpose of, 99, 102–103,
        281
    group home interactions, 102
    integrative counseling, 96
    multiple meaning and function, 281
    phases of treatment, 39–40, 41, 100
    Phase Two processes, 8, 9
    positive discipline, 193, 201
    resistance issues, 54
    rewarding misbehavior, 193
    staff interactions and, 93, 98, 286
    staff responses, 49
    treatment impasses, 52
Activities/activities programs, 284–285
    behavior modification, 154
    Four Phase System program
        components, 22
    group counseling, 104, 106
    interests and hobbies, 82–83
    program components, 22
    programming, therapeutic, 213–214
        games and sport, 221
        theory of therapeutic activities,
        215
        therapeutic effects, 221–222
    psychosocial assessments, 32, 82–83

staff role, 170, 171, 172–173, 177, 189
Adaptation
  assessment process, 66
  behavior modification, 140, 141, 145
  childhood development theories, 63
  conduct disordered adolescents, 262
  contracts and, 92
  defense system assessment, 84
  emphasis on, 88
  mechanisms of change, 42–43
  staff role, 177
Adaptation measures, Four Phase System, 9
Adaptive capacity
  discharge from treatment, 42
  psychosocial assessments, 31
Adherence, treatment, 44
  contracting as tool, 92
  integrative counseling, 100
Adjustment, developmental, 8
Adjustment, psychological
  assessment process in residential treatment, 67
  developmental, assessing, 179
  family dynamics, 117, 118
  Four Phase System, 6
  life skills program focus, 214
  phases of treatment, 39
  program components, 23
  psychosocial assessments, 61, 89
  self-control and self-correction as indicators, 154
  staff role, 182
  treatment outcome measurement, 10–11
Adler, A., 76
Administration
  Four Phase System, 2, 6
  organizational, resource allocation, 67
  skills teaching, 182
Admission criteria, Four Phase System, 8
Advocacy approach, Four Phase System disagreements, 15
Affect expression/regulation; See also Emotion(s); Self-control/regulation
  ego functions, 77

evaluation, 57–59
  integrative counseling, 96–97
  power struggles, 97
Affective behavioral expectations, 144
Affective life
  group work, 180
  positive discipline, 197
Aftercare, 4, 8, 10, 13
Agency (personality aptitude), 265
Agency network, Four Phase System, 1–2
Aggression
  conduct disordered adolescents, 263, 264
  ego functions, 77
  power struggles, 97
  reinforcement categories, 161
  self-control indicators, 78
Aggressive clients
  adolescent services in Ontario, 3
  integrative counseling, 96
Ainsworth, F., 46, 114, 120
Ainsworth, M. D. S., 64, 205
Aldridge, M., 29, 40, 58
Algozzine, R., 144
Alliances
  cooperative, classroom, 282
  deviant, 181
  therapeutic; See Therapeutic alliance/staff–client relationship
Allyon, T., 138, 141, 233
Alpert, S., 30
Alternative narratives, 128
Alternative treatments, systems approach, 143
Alternatives to institutionalization, 2
Amanat, E., 17
Anderson, C., 121, 123, 126, 201
Anderson, G., 123, 125
Anderson, J. A., 17, 200
Anderson, P. M., 228
Andreasen, N. C., 76
Andrews, J., 2
Anger
  causes of maladaptive behavior, 191
  confrontation, responses to, 195
  contextual counseling, 208
  counseling stages, 197
  counseling strategies (psychotherapy), 200

directed at youth workers, 54–57
family work, 131
psychosocial assessments, 73
Anger management, 42
  conduct disordered adolescent study, 268
  evaluation and behavior management, 279
  family work, 131, 289
Animal abuse, 78
Antisocial groupings; See
    Countercultural identification/ antisocial groupings
Antisocial symptoms/behaviors
  adolescents in residential facilities, 91
  causes of maladaptive behavior, 191–193
  group work, 102, 180
    hidden behaviors, 181
Anxiety
  activity participation and, 214
  anger as coping mechanism, 56
  behavior modification, 147–148
  conduct disordered adolescents, 261
  dealing with conflict contextually, 53
  family dynamics, 116
  front-line interactions, 98–99
  group counseling, 105
  integrative counseling, 96
  reinforcement categories, 162
Anxiety disorders, comorbidity, 85
Anxious attachments, 259
Archer, J., 30, 45, 56
Arches, J., 25
Argumentativeness/bickering
  behavior modification
    contracting process, 139
    reinforcements, 141, 155, 161
  confrontation and, 194
  group processes, 107, 109
  positive discipline, 197
Ariel, M., 36
Assertiveness
  encouragement of, 142
  family dynamics and, 259
  group work, 180, 181
  treatment classes, 284
Assessment
    activities and, 284

activities as aid in, 224
Four Phase System Phase Two programs, 8
in residential treatment, 66–67
structured activities as tool, 218
treatment progress; See also Progress assessment
family
  family work, 123–124
  Four Phase System intake procedure, 7–8
  psychosocial; See Psychosocial assessment
Atmosphere, group home, 108
At-risk adolescents, 91, 92
At-risk behaviors, family work, 116–117, 118, 132
Attachment
  affect and its expression, 57
  anxious, 259
  childhood development theories, 64
  ego functions, 77
  preventing deterioration, 205
  reactive, 114
  strategies for emotional interventions, 199
Attachment theory, 50, 199
Attention, 84
Attention deficit hyperactive disorder (ADHD), 78, 140, 257, 261
Attention deficits, 194
Attention seeking, 62, 163
Attention span, 77, 164
Attitudes, client
  behavior modification, 145, 146
  confrontation versus control, 193–194
  contracting process objectives, 137
  Four Phase System treatment approach, 135
  group work
    positive peer pressure, 108
    prosocial attitude development, 181
  positive discipline, 199
  psychosocial assessments, 74
  staff awareness of, 98
  staff role, 171
  toward placement, 123
  toward school, 84

Attitudes, family work, 125, 130
    family dynamics, 91, 118
    hostility to counseling, 127
    treatment issues, 118–120
Attitudes, staff
    counseling strategies
        (psychotherapy), 200–201
    countertransference, 172, 201–202
    difficult relationship with parents,
        127–128
    hostility toward clients, 145
    negative responses to clients, 184
    socialization process, 7
    toward family, 121
    and unit functioning, 185
Authoritarian leadership, family, 132
Autonomy, Four Phase System agencies,
    15
Autonomy, individual; *See* Self-
        determination/autonomy
Avoidance behaviors, 163–164
    with behavior modification program,
        145
    positive discipline, 201
Awareness, staff teaching, 181
Awareness of others, 144; *See also*
        Empathy
    conduct disordered adolescents, 261
    family dynamics and, 288
Axline, V. M., 58
Azrin, N. H., 138, 141, 233

                    B

Baker, L., 82
Ball-Rokeach, S. J., 247
Bandstein, K. K., 15, 274
Bandura, A., 12, 64, 138, 139, 206, 220,
    249
Banyon, F., 230, 237
Banyon, R., 230
Bardach, E., 15
Barkley, R. A., 78, 117, 140, 247
Barnes, G. M., 129
Barton, W. H., 88
Beardon, W. O., 109
Beaumeister, R. F., 42, 218, 219
Behavior(s)

    anger directed at youth workers,
        54–57
    assessment process in residential
        treatment, 67
    behaviorist model, 62–63
    causes of maladaptive behavior,
        191–193
    defense system assessment, 84
    discharge summary writing
        guidelines, 87
    goal-directed, 77
    group home interactions, 35–37
    hard-to-service adolescents, 2–4
    mechanisms of change, 42–43
    mirroring, 50
    personal characteristics, 79–82
    present and future, 6
    problematic, group versus
        community standards, 107
    psychosocial assessments, 61, 73, 89
    self-control indicators, 77–78
    social history, 70
    treatment classes
        classroom behavior scale, 253
        control of students, 233–235
        role of teacher, 247–249
    treatment motivation, 43–45
    treatment planning procedures, 19
    treatment practices, 20
Behavior adjustment, program
        components, 23
Behavior changes
    strategies for emotional
        interventions, 199
    treatment outcome measurement,
        10–11
Behavior control
    Four Phase System, 1
    students, 233–235
Behavior management
    channeling oppositional behavior, 58
    evaluation and, 278–280
    family work, 130
    treatment approach, 136
Behavior modification, 136–138
    activities and, 213–214
    contracting as tool, 12
    program components, 22
    psychosocial assessments, 32
    staff role

methods, 176
relationship building, 95
Behavior modification, level/
        reinforcement system,
        135–144, 274
    application of, 280
    applications of reinforcements,
        138–139
    behavior modification, 136–138
    behavior shaping, 138–140
    benefits of reinforcements, 140–143
    confrontation and, 194
    critical factors of reinforcements,
        146–148
    integrative approach to
        reinforcements, 38–39
    limitations of behavior management,
        148–152
        credit and point scale, 150
        explanations of levels, 149–150
        variable factors, 150–152
    point scale, 160
    rationale of reinforcements, 144–146
    reinforcement categories, explanation
        of, 161–164
    reinforcement scale, 155–156
    systems approach, 143–144
Behavior patterns, 57, 67
Behavior problems; See also
        Argumentativeness/bickering;
        Passive-aggression
    adolescent services in Ontario, 3
    attitudes toward placement and, 123
    cause–effect relationships, 143
    causes of maladaptive behavior,
        191–193
    as competency deficits, 142
    corrective teaching practices, 145
    hidden behaviors, 181
    parental monitoring and, 115
    referral information, 29–30
    responses to placement, 120
Behavior shaping, 138–140
Behavior theories, 100
Behavior therapy, 2, 7, 135; See also
        Behavior modification, level/
        reinforcement system
    conduct disorder treatment, 140
    with other treatment approaches, 141
Behavioral expectations, 144

Behaviorism, 279
Behaviorist theory, 62
Beker, J., 139, 142
Belief system
    creation of emotions, 260
    ego functions, 76–77
    group counseling, 105
    insight into, 209
    integrative counseling, 96
    staff awareness of, 98
Bell, J. E., 121, 288
Bellak, L., 75, 195
Bellanca, J., 231
Benjamin, M .P., 16
Berenson, B. G., 174
Berger, R., 48, 200, 282, 290
Bergstram, S. C., 173
Berman, P. S., 179, 260
Berne, E., 180
Bernheim, K., 119
Bernstein, N., 207, 258
Berry, M., 20
Bertolino, B., 30
Best practices, 165
Bettelheim, B., 35, 274
Bickering; See Argumentativeness/
        bickering
Blaskfield, R.K., 68, 86
Blau, G. M., 235
Blehar, M. C., 64
Bleiberg, E., 57
Blended families, 129
Bonding; See Therapeutic alliance/staff-
        client relationship
Bonuses, 150
Borderline personality disorders, 148
Borum, R., 202, 203, 208
Boszormenyi-Nagy, I., 121, 209, 288
Boundaries, 281–282
    affect and its expression, 57
    family work, 118, 124, 125, 129
    group home interactions, 36
    psychosocial assessments, 71, 72–73
    staff role, 184
        awareness of, 98
        counseling approaches, 175
        methods, 176
        social skills development,
            169–170
Bowen, M., 124

Bowlby, J., 50, 64, 114, 166, 205
Boyd-Franklin, N., 132
Boyd-Webb, N., 116, 123, 125, 288
Boyle, M. C., 85, 258
Breggin, P. R., 175
Brendtro, L. K., 41, 46, 107
Brodie, B. R., 42, 43, 45, 101, 194, 196,
        197, 207, 234
Bromfield, R., 79
Bronfenbrenner, U., 65, 272
Brown, S., 12
Bry, B. H., 132
Bullying
    abuse history and, 263
    behavior modification, 164
    classroom, 242
    conduct disordered adolescent study,
        267
    evaluation, 45, 48, 52
    group work, 103, 109, 180, 181
    psychosocial assessments, 71
Burnout, staff, 25
Burt, M. R., 154
Burton, D., 219, 221
Butler, T. L., 173
Butterfield, W. H., 147

                        C

Cain, H., 288
Cameron, J., 192, 193
Campbell, J., 228, 233, 234
Campbell, J. M., 29, 30, 277, 278
Campbell, L., 103
Campbell, N. R., 268
Camras, L. A., 262
Cantwell, D. P., 82, 116, 261
Carkhuff, R. R., 174, 175
Cartledge, G., 251, 278
Case formulation; See Treatment plan/
        planning
Case histories, typical client profile, 12
Case management approach, 15
Case management standards, 5, 13
Case notes; See Documentation/record
        keeping
Case study, conduct disorder, 263–266
Castonguay, L. G., 273
Catholic Charities, 3

Cause–effect relationships, 66
    behavior problems, 143
    conduct disordered adolescents, 258
    conduct problems/behavioral
        disorders, 78
    defense system assessment, 85
    general principles of treatment, 12
    psychosocial assessments, 74
Chamas, J., 258, 259
Chandler, S. M., 15
Change
    dynamics of, 42–43
    family work, 123–124, 129
Change, therapeutic
    behavior modification, 146, 154
    internalization failure, 146–147
    treatment approach, 136–137
Change models, Four Phase System, 5, 6
Chaotic home environment, 259
Char, W. F., 116, 119, 128
Charting, 139, 140, 142–143
    feedback to clients, 146
    limitations of behavior management,
        148–149
Chescheir, M., 258, 259
Child, D., 231
Child abuse; See Abuse
Child and Adolescent Services System
        Program (CASSP), 14
Child care work methodology, staff role,
        175–177
Child Protective Services, 92
Childhood development, 62–66
Children's Aid Societies, 2–3, 4, 14, 92
Children's mental health centres, 11
Choices; See also Decision making
    behavior modification
        effects of, 139
        reinforcements, 141
    impacts of, 66
    treatment emphasis, 136
Chores
    compliance problems, 162–163
    staff role, 169
Christenson, S. L., 84
Christopherson, E. R., 140
Cicchetti, D., 68, 266
Circular causality, 180
Circular conflicts, 175
Clark, A. J., 84, 261

Classes, treatment, 227, 282–284
   curriculum design of treatment
      center class, 243–244
   education, role in residential
      treatment, 239–241
   Phase Four, 9
   role of teacher, 247–249
Classroom behavior scale, 253
Clausen, J., 74
Clayton, R., 55
Client history, 53–54
Clinical codes, 24
Clinical direction
   Four Phase System, 4
   public policy and, 17
Clinical outcome; *See* Outcomes
Coalition of service providers, 1–2, 16
Cobb, N. H., 147
Code of conduct, worker, 167
Coe, W., 152
Coercion/coercive behaviors
   antisocial behaviors, 181
   family dynamics, 133
   group living, 103
   placement as, 54, 123
   psychosocial assessments, 72, 80, 81
   staff caveats, 198
Cognitive abilities
   abstract reasoning skills, 44
   academic functioning, 83
   activities and, 221
   assessment process in residential
      treatment, 66, 67
   behavior modification
      efficacy of system, 146
      enhancement of reasoning skills,
         141
   conduct disordered adolescents, 268
   ego functions, 75–76
   psychosocial assessments, 61
   referral information, 29
   staff role, 170
Cognitive distortions, 196, 208
Cognitive operations
   assessment process, 279–280
   behavior modification effects, 137,
      139
   family dynamics and, 287–288
   games and sport and, 221
Cognitive restructuring, 136

Cognitive structure, Piaget's theory, 63
Cohen, J., 16, 72
Cohen, J. J., 228, 232, 236, 237
Cohen, N. J., 259
Cohen, P., 72
Cohen, R., 16
Cole, R. E., 27
Coleman, M., 129
Collaboration, Four Phase System, 5,
   10, 13
Communication
   affect and its expression, 57–58
   conduct disordered adolescents, 267,
      268
   family work, 124, 125, 178
   Four Phase System, 1, 4, 6
      general principles of treatment,
         12
      strengths of, 10
   front-line interactions, 99
   group work
      activities, 217
      with conduct disorders, 262
      counseling, 104
   integrative counseling, 100
   policy and procedure manual, 167
   program components, 22–23
   psychosocial assessments, 32
      language, 76
      social history, 69
   staff role, 183, 184–185
      worker skills, 51–52
   task-oriented relationship, 145
Community
   living and learning environment, 101
   placement decisions, 119
   systems of care, 10
Community activities, 219–220
Community agencies, 8
Community-based programs, 9, 16–17
Community conflicts, 29
Community-level change, 229
Community reintegration
   conduct disordered adolescent study,
      268
   discharge from treatment, 42
   family work, 131–132
   Four Phase System, 5, 10
   integrative counseling, 101
   typical client profile, 13

Community resources
  life skills program focus, 215
  postdischarge family support, 134
  social skills development, 216
  staff role, 182–183, 188, 190
Community restrictions, 152
Community standards/norms
  behavior management system and,
    143
  problematic behaviors, 107
  socialization process, 7
Comorbid disorders, 85, 88
  conduct disordered adolescents, 261
  with conduct disorders, 257
  integrative treatment model, 274
Competence
  parental, 122
  treatment class goals, 283
Competency-based approach, 11, 136,
    137, 142
  reinforcements, 280
  staff role, 166
Competition
  group activity goals, 220
  structured activities, 218
Compliance, treatment; See Adherence,
    treatment
Concentration
  academic functioning, 84
  self-control indicators, 77
Concurrence with treatment process,
    114
Conditioning, 62
Condrell, K. N., 127
Conduct disorder (CD), 257–269
  behavior therapy, 140, 148
  case study, 263–266
  comorbidity, 85
  family dynamics, 258–259
  formulation, 266–267
  group interactions, 262
  integrative counseling, 96
  residential treatment, 260
  treatment issues, 260–261
Confidentiality issues, 183–184
Conflict, emotional; See Affect
    expression/regulation;
    Emotion(s)
Conflict resolution, 34, 269
  activities and, 224

education program, 237
  group work, 180
  power struggles, 97
  reinforcements and, 146
  within staff, 187
  staff role, 52, 106, 169
Conflicts, interpersonal
  behavior modification
    levels system, 146
    program effectiveness, 146
    strengths of modifying economy,
      147
    systems approach, 143
  conduct disordered adolescents, 257
  evaluation, 52–54
  family dynamics, 259
  family work, 113, 124, 125
    family dynamics, 115, 116
    reactive attachment, 114
  group home interactions, 181
    avoidance, 94
    group dynamics, 109, 111
  positive discipline
    counseling strategies
      (psychotherapy), 200–201
    nature of conflicts, 207–208
  within staff, 186–187
  staff responses, 207
    confrontation, 46–48
    dealing contextually, 52–54, 106
    difficult youngster, 45–46
    treatment impact, 48–50
    treatment impasses, 50–52
    treatment resistance, 43–45
  staff role, 169, 173
Confrontation
  counseling
    group, 105
    staff role, 174
  discipline, positive
    versus control, 193–194
    as encounter, 194–195
    supportive, 196–198
  evaluation, 46–48
  family work, 127
  group home interactions, 94, 105
  reinforcement categories, 164
  staff role, 174, 182
Conger, R. D., 56
Connectivity, 102, 109, 110

Conscience formation, 65
Consensus
    group process, 107
    treatment plan (plan of care), 5–6
Consequences
    behavior modification, 145
    causes of maladaptive behavior, 192
    conduct disordered adolescents, 264, 268
    positive discipline, 200
    reality testing, 79
    staff counseling approaches, 175
Consistency, 192
Conspiracy, 108
Constantino, G., 93
Construction of reality, 145
Consultation
    Four Phase System, 8
    recognition of need for referral, 181–182
Containment procedures, 9
Contextual counseling, 208–210
Contingencies of reinforcement, 138
Contingency management, 39, 137, 141–142, 145, 152, 193
Continuing education, staff, 199
Continuum of care, 2, 6
Contract, treatment, 92, 274
    behavior modification, 145
        behavior shaping, 139–140
        effects of contracting approach, 136–137
    family work, 121
    general principles of treatment, 12
    preplacement interview, 30
    psychosocial assessments, 32
    staff role, reviewing, 176
Control issues
    adult relationships, 72
    confrontation versus control, 193–194
    deception, 59
    disruptive behavior, 286
    family work, 126, 127
    manipulation as, 58
Control strategies, 164
Controls
    behavior modification
        reinforcements, 140–141
        staff caveats, 137

discharge from treatment, 42
family work, 124, 130
general principles of treatment, 11
group counseling, 104
mechanisms of change, 42–43
secure areas, 9
self-control and, 77–78, 262
treatment practices, 20
Convergence; *See* Integrative treatment
Cooperation, 144
    activities and, 284
    causes of maladaptive behavior, 193
    concurrence with treatment process, 114
    group dynamics, 109
    group home interactions, 37
    reinforcements, 141, 142
    teamwork, 186–187
    therapeutic activities theory, 215
Coordination of services
    adolescent services in Ontario, 3
    efficacy of system, 13
    Four Phase System, 1–2, 4, 5–6
Coping abilities
    activities and, 222
    defense system assessment, 85
    discharge summary writing guidelines, 87
    family work, 124, 125, 130
    typical client profile, 11
Corder, B. F., 106, 264
Corrections system, 3, 4
Corrective teaching practices, 145
Cost containment, 10, 17
Costello, J., 9
Cottle, T. J., 229, 249
Cotton, N. S., 44, 54
Counseling
    contextual, 208–210
    family, 114, 122, 123–124, 127, 130–131
    Four Phase System program components, 23
    person-centered, 136
    program components, 23
    psychotherapy, 199–202
    social history, 70
    staff roles contextually, 106
    staff support, 25
    stages of, 197–198

Countercultural identification/antisocial
groupings
conduct disordered adolescent study,
266–267
group work, 180
preventing deterioration, 206
psychosocial assessments, 71
referral information, 30
staff role, 171
Counterdelusional approach, 175, 195
Counterresistance, 50, 200
Countertransference, 99–100, 172,
201–202, 264
Crain, W., 63
Credits, 150
Creighton, A., 263
Crenshaw, D. A., 32, 52, 55, 214, 216,
219, 225, 284, 285
Crisis in childhood, 229
Crisis intervention, 9
Crisis management, 82
Critical thinking, 71, 284
conduct disordered adolescents, 261
education program, 246, 249
living and learning environment, 101
Criticism, staff, 183
Crocket, K., 137
Cultural processes
childhood development theories, 65
culturally congruent services of
publicly funded organizations,
16
family assessment, 123
personality development, 259
pop culture, 229
social history, 69–70
Cultures, organizational, 10, 34
Curriculum design of treatment center
class, 243–244
Curry, J. F., 10
Custodial rights, parental, 120
Cycles, groups, 105

D

Daily bonuses, 150
Daley, D. C., 103
Dana, R. H., 93
Dangel, R. F., 145

Danish, S. J., 221
Darling, N., 115
Darling-Hammond, L., 232
Data collection, 186
Davidson-Methot, D., 25, 26
Davine, M., 259
Davis, G. L., 107
Davis, J., 145
Davis, N. J., 229, 250
Davis, T. E., 183
Day treatment programs, 8, 23, 227; See
also Classes, treatment
Deal, T. E., 230, 246
Debriefing, 175
Deception, 58, 59
Deci, E. L., 192
Decision making
client; See also Choices
behavior modification effects, 139
family work, 124
group counseling, 104
positive peer pressure, 107
self-determination, 18–19
social functions, 70–71
clinical, assessment linkage to, 69
Four Phase System agencies, 13, 15
group work, 180
Deductive reasoning, 181
Defenses
activity participation and, 214
with behavior modification program,
145
conduct disordered adolescent study,
265, 268
conflicts, nature of, 207
confrontation as intervention, 195
and counseling, 174
diagnostic formulation, 84–85
discharge summary writing
guidelines, 87
ego functions, 78–79
family dynamics, 118, 124, 133
group counseling, 105
power struggles, 97
preventing deterioration, 206
psychosocial assessments, 73
subgroup formation, 109
Defensive youth work, 170
Defensiveness, 92, 93

Defiance; *See* Oppositionalism and
    defiance
Definitions, Four Phase System, 5
Dehle, C., 191
DeKlyen, M., 258
Delusions, 79
Delworth, U., 165
Denial
    confrontation as intervention, 195
    counseling stages, 197
    fears, 81
Deol, A., 119, 130
Dependency, 162–163
    activities and, 214
    conduct disordered adolescent study,
        265
DeSalvator, G., 55
deShazer, S., 121, 133
Deshler, D. D., 244
Devaney, A., 7
Development
    assessing developmental adjustment,
        179
    family dynamics, 114, 115
    Four Phase System, 5, 6
    psychosocial assessment by child
        and youth care workers,
        62–66
    psychosocial assessments, 68, 69
    social skills, 6
    theories of, 62–66, 73–74
Developmental delays, 42–43
Developmental disorders, conduct
        disordered adolescents, 261
Developmental levels
    behavior modification, program
        effectiveness, 146
    systems approach, 143
Developmental tasks, 7
Deviant peer groups
    conduct disordered adolescent study,
        267, 268
    group work, 181
Deviant values, 72
Devine, P. G., 193
Diagnosis, 88
    assessment process in residential
        treatment, 67
    discharge summary writing
        guidelines, 87

Four Phase System, 7
    psychosocial assessments, 68
*Diagnosis and Statistical Manual of
    Mental Disorders (DSM-
    IV-TM)*, 61, 262
Diemer, R. A., 264
Diet/nutrition, 186, 215
Differential diagnosis, 85
Difficult youngster, 45–46
Dinkmeyer, D., 130
Direct care staff role, 165–190, 285–286
    child care work methodology,
        175–177
    communication skills, 184–185
    community resources, 182–183
    ethics, standards, identity, and
        responsibility, 183–184
    family work, 177–178
    Four Phase System, 1, 2, 7
    general principles of treatment, 12
    goodness-of-fit, 114
    group home management, 188–190
    group work; *See also* Group work
    interpersonal skills, 185
    interviewing and counseling skills,
        173–175
    job responsibilities, 186
    organizational myths and metaphors,
        16
    parenting skills, 168–172
    policies and procedures, purpose of,
        165–166
    policy and procedure manual,
        166–168
    positive discipline; *See* Discipline,
        positive
    psychosocial assessments, 31
    teamwork, 186–187
    theory and practice of therapeutic
        activities, 172–173
    theory and practice of working with
        groups, 180–182
    treatment plan (plan of care),
        179–180
    treatment planning, 187–188
    treatment principles, 18
    unit functioning, 185
    youth worker role, 188
Discharge
    family work, 131–132

Four Phase System, strengths of, 10
Discharge goals
    efficacy of system, 13
    general principles of treatment, 11
    integrative counseling, 101
    parental support for, 120
    preplacement interview, 30
    treatment planning procedures, 19
Discharge issues
    family work, 127
    group counseling, 105
Discharge planning, 42, 188
    conduct disordered adolescent study,
        266, 268
    Phase One, 8
    program components, 22
Discharge summary writing guide,
        86–87
Discipline, positive, 145, 191–211; See
        also Behavior modification,
        level/reinforcement system
    causes of maladaptive behavior,
        191–193
    conflicts, nature of, 207–208
    confrontation as encounter, 194–195
    confrontation versus control,
        193–194
    counseling in the here and now
        (contextually), 208–210
    counseling strategies
        (psychotherapy), 199–202
    general principles of treatment, 135
    group home environment, 202–203
    integrative practitioner, 203–205
    preventing deterioration, 205–206
    strategies for emotional
        interventions, 198–199
    supportive confrontation, 196–198
Discipline, staff, 168
Disequilibrium, group, 105
Disobedience, reinforcement categories,
        164
Displacement, family dynamics, 116
Disputes, staff role, 176
Disruptive behavior
    integrative counseling, 272
    reinforcement categories, 164
    staff role, 286
Distancing, 203

with behavior modification program,
        145
    power struggles, 97
Documentation/record keeping
    adherence to treatment plan, 33
    charting, 139, 140
    communication skills, 184–185
    staff development and training, 24
    staff role, 186, 187
    treatment planning procedures, 19
Dodge, K. A., 268
Doherty, W. J., 266
Donovan, D., 78
Doren, D. M., 179
Double binds, 117
Drake, R. E., 274, 291
Dreikurs, R. B., 77, 81, 233, 276
Drives, behaviorist model, 62–63
Dror, Y., 40
Drug therapy, 82
Drug use/substance abuse, 281
    comorbidity, 85, 261
    conduct disordered adolescents, 261
    conduct disordered adolescent study,
        267
    family dynamics, 116–117
    family work, 132
    hidden behaviors, 181
    parental monitoring and, 115
    positive discipline, 201
    psychosocial assessments, 81
    as response to fear, 264
Dryden, M., 258
Dryden, W., 15, 206, 258, 260, 265, 273
Dukes, M., 240
Dumphrey, D., 13, 16
Dunst, C., 119, 130
Duplication of services, 4, 10
Durkin, E., 25
Durrant, M., 95, 235, 237, 239, 247, 248,
        251
Dutta, A., 152, 262
Dyer, C., 31

E

Eating habits, 80
Eclecticism; See Integrative treatment

Economy, modifying, 135, 141, 143,
        146, 147, 153, 154; *See also*
        Behavior modification, level/
        reinforcement system
Edelbrock, C. S., 78, 247
Education, role in residential treatment,
        227–255
    academic assessment, 244–247
    behavior control of students,
        233–235
    classroom behavior scale, 253
    curriculum design of treatment
        center class, 243–244
    educational options, 231–232
    Four Phase System Phase Four, 9
    parental influence on learning,
        235–237
    program components, 23
    public system of education, 228–231
    role of treatment class teacher,
        247–249
    special education, need for, 237–239
    student progress report, 254–255
    treatment classes, 239–241
    treatment planning, 187
    types of clients requiring treatment
        class, 241–243
Education and training (agency), 8
Edwards, S., 129, 131
Efficacy, program; *See also* Evaluation,
        program
    charting and, 140
    Four Phase System, 13–15, 16–17
    measures of, 17, 26
    treatment practices, 20–21
Egan, K., 230, 231
Egeland, B., 259
Ego functioning
    assessment process in residential
        treatment, 67
    conduct disordered adolescents, 261
    defense system assessment, 85
    discharge summary writing
        guidelines, 87
    family dynamics, 115
    Four Phase System treatment
        approach, 135
    integrative counseling, 204
    psychosocial assessments, 61, 75–79,
        89

strengths-based interventions, 85
Ego psychological theory, 278
Ego-supportive models, 280
Eisenberger, R., 193
Elder, G. H., 56
Elias, M. J., 228, 229, 236
Elkind, D., 71, 91, 214, 215, 218, 222
Elliot, A. J., 193
Ellis, A., 36, 37, 41, 46, 50, 54, 56, 59,
        94, 95, 96, 98, 102, 115, 148,
        154, 201, 206, 208, 209, 216,
        260, 265
Elmore, R. F., 228
Elson, M., 115, 206
Emotion(s)
    adaptive, 196
    affect and its expression, 57–59
    assessment process in residential
        treatment, 75, 85
    behavior modification, systems
        approach, 143
    behaviorist model, 62–63
    client hostility to staff, 54–57
    conduct disordered adolescents, 262
    confrontation, responses to, 195
    counseling
        contextual, 208, 209
        group, 105
        integrative, 96
        staff role, 173, 175
        stages of, 197–198
    creation of, 260
    defense system assessment, 85
    ego functions, 77
        assessment process, 75
        triangulation of, 79
    family dynamics, 115–118, 259
    games and sport and, 221
    group dynamics, 109
        group counseling, 105
        subgroup formation, 109
    mechanisms of change, 42–43
    power struggles, 97–98
    reflectiveness, second-order
        personality traits, 95–96
    of staff
        client responses to, 200
        countertransference, 99–100, 264
        hostility to clients, 145, 198, 207,
        208

management of, 50
power struggles, 98
psychosocial assessments, 73
self-preservation, 184
staff role, 166, 170–171
assessment of, 184
awareness of client moods, 201, 208
counseling, 173, 175
symptoms of adolescents in residential facilities, 91
treatment class performance and, 284
treatment motivation, 43–45
treatment principles, 18; *See also* Counseling
Emotional adjustment
mechanisms of change, 42–43
program components, 23
referral information, 29
Emotional-cognitive development, 6, 146
Emotional tone, 100
Empathy
development of, 65
family dynamics, 115
goals of program, 137
integrative counseling, 96
psychosocial assessments, 71
staff emphasis of, 285
staff role, 189
staff teaching, 181
Employment; *See* Work/occupational preparation
Empowerment, 104, 109, 137, 169
of family, 126
goals of program, 137
social skills development, 216
Encoding, 146
England, M. J., 27
Environment, work, 4
Environmental factors, childhood development theories, 65
Eppright, T., 258
Epps, J., 144
Epps, K. J., 144, 148, 195, 196
Epstein, L., 122, 136, 145, 146, 210
Epston, D., 137
Erikson, E., 63, 73, 115, 231, 237, 249, 250

Erker, G. J., 17
Erwin, E., 142
Esman, A. H., 278
Esterson, A., 115, 259
Ethics, 146, 183–184
Ethnographic interviewing, 69
Evaluation, client, 29–59
activities and, 284
affect and its expression, 57–59
anger directed at youth workers, 54–57
and behavior management, 278–280
conflict, dealing contextually, 52–54
confrontation, 46–48
difficult youngster, 45–46
Four Phase System, 7–8
group home interactions, 35–37
group home layout, 34–35
how change occurs, 42–43
integrative approach to reinforcements, 38–39
phases of treatment, 39–42
psychological assessments, 30–31
psychosocial assessment, 31–32
referral information, 29–30
residential placement, 33–34
treatment impact, 48–50
treatment impasses, 50–52
treatment motivation, 43–45
treatment plan (case formulation), 32–33
Evaluation, program, 10, 25–26, 140
Evidence-based practice, 15
Evolution of treatment needs, 5, 14
Executive skills, staff role, 190
Executive subsystem, family, 124
Expectations
behavior modification, 144, 145
family work, 124, 130
Exploitation, hidden behaviors in groups, 181

F

Fainsibler, L., 133
Fairness, 146, 153, 191, 192
False accusations, 170, 171, 198, 200
Falsification, 43, 111

Family
    assessment process in residential
        treatment, 67
    discharge summary writing
        guidelines, 87
    and education, 229
    general principles of treatment, 11
    living and learning environment, 101
    psychosocial assessments, 61, 71–72
    referral information, 29, 30
    residential environment as, 102
    social history, 69–70
    socialization process, 91
    typical client profile, 12
Family counseling, 123
Family dynamics
    causes of maladaptive behavior, 191
    conduct disordered adolescents,
        258–259
    family work, 115–117
Family history
    assessment process in residential
        treatment, 67
    ego functions, 78
    and expectations of staff, 154
    social history, 69–70
Family work, 113–134, 288–289
    assessment of family, 123–124
    conduct disordered adolescent study,
        265–266
    counseling, 288–289
    counseling, family, 130–131
    discharge from treatment, 131–132
    efficacy of system, 13, 14
    family dynamics, 115–117
    family work, 124–126
    Four Phase System, 7–8
        assessment, 8
        Phase Four, 9
        treatment approach, 5
    group participation skills
        development, 7
    integrative counseling, 272
    placement conditions, 121–123
    preventing deterioration, 205
    residential placement, 117–118
    staff role, 177–178, 286–287
    treatment emphasis, 126–128
    treatment issues, 118–120
    treatment plan

        family, 128–130
        procedure, 19–20
    treatment practices, 20
    treatment principles, 18
Fantasy life, 57, 67, 79, 82, 84, 93, 98,
        111, 164, 193, 225
    coping mechanisms, 81–82
    diagnostic formulation, 84
    staff awareness of, 98
Farber, E. A., 259
Farrell, M. P., 129
Farrington, D. P., 56
Fashimpar, G., 145
Fausel, D. F., 134
Fears
    defense system assessment, 85
    front-line interactions, 98–99
    psychosocial assessments, 81–82
Feedback, 137
    behavior modification, 141
        charting and, 146
        staff–youth discussions, 145
    family work, 178
    Four Phase System, 1, 2
    group activities and, 220
    group home interactions, 94
    learning-based approaches, 144
    program components, 22–23
    reinforcement system, 280
    staff role
        group work, 180
        treatment planning, 179–180
    structured activities, 219–220
Feelings, behaviorist model, 62–63
Feital, B., 258, 259
Feldman, L. B., 122, 125
Ferguson, E. D., 65
Fernandez, J. A., 228
Fetal exposure to toxins, 65
Feuerstein, R., 133, 139, 142
Fewster, G., 36, 41, 97, 98, 108, 137,
        168, 186, 197, 281, 287
Fight-or-flight response, 147, 196, 208
Fighting, verbal; *See* Argumentativeness/
        bickering
Finances, staff role, 170
Finch, J. H., 14
Fincham, F. D., 56
Fine, M. A., 115
Finlay, D., 4, 7, 12, 15

Finney, J. W., 140
Fischer, M., 78, 247
Fish, M. C., 228, 232, 236, 237
Fisher, D., 283
Fishman, C., 123, 124, 125, 289
Fitzgerald, A. J., 78
Flaherty, L. T., 73
Flanagan, C. A., 230
Fletcher, A., 115
Fletcher, J. M., 68
Flexibility, second-order personality
    traits, 95
Flooding tactics, 177
Flores-Gonzalez, N., 230
Focus, 144
Follow-up, 175
Fonagy, P., 71
Forehand, R., 137, 142, 154
Forester-Miller, H., 183
Foster, S., 115
Foster care, 266, 268
Four Phase System, 1–27, 61, 272–273
    efficacy of system, 13–15
    hard-to-service adolescent, 2–4
    integrative treatment, 17–26, 273
        principles, 18–19
        treatment planning procedures,
            19–20
        treatment practices, 20–26
    limitations of, 273
    organizational relationships, 7–9
    phases of treatment, 5
    program components, 21–26
        activities, 22
        group interactions, 22–23
        individual counseling, 23
        life skills, 22
        milieu development, 24
        program evaluation, 25–26
        psychosocial assessments, 24
        school, 23
        staff support, 25
        staff training, 23–24
    strengths of, 10–11
    theoretical principles, 4–7
    treatment
        general principles, 11–13
        phases of, 10–11
France, K., 40, 95
Frankel, F., 261

Frankel, N. R., 278
Frankl, V., 154, 166, 175
Franklin, C., 69
Franks, C. M., 277
Freeman, A., 43, 106
Freiberg, R. D., 15, 274
Freidman, R., 138, 140, 142, 148
French, J., 232
Freud, S., 62
Freud's theory of child development, 62
Frey, K. S., 228, 229, 236
Friedman, R. M., 14
Fronting, 111
Front-line interactions, group dynamics,
    98–100
Frustration tolerance
    activities and, 284
    conduct disordered adolescents, 261
    conduct disordered adolescent study,
        268
    reinforcement categories, 162
Fukuzawa, R. E., 231, 250
Fulcher, L. C., 186
Fuller, F., 68
Fullerton, C. S., 138, 140, 142, 148

G

Gagnon, L. H., 129
Games, 221, 223; See also Activities/
    activities programs
Gang activity, 116, 132, 267
Garbarino, J., 111
Garcia-Lopez, S. P., 232
Garfat, T., 36, 97, 98, 108, 137, 168,
    197, 281, 287
Garmezy, N., 263
Gatekeeper function, Four Phase
    System, 7–8
Gatz, M., 247
Gaucher, R., 103
Ge, X., 56
Gediman, H. K., 75, 195
Gelso, C. L., 264
Gender relationships, 71–72
Gender roles, 171
Generalization of learning, 285
Genetics, 65
Germain, C. B., 114, 122

Gershman, K. W., 230
Ghent, E., 281
Ghurman, H. S., 47, 95
Gibbs, J. C., 216, 268
Gilmor, T. M., 154
Giuliani, G., 232, 240
Glasser, W., 9, 53, 71, 139, 176, 209,
        232, 233, 235, 237, 239, 245,
        246, 282
Glenn, J., 235, 242, 244, 245
Goal-directed behavior, 77
Goal-oriented approach, behavior
        modification, 146
Goal setting
    behavior modification, 146
    ego functions, 79
    staff focus on, 114
Goals, client
    family work, 114
    staff awareness of, 98
    treatment approach, 137
Goals, education, 83
Goals, family members, 129
Goals, program, 5
    organizational issues, 16
    service dilemmas, 15
Goals, treatment, 136–137
    behavior modification, 142, 154
    conduct disordered adolescent study,
        268
    counseling benefits, 209
    efficacy of system, 13
    family counseling, 122
    Four Phase System, 2, 6–7
    general principles of treatment, 11
    group process, 109
        group activities and, 217
        group counseling, 103, 104
        group dynamics, 91–92
    integrative counseling, 101, 273
    positive discipline, strategies for
        emotional interventions, 199
    psychosocial assessments, 88
    staff role, 288
        revising, 176
        treatment planning, 179
    treatment planning, 19, 179, 187
Goldfried, M. R., 273
Goldstein, A. P., 216, 268

Goldstein, E. G., 77, 81, 87, 123, 216,
        265
Gondoli, D. M., 66
Gonso, J., 71
Good habits, 141
Goodness-of-fit
    placement decisions, 10
    resident-staff, 114
Goorich, W., 138, 140, 142, 148
Gordon, C., 93
Gottman, J., 71
Gottman, J. M., 133
Gow, J. G., 262
Graphs; See Charting
Graziano, A., 154
Green, C., 140, 143, 148
Green, W. H., 82, 140
Greenberg, M. T., 228, 229, 236, 258
Gronlund, N. E., 244
Group cohesion, 188
Group counseling, 103–106, 176–177
Group home
    interactions in, evaluation process,
        35–37
    layout of, 34–35
    management of, 188–190
Group theory, 2
Group work, 91–111
    actions that sustain group, 102–103
    activities, 214, 216–218, 223
        goals of, 220
        sustaining interest, 220–221
    assessment process in residential
        treatment, 66–67
    chaotic, 106–107
    conduct disordered adolescents, 262
    conduct disordered adolescent study,
        266–267, 268
    contextual goals of treatment, 91–92
    disequilibrium, 105
    Four Phase System goals, 7
    front-line interactions, 98–100
    general principles of treatment, 12
    group dynamics, 103–106
    group dynamics summary, 110–111
    group interactions, 103–106
    integrative counseling, 96–97,
        271–272
    living and learning environment,
        101–102

Phase Four, 9
positive discipline, 202–203
positive peer pressure, 106–108
power struggles, 97–98
program components, 22–23
psychosocial assessments, 61
socialization process and
      development of values, 92–94
stabilizing interactions, 100–101
staff development and training, 25
staff role, 106, 188
    methods, 176
    relationship building, 94–96
subgroups, 108–109
summary, 110–111
Growth, assessment process in
      residential treatment, 66
Gruber, J. J., 217, 218
Grunwald, B., 77, 233, 276
Grych, J. H., 56
Gulotta, T. P., 235

H

Habits, 141
    discharge summary writing
      guidelines, 87
    psychosocial assessment, 80–82
Haley, J., 118
Hamilton, S. F., 265
Hanna, C. A., 72, 261, 268
Hanna, F. J., 72, 261, 268
Hard-to-serve clients, 290
    demand for services, 16
    efficacy of system, 14–15
    Four Phase System, 2–4
    general principles of treatment, 11
    program evaluation difficulties, 10
Hardy, K. V., 32, 57, 66
Hardy, L., 111
Hargrove, E., 15
Harmain, M., 241
Harrington, R., 261
Harris, J. D., 268
Hartup, W. W., 30, 45, 56
Hayden, D. C., 84
Hayes, K., 228
Haynes, N. M., 228, 229, 236
Health, 170, 215

Healy, M., 231, 232
Hebb, D. O., 73
Helgerson, J., 25
Hernandez, M., 5
Hewling, D. G., 14
Heymans, P. G., 83
High-risk adolescents, 7
Hill, C. E., 68
History, client, 53–54
History, family, 67
History, treatment, 29
Hobbies, 82–83, 95
Hodges, S., 5
Hodges, V. G., 131
Hoffman, L., 121, 125, 127
Hoffman, R. G., 107
Hoge, R. D., 67
Holding environment, 9
Hollin, C. R., 148, 195, 196
Hollis, S., 126
Home care, 4, 8
Honesty, 171
Honig, A., 64
Hooper, S. R., 7
Hoover, C., 133
Hopkins, R. L., 230, 239, 248
Horner, R. H., 88
Horowitz, H. A., 73
Hospital-based programs, 5, 8, 9
Hostility, client
    responses to, 198
    staff role, 175
Hostility, staff
    family work, 127–128
    toward clients, 145, 208
Housekeeping duties, staff role, 169
Huges, J. A., 264
Hughes, D. A., 114, 117
Hultman, J., 7
Hultsch, D. P., 250
Humor, 180, 201
Hundleby, N., 288
Hurrelmann, K., 265
Hurvich, M., 75, 195
Husain, S., 116
Hyperactivity, 164
Hypochondria, 82
Hyson, M. C., 246, 248

I

Identity, 59; *See also* Selfhood/sense of
        self
    conduct disordered adolescent study,
        266–267
    family dynamics, 115
    school kid versus street kid, 230
    socialization process and
        development of values, 93
    staff role, 183–184
Impulse control
    causes of maladaptive behavior, 193
    conduct disordered adolescents, 257
    ego functions, 75, 77–78
    referral information, 29
    self-control indicators, 78
    sustaining, 280
    treatment practices, 20
Inclusiveness, 108
Independent living, 11–12
Independent service providers, Four
        Phase System, 1–2
Individual counseling, 23
Individualization
    staff role, 189
    treatment principles, 18
Individuation/separation phase, 39,
        41–42, 70
Information processing skills, 83
Informed consent, 20
Inner dialogue, 96
Inner world, 145
Insight, 6, 96, 207
    confrontation and, 195
    counseling stages, 197–198
    goals of program, 137
    integrative counseling, 100
    psychosocial assessments, 71
Institutionalization, 3, 4
Instrumental behavioral expectations,
        144
Intake procedure, 7–8
Integrative approach to reinforcements,
        38–39
Integrative capacity, 95
Integrative treatment, 7, 136, 271–272,
        273–274
    conduct disordered adolescents, 269
    Four Phase System, 17–26, 273

    principles, 18–19
    treatment planning procedures,
        19–20
    treatment practices, 20–26
group dynamics, 96–97
positive discipline, 203–205
staff role, 177
Intellectual functioning, 66; *See also*
        Cognitive abilities
Intellectualization, 79, 195
Intelligence, 66, 75; *See also* Cognitive
        abilities
Interaction patterns, 268
Interaction style, family work, 128–129
Interactional skills, 6, 32
Interdependence phase, 41, 188
Interests, 82–83, 95
Interference in others' affairs, 47, 75,
        156, 163, 201
Internal experiences, behaviorist model,
        62–63
Internalization
    counseling stages, 197
    failure of, 146–147
Interventions
    client perceptions of fairness, 153
    confrontation, 46–48; *See also*
        Confrontation
    family work, 114–115, 125
    Four Phase System, 7
        family assessment, 8
        Phase Two programs, 9
    integrative counseling, 272
    prioritizing, assessment and, 66
    staff role
        methods, 175, 176
        strategies for, 198–199
    variability of, 136
Interviewing skills, staff, 173–175
Interviews
    preplacement, 30
    psychosocial assessments, 69
Intimacy
    ego functions, 77
    psychosocial assessments, 72
Intimidation, 181
Irrational action/behavior
    causes of; *See also* Maladaptive
        behavior
    family dynamics, 115

Irrational thinking/beliefs/attitudes; *See*
    Thinking errors and irrational
    attitudes/beliefs
Irvin, J. L., 240
Isaacs-Shockley, M., 16
Isolation, 163–164
Israel, A., 117, 233
Issacs-Shockley, M., 16
Ivey, G., 283
Izzo, R. L. Y., 265

J

Jacobs, D. T., 228, 236
Jacobs-Spencer, J., 228, 236
Jeynes, W., 229
Jeziorski, R. M., 82
Johnson, J. H., 95
Johnson, T. C., 263
Jordan, C., 69
Juvenile justice system, 91

K

Kagan, R., 33, 39, 41, 57, 66, 111
Kamphaus, R. W., 29, 30, 277, 278
Kandel, E. R., 30, 193
Karp, C. L., 173
Kashani, J., 258
Kashubeck, S., 74
Kassimir, R., 230
Kazdin, A. E., 138, 141, 144, 181, 259,
    268, 274, 279
Keane, A., 288
Kegan, R., 65
Kein, J. P., 127
Kelly, F. D., 127
Kendall, P., 144
Kendall, S., 93
Kendricks, D. J., 148, 195, 196
Kernberg, O., 42
Kettler, J. A., 110
Keys, S. G., 72, 261, 268
Kincheloe, J. L., 228
Kingery, P. M., 55
Kipnis, A., 229, 243
Kiraly, M., 37
Kitchener, R. F., 141
Kivel, P., 263

Klein, M., 64, 117
Klein, R. E., 66
Klinger, E., 268
Kohlberg, L., 63, 65, 66, 70
Kohut, H., 43, 47, 64, 73, 115, 116, 197,
    198, 207, 258
Kooreman, H., 17
Kreisher, K., 25
Kronenberger, W. G., 45
Krugen, M. V., 46
Kruger, M. A., 96, 288
Kurdek, L. A., 115
Kwantes, C., 288

L

Labels
    group work, 180
    hard-to-service adolescents, 14–15
    relabeling, 174
Laborde, P. R., 122
Lahey, B. B., 261
Laing, R. D., 115, 116, 117, 126, 259
Language
    affective life, descriptions of, 77
    comprehension versus production
        abilities, 76
    descriptions of self, 74
    group home interactions, 103
    integrative counseling, 100
    negotiation of relationship, 93
    power struggles and disruptive
        behaviors, 51, 98, 102, 103,
        161–162, 171
    psychosocial assessments, 69, 76
    reinforcement categories, 161–162
Language skills, 283
    activities and, 172, 215, 218, 221,
        222
    communication skills, 44
    conduct disordered adolescents, 259,
        277
    education goals, 246
    and problem solving competency, 63
    staff role, 285
LaPointe, J. M., 56
Larsen, D., 191
Last restrictive environment, 7
Laszloffy, T., 57, 111

Laub, J. H., 132, 259
Laursen, E. K., 30, 85
Lavee, Y., 132
Lazarus, A. A., 271
Lazor, A., 2, 4, 7, 8, 10, 11, 12, 13, 14, 16, 17, 27, 42, 54, 117, 118, 119, 127, 154, 180, 202, 205, 272, 291
Leadership
    family work, 124, 125, 132
    games and sport and, 221
    group work, 108, 180, 182
    staff role, 182, 190
Learning
    academic functioning, 83
    childhood development theories, 63, 64
    relearning, 6
Learning, staff, 199
Learning-based approaches, 144, 145
Learning disabilities, 194
    comorbidity, 85
    conduct disordered adolescents, 258
    family dynamics and, 259
    integrative counseling, 96
    treatment classes; See Education, role in residential treatment
Learning environment, group dynamics, 101–102
Learning from experience, 42
    activities and, 224
    assessment process in residential treatment, 70
    conduct disordered adolescents, 258
    group activities and, 220
    positive discipline, 199
    staff role, 166
    therapeutic programming and, 213
Learning style, 23
Learning theory, 135
Leary, M. R., 42, 218, 219
Lee, M. Y., 103
Lee, R. E., 107
Lefcourt, H. M., 135, 154
Legal status, client, 29, 69, 91
Legault, F., 56
Length of stay, typical client profile, 12–13
Lerner, R. M., 250
Letendre, G. K., 231, 250

Levels; See also Behavior modification, level/reinforcement system
    explanation of, 149–150, 151
    reinforcements, 142, 143, 146
Levy, T. M., 114, 131
Lewis-Palmer, T., 88
Licensing regulations, 183
Life plan, 137
Life skills
    Four Phase System program components, 22
    therapeutic programming, 214–215
Life skills teaching, 7
    Four Phase System, 1, 5
    general principles of treatment, 12
    program components, 22, 23
    staff development and training, 25
    staff role, 170, 172
    treatment classes, 283
    treatment practices, 21
Lifestyle, family, 123
Lifestyle differences, 169
Lilberman, M. A., 47, 48
Limit setting
    behavior modification, 145
    family work, 130
    staff role, 188
        counseling approaches, 175
        methods, 176
Lipman, C., 258, 259
Listening skills
    family work, 124, 130
    group work, 180
    staff teaching, 181
Literacy, 283
Littky, D., 228
Living and learning environment, 101–102
Living space, 168, 169
Locked settings, 5, 8
Loeber, R., 261
Long-term residential treatment, 5
Loreng, F. O., 56
Loss of privileges, 56
    conduct disordered adolescent study, 264
    reinforcements, 139
Lowman, R., 186
Loyalties, group work, 182
Luborsky, L., 122

Ludburg, A. M., 79
Lupton, D., 174
Lupton-Smith, H., 107
Luthans, F., 200
Lying
    behavior modification, 139
    conduct disordered adolescents, 257,
        264
    evaluation, 48, 58
    psychosocial assessment, 81
    reinforcement categories, 164
Lymann, R. D., 268
Lynch, M., 266
Lyons, J., 25

M

Macciomei, N. R., 230, 233, 234
Mack, A., 259, 264
MacKinnon, R. A., 66
Madanes, C., 125, 127
Madsen, W. C., 126, 127, 128, 178
Magical thinking, 40
Mahler, M. S., 39
Maier, H. W., 34, 44, 54, 280, 289
Maintenance behaviors, 38
Maintenance (stabilization) skills, 180
Maintenance tasks, staff, 189
    policy and procedure manual, 167
    record keeping, 168
    unit, 189
Maladaptive behavior
    causes of, 95, 191–193, 204
        family dynamics and, 115
        peer relationships, 71
    psychological assessments, 30–31
Malan, D., 126
Malgady, R. G., 93
Mallinkrodt, B., 259
Maluccio, A. N., 114, 120, 131, 132
Management, contingency, 39, 137,
        141–142, 145, 152, 193
Management of behavior, evaluation
        and, 278–280
Management of home, 188
Management skills, parent, 131
Mandate, agency, 183
Manguel, A., 137

Manipulation/manipulativeness
    acting out as, 281
    adult relationships, 72
    affect and its expression, 58
    anger as, 56
    conduct disordered adolescents, 257
    front-line interactions, 99
    group dynamics, 111
    power struggles, 97
    responses to staff, 200
    staff role
        methods, 175, 176
        responses to, 48–49, 51
Manly, J. T., 266
Mann, J., 115
Margetson, N., 258, 259
Martinovich, Z., 25
Maslow, A. H., 64
Masterson, J., 9
Mathematics, 283
Maturation process, 5
McCoy-Simandle, L., 55
McDermott, J. F., 116, 119, 128
McIntyre, D., 78
McKay, G., 130
McLeer, S., 144
McLeod, J., 69
McNeill, B., 165
Meaning, 83–84, 96, 138, 155
    of behaviors, assessing, 179
    conduct disordered adolescents, 262
    counseling strategies
        (psychotherapy), 199
    integrative counseling, 100
    staff emphasis of, 166
Medical disorders
    comorbidity, 85
    staff qualifications, 170
Medical history, 70
Medication, 9, 82
Meichenbaum, D., 145
Meloche-Kelly, M., 259
Meltzer, J., 240
Memory
    academic functioning, 83
    and academic performance, 83
    activities and, 221
    cognitive functions, 75
    group work and, 110
    reinforcements and, 163

Mental health issues, 91
Mental health system, 92
Mental illness
    comorbidity, 85
    drug therapy, 82
    placement decisions, 119
Menzies, I., 10
Messner, M. A., 247
Meta-analysis
    behavior approach effectiveness, 148
    conduct disorders, 262
Metamessage, integrative counseling,
        100
Meyer, R., 70
Meyer, R. E., 245
Meyer, R. G., 45
Michaels, R., 66
Milburn, J. F., 251, 278
Miles, M. B., 47, 48
Milieu development, 24
Milieu interactions, 94
Milieu therapy, 7
Millspauch, C. M., 55
Milner, J. J., 259
Milofsky, C., 232
Minkoff, K., 274
Minuchin, S., 69, 115–117, 123, 124,
        125, 128, 129, 178, 288, 289
Mirroring, 50, 106
Mission statement, agency, 167
Modeling; See Role models
Modifying economy, 135, 141, 143,
        146, 147, 153, 154; See also
        Behavior modification, level/
        reinforcement system
Mohr, W. K., 17
Mollerstrom, W., 259
Money management
    life skills program focus, 215
    psychosocial assessments, 84
Monitoring, client
    behavior modification, 140–141
    specific criteria, 143
    staff role, 170, 171
Monitoring, parental, 115–116, 118,
        229, 266
Monitoring, patient; See Progress
        assessment
Monitoring, progress; See Progress
        assessment

Monk, G., 137
Mood
    assessment of, 180
    psychosocial assessments, 76
    reinforcement categories, 162
    staff counseling, 173
Mood disorders, 207
    comorbidity, 85
    family dysfunction and, 259
Mood swings, 196
    conduct disordered adolescent study,
        267
    integrative counseling, 203, 204
    positive discipline, 201
Moody, E., 107
Moral emotions
    developmental mechanisms, 65
    psychosocial assessments, 75
Morality issues
    parental response to changing
        standards, 229
    placement process, 191–192
    social construction of morality, 266
Mordock, J. B., 52, 55, 214, 216, 219,
        225, 284, 285
Morris, R. J., 140, 141, 147, 148
Morton, W. J., 2, 4, 7, 8, 10–14, 16, 17,
        25, 27, 31, 42, 54, 67, 71, 73,
        116–119, 127, 136, 154, 180,
        202, 205, 229, 249, 250, 259,
        272, 276, 287, 291
Moss, R. H., 13
Motivation
    activities and, 224
    assessment process in residential
        treatment, 70–71
    group counseling, 104
    socialization process and
        development of values, 93
Motivation, treatment
    behavior modification, 141, 146
    evaluation, 43–45
    socialization process and
        development of values, 92–93
    therapeutic relationship with parents
        and, 119
    treatment practices, 20
Motivation issues, behavior
        modification, 142, 146
Motives, group counseling, 105

Motor skills, 76
Mueser, K. T., 274, 291
Multidimensional approach to
        treatment, 6, 269
Multimodal treatment, 267
Multiple placements, conduct disordered
        adolescents, 263
Munger, R. L., 241
Murphy, J., 7
Murphy, S., 12
Myatt, R., 261
Myths and metaphors, organizational,
        13, 16

                    N

Narcissistic defenses, 85, 265
Narratives, alternative, 128
Narratives, personal, 199
Negative alliance, subgroup formation,
        108, 109
Negative dynamics, group process, 107
Negotiation skills, 7
        group work, 180
        life skills program focus, 215
        staff role, 183
        treatment emphasis, 136
Nellen, V., 221
Nervous habits, 80–81
Nesman, T., 5
Network, agency, 1–2
Newman, B. M., 104
Newman, P. R., 104
Nichols, M., 128
Noncompliance, 154
        confrontation versus control,
                193–194
        contextual management, 54
        treatment resistance, 44
Nonparticipation, 152
Norcross, J., 6, 11, 12
Normalcy, principle of, 34
Normalization, 153–154
        group norms and rules, 103
        psychosocial assessments, 89
        staff role, 189
        treatment principles, 18

Norms, community
        behavior management system and,
                143
        family and, 91
        socialization process, 7
Norms, group, 35–36, 103
Norms, social, 117
Noshpitz, J. D., 34, 55
Note taking; See Documentation/record
        keeping
Nothing to lose attitude, 39–40
Novich, E., 154
Nugent, F. A., 184
Nurmi, J., 75
Nutrition, 186

                    O

Object relations theory, 64–65
Objectives; See Goals, treatment
Obligations, 142
Obsessions, 147
Occupational skills; See Work/
        occupational preparation
Oei, T., 86
Offerd, D. R., 85, 258
Ogden, T. H., 65
Olson, D. H., 123, 132
Operant conditioning, 62
Operations, group home, 166, 167, 182,
        189
Oppositionalism and defiance, 92,
        280–282
        affect and its expression, 58
        behavior modification, 141
        causes of maladaptive behavior, 191
        conduct disordered adolescent study,
                265
        contextual management, 54
        counseling stages, 197
        deception as, 59
        defense system assessment, 84
        family work, 118, 131
        front-line interactions, 99
        group home environment, 37, 203
        integrative counseling, 203, 204
        phases of treatment, 40
        positive discipline, 201, 203
        power struggles, 97

preventing deterioration, 206
responses to staff, 200
socialization process and
        development of values, 93
staff responses, 49–50, 51
staff role, 49, 180, 286
staff skills, 170
Organic disorders
    central nervous system, 78
    comorbidity, 85
Organizational culture, dysfunctional,
        10
Organizational metaphors/myths, 13, 16
Organizational skills teaching, 182
Organizational structure/relationships,
        Four Phase System, 1–2, 3, 6,
        7–9, 13
Organizing roles, family work, 129
Orlans, M., 114, 131
Oshawa/Whitby Crisis Intervention
        Centre, 23, 61, 135, 165, 166,
        187, 275
Outcomes
    conduct disordered adolescents, 258
    discharge from treatment, 42
    Four Phase System, 5, 10–11, 13
    measures of, 17
    psychosocial assessments, 88, 89
    therapeutic relationship and, 33–34

P

Page, R. C., 103
Palliative nature of behavior therapy,
        147
Paperwork; See Documentation/record
        keeping
Parenting skills
    family dynamics, 115–118
    staff role, 168–172
Parents; See also Family work
    behavior principles, 136
    childhood development theories, 64,
        65
    influence on learning, 235–237
    social history, 69
Parent–worker alliance, 119, 121
Parsons, M., 140, 143, 148
Participant-observation, 69

Passive-aggression
    behavior modification, 141, 161
    positive discipline
        confrontation, 196
        counseling, 200, 201
    psychosocial assessments, 72, 78
    reinforcement categories, 161
    responses to staff, 200
    treatment class candidates, 242
Passive-dependent client, 161
Patchner, M. A., 259
Pathology, placement decisions, 10
Pathology-based interventions, 85
Patterns of behavior, 57, 67
Patterson, G. R., 115
Patterson, L. E., 116, 127
Pazaratz, D., 2, 4, 7–14, 16, 17, 20,
        23–27, 31–34, 37–40, 42, 46,
        49, 51–58, 61, 67, 68, 71, 73,
        92, 94, 96, 100, 103, 114, 116–
        118, 120, 121, 127, 129, 131,
        136–148, 152, 153, 165–174,
        176, 179–182, 185, 187, 195,
        198, 202, 204–208, 213,
        215–217, 229, 232, 240–246,
        248–252, 258–262, 268,
        272–274, 276–278, 281–285,
        287, 291
Pearce, J. W., 131, 281, 286
Pecora, P. J., 131, 132
Peer pressure, negative, 36, 171; See also
        Countercultural identification/
        antisocial groupings
    deviant peer groups, conduct
        disordered adolescent, 267,
        268
    subcultural attachments, 92
        family dynamics, 117
        psychosocial assessments, 71
        typical client profile, 12
    subgroup formation, 7, 92, 108, 109
Peer pressure, positive
    actions sustaining group, 102
    Four Phase System
        general principles of treatment,
            12
        Phase Four, 9
        program components, 22–23
    goals of treatment, 137
    group dynamics, 106–108

group home interactions, 35–37
group work, 181
psychosocial assessments, 32
Peer relations
    activities and; *See also* Activities/
        activities programs
    confrontation; *See* Confrontation
    goals of treatment, 137, 154
    group home interactions, 102
    group process, 110
    institutional culture and, 34
    psychosocial assessments, 61
    social interest, 76–77
Pelletier, L. G., 192
Penn, P., 125
Pennell, J., 123, 125
Pepper, F., 77, 233, 276
Perlman, H. H., 119
Perls, F. S., 55, 66, 137, 141, 206, 263
Person-centered counseling, 136
Personal attacks, responses to, 198
Personal possessions, 177
Personality development, 65, 259
Personality disorders, 54
Personality growth, 154
Personality pathology, continuum
        models, 2
Personality structure, 67
Personality traits, second-order, 95
Peterson, K. D., 230, 246
Pezzot-Pearce, T. D., 131, 281, 286
Pfeiffer, S. I., 8, 10, 114
Phases of treatment, 39–42
Phelan, J., 280, 288
Philion, C. A., 286, 291
Phillips, J., 88
Phillips, V., 233, 234, 235, 237, 251
Philosophical conflicts, Four Phase
        System clinicians, 15
Philosophical shifts, living and learning
        environment, 101–102
Philosophy, family, 123
Philosophy, organizational, 167
Philosophy, treatment, 4
Physical illnesss, 82, 163
Piaget, J., 63, 68
Pierangelo, R., 232, 240
Pierce, W. D., 192
Pike, D. R., 55
Pinsof, W. M., 129

Pittman, T. S., 213, 220
Placement conditions, family work,
        121–123
Placement decisions
    adolescent services in Ontario, 2–3
    evaluation, 33–34
    family work, 117–118
    Four Phase System, 2
        goodness-of-fit, 10
        Phase One, 8
        strengths of, 10
    hard-to-service adolescents, 4
    preplacement interview, 30
Planned discharge, 42
Planning
    adolescent services in Ontario, 3
    behavior modification,
        reinforcements, 146
    discharge; *See* Discharge planning
    strategic, 5–6
    treatment; *See* Treatment plan/
        planning
Play, 215, 217
Point scale, 149, 150, 160
Policies and procedures
    counseling approaches, 200
    purpose of, 165–166
Policy and procedures manual, 166–
        168, 183
Policy makers, 15
Politics, Four Phase System agencies, 15
Polsky, H. W., 6, 48, 200, 282, 290
Pop culture, 229
Portner, J., 132
Positive discipline; *See* Behavior
        modification, level/
        reinforcement system;
        Discipline, positive
Positive peer pressure; *See* Peer
        pressure, positive
Postdischarge planning, 268
Pottenbaun, S. M., 74
Potter, G. B., 216, 268
Powell, M., 86
Power
    bullying behavior, 263
    empowerment, 104, 109, 169
        of family, 126
        goals of program, 137
        social skills development, 216

family dynamics, 118, 119, 122, 124, 126, 132, 177
   conduct disordered adolescent study, 266
   empowerment of family, 126
   power structure of family, 124, 132
  of staff/workers, 98, 122
Power seeking, 99, 102, 233
  conduct disordered adolescents, 48, 263, 265
  manipulation as, 58
  subgroup alliances, 108, 109
Power struggles, 59
  behavior modification, 141, 144, 145
  classroom, 145, 234, 242, 248
  conduct disordered adolescents, 264
  confrontation as, 194
  family dynamics, 119
  front-line interactions, 99
  group dynamics, 97–98, 99, 109, 111
  group home interactions, 202
  manipulation as, 58
  positive discipline, 194, 196, 197, 200
  psychosocial assessment, 73
  responses to staff, 200
  staff responses, 48–49, 50, 51, 52, 184
  subgroup formation, 109
Practical skills, 23
Praise, 145
Predators, 48, 80, 96
Preplacement interview, 30
Preston, D., 12
Preventing deterioration, 205–206
Preventive approaches, 16
Privacy issues, 183–184
Privileges
  reinforcements, 56, 139, 141, 149, 151, 152
  staff role, 178
Proactive teaching, 145
Problem definition, contextual counseling, 209
Problem identification
  behavior modification, 141
  counseling benefits, 209
  family work, 124
  treatment planning, 187

Problem resolution, 34
Problem solving
  activities and, 224, 284
  assessment process, 66, 280
  behavior modification
    effects of, 137, 139
    goals of treatment, 141
    program effectiveness, 146
  causes of maladaptive behavior, 193
  conduct disordered adolescent study, 268
  conduct disordered adolescents, 268
  counseling benefits, 209
  family work, 125, 129
  group activities and, 217
  group activity goals, 220
  group counseling, 103, 105
  group home interactions, 36–37, 94
  integrative counseling, 100
  life skills program, 214
  living and learning environment, 101
  power struggles, 98
  social skills development, 216
  Thorton's theory, 63
  treatment emphasis, 136
  treatment motivation, 44
Process in residential treatment, 66–67
Process models, 5
Prochaska, J., 6, 11, 12
Proctor, R. W., 152, 262
Program evaluation, 10, 25–26
  charting and, 140
  policy and procedure manual, 168
Programming, therapeutic, 213–225
  activities program, 213–214
  Four Phase System strengths, 10
  games and sport, 221
  group activities and community use, 216–218
  life skills program, 214–215
  psychosocial assessments, 32
  residential environment, 114
  social skills development, 216
  structured activities, 218–220
  sustaining interest, 220–221
  theory of therapeutic activities, 215
  therapeutic effects of activities, 221–222
  treatment components, 213

Progress, evolution of treatment needs
    in Four Phase System, 5
Progress assessment
    behavior modification
        charting, 139, 140, 149
        levels system, 149–150
    general principles of treatment, 11,
        12
    group work, assessment of, 180
    psychosocial assessments for, 88
    staff role, 179–180, 185, 188
    student, 254–255
    treatment planning, 19–20, 179–180,
        187
    treatment practices, 21
Progress report, student, 254–255
Property management, staff role, 189
Prosocial attitude development, 181
Protocols, treatment, 107, 109, 178
Psychiatric disorders, 207
Psychiatric hospitalization, 4
Psychiatric symptoms, 91
Psychiatric treatment, 8
Psychoanalysis, 7
Psychoanalytic theory, 63
Psychodynamic approach, 274
    with behavior modification program,
        280
    general principles of treatment, 12,
        135
Psychodynamic theory, 278–279
Psychoeducational therapy, 7
Psychological assessments, 30–31
Psychological functioning
    psychosocial assessments, 73–75
    referral information, 29
Psychological testing, 92
Psychological theory, 278
Psychosocial adjustment, 10–11
Psychosocial assessment, 274, 277
    by child and youth care workers,
        61–89
        adult relationships, 72–73
        childhood development, 62–66
        guide for writing discharge
            summary, 86–87
        peer–sibling relationships, 71–72
        personal characteristics, 79–86
        procedure, 68–79

    process in residential treatment,
        66–67
    social functions, 70–73
    social history, 69–70
    evaluation, 31–32
    Four Phase System program
        components, 24
    overview, 275–276
    personal characteristics
        diagnostic formulation, 84–85
        drug therapy, 82
        habits, 80–82
        interests and hobbies, 82–83
        school (academic functioning),
            83–84
        treatment plan, 85–86
    procedure
        background (social history) of
            youth, 69–70
        ego functions, 75–79
        psychological functioning, 73–75
        social functions, 70–73
Psychosocial Assessment model
    application of, 280
    conduct disordered adolescents, 269
    theoretical principles, 278–279
Psychosocial functioning, integrative
        counseling, 96
Psychosomatic disorders, 82, 170
Public funding, 16
Public policy, 15, 17
Public system of education, 228–231
Punishment
    causes of maladaptive behavior, 191,
        192
    childhood development theories, 64,
        65
    front-line interactions, 99
    perception of, 153
    policy and procedure manual, 168
    positive discipline, 200
Purpose, 104, 262
Putman, F., 78, 81, 214

Q

Quigley, R., 107

R

Racine, Y. S., 85, 258
Rand, K., 105
Rand, Y., 133
Randall, D., 2, 4, 7, 8, 10–17, 27, 42, 54, 117, 118, 119, 127, 153, 180, 202, 205, 272
Rapp, C. A., 8
Rappaport, J., 16
Rapprochement; *See* Integrative treatment
Rasbury, W. C., 95
Rasmussen, B., 71
Rathvon, N., 230, 235, 238, 245, 246
Rating, behavior, 148–149
Rating scale, level/reinforcement system, 148–150, 153, 277–278; *See also* Behavior modification, level/reinforcement system
Rational emotive therapy, 7, 265
Rationalization, 79, 265
Reactive attachment, 114
Read, N. O., 74
Reality
    construction of, 95, 145
    sense of, 79
Reality, acceptance of, 21
Reality testing, 75, 79, 195, 196
Reality therapy, 7
Reasoning skills, 181
Reber, M., 144
Reconstituted families, 129
Redl, F., 41, 58, 71, 148, 166, 173, 196, 206, 208, 248, 280, 286
Reentry programs, 5, 7, 9
Referral agencies, 5
Referral information, 29–30, 69
Referrals, 92
    discharge summary writing guidelines, 86
    hard-to-service adolescents, 14–15
    placement decisions, goodness-of-fit, 10
    psychosocial assessments, 69
    recognition of need for, 181–182
    social history, 70
Reflection/self-awareness; *See* Self-awareness/reflection

Reflectiveness, staff skills, 174, 184, 208, 210, 280, 285
    counseling, 199
    family work, 288
    methods, 177
    staff–youth relationship building, 95–96
    teaching, 181
Reframing, 113, 174
Regional programs, Canada, 3–4, 5, 7–8
Regression, 78–79
Regulatory requirements, 166, 183
Reid, D., 140, 143, 148
Reid, J., 258
Reid, W. J., 129
Reinecke, M. A., 43, 106
Reinforcement(s), 274, 276–278; *See also* Behavior modification, level/reinforcement system
    application of, 280
    behavior modification, 163
        applications, 138–139
        benefits of, 140–143
        categories, explanation of, 161–164
        credit and point scale, 150
        critical factors of, 146–148
        levels system, 149–150
        limitations of behavior management, 149
        rationale of, 144–146
        stimulus-response equation of behaviors in residential settings, 148
        time outs/removal of, 143–144, 145, 151
        variable factors, 150–152
    behaviorist model, 62–63
    causes of maladaptive behavior, 191, 192
    childhood development theories, 64
    confrontation and, 194
    family work, 130
    group home interactions, 94
    integrative approach to, 38–39
    meaningful rewards, 280
    positive discipline, 200
    psychosocial assessments, 31
    staff role, 177, 189
Reinforcement scales, 151, 155–160

Reintegration; *See* Community
        reintegration
Reiser, M. E., 66
Reiss, D., 114
Relabeling, 174
Relationship, staff–youth; *See*
        Therapeutic alliance/staff-
        client relationship
Relationship problems, group work, 181
Relationships
    activities and, 213–214, 222
    conduct disordered adolescents, 257,
        258
    family dynamics, and personality
        development, 259
    group dynamics, 93
Relearning, 6
Relevance of treatment, 19–20
Remediation, 6
Rennie, D. L., 265
Repression, 78, 81
Residential placement; *See* Placement
        decisions
Residential programs, 11; *See also*
        Group work
    assessment process in, 66–67
    conduct disordered adolescents, 260
    Four Phase System, 7
    psychosocial assessments, 69
Resiliency, 11, 82, 136
Resistance to treatment, 44–45, 92
    conduct disordered adolescent study,
        265
    contextual management, 54
    family work, 122, 123, 266
    front-line interactions, 99–100
    group dynamics, 109
    preventing deterioration, 206
    treatment plan, 86
    treatment practices, 20
    typical client profile, 12
Resistive stage, counseling, 197
Resnick, G., 154
Resocialization, 6, 284
Resolution, counseling stages, 198
Resource allocation, 10, 67
Resource sharing, 6
Response cost, 150–151
Response to treatment; *See* Outcomes

Responsibility
    conduct disordered adolescents, 261
    family work, 127, 128, 129
    group counseling, 105
    positive peer pressure, 108
    psychosocial assessments, 32
    staff role, 183–184
    treatment practices, 21, 136
Responsiveness, staff role, 189
Restitution, 175
Restraint procedures, 171–172
Restrictions
    community, 152
    conduct disordered adolescent study,
        264
    Phase Two secure areas, 9
Revocation of privileges, positive
        discipline, 200
Rewards
    behavior modification, 152–153; *See
        also* Reinforcement(s)
    causes of maladaptive behavior, 191,
        193
    childhood development theories, 64
    psychosocial assessments, 32
Reynolds, M. C., 238, 247
Ribordy, S. C., 262
Richin, R., 230
Riegel, K., 79
Rights, 142, 175, 183
    group counseling, 104
    social skills development, 169
Rippel, L., 123
Risk factors, family dynamics and
        parenting, 115
Risk taking
    encouragement of, 142
    group work, 181
    psychosocial assessments, 73
Risky behaviors, 116–117, 132
Rituals, family, 67
Robbins, S. P., 25
Roberts, A. R., 266
Robin, A., 115
Robinson, B., 258
Robinson, H., 123, 126
Rodriguez, E. R., 231
Rogers, C. R., 59, 67, 145, 173, 199, 200,
        208, 231

Role models, 199, 207
   group work, 103, 181
   preventing deterioration, 205
   psychosocial assessments, 32
   staff role, 287
   worker awareness of, 200
Role playing, 82, 111
Roles
   family work, 124, 129, 132
   group work, 180
Ronan, K., 144
Room maintenance, 163
Rose, K., 228
Rose, R. L., 109
Rose, S. D., 96, 103, 105, 107, 144, 180,
     243, 247, 262
Rosenfield, E., 278
Ross, D. M., 59, 264
Ross, R. R., 265
Rothstein, A., 235, 242, 244, 245
Routines, 162–163
Rowe, J., 288
Ruben, D. H., 230, 233, 234
Rule breaking, 58
   power struggles, 97
   psychosocial assessments, 74–75
   reinforcement categories, 161
Rule compliance, during activities, 83
Rule creation, group dynamics, 109
Rule enforcement, staff role, 184
Rules
   causes of maladaptive behavior, 192
   family work, 118, 125, 129
   group activity goals, 220
   worker behaviors, 200
Running away, 74, 97, 147
Rural environments, Four Phase System,
    9
Russel, L., 17
Russell, C., 123
Rutter, M., 263
Ryan, R. M., 192
Ryan, T., 229, 231
Rye, D. R., 228, 229
Rynders, J. E., 133

S

Sabotage, 109, 111

Safety issues
   group process, 107
   placement decisions, 119, 129
   staff role, 170, 184
Sampson, R. J., 132, 259
Sanderson, W. C., 85, 261
Sanfran, J. D., 273
Sarles, R. M., 47, 95
Satiation tactics, 177
Satir, V., 117, 124, 133
Sattler, J. M., 31
Scapegoating
   family dynamics, 116, 126–127
   group work, 109, 180
Schepis, M., 140, 143, 148
Scherer, M., 88
Schoenberg, S., 101
School component; *See also* Education,
    role in residential treatment
   Four Phase System, 23
   living and learning environment, 101
School performance, psychosocial
    assessments, 83–84
School plan, treatment planning, 187
Schumaker, J. B., 244
Schwartz, R., 128
Scull, A., 17
Searight, H. R., 17
Second-order personality trait, 95
Secure units, 8, 9
Security, 168
Self-acceptance, 9, 94, 137, 142
   behavior modification, 148
   positive discipline, 197
   staff, and responses to clients, 198
Self-agency, 9
Self-assessment/evaluation
   body image, 80
   integrative approach to
     reinforcements, 38
   living and learning environment, 101
   negative, parental influence on
     learning, 235, 236
   as postive characterological
     development, 154
Self-awareness/reflection, 264–265, 279
   activities and, 215, 219, 294
   behavior modification
     effects of, 138–139
     systems approach, 144

conduct disordered adolescents, 261,
    265
confrontation and, 194
Four Phase System treatment
    approach, 5
goals of program, 137
overload and, 194
staff responses to clients, 198
staff teaching, 181
staff–youth relationship building,
    95–96
strategies for emotional
    interventions, 199
therapeutic activities theory, 215
treatment classes and, 237, 243
Self-care
    behavior modification
        effects of, 137
        reinforcements, 142
    contracting process objectives, 137
    general principles of treatment, 12
    group counseling, 104
    living and learning environment, 101
    psychosocial assessments, 74
    reinforcement categories, 163
    staff role, 168
Self-concept/esteem/image
    conduct disordered adolescents, 259,
        262
    conflicts, nature of, 207, 208
    discharge summary writing
        guidelines, 87
    family dynamics and, 115, 259
    Four Phase System treatment
        approach, 11
    general principles of treatment, 11
    integrative counseling, 96
    interests and hobbies and, 82–83
    psychosocial assessments, 73–75
    treatment practices, 20–21
Self-control/regulation
    behavior modification
        reinforcements, 140–141, 142
        systems approach, 143, 144
    conduct disordered adolescent study,
        265
    conduct disordered adolescents, 262,
        269
    family dynamics and, 117, 287–288

Four Phase System treatment
    approach, 5
front-line interactions, 98–99
indicators of, 77
as postive characterological
    development, 154
psychosocial assessments, 61
strategies for emotional
    interventions, 199
and treatment class benefits, 284
treatment practices, 21
Self-correction
    causes of maladaptive behavior, 193
    as postive characterological
        development, 154
Self-determination/autonomy
    behavior modification
        positive characterological
            developments, 155
        program effectiveness, 146
        reinforcements, 141
    ego functions, 75, 76–77
    family dynamics, 117
    Four Phase System treatment
        approach, 9
    staff role, 170, 189
    treatment principles, 18–19
Self-expression, reinforcement
    categories, 164
Self-harm/self-mutilation, 74
    behavior modification, 153
    causes of maladaptive behavior, 193
    Four Phase System Phase Two
        programs, 8
    psychosocial assessments, 81
    reinforcement categories, 161
Self-help, staff role, 171
Self-management
    behavior modifcation objectives, 137
    reinforcements, 280
    self-control indicators, 78
Self-rating, 94
Self-soothing, 196, 222, 280
    self-control indicators, 78
    strategies for emotional
        interventions, 199
Self-sufficiency, staff role, 188
Self-talk, negative
    changing, 98, 207, 278

conduct disordered adolescent study,
265
confrontation, 196
and emotions, 206, 210, 260, 278
focusing on, 196
integrative counseling, 96
Selfhood/sense of self; *See also* Identity
behavior modification
reinforcements, 142
systems approach, 144
bonding and, 199
development of, 73–74
family dynamics, 91, 116
autonomy/self-determination, 117
and ego development, 115
group activities and, 217
group counseling, 104
mechanisms of change, 42–43
power struggles, 98
Seligman, M., 122
Sense of self; *See* Selfhood/sense of self
Sensitivity, 181
Separation and loss, 115, 119–120, 260
Serin, R., 12
Seruya, B. B., 124
Service agreements, 4
Service provider coalition, 1–2
Severe, S., 125
Sexual activity
conduct disordered adolescents, 261
family dynamics, 116–117
reinforcement categories, 162
staff role, 170
Sexual development, 80
Shafir, M., 78
Shafir, S., 78
Shahbazian, M., 41, 46, 107
Shanahan, M., 56
Shapiro, J. P., 15, 274
Shapiro, S., 257
Shectman, F., 66
Sheldon, B., 274
Sherradan, M., 6
Sherrod, L. R., 230
Shervin, H., 66
Shiller, V. M., 136
Shirk, S., 88
Shonk, S., 266
Short, R., 257
Short-term treatment, 5

Shulman, I., 48
Shulz, K., 258, 259
Siegel, L. J., 95
Siegler, A. I., 81
Silver, A. A., 68
Silverberg, S. B., 66, 70
Sinclair, R. J., 115
Single-parent families, 129
Sizer, N. F., 248, 250
Sizer, T. R., 248, 250
Skills, staff, recognition of limitations,
181–182
Skills acquisition
classroom, 283
interests and hobbies and, 82–83
positive discipline, 199
reinforcements, 141
task-oriented relationship, 145
therapeutic programming and, 213
Skills-based approach, 144, 145
Skills teaching
Four Phase System, 1
general principles of treatment, 12
group work, 180–181
psychosocial assessments, 32
treatment emphasis, 136
Skinner, B. F., 62, 147, 148
Skinner, H. A., 68, 86
Sleeping habits, 80
Slot, N. W., 145
Small, R. W., 114, 120
Smallish, L., 78, 247
Smelser, D., 127
Smith, D. G., 128
Social assistance programs, 17
Social dynamics, group home
interactions, 35–37
Social functioning
personal characteristics, 79–82
referral information, 29
Social history, psychosocial
assessments, 69–70
Social interactions
assessment process in residential
treatment, 67
living and learning environment, 101
psychosocial assessments, 32, 89
staff duties, 114
Social interest, ego functions, 76–77

Social learning
    behavior modification, 145
    Four Phase System, 2, 6–7, 135
    institutional culture and, 34
    psychosocial assessments, 32
    resocialization, 6
Social learning theory, 278
Social milieu, therapeutic, 12
Social network establishment,
            community reintegration, 268
Social norms
    family and, 91, 117
    normalization, 153–154
Social problem solving, conduct
            disordered adolescents, 268
Social services agency network, 1–2
Social services referrals, 92
Social skills
    family dynamics and, 259
    staff role, 185
Social skills development, 6
    activities and, 223, 224
    conduct disordered adolescent study,
            268
    discharge from treatment, 42
    family and, 91
    Four Phase System, 1
    goals of program, 137
    group activities and, 216–218
    group home interactions, 35–37
    learning disabilities, indicators of, 85
    programming, therapeutic, 216
    psychosocial assessments, 61
    reinforcements, 280
    staff role, 169–170, 183
    structured activities, 218–220
Social support system, 8, 9
Social system
    actions sustaining group, 102
    peer group as, 106–107
Socialization
    conduct disordered adolescent study,
            266
    family and, 229
    family dynamics, 115–116, 118
    group activities and, 92–94, 218
    staff roles, 106, 169
Sociocultural processes
    Four Phase System, 17

    treatment planning procedures,
            19–20
Solutions-based approach
    family work, 126
    group counseling, 105
    integrative counseling, 100
Space, private, 35
Spark, G., 121, 288
Sparks, R., 228, 229
Sparrow, S. S., 68
Special education, need for, 237–239
Special education model, 227
Speech assessment, 76
Spekkens, J. F., 2, 4, 7, 8, 10–14, 16, 17,
            27, 42, 54, 117–119, 127, 154,
            180, 202, 205, 272, 291
Speltz, M. L., 258
Sport, 221, 223
Sprenkle, E., 123
Springer, D., 108
Stabilization
    maintenance skills, 180
    Phase Two programs, 8
Stabilizing interactions, group
            dynamics, 100–101
Stadden, J., 278
Staff; See also Direct care staff role;
            Group work
    anger directed at, 54–57
    behavior modification, charting, 139,
            140
    conduct disordered adolescent study,
            267–268
    confrontation, 46–48
    countertransference; See
            Countertransference
    dealing with conflict contextually,
            52–54
    demoralization, 10
    development and training
        Four Phase System, 7
        program components, 23–24
    evaluation of client
        case formulation, 32–33
        group home interactions, 35–37
        integrative approach to
            reinforcements, 38–39
        psychological assessments, 30–31
        residential placement, 33–34

family work, difficult relationship
    with parents, 127–128
Four Phase System, 1, 7
goodness-of-fit, 114
group dynamics
    contextual role, 106
    group process, 109
    staff–client relationship, 94–96;
        See also Therapeutic alliance/
        staff–client relationship
high turnover, 16
life skills teaching, 7, 172
organizational issues, 16
psychosocial assessments, adult
    relationships, 72–73
responses to manipulation attempts,
    48–49
responses to oppositionalism and
    defiance, 49–50, 51
role of, 188, 285–288
support of, 25
Staff–client relationship; *See*
    Therapeutic alliance/staff–
    client relationship
Stage flexible intervention, 6
Stages of counseling, 197–198
Stages of development, 39
Stages of treatment, 5, 20
Standardized treatment approach,
    behavior modification, 146
Standards, 183
    academic functioning, 84
    community, behavior management
        system and, 143
    Four Phase System, 5
    policy and procedure manual, 166
    staff role, 183–184
Stark, K., 174
Stein, J. A., 44, 108
Stein, M., 230, 237
Stein, R., 230, 237
Steinberg, L., 70, 115
Sterba, M., 145
Stewart, S., 121, 123, 126, 201
Stierlin, H., 116, 124
Stimulus-response equation, 148
Stoltenberg, C. D., 165
Stoner, R. J., 14
Stouthamer-Loeber, M., 115

Strategic planning, Four Phase System,
    5–6
Strategies for change, 136–137
Strategies for emotional interventions,
    198–199
Strengths
    emphasis on, 88
    Four Phase System treatment
        approach, 5
Strengths-based model, 114
    contracts and, 92
    efficacy of, 85
    family work, 8, 126
    Four Phase System, 5, 8
    psychosocial assessments, 88
    staff role, 176
Stress
    client
        integrative counseling, 96
        staff awareness of, 98
    cultural ways of dealing with, 259
    family work, 130
    staff, 25
Stress management, family work, 125
Stress tolerance
    causes of maladaptive behavior,
        192–193
    family dynamics and, 259
Stroul, B. A., 14
Structural intervention, family work,
    125
Structural organization, psychosocial
    assessments, 73
Structure
    family dynamics, 118
    organizational, 16
    residential environment, 114
Structured activities, 218–220
Structured learning, behavior
    modification, 145
Student progress report, 254–255
Subcultural attachments, 92
    family dynamics, 117
    psychosocial assessments, 71
    typical client profile, 12
Subgroups, 102, 272
    group dynamics, 108–109
    preventing deterioration, 206
    staff role, 171, 176, 181, 182

Substance abuse; *See* Drug use/
          substance abuse
Substitute behaviors, 177
Subversion, 164
Sugai, G., 88
Suicidal clients, 8, 30, 70, 81, 86, 202
Sullivan, H. S., 71, 275
Superego, 79
Superficial behavior changes, 153
Supervision, parental, 115–116
Support, family, 134
Support, staff, 25
Support systems, client
     Four Phase System
          Phase Four, 9
          Phase One, 8
     phases of treatment, 40
     psychosocial assessments, 32
     social skills development, 216
Supportive confrontation, 196–198
Survival skills, 171
Sustaining interest, 220–221
Swann, W. B., 213, 214, 220
Swearing, 161–162
Symptomology
     adaptation to fit admission
          parameters, 15
     clinical goals, 6
     intake procedure, 8
Systems approach, behavior
          modification, 143–144
Systems of care, 10, 17
Systems theory, 13, 278
Syvesten, A. M., 230

T

Taibbi, R., 114, 288, 289
Tannehill, R. I., 107
Tannen, D., 93
Target, M., 71
Target behaviors, 151–152
Task-centered contract, 136
Task orientation
     group home interactions, 102–103
     maintaining, 145
Task performance, self-control
          indicators, 77
Taylor, D., 30

Teachers, treatment class
     control of students, 233–235
     cooperative alliance, 282–283
     role of, 247–249
Teaching
     confrontation as, 47–48
     corrective, 145
     Four Phase System, 1
     staff role, 176
Teamwork, 188
     case formulation, 33
     Four Phase System, 5, 13
          team meetings, 5
          treatment planning procedures,
               19
     staff role, 184, 185, 186–187
Teel, J. E., 109
Temperament, 192, 208
Terminology, psychosocial assessments,
          69
Testing behavior, 175
Tharp, R. G., 139, 146
Thase, M. E., 103
Thatcher, R. W., 65
Theory
     childhood development, 62–66
     Psychosocial Assessment model,
          278–279
Theory and practice of therapeutic
          approaches
     activities, 172–173, 215
     group work, 180–182
     theory versus practice, 51–52
Therapeutic activities; *See* Activities/
          activities programs
Therapeutic alliance/staff–client
          relationship, 9
     activities and, 221
     behavior modification, 152
     confrontation and, 195
     family work
          family dynamics, 121
          with parents, 119, 121, 134
     integrative counseling, 100–101
     intervention strategies, 198
     phases of treatment, 41
     psychosocial assessments, 72
     responses to oppositionalism and
          defiance, 49–50, 51
     staff caveats, 146

staff–youth relationship building, 33–34
Therapeutic programming; *See* Programming, therapeutic
Thinking about thinking, 144
Thinking errors and irrational attitudes/ beliefs
causes of maladaptive behavior, 95, 193, 204
family dynamics and, 115, 259
peer relationships, 71
conduct disordered adolescent study, 268
contextual counseling, 208
group treatment, 105
Thinking strategies, social skills development, 216
Thomas, C., 261
Thomas, G., 129
Thomas, R. M., 234
Thompson, K., 30
Thorton, S., 63
Thoughtfulness, 181
Thought processes; *See also* Critical thinking
ego functions, 75
psychosocial assessments, 76
Threats, defense system assessment, 78–79
Thurow, C., 57, 94
Tichy, N., 13
Time-outs, 127
positive discipline, 201
from reinforcements, 143–144, 151
staff counseling approaches, 175
Time sense, 79
Todd, A. W., 88
Token economy, 39, 152
Tomm, K., 127
Training, staff, 7, 23–24
Transaction redirection, 107
Transactional analysis, 7
Transference, 285
Transition phases, group work, 180
Transportation, life skills, 167–168, 215
Trauma
Four Phase System phases Three and Four, 9
psychosocial assessments, 73
Trauma history, fears, 81

Treatment, prioritizing, assessment and, 66
Treatment classes; *See* Classes, treatment
Treatment contract; *See* Contract, treatment
Treatment failure, staff responses, 199
Treatment goals; *See* Goals, treatment
Treatment history, 29
Treatment impact; *See also* Progress assessment
evaluation, 48–50
outcomes; *See* Outcomes
Treatment impasses
evaluation, 50–52
group work, 180
social history, 70
Treatment issues
conduct disordered adolescents, 260–261
family work, 118–120
Treatment methodology, 7
Four Phase System, 4, 6
placement decisions, goodness-of-fit, 10
Treatment motivation, 43–45
Treatment phases, 4
Four Phase System, 5, 6
integrative counseling, 100–101
Treatment plan/planning
activities, 214
assessment process, 67
behavior modification
adjustment with changed behaviors, 140–141
monitoring, charting and, 140
discharge summary writing guidelines, 87
evaluation process
case formulation, 32–33
psychological assessments, 30–31
staff monitoring of adherence, 33
family work
family treatment plan, 128–130
parental participation in, 120
Four Phase System, 5–6, 7
development of, 7–8
integrative treatment principles and practices, 19–20
Phase One, 8

procedures, 19–20
strengths of, 10
treatment plan (plan of care)
    development, 7–8
treatment principles, 18–19
procedures, 19–20
psychological assessments, 30–31
reviewing, 188
staff role, 187–188
    plan of care, 179–180
    reviewing, 185
treatment approach, 136
treatment principles
    general, 12
    self-determination, 18–19
Treatment practices, program
    components, 21–26
Treatment protocols, 107
Treatment stagnation, 5
Tremblay, R., 30, 45, 56, 269
Triangulation of emotions, 79
Trivette, C., 119, 130
Trust, 175, 203
    actions sustaining group, 102
    conduct disordered adolescents, 261
    family dynamics and, 259
    front-line interactions, 99
Tuma, J., 11
Turnell, A., 129, 131
Turnover, staff, 16
20-day treatment, 8

U

Ulrich, D., 13
Unconditional positive regard, 199
Unconscious material
    conduct disordered adolescents, 265
    diagnostic formulation, 84
    evaluation, 29
    group living, 93, 99
    positive discipline, 197, 206
    therapeutic programming and, 213
Underwood, J., 228
Unit operations, staff role, 185, 189
Urberg, K. A., 104

V

Vallerand, R. J., 192
Value-laden issues, group work, 181
Values
    alternative, 92–93
    countercultural, 171; See also
        Countercultural identification/
        antisocial groupings
    deviant, 72
    ego functions, 76–77
    family and, 91
    family dynamics, 117, 118
    Four Phase System program, 5
    group counseling, 106
    group home interactions, 103
    socialization process, 7
    staff awareness of, 98
Van Lieshout, C. F., 83
Van Wagner, S., 264
Verbal fighting; See Argumentativeness/
        bickering
Verhaagen, D., 202, 203, 208
Vernon, A., 116
Vetere, A., 130, 265
Violence
    conduct disordered adolescents, 258
    ego functions, 78
    fears, 81
    psychosocial assessments, 73
    school, 230
Vitario, F., 269
Vorath, H. H., 107

W

Wachtel, E. F., 91, 121, 125, 126, 133,
        191, 263
Walberg, H. J., 238, 247
Wall, S., 64
Walsh, J. M., 140, 148
Walters-Leeper, G., 259, 264
Wang, M. C., 238, 247
Waters, E., 64
Watson, D. L., 139, 146
Watson, J. B., 62
Webb, W., 122
Weisber, R. P., 228, 229, 236
Weisz, J. R., 274
Welfel, E. R., 116, 127

Well, K., 10
Wetzer, S., 85, 261
Wexler, D. B., 77, 202, 208
White, P. D., 17
White, R. W., 155
Whittaker, J. K., 8, 10, 114, 131, 132, 289
Wicka-Nelson, R., 117, 233
Wierson, M., 137, 142, 154
Wilder, D. C., 103
Wilderness environment, 9
Williams, A., 57, 94
Williams, S., 200
Wineman, D., 41, 58, 71, 148, 166, 173, 196, 206, 208, 280, 286
Winnicott, D. W., 4, 9, 66, 118, 206, 258, 274, 276, 281, 290
Winslade, J., 137
Withdrawal
    counseling stages, 197
    defense system assessment, 84
    power struggles, 97
    reinforcement categories, 162
Wolf, E., 116, 207
Wolfensberger, W. C., 18
Wolpe, J., 147
Wood, J., 29, 40, 58
Woods, M. E., 123, 126

Workers; See Direct care staff role; Staff
Work ethic, 185
Work history, psychosocial assessments, 84
Work/occupational preparation, 23, 214, 215
Work plan, treatment planning, 187
Wozner, Y., 207
Wrap-around programming, 4
Wright, E. R., 17, 259
Wright, N., 264

Y

Yalom, I. D., 47, 48, 103, 105, 173, 180, 194
Youth justice system, 91
Youth worker role, 188; See also Direct care staff role; Staff
Ysseldyke, J. E., 84
Yu, M., 145

Z

Zero tolerance policy, 230
Zins, J. E., 228, 229, 236
Zoccolillo, M., 269